NEW GILL HISTORY OF IRELAND 5

Nineteenth-Century Ireland:
The Search for Stability

NEW GILL HISTORY OF IRELAND

The Gill History of Ireland originally appeared in eleven paperback volumes between 1972 and 1975. It was immediately acknowledged as the most authoritative multi-volume history of Ireland. Now, because of the continuing evolution in the writing of Irish history, it is being succeeded by the NEW GILL HISTORY OF IRELAND. The format is different—six longer volumes rather than eleven short ones—but the intention is the same: to offer the general reader an accessible and up-to-date survey of Irish history.

NEW GILL HISTORY OF IRELAND
5

Nineteenth-Century Ireland: The Search for Stability

D. GEORGE BOYCE

GILL AND MACMILLAN

Published in Ireland by
Gill & Macmillan Ltd
Hume Avenue, Park West
Dublin 12
with associated companies throughout the world
www.gillmacmillan.ie

© D. George Boyce 1990

Print origination by Irish Typesetters, Galway
Printed by ColourBooks Ltd, Dublin

*The paper used in this book comes from the wood pulp of managed forests.
For every tree felled, at least one tree is planted, thereby renewing
natural resources.*

British Library Cataloguing in Publication Data

Boyce, D. George (David George) *1942–*
    Nineteenth-century Ireland : the search for stability. -
    (New Gill history of Ireland;5).
    1. Ireland. Social conditions, 1800-1899
    I. Title
    941.5081

    ISBN 0-7171-1620-4
    ISBN 0-7171-1621-2 pbk

8 10 11 9 7

To J. C. B.

Contents

Acknowledgments

I AM grateful to the following copyright owners for permission to publish material: the Earl of Belmore (D 3007); the Marquis of Downshire (D 607); Guy J. Darell, Esq. (D 929); the Linen Hall Library, Belfast (T 2771/7); Major J. W. R. Madden (D 3465/J/27/8 and D 3465/J/27/19); Lieutenant-Colonel G. E. Liddle, O.B.E. (D 1402/1). All these documents are kept in the Public Record Office of Northern Ireland. I am grateful to Dr A. P. W. Malcomson, Deputy Keeper of the Records in the Public Record Office of Northern Ireland, for his help in tracing copyright owners and for giving me permission to quote from documents where appropriate.

NOTE ON TERMINOLOGY

The Irish Parliamentary Party was also known as the Home Rule Party, the Nationalist Party, or simply as the Irish Party. All these names are used interchangeably in this book.

The terms 'Nationalist', 'Liberal', 'Radical' and 'Conservative' appear with an initial capital when they are used predominantly in the sense of denoting membership of specific political parties or groups. They appear in lower case when used predominantly in the sense of denoting allegiance to or support for each particular movement or ideology in general.

The term 'Protestant' tended to be used by contemporaries (particularly in the earlier part of the nineteenth century) to apply exclusively to members of the Church of Ireland. In this book this sense of the word is retained in variations of the well-known phrase 'Protestant, Catholic and Dissenter', but is otherwise avoided. The terms 'Anglican' and 'Episcopalian' are instead used interchangeably to describe the Church of Ireland, which is also occasionally referred to (before 1871) as the Established Church.

ix

Letterkenny • Derry DERRY • Ballymena
DONEGAL U L S T E R ANTRIM
Donegal • Omagh • Belfast
TYRONE DOWN
FERMANAGH Armagh • Downpatrick
Sligo • Enniskillen ARMAGH
MAYO R.Erne MONAGHAN Newry •
SLIGO LEITRIM Cavan •
Castlebar • ROSCOMMON Leitrim CAVAN • Dundalk
Longford LOUTH
Roscommon • LONGFORD Navan •
C O N N A U G H T Mullingar • MEATH R.Boyne
WESTMEATH DUBLIN
Ballinasloe • Athlone KILDARE Dublin •
Galway • OFFALY Tullamore • Kildare R.Liffey
GALWAY R.Shannon Port Laois • WICKLOW
CLARE L E I N S T E R Wicklow •
Ennis • LAOIS WICKLOW
Nenagh • Carlow •
Kilkenny • CARLOW
Limerick • Thurles •
LIMERICK TIPPERARY KILKENNY
M U N S T E R Clonmel • WEXFORD
KERRY • Tralee R.Suir Wexford •
CORK Mallow • WATERFORD Waterford •
Killarney • R. Blackwater
Cork •
R. Lee

Border between Republic of Ireland
and Northern Ireland
.... County Boundaries
0 ————————— 75 km

Introduction

THE period covered by this book (1798–1923) both began and ended with a rebellion followed by civil war. In between stretched the Union linking Ireland to Great Britain.

One of the inescapable penalties of writing history is that the historian knows not only the starting-point of his or her journey but also the destination; and this knowledge invariably influences the choice of what are selected as important and significant events. The Union which was formally inaugurated with the creation of a United Kingdom parliament and a new Union flag on 1 January 1801 was broken in 1921 with the establishment of two new states, Northern Ireland and the Irish Free State. The failure of the Union colours subsequent perception of it. It is tempting to regard it as in some sense doomed to impermanence; and this sense of failure influences its interpretation. 'Turning-points' and 'crises' are selected on the basis of Ireland's eventually giving notice of leaving the Union; and a false unity is imposed on the period: the British context of Irish history sets the framework of discussion, even among those who regard its inception as an imposition and its ending as a blessing.

Certainly the political framework was very different. Ireland no longer had a parliament of her own, and was governed (through a species of administrative devolution) by Westminster. But Ireland, and therefore Britain, brought into the United Kingdom a whole set of special social, economic, political and religious developments, or half-developments, or suppressed developments, that make the dividing-line of 1800 less absolute than it at first sight appears. Irish society in the late eighteenth century was growing more complex, and certainly more volatile. Protestant, Catholic and Dissenter experienced new circumstances and explored different political options—options denied them in the more tranquil years after the Glorious Revolution. Protestants were obliged to defend their political privileges, not only against Presbyterian radicals but also

against the hitherto dormant Roman Catholics, increasingly embol-
dened by the support afforded them by the British government in
their campaign for the removal of penal disabilities. And these were
not only matters of high politics, to be decided between London
and Dublin; they involved real public political debate, and eventually the intervention of radical societies. And they spread beyond
normal political activity, as Catholics, for their part, developed a
sense of solidarity in the face of Protestant opposition and government repression. What followed can be summed up without doing
too much injury to the complexity of the problem: Ireland in the
1780s and 1790s witnessed the weakening of deference among many
of her peoples, not least among the Catholics who formed the vast
majority of her population.

This posed an important question: would the new habits of
thought and behaviour find some sort of accommodation within the
eighteenth-century Irish constitution? Or would they drive Ireland
towards yet another confrontation, setting her divided people at
each other's throats and plunging the country into political crisis? It
is possible to argue that the existing Irish constitution might have
provided a framework within which a healed and settled constitution might have been created; that gradual reform (or even the
speedier pace of reform that was seen from the late 1780s) would
have brought within the boundaries of the political system those
elements, mainly of middle-class status, from Catholic and Dissenter society that were foremost in demanding political change.
But this is to ignore two important circumstances. The British
government's desire to push reform onwards, even to the point of
compelling the Irish parliament to pass a measure of Catholic
Emancipation, collapsed in mutual recrimination in 1795.[1] Catholic
hopes, raised and then suddenly dashed, created an unstable
political environment. This was worsened by the growing disorder
in the Irish countryside, as Catholic Defender clashed with Protestant Peep o' Day Boy and his like, especially in the border
counties of Ulster. Long before the 1798 rebellion large areas of
Ireland were seething with discontent, with groups of people either
successfully standing their ground or being dislodged by their
enemies. This enmity was inspired by the desire of local groups to
dominate, to stake their claim to territory, and to drive their foes
from their areas; but it was based on the old enmities between Protestant and Catholic; and in these volatile times even the would-be

Presbyterian radical might find himself switching his allegiance from radical United Irish Society to Protestant Orange Society—sometimes belonging to both at the same time.

When, in 1798, these crises came to a head, they resulted in a succession of bloody and confused events, dominated by a series of insurrections, local in nature, lacking in central co-ordination or unified aim, but administering a shock to the whole Irish political system. Britain felt that the confusion was not to be borne, and determined that the Irish parliament must be wound up and Ireland merged in the wider context of a United Kingdom. This would have the double advantage of restoring order to Ireland, while at the same time ensuring that she would not again offer a threat to British security in time of danger. It might also provide a remedy for that political deficit that Ireland always seemed to carry forward, namely her failure to discover what Edmund Burke called the 'ground-work' of a constitution:[2] a settled form of government based upon shared political perceptions. If the Union were accompanied by Catholic Emancipation (the right of Catholics to sit in parliament), then Catholics would reconcile themselves to its permanence, and Protestants of whatever kind would feel secure in a political arrangement that would leave them still a majority—a majority, that is, in the overwhelmingly Protestant United Kingdom with its Protestant king and constitution.

The Union, in this view, would place Irish Catholics rather in the position of the Protestant Huguenots in France; they would be a minority and therefore at the behest of the majority of British citizens. They could be advanced to full political rights. Or, then again, perhaps they might not be thus advanced. For if they were indeed like the Huguenots in France, then they might be regarded as an alien body, responsible in the past for civil war, insurrection and maybe even revolution: an 'unassimilable minority'.[3] All this rendered the making of a settled constitution by no means certain or easy to attain. Yet there was confidence that the Union would indeed attain it. In Ireland Catholics were in proportion to Protestants as three to one; in the United Kingdom they would be as three to eleven. This would persuade Catholics that they could not get rid of Protestants, and Protestants that they need not fear Catholics. 'Strength and confidence', Lord Castlereagh predicted, would produce 'liberality'.[4]

This proposition was soon to be tested in the great struggle over

Catholic Emancipation. The long and ultimately successful campaign revealed for the first time how British and Irish politics could interact, with significant results, in the new context created by the Union. Daniel O'Connell has, justly, been given the accolade of 'Liberator' because of his powerful and dynamic leadership of the Catholic cause. But that cause could not have triumphed but for the steady erosion of British public opposition through the efforts of Emancipationists in the British House of Commons. These supporters held it axiomatic that the Union was now permanent. This was the view of Henry Grattan, the doyen of Protestant Irish patriotic feeling in the late eighteenth century.[5] But O'Connell implicitly, and later explicitly, challenged this idea, or at least the basis of the idea. For Grattan had always held that Roman Catholic freedoms were compatible with Protestant security, and he always assured the Irish parliament that he would not otherwise have supported the Catholic demand. O'Connellism held that, notwithstanding the Act of Union, the Catholics were the real majority in Ireland, and that the Protestants were an 'artificial' ascendancy in view of the fact that they depended for their position on the support and encouragement of Great Britain.

This would reverse the poles of Irish politics, for it would relegate the Protestants into the position of the Huguenots. They would be the minority, dependent upon the sufferance of the Catholic majority. And yet, if Protestants denied this and clung to the Union, with its Protestant and British majority, then Catholics would continue to fulfil the Huguenot role. This great central question lay at the heart of Irish political life in the nineteenth century; its character and its resolution—or lack of resolution—helped to shape not only Irish but British politics under the Union.

It would be wrong to imply that the outcome of the conflict must be union or separation. The choices were never as simple as that. O'Connell himself pointed the way to another alternative in his practice of co-operating with the Whigs in the 1830s; and this policy of working within the context of the United Kingdom to create special local Catholic institutions was adopted by later generations of Irish political and religious leaders; religious, for in the course of the nineteenth century another great central force emerged: the Roman Catholic Church, which assumed the role not only of moral and religious teacher to its people, but also of its political mentor and its guide, if never its driver. The church was prepared to negotiate on behalf of the Irish Catholic, and to negotiate also with any political movement that purported to represent his interests. This meant in practice that Irish political leaders, from O'Connell to Redmond (and beyond), had to make a concordat with the church. It also meant that they had to bargain with British governments, since separatism was unsupported by the people, opposed by the hierarchy, and denied by the British, until the revolutionary era ushered in by the Great War. It was therefore not the least of the many skills demanded of nationalist politicians that they acquire the ability to prepare their people for disappointing news.

This gave Irish politics a particular style. Rhetorical battles had to be won even when real political causes were lost or temporarily overthrown. The Irish Parliamentary Party, which represented Catholic Ireland for some fifty years from the 1870s, did so because it was able to maintain its hope of a promised land—a self-governing, majority-ruled Ireland—and because it negotiated real and tangible benefits for its people, and especially for the church, and for the solid core of its supporters, namely the tenant farmers. Yet it would be misleading to assert that political leadership in Ireland always came from the top, or that it was merely a question of manipulating the machinery of high politics. Ireland was a country where political leaders had to maintain the closest possible contact with their followers. For the fact that Irish political demands were put into the Westminster political system must not obscure the vitality of local political life. Irish Catholics, Protestants and Dissenters had clear and definite views about what they wanted, especially on the central issue of their livelihood—the question of the land.

Ireland in the nineteenth century was an overwhelmingly rural country. It was so not only in the sense that most of its people gained their living from the land, but also in the sense that rural values and ways of life shaped the thinking of the vast bulk of its people. In 1800 Ireland's population was about 5 million, or one-fifth of the total population of the British Isles. This was to alter radically in the course of the century as the Great Famine and the ongoing process of emigration took their toll. Irish towns in 1800 were small. Dublin was the largest with a population of nearly

200,000. Outside Dublin, the next largest was Cork with 80,000; Limerick with 60,000; Belfast with 20,000; Drogheda and Waterford with the same.[6] The balance shifted during the course of the century, and the great industrial city of Belfast rose to put Dublin into second place as the main port of Ireland. But this did not alter the fact that Ireland was the land of the small town; and the town acted as the market for the surrounding agricultural population, and the supplier of its needs. Town and country were not opposites, despite the efforts of romantic nationalists to depict them as such; they were complementary, and when rural areas faced recession or crisis, so did urban dwellers, or at least those of them who counted for most—shopkeepers, publicans and the like—as farmers sold less and spent less.

Rural Ireland was itself divided into different, and indeed contrasting, sets of people. At the top were the landlords, forming 0.2 per cent of the population in 1861 but owning the vast bulk of the land;[7] twenty years after the famine some 2,000 of them, each with 2,000 acres or more, held two-thirds of the land of Ireland.[8] Landed property was to decline as a valued resource (political and economic, but not perhaps social) in the course of the century; but it was a long and slow decline, and even as late as the 1870s landlords could still envisage a future where their property provided them with a substantial living. This was less certain in the case of the tenant farmers, whose interests were at the centre of most political debate in the nineteenth century. The Great Famine opened up a more hopeful future for the tenant farmer, in that it encouraged the consolidation of his holdings and greatly depleted the ranks of the labourer and the cottier. Cottiers held small areas of land under a tenant; labourers held only cabins, usually without plots, though occasionally with very small plots of perhaps an acre or less in extent.[9] Labourers became marginal figures after the famine, and although their smaller numbers often enabled them to negotiate better wages, yet their political influence was negligible. Their gaining of the vote in the franchise reform of 1884–5 made no difference in the south; only in the north, where the nationalist threat called for Protestant solidarity, did their membership of the Orange Order and their electoral influence elicit at least promises (if little else) from the Unionist leadership.

The decline in the cottier class after the famine enabled tenant farmers to consolidate holdings of land; and while tenant farmers themselves varied greatly in their wealth and position, being substantial in some areas such as Munster and poor in the west, yet their interests were placed in the forefront of Irish life, for they formed a reasonably homogeneous and identifiable set of people, whose votes counted above all others. Even in the north, where sectarianism was most influential, the wishes of Episcopalian and Presbyterian tenant farmers could not be ignored, and not least by Protestant and Unionist leaders intent upon creating a solid front against the threat of Catholic domination.

The tenant farmers formed a kind of political and social ballast, and after 1882 became an increasingly conservative force in Ireland. The heady days of the Land League seemed to promise some sort of social revolution in Ireland; but its issue was a stabilising one, as farmers won, and then consolidated, their gains: first in the shape of rent rebates, then through land purchase. This gave Ireland a core of social stability; yet political stability eluded her. For the great central question remained unresolved: if Ireland were to have self-government, which of the major groups in Ireland was to inherit the future?

This question was different in kind from the controversies aroused by land reform, the reform of the Church of Ireland, municipal reform, educational reform. It was true that it was perhaps implicit in these other issues, in that they all raised in some degree the question of which tradition was to prevail in Ireland. The disestablishment of the Church of Ireland, for example, was treated by both Protestants and Catholics as a kind of 'national' question, one with implications for the future mastery of the country. But self-government, or 'Home-Rule', was of a different order. It threatened to deprive Irish Protestants of their status; and, what is crucial, it was a threat that touched *all* Protestants, the middling tenant farmer in County Cork, the working-class labourer in Derry, the skilled artisan in Belfast. It was not merely a matter of economics, though Protestants held that their prosperity depended upon the maintenance of the Union; nor did it involve religion alone, though again Protestants insisted that they would suffer religious persecution under a Dublin parliament. It included all these considerations, yet the whole of the opposition to Home Rule was greater than the sum of the parts. Protestants knew that it was at bottom a challenge to their whole identity and survival; and they knew it was so because Home Rule would degrade them to the unenviable status of the permanent minority in Ireland. This would mean a real revolution, for it would affect not only their long-term future, but their immediate self-concept: that of a people who had wrested victory from the jaws of defeat in 1690 and who now stood on the brink of another round of the old struggle, when their lives and liberties were to be placed at the mercy of those whose own experience hardly disposed them towards sentiments of liberality and tolerance. It was, then, the same predicament as that summed up in the words of Archbishop William King in 1688: 'There was no medium, but that we or they must be undone.'[10]

This was the most extreme position; but for most of the century there was a 'medium', and that medium was the Union, with a British government that played the role of arbiter—not, of course, a disinterested arbiter, for British politicians had their own priorities and their own self-interest to consult. But the Union provided a constitutional framework which contained, and even constrained, conflict between the different groups of people in Ireland, without, however, finally smothering the debate on the constitution itself. Thus the Presbyterians of Ireland, at the beginning of the century, were content to turn in upon themselves, enjoy a sense of exclusiveness, fulfil their lives with deep theological disputes, advance themselves in economic and social terms, and play almost no discernible political role; yet when the Union was in danger, as it appeared to be in 1843, 1886, 1893 and 1912, the vast majority of Presbyterians sprang to its defence, abandoning both their political indifference and their political radicalism (or what was left of it).

The debate on the constitution was itself a cause of instability; yet it was debated in mainly constitutional ways—through elections, parties, the British parliament, the press. But this debate had a Janus face, for the idea of violence, though it made little headway in practical terms until just before the Great War, was one that the contending political groups in Ireland did not, ultimately, rule out. It was indeed the last argument of Irish politics, the ultimate appeal, if matters came to a head, when one side or the other must be ruined. It helped to shape not only the form but the very establishment of the two new states that were built upon the wreckage of the Union in 1921–2. The 'troubles' which gave birth to twentieth-century Ireland, however, did not jeopardise that fundamental stability that was the product of the long revolution of the preceding century, when Britain sought to mediate the pace of change, and did so with some degree of success. The British parliament gave Ireland not only reforms but also a long experience of political and constitutional government. Ireland's own political leaders were skilled in using that British system, while at the same time seeming to reject its 'Saxon' values, or, in the case of the Protestant Conservatives and Unionists, exploiting it as best they could, while embracing (apparently) those values. Yet neither side ultimately controlled that parliament and government, however much they might exert influence over the British Conservative and Liberal parties. This meant that at various times, and especially when British parties thought in terms of the 'national' interest (that is, the interests of England, the predominant partner in the kingdom, as Lord Rosebery termed it), all political groups in Ireland were capable of feeling persecuted, by each other and by the British. This helped to create a strong sense of grievance, as both Catholics and Protestants felt uneasy about the intentions of a government which they did not elect but which could play a decisive role in their future.

Many of the problems of nineteenth-century Ireland were carried over from the conflicts of the 1790s. But the Union placed them in an entirely new context. Ireland was deeply influenced by British government, society and culture. Her politics, economics, literature, all were dominated by her powerful neighbour. This domination was to continue beyond the end of the Union and was to shape the destinies of the states that were founded in its shadow.

The Union:
Prelude and Aftermath,
1798–1808

On 9 January 1798 the first session of George III's sixth and last Irish parliament opened. A few months later it stood as helpless witness to the outbreak of the most ferocious and dangerous rebellion in Ireland since the seventeenth century; and within two years it was to undergo dissolution and the absorption of its members into the united parliament of Great Britain and Ireland.

The rebellion not only ended the life of the Irish parliament; it ended too the assumptions that the average educated and politically aware observer might have entertained about the likely future of his society: that on the whole the end of the eighteenth century was better than the beginning; that by and large Irishmen were settling down into a tolerable, if not yet tolerant relationship with one another; and that, as the author of a preface to an edition of Molyneux's *Case of Ireland's being bound by Acts of Parliament in England* put it in 1770, 'the two sects are insensibly gliding into the same common interests'.[1] Positive evidence was to be found in several important manifestations of the new spirit. When Catholic political activity began to revive in an organised form after 1759, it was eased towards a spirit of loyalty by the papacy's decision to withhold recognition in 1766 from the heir of the Old Pretender;[2] a good Catholic could, and indeed should (in the eyes of his church), support his lawful sovereign, George III; and Catholic bishops warned their flocks of the danger to the king's happiness threatened by the American rebels in 1778.[3] The Volunteer movement, which swept across Protestant Ireland at the time of the American War of Independence, revealed not only a spirit of self-reliance on the part of its members, but also a commendable openness to the claims of Catholic and Dissenter to a share in political power. It might even

be claimed that Ireland was more tolerant than England, notwithstanding that English Protestantism and constitutionalism rested
upon a surer foundation. For, despite the anxiety of many members
of the Irish parliament at the Catholic relief acts drawn up by the
British government and passed in 1778 and 1782,[4] there was no Irish
equivalent of the Gordon riots that reduced parts of London to ruin
and cost the lives of some 450 people in June 1780.

Ireland's failure to follow the English example of frequent rioting
must not, however, obscure the great dilemma in which the Irish
political ruling class found itself in the last quarter of the eighteenth
century, and which England did not share. The Irish political
nation, the people who held exclusive membership of the Irish
parliament, were like their English counterparts in general social
background and outlook. They moved easily in society on both
sides of the Irish Sea; they were, like the English gentry, both
cosmopolitan and yet highly parochial. They too had the sovereign,
King George, as their monarch in their kingdom of Ireland; they
also had their state church, the Church of Ireland, to which they
gave unenthusiastic but formal support as a pillar of the constitution. In contrast, Protestant Dissenters, in Ireland as in England
and Wales, were effectively excluded from political power, from
holding civil and military office under the crown (in Ireland until
1780), and from municipal corporations. They were not subject to
the same legal disabilities as Catholics, but no Dissenters sat in the
Lords and very few in the Commons. Their social and economic
status in any event precluded them from any effective political role,
except as members of the county electorate in counties in the north
of Ireland. Furthermore, they had to pay tithes to the Church of
Ireland. But they could be relied upon to support the Protestant
interest, especially in time of trial; and they were a people whose
general respectability seemed to deny Jonathan Swift's claim that
they were an angry cat in full liberty. (In fact most of those who
were liberty-minded emigrated to America.)

But Irish Anglicans were not in other respects as happily
circumstanced as their English brethren. The distribution of population in Ireland showed marked imbalances. Anglicans claimed
about 14 per cent of the population of Leinster and had a strong
representation in Dublin; but in the south and west they comprised
only about 3 to 5 per cent and lived amongst an overwhelmingly

large Roman Catholic population. And even in Ulster, where 45 per cent of Anglicans lived, they were surrounded by a Presbyterian community that made up 99 per cent of the total of Irish Presbyterians.[5] Where Anglicans were strongest, so therefore were Presbyterians. And in the late eighteenth century Presbyterians could no longer be relied on to behave themselves. They were becoming politically alert, active in radical politics, and critical of the unreformed and unrepresentative nature of the Irish parliament.

Nevertheless, it was impossible to envisage a state without a state church; and while the Church of Ireland had its critics, it could take comfort in its constitutional security and in the general, if unfounded, belief that the obvious errors of Roman Catholicism would, in an age of enlightenment, erode the religion of the overwhelming majority of the people of Ireland. But by the end of the century it was clear that the Irish Catholic would not suffer the fate of a disappearing species. On the contrary, his faith and endurance, his support of his religion, his courage in the face of adversity, held out new and alarming possibilities for the Church of Ireland, and indeed for Protestants in general. The hierarchy was loyal; but it was hard to know what kind of sentiments and beliefs lurked below the surface, and what kind of impact these might have on the social fabric of Ireland. And this was not only a matter of the Catholic religion; Irish Protestantism too was beginning to undergo a change that was to make the politics of religion a major concern in the Union period. The easy latitudinarianism of the Church of Ireland invited the attention of those, inspired by the English Methodism of John Wesley, now active in Ireland, who held that faith, salvation, and a probing attitude to religious truth were inseparable from the life of the church. And when to this evangelical movement was added the special character of Ireland, the awareness of the vast bulk of the unconverted Roman Catholic people still stubbornly clinging to their religion, the threat to the truth of revealed religion from these people, then the evangelical tendencies noticeable in the late eighteenth century had important implications for the relationship between the religious denominations of Ireland.[6]

The Roman Catholic was, therefore, the object of attention from many quarters in the decade before the Union. Above all, he was the object of attention from a British government anxious to enlist his support in the years of crises as the French Revolution stood forth as the enemy of political establishments all over Europe; and he was the object of attention too from those sections of Irish Anglican and Presbyterian opinion which hoped to relieve him of his remaining political burdens either for the sake of liberty and enlightenment or as a means of enlisting his political support for a radical reform of the whole Irish representative system. Radicals hoped that the instrument of reform would be the Volunteer companies formed during the American crisis and now infiltrated by men from the lower orders of society.

Some Catholics were willing to acknowledge that the atmosphere had changed, or was changing, for the better: in 1792 Bishop MacMahon of Killaloe declared that the generous subscription of the grand jury of Clare towards a school which he had set up in Ennis was an example of 'what liberal sentiments at present subsist betwixt Roman Catholics and Protestants'. But, again, there were signs of the crucial shift in posture that would shape Irish religion and society under the Union. Just as Protestant evangelicals were unhappy about the latitude of their practitioners of religion, so a first sign of the new aggressive style was detectable in the person of Thomas Hussey, who became Bishop of Waterford in 1797. Hussey expressed strong displeasure at Catholic children attending Protestant schools, and he believed that denominational differences were central to Irish life. In the wider political sphere, he was also a characteristic figure, in that while he was a conservative abroad, he cast himself as a radical at home—radical, that is, in his criticism of government policy, and contemptuous of any deferential sentiment that the government hoped might follow from concessions made to Catholics.[7] It would have been difficult, in any case, for a society so divided as Irish society was in the eighteenth century, with a clear line distinguishing those who were within the constitution, enjoying legal and civil rights, and those who were not, to cope with the tides of change. It was even more difficult for such a society to adapt to change in an age of radical thought and revolutionary fervour.

In general, Catholics seemed a passive people, willing to wait gratefully for what the Irish parliament, prompted by the British government, would concede to them, or willing to co-operate with the Volunteer movement in such a way as to demonstrate their virtue as active but not over-demanding suppliants. But Catholic political activity was not narrowly confined to the world of high

politics and government decisions, nor even to the popular movement of the Volunteers. The Catholic Church was not usually
associated with populist or democratic behaviour in the history of
Europe; but in Ireland the case was different. The experience of a
large, universal church, representing the majority of the people, but
deprived of its livings, administrative arrangements and any state
connections, was an unusual one, and one which shaped the special
role of the Catholic Church in Ireland. The church depended upon
popular support; and even though this at times was lacking, even
though priest and people could find themselves locked in conflict
when clergy sought to condemn or suppress agrarian organisations,[8] it survived bad times and gave Irish Catholicism its peculiar
character as a deeply emotional, non-intellectual and democratic
force. Irish priests, and even Irish bishops, were all too often found
on the side of the underdog. But this democratic experience was
combined with a strong sense of history and past wrongs and
humiliations; injustice, when based on the past, was not easy to
remedy in the present, because concessions scarcely compensated
for wrongs which ought never to have happened in the first place: a
sense of grievance was not the same thing as a complaint, and was
not necessarily subject to legislative solutions.

Two other social developments were to influence Irish politics
both before and after the Union, as far as Catholicism was
concerned. The first was the tendency of peasant communities to
form agrarian secret societies for mutual protection and, if need be,
for mutual aggression against their enemies: these being variously
defined, and including Catholic as well as Protestant farmers;
Protestant landlords; and Anglican tithe-gatherers. These societies,
of course, invited the hostility of the Catholic clergy, but they were
nonetheless associated with the Catholic religious/political experience, with the sense of past expropriation—even when that
expropriation was, strictly speaking, the lot of the Catholic land-
owner, not the landless labourer, cottier and peasant. To win for
Ireland the double victories of 'one religion' and 'ownership of the
soil' seemed a natural conjunction of aspirations.[9] And after the
Union, when the grand design of religious and economic triumph
faded, secret societies still existed and brought areas of the country
into disorder and a kind of primitive terror.

The second development was almost the opposite of peasant
organisation. Ireland had developed a Catholic middle class,

excluded from the parliamentary and municipal franchise, from state and municipal office, and from the commission of the peace, but able to make money out of respectable activities such as medicine and commerce (though not yet the law). Catholics also profited from the cattle-grazing business. Such people were bound to question the ground of their exclusion from all political life. The Catholic middle classes were soon to achieve prominence in the campaign for the mitigation of civil and legal disabilities. In the process they shouldered aside the less vigorous, more deferential Catholic landowners who up to 1792 were the leaders of the Catholic Committee, a body founded some years earlier to represent Catholic political interests. Ultimately this newly emerged class would comprise Daniel O'Connell's most fervent supporters and loyal lieutenants. This experience, this participation in group activity, in signing petitions, in urging the Catholic case to both the Irish and, above all, the British parliament, helped to build a sense of solidarity that straddled the Union but was profoundly changed by it. The Union, with its guarantee of at least a framework of political stability, enabled vigorous, disruptive and even illegal means to be employed without the danger of a breakdown of order and a dissolution of the fabric of the state, such as happened in 1798.

A breakdown was not far away when the Irish parliament met in session in January 1798. Indeed, it had been threatened for the past decade, and in some areas of the country had actually occurred. County Armagh in particular was notorious for disturbances and sectarian clashes, with Protestant Peep o' Day Boys and Catholic Defenders contesting territory, or at least the domination of territory, in an area where the two religious groups were so evenly balanced that each might with confidence engage his opponent. In September 1795 the most serious engagement, the so-called 'Battle of the Diamond' in the north of the county, precipitated the foundation of the Orange Order, a body drawing its main strength from the lower orders of society, but with the gentry willing in many cases to give its approval to a movement which it could hardly resist and which it might with profit aspire to lead.

The increasing instability of certain parts of Ireland, and of Irish society, altered both the membership and tactics of the United Irishmen, who had derived their concern for radical political reform from the political excitement and opportunity created by the

American and French revolutions. The United Irishmen were originally typical of radical political societies, drawing their support mainly from the Protestant mercantile and professional classes of Belfast and Dublin, and impatient of the corruption and lack of democratic politics found in Ireland, Britain and, for that matter, around the world. Like the doyen of radicalism, Thomas Paine, the United Irishmen had only vague and general ideas of what the Ireland they sought to create would look like; they knew, however, that it would be clean, pure, parsimonious of public money, and based upon the 'people'—which, in the Irish context, meant, of course, including Catholics in the government of the nation. Some United Irishmen (for example, William Drennan) harboured doubts about the latter reform, considering the Irish Catholic a somewhat alarming figure, but one whose 'dark' mind must nonetheless be explored or, better still, freed from its medieval chains. The United Irish leadership did not initially wish to break the connection with Britain; they had no clear intention of resorting to arms.[10] But by the mid-1790s they were a movement under pressure as the British government, alarmed by the spread of radicalism throughout the British Isles, sought to infiltrate their organisation by spies and to use (often brutal) force to break the movement before it should be able to organise for any kind of armed uprising.

These measures were welcomed by Protestants in areas where Defender activity was most intense, in Down, Cavan, Meath, Monaghan, Kildare and Dublin. Protestant fears were heightened by the rumours sweeping the country, reviving memories of past confiscations and revenge for the great defeat of Catholic Ireland in 1690. Some United Irishmen were moved to write pamphlets assuring Protestants that no such reversal of the verdict of the past was contemplated by them, and that Protestant land titles, in particular, were safe. But their growing desperation caused the United Irish leadership to seek an alliance with the Defenders, whose numbers and discontent could hardly be ignored by any would-be radical or revolutionary body. And the hopes of Catholics (enfranchised on the same terms as Protestants in 1793) for a peaceful attainment of their outstanding political goal, the right to sit in parliament, were dashed when the ambitious but over-eager viceroy, Lord Fitzwilliam, was dismissed and recalled in February 1795 because he had exceeded his instructions and made too close an alliance with supporters of Henry Grattan.

By 1796 the United Irish movement had been transformed: it was now committed to the Defenders, and it was also disintegrating as a coherent political force. The Defenders were difficult to control, and co-ordination of effort, already doubtful, was rendered even less likely by the government's repressive measures, which made the planning of a centrally directed uprising most uncertain. Moreover, the obviously sectarian nature of the Defender organisation frightened away many of the early United Irish leaders. But the government's determination to suppress the subversive elements only made it more imperative for the United Irishmen and Defenders to hazard all on some rebellious gamble, however risky an enterprise that might prove to be. And, with the possibility of French help, it might have a chance of success. In September 1796 John Goddard of Newry wrote to the Marquis of Downshire about 'four young men' who were overheard singing 'Let us unite with France, / And our right advance'—and to the tune of 'God Save the King'.[11]

It was felt by some, particularly in the north, that a 'great deal of hanging' would 'keep the stiff *Presbyterians* in that quarter in order'.[12] General Lake's severe repression in the north weakened the United Irishmen's chances of a successful rising; similar methods were employed in Munster and Leinster; and in Dublin some leading conspirators were arrested. The rebels must now act, or give up the game; and in May 1798 the rising began. It made most progress in County Wexford, which, however, became the scene of a ferocious sectarian conflict. Both sides threw compassion aside, as soldiers, rebels, Catholic militia and Protestant yeomanry vied with each other in atrocity. The reason is not hard to find. Habits of servility on the one hand, and mastery on the other, afforded little room for mercy and restraint. There were growing fears and rumours of extermination, with Protestant and Catholic casting each other in the role of exterminators. Atrocities were encouraged by the whirlwind effect of rebellion itself, when reprisal and cruelty suddenly became possible, and command from above broke down in the murderous atmosphere of civil war. 'You may rely on this war being considered a religious one,' wrote Richard Annesley to Downshire in June 1798. 'The priests exhort them, lead them and make them desperate.'[13] As for the Presbyterian rebels of County Antrim, they were described by a contemporary as 'cloven-footed'.[14] Even after the rebellion appeared to be crushed, by the middle of June, Lord Cornwallis, the British commander-in-chief, wrote in exasperation of the indiscipline of the militia and their ferocity against the people, and of the Irish parliament's overwhelming feeling against any kind of clemency: 'By their unaccountable policy, they would drive four-fifths of the community into irreconcilable rebellion.'[15]

It was the firm belief of the overwhelming mass of Protestants that the 'four-fifths' of the Catholics were already in irreconcilable rebellion; and this was given fresh credence when in September 1798 the French did at last land at Killala Bay, in the west of Ireland. Such an expedition had been the subject of rumour in April 1798;[16] but when the landing took place, it once again threw the country into a panic, and the suppression of this bold enterprise was accompanied by ferocity, revenge and reprisal. As far as the Protestants of Ireland were concerned, the whole incendiary business had been a narrow escape; and despite their proclaimed belief that the 'loyal gentry' had saved their country by their example, no one could doubt that the British government had through its exertions done its bit to save the loyal gentry. And the terrible events of '98, the casual slaughter of combatant and non-combatant alike, checked the growing confidence of Irish patriots like Henry Grattan that Ireland could look to a future when the sects would cease to rail against each other. More significantly, it marked the culmination of that process by which the British government was coming to acknowledge that Ireland could not, with safety, be left to her own devices and trusted, by and large, to manage her own political affairs. By intervening in Irish politics in the 1790s the British government had in a real sense contributed to the growing instability of Ireland, since each group looked with hope or fear, depending on its own perception of where its best interests lay, on the intentions and policy of the British. Had the government carried out its determination to remove the remaining penal statutes affecting Catholics, it might have achieved some major victory in its desire to detach Catholics from revolution. But the Defenders were in any event locked in battle with their Orange enemies; and the Presbyterian radicals of the north sought a thorough reform of the whole parliamentary system, which no British government was prepared to countenance. The policy, therefore, of mediating Irish politics through the device of the Irish parliament had failed, and failed disastrously. And its failure had plunged not only Ireland but the whole British Isles into a major political and strategic crisis.

Ireland could not remain in a state of smothered rebellion; nor could she continue to pose a threat to Britain's western flank in time of international crisis and war. The only alternative that seemed to meet British needs was some form of union between the two countries, for union would give strength and direction to British policy, unite the resources of the two countries, end the kind of confusion and policy divergences typical of the 1790s, and bring Ireland peace and prosperity under a single government—for Ireland was regarded as a rich country rendered poor through political instability. All this a union could achieve, providing that an essentially Protestant constitution could be reconciled with the pragmatic and enlightened need to accommodate Catholics within its framework.[17]

These were persuasive arguments; and given the fact that in a United Kingdom the Protestants would form part of a great majority of their co-religionists, with British citizenship offering them a kind of permanent majority status, it would seem certain that the Protestants of Ireland would immediately perceive where their true interest lay and at once accept the new constitution. This might appear even more likely when the terms upon which the British government sought union were drawn up. Ireland was to have a generous representation in the new parliament of the United Kingdom, with 32 peers and 100 M.P.s. The churches of England and Ireland were to be united as an established church. Ireland was to contribute to the expenses of the United Kingdom in the proportion of two to fifteen, that is to say she would pay two-seventeenths of the whole. This would be reconsidered at the end of a twenty-year period. Ireland and Great Britain were to retain their own responsibility for their national debts, and when the two national debts stood in proportion to each other of two to fifteen, then the two fiscal systems could be fused. There was to be free trade between the two countries, with two exceptions: as long as there were two fiscal systems in existence excisable articles were to be subject to countervailing duties; and for twenty years a number of Irish-manufactured products were to be protected by a 10 per cent duty.[18]

When the details of the proposed union are examined, they reveal a remarkably fair treatment of the Irish: remarkable in that the terms were not only quite generous, but also in that they were drawn up solely by the British government and were not the subject of negotiation as the Anglo-Scottish Union had been. The only major complaint—that Ireland's share of responsibility for United Kingdom expenditure was too large—became a reality only because of the long-drawn-out and unforeseen war with France, which imposed a financial burden on both countries, but one especially felt by the poorer classes in both. Yet in January 1799 the Marquis of Downshire was told that 'The idea of a Union engrosses the public mind, and the warmth with which argument is carried on becomes very disagreeable. The generality of the people wish to combat the principle—consequently not to have the merits brought forward. The most violent of the corporations say they will sue for Catholic Emancipation in preference.'[19] This seems astonishing in the light of the recent narrow escape of Protestant Ireland. But the Protestants had a sense of tradition and a keen perception of what they regarded as the grandeur of their nation's political heritage. Protestant Ireland was won in the general war for religious and civil liberty in 1689–90. Nature never intended Ireland to be a province; she had 'the outlines of a kingdom'. Under the benign influence of her parliament, Ireland had witnessed the flourishing of her arts, her commerce, her genius. Her parliament had given inspiration to the Irish gentry to defend themselves in the late rebellion. If all this were thrown away, Ireland would suffer.[20] She would pay an economic price for the loss of her parliament. If the trade of both islands were to be thrown open to each 'unclogged with duty', then 'the enlargement must instantaneously ruin, if not extinguish utterly, some of our best manufactures'.[21] There were other, more immediate, reasons for anti-Unionism. Cavan, Monaghan, Armagh, Tyrone and Fermanagh were centres of Orange anti-Unionist sentiment, counties where sectarian feeling ran highest, and where the exclusively Protestant yeomanry force had gained many recruits, fired by a distrust of the British government's tendency to be 'soft' on Catholics. Anti-Unionist sentiment was also strong in Wexford, Kildare, Carlow and Wicklow, where Protestants had suffered in the '98 rising.[22] But whatever the range of motives, there were still to be found Protestants in Dublin who were talking of petitioning for repeal of the Union as much as a decade after its passing.

Catholics, for their part, were uncertain of how to approach the great question of the day. Some, such as Daniel O'Connell, sympathised with the Protestant anti-Unionists' notions of Ireland's rights as a nation; but most were prepared to believe that their grievances might well be redressed by a British government anxious to win as much support for union as possible; and if such were to be the case, then, one observer wrote, it would be sufficient to 'gain them over to the Union'.[23] But while Catholics debated, anti-Unionist Protestants acted, and the opposition in parliament at the beginning of 1799 was lively enough to delete a paragraph in the address to the throne approving of union, by 109 votes to 104. The government then set to its task of winning a majority for its policy, by any means within the political tolerance of the time—means which later generations branded as 'corruption'. But in any event it was clear that the anti-Unionists in the Irish parliament could never hope to achieve the success that the patriots led by Henry Grattan had enjoyed in 1782, for the simple reason that there was clearly not going to be a repetition of the conditions of 1782, when a sympathetic opposition party in the Westminster parliament took office with a whole series of measures already promised to the patriots at College Green. Pitt was secure; and perpetual opposition to the Union would mean exclusion for an ambitious Irish politician from any hope of future political advancement. When the session of 1800 began, the government knew that it had a majority for the Union; resolutions embodying its scheme were adopted by the Irish Commons and Lords by 28 March, and by the British parliament by the second week of May. On 6 June the Irish House of Commons received and approved its committee report of the Union bill by 153 votes to 88. The bill was then laid before the British parliament; and after each parliament had made final minor amendments which the other accepted, the terms were embodied in identical bills and given the royal assent on 2 July, in the British parliament, and 1 August, in the Irish. By now, the great public excitement of 1799 had evaporated, and the Union was carried against a background of apathy.

The 100 Irish M.P.s who took themselves across to the Union parliament sat for a mixture of county seats (64), borough seats (35), and Dublin University (1). They fitted easily enough into the society and working of the Westminster institution and proved themselves loyal supporters of the administration in a true eighteenth-century fashion. In 1806–7 no fewer than fifty of them seem to have given their support to Pitt, to the 'Ministry of All the Talents', and to the Duke of Portland. The great landed families— the Beresfords, Ponsonbys and Fosters—maintained their political interest, dominated their localities, and dispensed patronage to all and sundry; in short, they behaved as most political families did in the pre-reform era (much to the frustration of historians who regard non-ideological politics as highly unsatisfactory). Those who had been strenuous opponents of the Union, like the Marquis of Downshire and John Foster, Speaker of the Irish House of Commons, were not victimised for their behaviour, but compensated for their pecuniary loss. Even messengers and doorkeepers of the now defunct Irish parliament buildings were given compensation for loss of earnings. Henry Grattan was elected to the British parliament in 1805, where he soon established himself as an orator whose performances earned him as much admiration in London as they had in Dublin.[24]

Eighteenth-century Ireland had been part of the wider cultural world of the British Isles; and almost all her writers addressed themselves to themes that were of a more general interest, with little or no specifically Irish content. Now, however, the early years of the Union saw the beginnings of a literary development that was to have important effects on both English and Irish cultural and political perceptions. Maria Edgeworth's *Castle Rackrent* (1800) was the first Irish novel to address itself to an Irish theme but also to an English audience, for she was careful to assure her readers that the events she unfolded bore no resemblance to the Ireland of her own time. She looked forward to an era when, under the Union, Ireland would lose her identity and thereby free herself from the dislocations of eighteenth-century society. But there was another Ireland that was being forged in the new century, and under—and directly as a result of—the new political system created by the Union. Thomas Moore's *Melodies* (1808) looked back with fond regret to an ancient Irish civilisation which, perhaps, found echoes in the recent period of 'Grattan's Parliament', when there was a brief moment of love of country, fond patriotism and gentle ruination. But Moore was not merely a drawing-room, calling-card Irishman. He was capable of writing a powerful indictment of British policy in Ireland at the close of the eighteenth century. In

Corruption, and Intolerance: Two Poems: Addressed to an Englishman by an Irishman, published anonymously in 1808, he attacked both Whigs and Tories. Whigs were ridiculed because

> As bees, on flowers alighting, cease their hum,
> So, settling upon places, Whigs grow dumb.

But Tories were the main target of his verse:

> But, oh poor Ireland! if revenge be sweet
> For centuries of wrong, for dark deceit
> And with'ring insult—for the Union thrown
> Into thy bitter cup, when that alone
> Of slavery's draught was wanting—if for this
> Revenge be sweet, thou hast that daemon's bliss;
> For, sure, 'tis more than hell's revenge to see
> That England trusts the men who've ruin'd thee
>
> All that devoted England can oppose
> To enemies made friends and friends made foes,
> Is the rank refuse, the despis'd remains
> Of that unpitying power, whose whips and chains
> Drove Ireland first to turn, with harlot glance,
> Tow'rds other shores, and woo th' embrace of France.

Another version of the poem put the message of the last two lines even more fiercely:

> Made Ireland first, in wild, adulterous trance,
> Turn false to England's bed and whore with France.

Moore's savage indictment of English perfidy and policy revealed that, despite his dislike of the demagoguery and intolerance of Irish politics, he was capable of, as he put it, 'giving new forms to claims and remonstrances' which had been urged more eloquently before and 'would long ere now have produced their effect, but that the minds of some of our statesmen, like the pupil of the human eye, contract themselves the more, the stronger light there is shed upon them'.[25]

The method used by Moore—of addressing his poems 'to an Englishman'—was a common means of pamphleteering in the late eighteenth and early nineteenth centuries; it was used, for example, by Burke in his famous *Reflections on the Revolution in France*. It was also used by another celebrated writer of the day, who was able to combine the service of Ireland with a popularity in England. Lady Morgan (Sydney Owenson) contributed to the case of Ireland against English misconceptions, and to the idea of a lost 'Celtic' Irish identity—an identity more convincing to the English than the Irish (but which the Irish were adept at using when it suited them). Lady Morgan was something of a literary and social adventuress; her father had been an actor-manager at the Theatre Royal in Fishamble Street; and she claimed (in London) to be 'from the barony of Tireragh in the province of Connaught' and of an aristocratic line. Whatever the truth or falsehood of this, she was fascinated by what she saw as the feudal trappings of the west of Ireland; and when she came to write about this society in 1806, she chose a romantic subject: the 'Wild Irish Girl' Glorvina, the daughter of Myles MacDermott, 'Prince of Connaught'. This heroine's mysterious Celtic charm won the heart of Horatio Mortimer, a young man 'sent to a country against which I have a decided prejudice', and one which he supposed 'semi-barbarous, semi-civilised'. But Irish liberality, Irish wit, Irish learning, and the strange and glorious landscape soon dispelled his prejudice, and Mortimer ended up defending the country against all the calumnies of people like himself—Englishmen ignorant of Ireland. The story was related in a series of letters written by Mortimer to a friend; but equally significant were the references, taken from contemporary sources and printed at the foot of the page, describing traits and manners of the Irish, as noted by various learned observers. The author thus addressed the reader on two levels: on the fictional, through the plot; and on the factual, through the plentiful discussion and quotation that formed such a large part of the work.

Neither fiction nor 'fact', as it happened, bore much resemblance to the Ireland of Lady Morgan's day. But at least she gained for Ireland a sympathetic audience in England. Her book was published by the celebrated Sir Richard Phillips. Her readership responded to the sentimental side of Irish life (as it was later to respond to the gentle and gently nationalist ballads of Thomas Moore). It read about the loyalty of the Irish to their sovereigns, the Stuart kings. And it learned too about a dying or dead civilisation, one which touched its heartstrings in ways in which the reality of Irish life could not. Romantic Ireland was born as the Irish enlightenment drew to its close in rebellion. And the idea that there was indeed a 'fair Hibernia' that might be rescued from the clutches of conspirators, moonlighters, cruel peasants, irresponsible national leaders and the Roman Catholic Church exercised a certain fascination over the minds of many English people, including some politicians. The book even cast its spell over the ladies of the viceregal court, who commissioned jewellers to manufacture Glorvina brooches, despite Dublin Castle's reservations about its 'subversive' moral; and it ran through seven editions in two years.[26]

All this was far removed from the recent bloody and divisive rebellion, with its trail of burnings, hangings and shootings. Lady Morgan's rural arcadia might be located somewhere in Ireland; peasants were doubtless the generous and colourful people that were depicted in the pages of *The Wild Irish Girl*. But there was a peasant Ireland of the fact as well as of the mind, that was to engross the British authorities as they established themselves in Dublin Castle in 1801. For many of the poorest people in rural Ireland life was a steady struggle for existence, an existence always threatened by their social superiors armed with the full support of the law. Shortly after the Union there was a recrudescence of the violence perpetrated by secret societies whose presence had been endemic since the late eighteenth century: Threshers, Rockites and other clandestine groups whose ability to terrorise parts of the country-side, though it must not be exaggerated, was what most astonished English observers of Ireland. The targets of these societies were farmers, tithe-proctors who collected money due to the Church of Ireland, and on occasion priests whose demand for dues was considered unreasonable, sometimes even landlords, though they were a more remote and formidable prospect. Secret societies were organised by those at the bottom of the social scale, namely labourers or very poor tenants. They first resurfaced in 1806–7 in Connacht, and, though not political in outlook, they were a source of trouble to the government until the foundation of a professional police force by Sir Robert Peel in 1814 enabled the authorities to begin to gain the upper hand.[27]

Agrarian crime was carried forward into the new century; but the British government felt that at least it had scotched the radicalism of the United Irishmen. They were perhaps premature in their complacency. In 1803 Robert Emmet sought to raise the flag of rebellion again, this time without the help of the French. He planned to seize Dublin Castle and other important buildings, and then wait for the people to rally to the cause. On 23 July Emmet led a small force into the streets of the capital, engaged in a fight with some soldiers, and then fled, to be captured, tried and executed. He made an impressive speech from the dock, the first of the political performances that would later be repeated by the Fenians in 1867, by Roger Casement in 1916, and by others in the republican tradition: 'Let my character and my motives remain in repose in obscurity and peace, till other times and men can do them justice. *Then* shall my character be vindicated. *Then* may my epitaph be written.'[28] Emmet, like Lady Morgan, struck a chord not only in certain kinds of Irish but also English public opinion. As late as 1931 Raymond Postgate wrote that:

> As we think of the character of Robert Emmet we seem to be holding in our hands a prism of white, very clear glass. There is no distortion in it; the pellucid devotion to one idea prevents the many-coloured play of mixed motives. . . . Those who in their youth have been wholly devoted to a cause or an ideal, can see in young Emmet the boy that they once were, or, at least, hope that they once were. Nothing disturbed or distracted his devotion to Ireland; there were no distorting interests to flaw the clearness of the light.[29]

Emmet's recovery of insurrection from what another English admirer of a later age called the 'dismal period of violence, hatred, debauchery and self-interest'[30] had little relevance in the Ireland of 1803. Trees of Liberty were planted; the rebel resistance at Vinegar Hill was praised;[31] but republicanism as a serious popular force was dead.

It was dead, not only because the French were no longer 'on the sea', but because it could not offer any unifying ideology either to Catholics or to Presbyterians as it had in the years 1795–8. The experience of '98 had burned itself deeply into both the Presbyterian and Catholic consciousness, but in ways that were adverse to its repetition. Presbyterians were already shedding their radicalism before the rebellion: of 14,000 loyal yeomanry in Tyrone, Fermanagh, Down and Armagh, some 10,000 were Presbyterians, and, as one historian of their denomination put it, 'Not one of them was known to violate his oath of allegiance, as was done in other districts by some Roman Catholic members of this force.'[32] James

McKey of Belfast wrote to the Marquis of Downshire that 'To see Presbyterian ministers, with rich republican [i.e. radical Presbyterian] shopkeepers, sitting in the guardroom at daylight in the morning with their guns, had, in my eyes, a wonderful appearance.'[33] The sectarian warfare of the south caused them, in the words of a later commentator, to 'think it better to bear the oppression of landlords than to be piked by Papists. . . . Four generations had come and gone since the massacre of 1641, which was then almost forgotten; but fresh massacres in the South raised again the fears and excited the anger of the sturdy Ulster Presbyterians.'[34] The 'oppression of landlords' was, in time, to arouse again a spirit of radicalism in Presbyterian breasts; but it was of a different stamp from that of the United Irishmen, and was related to specific grievances rather than to the grievances of all Irish underdogs; and it could flourish—indeed, could *only* flourish—within the political context of the United Kingdom.

Catholics were also affected by the disaster of '98; and they, for the most part, did 'fear to speak' of it. Republicanism was an uneasy mixture of sectarian hatred and humanitarian philosophy; it had no clearly articulated political goal beyond that of making Ireland free, and even the nature of that freedom was not clearly defined: for some it meant the separation of Ireland from England, but others would have settled for less. And the rising star of Catholic politics, Daniel O'Connell, lost no opportunity to vilify the men of '98 and to characterise them as irreconcilably violent republicans.[35] But apart from O'Connell's efforts to prevent a repetition of the rebellion, there was the simple fact that '98 had produced enough horrors to frighten and offend the bulk of the Catholics of Ireland, who were far removed in sentiment from the Gothic bloodlust frequently attributed to them in the frenzied months of the rising.

Nevertheless, the Catholic role in the '98 rising was too tempting a target to be ignored by Protestant historians, intent on rewriting history that would conform to the old idea of the eternal enemy against whom all Protestants must be ever vigilant. One of the earliest writers in the field, Sir Richard Musgrave, aspired to blacken the entire Catholic community (while discreetly ignoring the Presbyterian role in the rising) in his *Memoirs of the Different Rebellions in Ireland, from the Arrival of the English*, published in 1801 and quickly reissued. Musgrave, an M.P. for a Waterford borough in the Irish parliament, declared that the concessions made

to Catholics for nearly twenty years, might reasonably have been
expected to attach them to the state and to their Protestant fellow-
countrymen. But this was far from the case, for not only the '98
rebellion but also 'incidents which daily occur' afforded proof 'that
the tenets of their religion, and the conduct of their priests, will
always make it impracticable'. Such tenets, infused into the minds
of the population, 'have been a fruitful source of discord and
rebellion ever since the introduction of the reformation'. Musgrave
excepted from his strictures the Catholic nobility, gentry and
business classes, who were 'loyal, generous and humane'; but these
were an 'inconsiderable part of the community'; and the Roman
Catholic religion was irreconcilably opposed to civilised government. Catholics should be satisfied with toleration and must not
interfere in the government of the kingdom, 'as such interference
would be incompatible with the Protestant ascendancy, which we
have resolved *with our lives and fortunes to maintain*'. Catholic and
Protestant could live side by side in perfect amity in Germany; but
different circumstances prevailed in Ireland, in that Catholics were
taught to keep alive the hope of recovering their forfeited estates.[36]

Musgrave's provocative essay did not go unanswered; it brought
forth a series of histories which set out to refute his version of the
remote and recent Irish past. Among these was the Rev. James
Gordon's *History of the Rebellion in Ireland* (1803). Gordon in his
preface expressed his disapproval of 'catholicity', but he 'rejoiced in
the repeal of penal statutes' and declared that 'Whenever the
government shall have manifestly shewn a resolution for the
concession for the catholics, counterfeit loyalists . . . will be seen
completely changing sides, and courting those against whom they
now rail, with marked assiduity.' These counterfeit loyalists, like
over-zealous Catholics, were, Gordon proclaimed, the enemies of
impartial history; and his efforts to counsel them to cultivate mutual
friendship brought forth 'the opposite of thanks from both'. But he
felt some degree of comfort in the reflection that those who
formerly boasted of their shocking atrocities now felt contrition for
these acts.[37] He hoped, in conclusion, that

> One of the happiest consequences reasonably expected to arise,
> in course of time, from the abolition of our national distinct-
> iveness, the removal of our local parliament, and its incorp-
> oration with that of Britain, is the subsidence of that rancorous

spirit of religious animosity, which has been the parent of so much mischief to this island.[38]

Francis Plowden, an English Catholic lawyer, also urged a proper union to counteract Musgrave and his like; and William Parnell in his *Historical Apology for the Irish Catholics* (1807) argued that the 1641 rising had broken out because of injustice to the Catholics. Dublin Castle, for its part, did not approve of Musgrave's attack on the loyalty of Catholics, or rather their disloyalty, through the ages, for it wished to ensure that past animosities would indeed be buried in the past. The Catholic historian Denis Taaffe, while attacking Musgrave, struck an otherwise conciliatory note urging that the Union be given a chance to justify itself.[39]

The Scottish Union, in this sense, had 'justified' itself, in that it had provided a framework within which Episcopalians could live in a toleration which they would not have enjoyed in an independent Scottish kingdom; and the hope was that, outside the narrower confines of the kingdom of Ireland, the same kind of toleration would ensue. James Gordon did not doubt that in the imperial parliament, 'as in a truly protestant assembly, the question will be decided in the spirit of liberality, justice, and true policy; over-ruling by an august determination the ominous croakings of little bigots'. He also listed some important reforms that were necessary to settle Ireland, notably the granting of long tenures to the peasants so as to encourage them to improve their tenancies, and also a fair and equitable commutation of tithes 'or such modification of them as would relieve the industrious cultivator, by obliging the lazy grazier, and the idle esquire, to bear a just proportion of the burthen'.[40] The Dowager Marchioness of Downshire, writing in 1804, feared that 'Without the interference of well-informed, independent Irish members . . . little can be done for Ireland, on account of the general want to particular information and know-ledge of its interests, which the English members cannot be supposed to possess.' But she took consolation from the reflection that 'No disposition in the government or parliament is wanting to meet and relieve all its wants, and much good is to be hoped for and expected.'[41]

This would be the real test of the Union. Not the manner of its passing, which later generations dismissed as 'corruption', but which was perfectly consistent with the political behaviour of the time; not the terms of the act itself, which were as fair and generous as the terms of union between England and Scotland more than a century before, despite the fact that the Scottish Union was negotiated between the two governments (though the Scottish Union, like the Irish, was regarded by Scottish Unionists as simply the lesser of two evils; lesser than standing alone as a satellite state).[42] Scotland did not, any more than Ireland, gain immediate economic benefits from her union with England. In Scotland trade and manufacture were on the fringe of a predominantly rural economy. The Scots were no more welcome in England after the 1707 act than were the Irish after 1801. And certainly the Irish had been more popular (or at least less unpopular) than the Scots in the eighteenth century. Dr Johnson noted that there was a ready hand of friendship for the Irish in England, whereas the Scots were held up to ridicule, their thick accents and their tendency to stick together derided.[43] It was not until the end of the eighteenth century that England and Scotland moved towards what A. V. Dicey and Robert S. Rait called 'moral unity'.[44] Yet even as late as 1781 Charles Macklin's dramatic masterpiece had as its central character Sir Pertinax MacSycophant, a hypocritical Scottish adventurer.[45]

Jonathan Swift believed that the Scottish Union was one that 'creates / Divided hearts, united states', and described it as 'our crazy double-bottom'd realm'.[46] Ireland entered a union with Irish and English hearts no more divided than those of Scotland and England were, and with a double-bottomed realm no more crazy than the Anglo-Scottish Union. But it had been widely anticipated that the one measure that would unite hearts and provide a steadying ballast to the Irish Union was the granting of Catholic Emancipation. Indeed, Union and Emancipation were two sides of the same policy, that of removing the festering discontent created by the British government's retreat from the Catholic cause after 1795, and of settling Ireland after the '98 rebellion. But when Pitt was involved in the long struggle to carry the Union, while at the same time absorbed with his conduct of the war with France, he found himself unable to modify George III's objection to Emancipation on the grounds that it would violate his coronation oath to maintain the Protestant constitution. On 6 February 1801 Robert Hobart wrote to the Marquis of Downshire describing 'Mr Pitt's, Lord Grenville's, Mr Dundas's and Lord Spencer's resignation' and explaining that 'The principle upon which the new administration is formed, is to resist what has been termed "Catholic Emancipation".'[47] This political episode revealed one of the obstacles confronting the confirmation of Irish Catholics as loyal British subjects; for if indeed the British constitution was a Protestant one, then Catholics were suspect, since their political tradition was one of sedition and disaffection. This was not true of the Catholic Church, which was anxious to reach an accommodation with the state; nor was it true of the Catholic gentry, who had led the reform movement since the 1780s. But the '98 rising left behind smouldering resentments and reminded each side in Ireland of its history. Thomas Cloney, in his *Personal Narrative* of the Wexford rising, referred to Protestants as a 'knot of descendants of Cromwellian settlers . . . who were ever tenacious about the tenure by which they held their possessions'; while a Protestant who had witnessed the summer of 1798 reminisced that 'Our farm . . . had been in our family since the Battle of the Boyne, for I am descended from a Williamite.'[48] The difficulty was that each side in Ireland felt badly used.

The British parliament in the late eighteenth and early nineteenth century was a powerful and respected body, and one which, moreover, was aware of the need to placate Catholic opinion, inasmuch as this could be done without raising the issue that had brought Pitt down in 1801. The government was concerned in 1807 with reports of disturbances in the rural areas of the west and midlands of Ireland, and it had been forewarned of a Catholic petition for Emancipation; it also hoped to raise new regiments among the Catholic Irish for service in the French war. It therefore seemed sound policy to look again at a whole list of Catholic demands which stopped short of Emancipation: extra money for the Catholic seminary at Maynooth; a measure of tithe reform; financial provision for the Catholic clergy. There was also the possibility of a commission to inquire into education in Ireland with a view to founding a general system of Irish education. But these hopeful plans were frustrated when King George objected to the government's proposal to enable Catholics to hold commissions in the armed services in Britain (they could already do so in Ireland under the terms of the relief act of 1793). The government intended to use Catholic levies to restore order in disturbed areas of Ireland, instead of the controversial Protestant yeomanry. And if the 1793 act were amended, they would be free to attend mass in Britain before being collected for dispatch to foreign service. The king's objections to the government's proposed course of action caused dissension in the cabinet between those who were most sympathetic to the Catholic claim and those who were prepared to resort to a compromise in the hope of accommodating the king's point of view. Grenville was himself by no means averse to leaving office, and when the king asked him for a pledge that he should not raise the Catholic question again, Grenville resigned.[49]

This was a disappointing setback for the high hopes entertained by some for the future of Ireland under the Union, and Henry Grattan was blamed by some for not clearly indicating his support for the ministry and thus strengthening its hand. He claimed that it was his belief that the Catholic question should be a non-party one.[50] But the episode revealed that a British government was prepared to adopt measures disliked by many Protestants in Ireland, especially, it must be said, if such measures were deemed vital to the interests of Great Britain and the empire. Whether this could be said to reveal that Westminster had wider horizons, or only a different set of equally narrow ones, remained to be seen.

As far as Catholics in Ireland were concerned, 'moral unity' would be put to the test over the question that followed hard upon the downfall of Grenville's ministry: the revival of the debate on Catholic Emancipation. The longevity and in the end the intensity of this controversy was to alter the political landscape of an Ireland that, a decade after the rising of 1798, seemed, if not tranquil, then at least politically manageable.

The immediate aftermath of the Union was as important as its prelude; it was not the 'political vacuum' which often occupies a sentence in history books. It saw the beginning or advance of some vital political, social and economic developments. There was the rapid decline of Presbyterian radicalism and, in addition, the shift of conservative Protestant organisations like the Orange Order from opposition to support of the Union—though the Orange Order, after its cantankerous fashion, managed to combine a refusal to respond to Emmet's call for its members to 'return from the paths of delusion' with complaints that an Irish parliament would not have been so neglectful as to allow such a conspiracy.[51] There was the general acceptance in Great Britain that the Union was the permanent constitutional framework of the British Isles; yet there was the continuation of a separate Irish administration that seemed to indicate that Ireland was British with a difference. The period saw the continuation of British uncertainty about the Catholic question, and a lost opportunity for the British state to place itself in the same kind of close relationship with the Catholic Church as other European states, Protestant in outlook, had managed to achieve. It witnessed the last flare-up of republicanism in 1803; it saw the beginning of republicanism as a cult, with Emmet's celebrated speech from the dock, and the 'respectability of insurrection'.[52] These years revealed that agrarian discontent and violence were not a thing of the past, but were an indication of the economic problem that Britain had now taken responsibility for; they also saw the beginning of the birth of 'romantic Ireland', a concept that made its way as much (if not more) into English as Irish sentiment, offering an image of a 'fair Hibernia' which helped overcome English anti-Catholic feeling and gain for Ireland a sympathetic audience. They witnessed too the founding of a myth: the idea of Grattan's Parliament as a sort of high-water mark of Ireland's political existence, when

> Though Britain's sunshine hour with thee be past,
> Ierne still one ray of glory gives,
> And feels but half thy loss while Grattan lives.[53]

It was a myth that was to inspire such diverse leaders of public opinion in Ireland as Daniel O'Connell, Isaac Butt, Charles Stewart Parnell, Arthur Griffith and William Butler Yeats. The years immediately following the Act of Union were as significant for the future of Ireland as the climactic rebellion of 1798 and the great constitutional change which was its consequence.

The Catholic Question and Protestant Answers, 1808–29

CATHOLICS had Irish Protestant champions in the British parliament in the early years of the Union; in particular they had the support of Henry Grattan, who, in his very first speech as newly elected member for Malton in Yorkshire in May 1805, disputed the claims of those who alleged that Catholics could not be loyal citizens. He argued that, since the extermination of the Catholics was out of the question, and since their partial adoption had failed, then there was no alternative but 'absolute incorporation': 'What the best men in Ireland wished to do but could not do . . . you may accomplish.'[1] And indeed it seemed that the British parliament could accomplish what the Irish parliament could not do: for both English and Irish members gave Emancipation increasing support, and even in the House of Lords opposition was diminishing. And in order to allay English fears about Catholic allegiance to a foreign pope, Grattan and his supporters suggested that Emancipation should be accompanied by the safeguard of government control over episcopal appointments, not on theological but on purely political grounds: the crown should be empowered to veto any candidate considered unsound. This would dispose of the prejudice that the papacy still held the power of excommunicating its adherents and thus maintaining its grip on their consciences and behaviour. In the future nomination of bishops the king could intervene to exercise his royal prerogative: 'In France the King used to name; in Canada the King names; it is by no means incompatible with the Catholic religion that our King should name; and I do not see any great difficulty on this head.'[2]

Grattan declared that the Catholics of Ireland had authorised him to press for Emancipation under the veto condition. But between 1800 and 1808 Catholic opinion was changing, and becoming more self-assertive. They had, after all, been politically active for decades; they were writing histories to vindicate their conduct in the turbulent politics of the last decade; and the lawyers, merchants and professional men who formed the emerging Catholic middle class were less deferential than the handful of aristocrats and landed gentry who had steered Catholic politics towards Emancipation since the 1790s. These leaders had practised the politics of deference, seeking to persuade the British government that neither it nor the Protestant people of Ireland and Great Britain had anything to fear from the admission of Catholics to parliament. But by 1808 the more restive elements in the Catholic Committee had found a leader who could represent both their impatience with the delay over Emancipation, and their determination not to accept it on terms other than their own: Daniel O'Connell.

O'Connell was himself from a landed background, a lawyer by training, and a politician to the tips of his fingers. His large figure, his robust style and his penchant for the wounding phrase made him a formidable opponent; his unapologetic Catholicism rendered him the butt of every anti-Catholic jibe in the religious politics of his day and made his verbal and physical armour essential to his chances of survival. He established his reputation as a lawyer, and as one whose extensive legal practice had as its central purpose the defence of Catholics against the rigours and prejudices of the Protestants of Ireland, whose key positions in the magistracy, the police and the judiciary made their power a real obstacle to Catholic advancement in the world. This earned him his early nickname of 'Counsellor'; and it was upon this reputation as a popular and successful lawyer that his political career was founded. In many ways O'Connell typified Catholic Ireland: his 'healthy, good-humoured face',[3] his expansive style, his wit and eloquence, even his large physical build, all invited caricature; and O'Connell was portrayed as the very epitome of the priest-ridden, irresponsible Catholic, whose penchant for scurrility was notable even by the lax political standards of his day.

This scurrility, however, could provoke resentment even among his Catholic followers as O'Connell set himself to persuade or dragoon his opponents in the Catholic Committee to follow his advice on the question of Emancipation, and more particularly on the veto. The veto was open to many objections, in the view of O'Connell and his supporters; these objections were not theological, but social and political. It was easy to arouse opinion about the sort of man who would accept the veto of an anti-Catholic English king: he would be tempted into the world of Dublin Castle, where he would become a spy or a sycophant; he would be a man of 'family connections' with an electioneering interest; he would be at the behest of Orange magistrates; he would even encourage his people to become Protestants or rebels.[4] But these prejudices, colourful and arousing though they might be, were by no means shared by all members or supporters of the Catholic Committee. Richard Lalor Sheil, in particular, spoke for the vetoists, arguing that the real value of the veto lay in that it would disarm Protestant and English objections. This became a difficulty when in 1813 the House of Commons approved of the principle of Catholic Emancipation with securities. The Catholic hierarchy, after much deliberation, decided that they could assent to the bill without incurring the sin of schism, and the Catholic Board (a new Catholic organisation created after the government raided meetings of the Catholic Committee in October and December 1811) supported them. This occasioned further dissension among Catholics, with vetoists and anti-vetoists arguing their respective cases.[5] All this dissipated Catholic energy and set back the cause of Emancipation. But within a few years the movement was assisted, and directed towards O'Connell's control, by events on the British political stage. This new trend started in 1821 when a prominent Protestant supporter of the Emancipation movement, William Conyngham Plunket, brought the case before the House of Commons yet again.

Plunket's speech on 28 February 1821 was significant not only for its eloquence but also for its argument that concessions to Catholics were inevitable and that the tide was flowing in the direction of Emancipation. Sir Robert Peel's attack on the proposal was equally significant, for he conceded that if he could be convinced that Emancipation would indeed effect a reconciliation between Catholic and Protestant in Ireland, he would give way; but he added that he did not see how a long struggle for power between the contending groups in Ireland could be ended by an alteration of the penal code. And he still denied that the Protestant British constitution could be safe in the hands of those who would not give security for their attachment to the reformed religion.[6] Plunket's motion was carried in the House of Commons by a majority of six: the first pro-Catholic majority since 1813. In the following April his bill, which included the veto and which gave to the state the right of access to information concerning all correspondence between Catholics in the United Kingdom and Rome, was carried in its third reading by nineteen votes. The anti-Emancipationists rallied and used the Lords to defeat the bill. The king took an inflexibly Protestant stance on the issue, and the Duke of York, who was expected to succeed George IV, contributed an anti-Catholic speech.[7]

Peel's anti-Emancipationist speech revealed that there was a body of thought that identified the Union openly and unequivocally with the Protestant interest in Ireland. This was dangerous in that it implied that if Catholics campaigned for political rights, they could only overcome the Protestant opposition by attacking the Union as well. But the Emancipationist success in the Commons indicated that there were those who insisted that the Catholic claim must be pressed in the face of Irish Protestant opposition. Protestants in Ireland now found their new circumstances revealed most clearly. They no longer controlled their own political destinies, as they had felt they did in the eighteenth century in their own kingdom of Ireland. They could for the moment take comfort in the reflection that sections of British public and parliamentary opinion were on their side. In Scotland, for example, the anti-Emancipationist campaign became a popular and highly charged affair, strident in its denunciation of the Catholic cause. Although Ireland lacked an independent political existence, the British preoccupation with the religious and constitutional settlement of 1688–9 nevertheless seemed to indicate that the Union and the Irish Protestant cause were safely, and inextricably, linked. But this was to overestimate the similarity between British and Irish Protestant perspectives.

The Plunket affair was a major blow to the vetoists in the Catholic camp. Their willingness to accept what O'Connell denounced as near-treason to their creed and their nation was discredited by the defeat of a vetoist bill. And since the institutions of Britain were biased by two-thirds (Lords and Crown) against one-third (Commons) on the anti-Catholic side, O'Connell now turned his attention to the possibility of creating a powerful engine of Catholic pressure within Ireland. This would have been an impossible concept for the moderate and conservative leaders of Catholic opinion before O'Connell, for it involved mobilising people whose political voice was muted by landlord power and whose numbers might include non-electors as well as electors—another dangerous precedent. But O'Connell was a radical as well as an Emancipationist; a parliamentary reformer as well as a defender of the Catholics of Ireland. And the power of parliamentary elections was revealed when in February 1823 a pro-Emancipationist Protestant candidate, Colonel Henry White, was narrowly elected for County Dublin. O'Connell participated in the campaign and enjoyed the spectacle of Protestants venting their frustration and fury on the successful candidate. Moreover, the experience convinced O'Connell and, equally importantly, Richard Lalor Sheil (who had earlier experienced deep differences with O'Connell over Emancipationist tactics) that the organisation and mobilisation of Catholics were needed. The campaign must become a popular cause, able to tap Catholic discontent and sense of grievance, yet contain that within legal and political bounds. After negotiations involving Catholic gentry and middle-class leaders a new organisation, the Catholic Association, was founded in 1823. This body did not immediately sweep into its ranks all the Catholics of Ireland; some spoke of it with contempt. But its choice of tactics was sound: it would press the claim for Emancipation; but it would not only do that (for, after all, Emancipation was to most of the Catholics of Ireland a rather abstract affair); it would in addition provide the role which O'Connell himself filled in his early career: that of 'Counsellor' to the Catholics of Ireland, the redresser of their immediate grievances, the defender of their rights.[8]

This anticipated the tactics of later mass democratic movements in Ireland, which combined a broad and not always popular political demand with an attention to the more pressing concerns of the Catholic people. Emancipation would be strengthened not only by its association with real and felt grievances, but also by the fact that these grievances, it was said, could be remedied by the achievement of the more abstract claim. Thus Emancipation would not simply be a battle for loyal royalist Catholics to sit in the British legislature and take their rightful place among its members; it would also be invested with a kind of millennial sentiment, a sense of a people coming out of bondage and casting down their foes. This in turn had implications for their 'foes'; for it placed liberal Protestants in a dilemma, since their sort were now inevitably associated with the enemies of the people, and could deem themselves so regarded. The radically-minded *Belfast Monthly Magazine*, drawing attention to the *Dublin Evening Express*'s description of itself as 'authentically Catholic', remarked sorrowfully on the implications of this and of such expressions as 'good old Catholic Ireland'. This would perpetuate 'a distinctiveness; a separating instead of an associating spirit; and a system of exclusion instead of assimilation'. It added that

> If Protestant bigots be desirous to drive down the stakes of a new Pale in Ireland, let not the Catholics be busied on their side, in the very same employment, but rather approve their liberality and wish to anticipate complete emancipation, by mixing as much as possible with their Protestant brethren, and not fall back, of themselves, into a sullen and suspicious seclusion.

The Catholic mind, it concluded, would 'be much benefited by *travel*'.[9] Political life in Ireland after 1823 was breaking the mould, ending the stagnation that had been its characteristic since 1808; but it was also entering a dangerous and divisive period, and one which would leave a lasting impact on the Catholic and Protestant consciousness.

There were other signs too that the mould was breaking. Britain stood by Protestant Ireland on the Emancipation question (or at least the Lords and Crown did); but this was because the Lords and Crown, and much of the Commons, were convinced that Emancipation would be dangerous to the British constitution. It was, however, a logical extension of that argument to maintain that the British constitution could be secured by other means as well: by holding the line on Emancipation, but also by using British administrative and legislative power to redress Catholic grievances in Ireland itself. This would not threaten the British state (though it might threaten its Protestant extension in Ireland itself), and it would be an earnest of the essential goodness of British intentions.

In 1821 the king made a conciliatory visit to Ireland and was, together with the new Lord Lieutenant, the Marquis of Wellesley, presented with loyal addresses by Catholic representatives. Plunket, the champion of Emancipation, was made Attorney-General in place of the anti-Catholic William Saurin. O'Connell himself described Wellesley as 'the harbinger of Emancipation' who was 'determined to put down the Orange faction'. And Wellesley, vain and an indifferent administrator though he was, showed himself willing to be conciliatory to the leader of Catholic Ireland, with whom he shook hands and exchanged civil words.

A reforming Lord Lieutenant would not be short of work. Among the objectives of the Catholic Association were listed the need to

> obtain legal redress for Catholics injured by Orange violence and oppression who were unable to obtain redress themselves. To prevent, legally, Orange processions, violence, etc., and to bring the perpetrators to court. To prosecute Orange murderers. To procure for Catholics all rights to which they were entitled by law but which for thirty years had been denied them.[10]

As well as the Orange question, there was a whole congeries of grievances which O'Connell could work up into an issue and then offer for redress. One was the question of Catholic burials in churchyards, which were then all in Protestant hands. In September 1823 the sexton of St Kevin's churchyard, Dublin, refused to follow normal practice and allow a Catholic priest to recite the *De profundis* over the grave of a parishioner. The Catholic Association acknowledged that this was indeed a departure from the usual Protestant attitude; but O'Connell exploited the controversy to arouse a sense of indignation among Catholics about the implications of the refusal.[11] It was certainly brilliant politics to spread a sense of grievance about a procedure which had been accepted as inevitable, but it raised the question of whether or not the creation of a 'grievance culture' would offer a secure and stable base for the union of Catholic, Protestant and Dissenter that O'Connell had made his declared aim.

Issues such as these had deeper implications. For O'Connell was pointing to the central anomaly of Ireland, the fact that its population and its politics were, in a manner of speaking, out of step with each other. The population of Ireland was, by the (not very accurate) census of 1821, some 6,801,827, of which the vast majority were Catholic. This majority was general, except in the north-east, and even there the local Protestant majority was divided between Episcopalian and Presbyterian. In the early years of the nineteenth century Irish Presbyterians were conspicuous by their political absence. They had their own church system, their own society, and had no desire to play a prominent role in politics. Nor were they to be numbered among radical agitators, for the memory of 1798 was as frightening and painful to them as it was to Catholics. Their preoccupations were limited to establishing their own college for the education of their ministers of religion, who were previously obliged to migrate to Scotland for that privilege. Their only comment so far on the Catholic Emancipation issue was to pass in 1813 a motion in the Synod of Ulster in favour of admitting Catholics to parliament. The intellectual energies of Presbyterians were absorbed by debates on the theory of the Trinity and the nature of Christ. But by the 1820s, as the O'Connellite pressure began to make itself felt, Presbyterians too began to exhibit what the *Northern Whig* admitted was 'an inveterate and determined hostility' against Roman Catholic claims. And the staunchly anti-Emancipationist *Belfast Newsletter* exhorted Presbyterians to come forward and oppose a measure 'the final issue of which will be the entire subversion of your political and religious rights'.[12]

Still, O'Connell cannot be blamed for the conditions that made this change of mood possible. As a witness giving evidence in 1824 to a House of Commons committee on disturbances in Ireland put it when he was asked if he thought these were 'political':

> Yes, I am sure political feeling always mixes with these disturbances; when there are disturbances arising from any immediate pressure upon the people, political causes always come in to aggravate and to increase those disturbances.
>
> What is the nature of those political feelings?
>
> I think they arise altogether out of the distinctions which the law makes betwixt Catholic and Protestant.[13]

O'Connell's desire was to bring such discontented opinion within the scope of his movement, where it could be profitably utilised; but his anxiety that Catholics should be given equality with Protestants arose also from his deep distaste for violence, whether social, sectarian or political. He must therefore attach as many people as possible, from as many social groups as possible, to his movement, as much for the sake of order as for the sake of political power. His method was to use the Catholic Association as a kind of popular club, which anyone could join on payment of a penny a month. This utterly changed the nature of the Association, which until 1824 attracted only limited support, with its subscription fee of one guinea. Now the 'Catholic rent' was collected on a Sunday with the aid of the parochial clergy. O'Connell, ever the modern politician, recruited newspaper owners and journalists to popularise his association, and he benefited both from the abusive reaction of some Protestants to his movement and from the willingness of Catholic bishops to emerge from their studied silence and put the case for what one of their number, James Doyle, Bishop of Kildare and Leighlin, called a reform of the 'state of the civil laws'. Doyle called for Catholics to be admitted to full equality under the British constitution, and he declared that Catholic clergy could no longer remain silent, however much they admired the British constitution, since 'our fetters are too galling, our chains are too closely riveted, our keepers are too unfeeling'. Doyle, like other leaders of Catholic opinion such as Sheil, Thomas Wyse, and indeed O'Connell himself, were certain of their loyalty to the crown and constitution; just laws, justly administered, would enable Catholics to give their ready acceptance to the Union and to be accommodated comfortably within it. Doyle admired Grattan as much as he admired O'Connell; and he appealed to the British government to redress Catholic grievances and establish the Union on a firm basis, instead of the system of coercion which was now, apparently, becoming one of its chief characteristics.[14]

The question was, however, whether or not the British government could satisfy Catholics, and at the same time avoid arousing the wrath of Protestants, whose idea of the Union was that it was instituted precisely to continue those privileges and advantages, those laws and institutions, which Doyle and O'Connell were asking Britain to remove. Not that all Protestants were against constitutional reform: far from it, for it was always a characteristic of Irish politics in this period that liberal Protestants were to be found among the Emancipationists, and that many Irish Protestants found the strident rhetoric and lively activities of the Orange Order offensive and embarrassing. The Orangeman was the butt of the Protestant writer Charles Lever, who in his highly popular novel *Charles O'Malley, the Irish Dragoon* (1840) depicted the Orange stereotype, Billy Crow, as a figure of ridicule, whose religious bigotry was only rivalled by his mental deficiencies.[15]

The state's official impatience with its extremist supporters came to a head in July 1822 when the Lord Lieutenant tried to dissuade the Orange Order from decorating the statue of King William III in College Green. In November he sought to prevent a breach of the peace by forbidding its decoration and thus became the target for a rowdy demonstration in the Theatre Royal. A number of the culprits were arrested and put on trial, though subsequently released. The fact that the jury was predominantly Orange in composition was a sort of triumph for the Catholic side, in that it vindicated all their complaints about the unfairness of the law in Ireland. In the following year the government passed an Unlawful Oaths Act to subdue all secret societies, including the Orange Order, and the Order, now a regular target for British parliamentary criticism, decided to dissolve and reconstitute itself to keep within the law. In 1824 the annual Twelfth of July parades were cancelled by the Grand Orange Lodge in Dublin; and it was clear that the tone of government, if not yet much of the substance, had changed.

It had changed because the Catholic Association was working with the grain of the British constitution. There was nothing specifically 'Irish' about the Catholic movement, if by that is meant some unique political shape or organisation or (for that matter) theory. Catholics based their claims on British liberal theory, on the idea of contractual government, whereby the crown had the right to a Catholic's allegiance but must in turn observe and respect the liberties of the subject. Sir Robert Peel noted that 'In this age of *liberal* doctrine we shall find it difficult to contend against emancipation, as they call it, unless we can fight with the advantage on our side of great discretion and forbearance.' Irish Protestants, therefore, should realise that their real strength lay 'in a conviction on the part of England that their cause is a just one and that the hostility which threatens them is the result of sheer religious bigotry and hatred and not the offspring of insulted and irritated feelings'.[16] But it was hard for Irish Protestants to maintain a calm and reasonable front when their character was depicted as synonymous with the ideas and actions of the Orange Order.

While the Orange Order was being driven from the centre of Irish political life in 1822–4 the Catholics were apparently in the process of being taken into favour; from 1823 O'Connell and other leading Catholics, lay and clerical, were becoming almost regular attenders at viceregal levees. Anti-Catholic Protestants might well be forgiven for regarding their plight as particularly vexatious: at a time when Catholicism was widely regarded as in the reactionary and conservative interest, in Ireland (a bastion of religiously conservative Catholicism) it was identified with contemporary liberalism. That there were strange bedfellows in this liberal movement could not be denied, for among the leading Catholic spokesmen of his day was the very anti-Protestant Archbishop MacHale, who in the next decade set his face against mixed Protestant and Catholic schools on the grounds that they were intended to sap the religion of the people 'under the specious guise of a liberal education'.[17] But the Catholic Association, though denounced by the anti-Catholic English press as 'beggars' led by their 'king', was essentially of middle-class organisation and leadership, and this gave it a purchase on sections of English opinion which O'Connell cultivated assiduously. He was the confidant of radicals such as Brougham and Cobbett and enjoyed the company of earls, barons and dukes at dinner.[18] 'Respectability', once the monopoly of the Irish Protestant, was now becoming the hallmark of that second-class citizen, the Irish Catholic.

All this seemed to augur well for the future not only of the Emancipation movement but even of Catholic–Protestant relations in general. If the British government was shifting in its attitude to the Catholic predicament, if indeed there were (as there always were) liberal Protestants willing to put themselves forward as advocates of the Catholic cause, then it might be expected that the outcome of this, the first and most prolonged crisis in Irish politics since the Union, would end in reasonable compromise. But 1825 revealed again the endless frustrations which the Emancipation saga seemed subject to. Dublin Castle, faced with what it regarded as a real danger of civil war in Ireland, decided to act against both the Catholic Association and its enemy, the Orange Order. Peel's government accordingly suppressed the Order and the Association in a kind of even-handed repression. But this could not disguise the fact that the most important opponents of Emancipation were coming to believe that they could hold the line no longer. In March 1825 the radical Sir Francis Burdett and the old campaigner William Conyngham Plunket drew up a Catholic relief bill with certain securities: the state payment of the Irish Catholic clergy and the disfranchisement of the Irish forty-shilling freeholder voters. O'Connell's support for the bill landed him in difficulties with a section of his own followers, led by John Lawless, and his embarrassment was increased when the bill was rejected in the House of Lords by forty-eight votes. O'Connell held, not unreasonably, that he had been betrayed, and he declared his intention of returning at once to Dublin to renew his agitation. In July 1825 he launched a new Catholic Association; but his eventual triumph was initiated not by himself but by an able young campaigner, Thomas Wyse, a member of a Catholic mercantile family in Waterford.[19]

The lively campaign for the County Waterford seats in the general election of 1826 revealed that the London social scene, where O'Connell was now something of a lion of British liberal society, was one thing; the excitement of the hustings in Ireland was quite another. Catholic leaders, in the absence of a native political tradition, or even any usable political tradition, might employ the language of Locke and British liberal ideology; but the rank and file who paid the Catholic rent, and many of their clergy, had other ideas. It was significant that Thomas Moore, whose sentimental songs paralleled Lady Morgan's books in popularising Ireland's illustrious past and its unhappy present, later denounced O'Connellism as a dangerous popular development, an aberration from his gentler and more romantic (and more acceptable) presentation of the cause of Erin against the Saxon. To the mass of O'Connell's followers, the guilt of the Saxon was denounced in rather more strident tones. In the election contest in Waterford (a liberal Protestant area) the Catholic Association used priests to canvass every freeholder, and despite the fact that the Association candidate, Villiers Stuart, was a liberal Protestant landlord, the campaign quickly assumed a sectarian character. The Beresfords, Villiers Stuart's Tory opponents, were denounced as 'Orange bloodsuckers', exploiters of the Catholic people, enemies and bigots. Catholic slogans referred to the pitch-cap and the flogging-triangle used by the government's troops in the 1798 rebellion. O'Connell's own electoral tour whipped up feeling further, with references to the 'bloody Beresfords' (though Lord George Beresford was generally regarded as a kindly and friendly man). Those who voted for Beresford in the first day of the poll were denounced as 'miscreants' and enemies of their religion. The election itself was peaceful and orderly; this only demonstrated that O'Connellism could combine extreme agitation with disciplined behaviour. Indeed, the very extremism of his language was what the electors and O'Connell's other supporters needed and wanted to hear, and it could prove an effective substitute for physical methods. The war of words, its sectarian character and its atmosphere of moral intimidation deterred Protestant voters from turning up at the polls and revealed the new sense of excitement and crusading spirit which the Catholic Association was capable of arousing and welding into a popular political force.[20] The Protestant in Waterford might well be forgiven for thinking that he was now on the defensive in the country which, since 1690, he had been able to call entirely his own.

The victory in Waterford was particularly important, for it convinced O'Connell that he could after all rally the freeholders (whom he had earlier despised as landlord lackeys whose vote might as well be deleted from the registers). Now they had shown their spirit and patriotism; and he accordingly inaugurated the 'new Catholic rent' to compensate freeholders who had been victimised by their landlords for voting for candidates of liberal outlook: 'The Catholics of Ireland form a nation—they should have national resources.'[21] The spectacle of freeholders defying their landlords was repeated in Louth, Westmeath and Monaghan.

The victories of liberal candidates in these hotly contested elections of 1826 were the first step on the road that led to the great personal triumph of Daniel O'Connell at the Clare election of 1828. It was clear that Protestants who opposed O'Connellism could no longer rely on the votes of their Catholic tenants as a natural aspect of their tenants' political obligations. Catholics could be mobilised to support pro-Emancipation candidates, including the unlikely example of Alexander Dawson in Louth, who professed himself a radical with a clearly expressed contempt for all religion, including what he called 'purgatory and Papacy, and all these fads'.[22] This was the beginning of a phenomenon which was to recur in Irish politics, when a constituency could vote for a candidate whose credentials were simply that a Catholic political organisation had issued an instruction that he should be voted for. Peel regarded the 1826 results with some disquiet, since they showed that Ireland stood in danger of experiencing the dissolution of 'one of the remaining bonds of society, the friendly connection between landlord and tenant'. This bond was not yet dissolved, however, as the well-disposed Protestant landlord was an essential element of O'Connell's strategy for success. But his movement was bearing increasing evidence of an idea that was implicit in his politics, and which was now becoming explicit: the claim that, as O'Connell declared to the Catholics of Ireland on 10 July 1826, they were 'the people, emphatically the people' and that 'the Catholic people of Ireland are a nation'. If the Catholics of Ireland formed a nation, and not just a group within a wider British nation (such as Protestants claimed both they and the Catholics formed), then, as the *Dublin Evening Mail* pointed out, O'Connell was working towards an 'imperium in imperio—a Roman Catholic nation subsisting independently in the bosom of a Protestant Empire'. Liberal Protestant supporters of Emancipation would eventually find themselves cast aside by the liberated Catholics.[23]

This was to touch Irish Protestantism on a very raw and exposed nerve indeed. When Henry Grattan spoke for 'Ireland a nation' in the 'patriot' era, he never doubted that his Irish nation was Protestant, joined in increasing numbers by (respectable) Catholics, so that its essentially Protestant character would become gradually modified, but not fundamentally altered. Emancipation, Grattan and other liberal Protestants held, could be granted as a matter of plain justice and sensible statesmanship; restrictions on Catholics belonged, after all, to a less enlightened age when men persecuted each other for religious reasons; it had no place in the modern world. But in the 1820s the world did not look as modern as heretofore, for both Catholics and Protestants were developing traits that contradicted the cool logic of Grattanism. Catholic Emancipationists were inclined to appeal not to the enlightened present but to the historic past, to their unbroken tradition of resistance, survival and re-emergence as a distinct people cruelly dispossessed of their country but now at last fighting back against their oppressors. A kind of millennial sentiment surfaced, with prophecies foretelling the exciting prospect of an extirpation of Protestantism and the expulsion of 'Harry's breed' from the land.

Protestantism itself was not standing still and passively awaiting its fate. On the contrary, Protestants became more than ever convinced of the righteousness of their religion, of its essential truth. The 1820s saw the quickening of the evangelical impulse, with its declared aim of subjugating 'Irish Popery to the faith of Christ'.[24] Methodists and Anglicans competed for this privilege, and organisations such as the British and Foreign Bible Society and the London Hibernian Society worked in the 'darkest' regions of Ireland to bring the light of the Gospel to her unfortunate people— and, thereby, to cement the Union of Great Britain and Ireland, for the basis of British nationhood was, of course, the Protestant faith.

This new reformation naturally provoked a powerful and bitter response on the part of the Catholic Church, now threatened by evangelicals in its own heartland. The struggle for the soul of Ireland was seen by the Catholics as an attack not only upon their religious faith, but upon their very existence as a people (perhaps even as a 'nation'). It was hardly to be wondered at that in the era of Emancipation tensions and mistrust between large sections of the religious groups were worse than at any time since the dreadful aftermath of 1798.

O'Connellism was not really a national movement, if by that is meant a movement which covered all Ireland uniformly and embraced all or most politically active Irishmen. It was strongest in the south-east, weakest in the north, and weak also in the west, where the organisation failed to make any significant inroad into that still hardly politicised region. Its electoral clubs were growing steadily between 1825 and 1829, but were fewest in Ulster, Connacht and the south-west. And while Emancipation could raise great excitement, as it did in 1826, the pattern was one of rise and fall, rather than a steadily ascending graph: after Villiers Stuart's great victory in Waterford he was alarmed by his rapidly declining popularity within a few weeks.[25]

The chief difficulty facing O'Connell, and indeed all political groups in Ireland—Catholic or Protestant, Whig or Tory—was that the franchise was extended only to a small and heterogeneous proportion of the population and prevented any party from forming a stable, reliable political base from which it could operate with confidence. Irish freeholders were in 1829 divided into four groups: 40s, £20, £50 and £100 freeholders, all with equal rights at the polls (though from 1795 the 40s freeholders had to live on or cultivate the freeholds from which they derived their qualification). The 40s and £20 freeholders must have registered within eight years of an election; the £50 freeholder might vote although he had not registered. In the boroughs the exercise of the franchise was varied: in some, such as Downpatrick, the electorate consisted of £5 householders; in others, such as Carrickfergus, there was a large electorate of freemen; but in all cases the electorate was hand-picked and under the control of the patron, who nominated the member to represent the constituency.[26]

No political party—or at least no party which sought to base its power on popular organisation and support instead of a traditional local interest—could be organised on a nationwide basis in these electoral circumstances. And this franchise was one which the landed families of Ireland, the almost exclusively Protestant landed families, could envisage remaining in their power for the foreseeable future. But the vulnerability of the system lay in the very complacency which it naturally induced in its upholders, and in the shock, therefore, that they felt when it was challenged and overthrown, as in Waterford in 1826. This sent a tremor not only through Protestant Ireland (or more correctly, anti-Emancipationist Protestant Ireland) but also through the whole British constitutional system, which was obliged to witness such unthinkable scenes as the defeat of a strong, traditional landlord interest by those who (in England, certainly) could have their votes in support of that interest taken for granted. A victory like that of Villiers Stuart might have its limitations; and it was certainly not the beginning of an Emancipationist clean sweep; but its symbolic importance was undeniable. One such victory—and there was more than one such victory in 1826—was worth a score of defeats or setbacks, for it stood as a warning to anti-Emancipationists that they could be defied in their own strongholds; and it sent a signal too to the British government that Emancipation was an issue that would simply not go away.

The weakening of the anti-Emancipationist case was not immediately evident; the new House of Commons elected in 1826 produced an anti-Catholic gain of about thirteen. But the British government and some Protestant observers in Ireland noted the new spirit abroad in the land, a spirit of self-reliance and even defiance; some even predicted another rebellion. And in Great Britain there was an increasing acceptance of the need for concession; when the Duke of Wellington became Prime Minister in January 1828 he was already searching for the means by which he could extricate the government and the country from the long and arduous controversy that threatened the political stability of the kingdom.

The tone of the new government was revealed in the appointment of the Marquis of Angelsey to replace Wellesley as Lord Lieutenant. Angelesy had been selected before Wellington took office, but now he was dispatched to Ireland with the self-confessed desire to 'go to Ireland determined to act impartially between [Catholic and Protestant] and without the least bias either one way or the other'. This meant, of course, that he was quickly perceived as acting *with* bias one way or the other, in his case the Catholic way and against the Protestant way; and his encouragement of leading Catholics at his levees (not to mention his penchant for wearing the shamrock—a large one, moreover—in his hat on St Patrick's Day) soon marked him out as a 'Catholic'.[27] There were other straws in the wind. In April 1828 the English Test and Corporation Acts were repealed, thus removing a principal disability for Dissenters, who up until then had been required to receive the sacrament according to the rites of the Church of England if they were to become office-holders under the government. Catholics were not, of course, on the same footing as Dissenters, for their loyalty was much more profoundly suspect; but it could not be doubted that a Protestant line of defence had fallen, and that, as Lord John Russell put it, the enemy, having been forced to give up his first line—that none but churchmen were worthy to serve the state—might soon be persuaded to concede also the second: 'that none but Protestants are'.[28] There was another way of looking at the issue, however, which was that Dissenters, once admitted to the constitution, would find their common Protestantism would now bind them to the anti-Catholic cause. English Catholics, aware that the Wellington administration was revealing itself as flexible on questions of loyalty and religion, were inclined to distance themselves from the dangerous and disreputable agitation of O'Connellism, and even blackballed O'Connell when he was put up for membership of a London Catholic club.[29] Nevertheless, the idea that church and state were synonymous and inseparable had been damaged.

On 8 May 1828 Sir Francis Burdett moved a resolution for a committee of the whole house to consider the restrictive laws on Catholics, and in a division on 12 May he received a small majority of six in favour of his motion. It was clear that the sheer persistence of the Emancipationists in parliament since 1808 was at last wearing down opposition, in terms of votes, but also in terms of the argument: if Ireland was to be governed at all, if politics were not to be eternally focused on this by now vexing and debilitating question, then it must be resolved. When in May Wellington reshuffled his cabinet to produce an anti-Catholic majority, it seemed as if all this effort was to be frustrated; but the duke, though he courted the anti-Catholic side, was really searching for a means to resolve the issue without at the same time splitting his party. His manoeuvres amounted to studied ambiguity rather than clear and decisive direction; in other words, they belonged firmly to the world of politics. However, while the duke gave out somewhat contradictory signals (signals which were taken by the anti-Catholic side as either a confirmation of his Protestantism or a sign that he was in danger of betraying it) events were moving in Ireland in such a way as to threaten to take the matter out of the government's hands and allow agitation to crown itself king of Ireland. For on 24 June 1828 O'Connell announced that he was a candidate in the by-election in County Clare.

In January 1828 the Catholic Association, dismayed by the apparent anti-Catholic trends in Wellington's cabinet, resolved to oppose the return to parliament of every supporter of his administration. This radical policy was met with some caution by O'Connell in May, after the repeal of the Test and Corporation Acts, which he rightly interpreted as a sign of a change in the atmosphere. But the Catholic Association was determined to put its policy into effect; and it got the opportunity to do so when William Vesey Fitzgerald, one of the members for Clare, was invited by Wellington to join the cabinet as President of the Board of Trade. He therefore had to offer himself for re-election in Clare. Fitzgerald was a popular man, an Emancipationist, an opponent of the Union in 1799, who had held his seat since 1818 without a contest. The original idea of the Catholic Association was to secure a Protestant to oppose a Protestant, as Villiers Stuart had done in 1826; but more radical members of the Association conceived the idea that a Catholic should stand, defy the opponents of Emancipation, offer a direct challenge to the British parliament, and display the depth of Catholic feeling on the issue. Clare was hardly, on the face of it, an ideal choice for the experiment: it was a county whose local landowning families were largely Gaelic or Norman in origin, but who had turned Protestant to save their estates; it was largely Irish-speaking, and few of the Catholic Association's young radicals had Irish.[30] Yet the Association, having resolved to do the daring thing, could not withdraw without its opponents' jeers ringing in their ears. It was not, of course, illegal for O'Connell to stand for parliament; what he could not do was to take his seat, or at least if he were to try to do so, he must take the oath required of all M.P.s, which Catholics could not in all conscience do, requiring them as it did to declare that 'the sacrifice of the mass, and the invocation of the Blessed Virgin Mary, and other saints, as now practised in the

Church of Rome, are impious and idolatrous'. O'Connell used this oath rather unscrupulously, pointing out that Fitzgerald had taken it and would take it again, while 'I would rather be torn limb from limb'. This set the tone for his campaign, which was Catholic in both the religious and political sense: Fitzgerald was a 'libeller of the Catholic faith', while O'Connell was 'ready to die, for the integrity, the honour, the purity of the Catholic faith'. Priests harangued the people, embracing those who voted on the 'right side', and 'marking' with a sign of the cross on their forehead those on the 'wrong side'. A 'national' note was struck: O'Connell pledged himself, if elected, not only to vote for every measure favourable to radical reform of the representative system, but also to work for the 'diminution and more equal distribution of the overgrown wealth of the Established Church in Ireland . . . and to bring the question of the Repeal of the Union at the earliest possible period before the consideration of the Legislature'.[31]

Now, at last, the truth was out—or so it must have seemed to the Protestants of Clare and of Ireland. Now Emancipation was seen as its enemies always saw it—as an attack upon the church and the state. O'Connell sought to modify the damage his words had done to the prospects of support from the liberal Protestants of Clare; but the conduct of the election, the strong sectarian note, the presence of Catholic priests as canvassers and supporters of O'Connell, his use of 'Irish' symbols, his flaunting of the green over the orange ('no party colour; it may, to be sure, be hateful in the eyes of our opponents, but that darling colour shall flourish when the bloodstained Orange shall fade and be trodden underfoot'), and, above all, his appeal to the historic experience of his people, to their degradation at the hands of Protestants, past and present: all this made the Clare election not only the 'birth of Irish democracy' (which of course it was), but the first modern election in Ireland, in that it was based upon the past and upon sectarian war-cries whose effectiveness was all too alarmingly demonstrated. Priests declared that a vote against O'Connell was a vote against the Catholic religion.[32] Irish democracy bore from its birth the mark of the Clare election, and it was a mark that was to remain, enduring and inescapable, throughout the rest of the nineteenth century.

The Protestant landowners of Clare watched with amazement the unprecedented behaviour of their freeholders, who marched to the polls behind their natural political leaders and then proceeded to vote for the 'Counsellor'. Landed power, not only Protestant power, was visibly overturned—and all this without violence, for O'Connell, as always, called for cheers for the troops sent to Clare to stand by in case of trouble. The electorate was not only defiant, it was also sober, for again O'Connell's supporters were careful not to allow their opponent any chance to discredit the ballot revolution that was clearly now on the way to success—a success declared when O'Connell won the seat by 2,057 votes to Fitzgerald's 982.

Yet all this obscured the solid and unobtrusive but steady groundwork laid by liberal Protestant supporters of Emancipation in the years before 1828; even the worsted candidate, Vesey Fitzgerald, revealed himself as a man of honour when he continued to support Emancipation after his humiliation. It was only human nature that Catholics should enjoy their triumph after years of defeat and powerlessness. It was, however, unlikely to reconcile the two religions in their politics.

O'Connell's victory produced feelings of alarm, not only in Ireland but also in Great Britain, where the social implications were as important as the religious, if not more so: for freeholders to defy landlords was to call in question the whole basis of political power and social stability. 'The Irish gentlemen have at present', Wellington admitted, 'none of the influence which belongs to men of property in a well-regulated society.'[33] It was essential, however, that the government respond to this distressing state of affairs; and the remedy could only be to concede Emancipation, since there was now a dangerous agitation in Ireland on its behalf, and a majority in the British parliament in its favour. But Wellington was determined to ensure that concession should not mean that the Established Church in Ireland, let alone the Union, would be placed at risk. In the autumn of 1828 he stressed the gravity of the Catholic question to the king and obtained his permission to lay it before the cabinet in January. When it was put to the cabinet, there was immediate acceptance that Emancipation must be conceded. The old safeguards which had been considered since 1808 were rehearsed yet again: state salaries for Catholic clergy, the licensing and registration of Catholic priests. But it was recognised that these would alienate the Catholics further, without pacifying the Protestants. It was also recognised, however, that Emancipation was in the end a political question, a question of political power; for it was accompanied by an act amending the election laws. This measure raised the freehold qualification in the counties in Ireland from 40s to £10, thus ensuring (it was hoped) that there would be no repetition of the Clare experience, and restoring to the gentry some of the influence which belonged to men of property. Wellington and his cabinet ignored the new Protestant political front now forming in Ireland and Great Britain against the Catholic cause—the Orange and Brunswick clubs; they acknowledged that this extremist stance was no firm basis upon which to found either a policy or a government.[34] An act was passed suppressing the Catholic Association by name, thus preventing it from evading prohibitive legislation through the previous device of dissolving and reconstituting itself. But this could not disguise the fact that, as the historian of the Catholic Emancipation movement put it, Clare was 'a new event in the history of the constitution—it was new in the history of Ireland' because 'a new order of things had *really* arisen in Ireland'.[35]

What was the nature of this new order of things? Peel recognised some of the problems posed by the Clare election with his usual shrewdness. A sense of common grievance and the sympathies of a common interest had begun to loosen the ties 'which connect different classes of men in friendly relations to each other'; and the basis of this development was not violence or disorder, but the peaceable and legitimate exercise of the franchise, the power of free speech, of public meetings, of lawful organisations, exercising what was essentially a moral force—all of which worked towards rendering irresistible 'the demand for civil equality'.[36] This method was frustrating and baffling for the authorities in Ireland; all the troops they could muster were rendered useless because there was nothing for them to put down (and they often showed an alarming tendency to exhibit sympathy with the Liberator's gatherings, and he with them).

If coercion could not put an end to this agitation, concessions might; but this also held perils for the British government and parliament. If Irish Protestants were the natural supporters of the Union, then their power—and their allegiance—might be undermined by a policy of concession. And to seek to remedy Catholic grievances would imply that the Union between Great Britain and Ireland was on a sort of permanent trial—that it was not something to be taken for granted, not natural, silent and discreet, but always in question, a matter for debate, an arrangement that could or should be subject to perpetual review. All this would prevent not only Ireland but the whole United Kingdom from having what was the foundation of any state's stability: a settled constitution. Moreover, who would be the judge and jury in this ongoing trial of the Union? O'Connell's answer seemed to be: the Catholic nation of Ireland. But it could be argued with equal force that it must be the British majority of the whole kingdom, of which the Protestants of Ireland constituted an integral part (according to their own reasonable claim). At any rate, if the Irish majority was the jury, the British majority and its government would be the judge. In one sense the anti-Emancipationists had logic on their side when they questioned the possibility of a Catholic nation existing in the bosom of a Protestant state. If Catholics were kept in their place, then the constitution would not be on permanent trial, and would attain in Ireland the status that it held in Great Britain: that of a permanent and fundamental law, unquestionable in its legitimacy. Protestants in Ireland could easily see themselves as the front line of defence of the British constitution, as established in 1689 and reformulated in 1801. The Protestant defensive posture was given tangible reality but events such as 'Honest Jack' Lawless's visit to the north in September 1828, when he boasted of his intention to enter 'Protestant' towns at the head of twenty or thirty thousand Catholics.[37] The only question after Emancipation had been conceded was whether or not Irish Protestants could rely on the second line of defence: the British public, its government and its parliament.

O'Connell's victorious campaign seemed to suggest that the Union was already in grave danger; but it would be mistaken to see O'Connell as the forerunner of separatism. O'Connell's language always merited careful study, for it was couched to arouse his supporters, frighten or even intimidate his foes, yet always to keep the peace and avoid bloodshed. Moreover, he was still in his own eyes a loyal man. In a remarkable speech at Clonmel in September 1828 O'Connell referred to Orangemen and Brunswickers talking of a second 1798. 'Oh,' he roared,

> would to God that our excellent Viceroy Lord Anglesey would but give me a commission, and *if* those men of blood should

attempt to attack the property and persons of His Majesty's loyal subjects, with a hundred thousand of my brave Tipperary boys I would soon drive them into the sea![38]

This, of course, saved him from prosecution under the law; but it also revealed his belief that Catholics could be 'loyal subjects', if only they were allowed to have their own way in their own land. The fact that O'Connell always saw Ireland as a distinct political entity did not mean that this entity must separate from Great Britain. In any case, O'Connell was not in a position to effect separation, even if he had wanted to; his supporters after 1829 were a minority in the House of Commons and could not shake the firm grip on Irish Catholic politics of a new political group which emerged under Emancipation: that of the Irish Catholic Whigs, vigilant enough defenders of their people's cause, but convinced, as the majority of Irish Catholics remained convinced, that the Union was likely to remain in existence, however much its working might be reviewed.

The Union could not rest upon the principles on which it had been established before 1829: that of the maintenance of Protestant privilege, in the administration, in the law, in the police forces, in local government, in the Established Church, in tithes, in matters affecting the condition of the Catholic people in general. Here was a formidable list of grievances which would provide much work for a British government if it was inclined to seek to remedy them—as, after 1829, it would almost certainly have at least to attempt to do. If these and other defects were put right, would then the Catholics of Ireland prove to be the loyal subjects that O'Connell claimed they were? Protestants doubted this; as one of their number put it, the question could be settled in a 'Protestant' fashion, that is by Catholics adopting an outlook which would enable them to 'shut their religion up within their own hearts—to leave the tenets of their church at the door of parliament, and shut the door upon it'; however, all 'past experience showed that the discipline and doctrine of the Roman Catholic Church were incompatible with the principles of the Britsh constitution'.[39] And for all Protestants the question remained: did Catholics demand to be put on one footing with Irish Protestants (which was bad enough for many Protestants), or was the equal footing merely a prelude to Catholic superiority? O'Connell's speeches and style seemed to indicate the latter. Still, from a British perspective, it could be argued that the Union might be stabilised by concessions and reform.

The 1830s and 1840s were decades when the middle classes were making their political influence felt: in England, on behalf of a collection of laws and regulations to improve society, public health and working conditions. In Ireland there were fewer, if any, philanthropic ideas of this kind. But O'Connell wanted Ireland to have its share of benefits in this age of improvement and reform. In 1825 he wrote to his wife:

> Oh, if we had English wealth pouring in upon us as it ought to do, what comforts would our poor people enjoy compared to their present misery.

Catholic Emancipation, in O'Connell's view, had been part of this process by which Ireland and England might yet be reconciled; otherwise there might be separation, for which he saw 'the growing materials'. O'Connell always kept sight of repeal of the Union as the highest bid that he could make; but he also spoke of the Union as a real and lasting possibility, which, however, would become a 'moral impossibility' if reforms such as Emancipation were delayed unduly: 'The disastrous struggle will be delayed by us who *now* possess influence, but come it will.'[40] Between 1829 and 1845 the Union was put to work, and British politicians and public were obliged to regard Irish affairs as integral to British politics, in the hope or expectation that Ireland would become a settled part of the United Kingdom.

Testing
the Union, 1830–45

THE decade and a half between Catholic Emancipation and the Great Famine were of deep significance for the Union. These years marked the development of the United Kingdom parliament as an instrument of government, a body which was looked to as a remedial and reforming institution, and one which was deeply influenced by the radical ideas fashionable at the time. It was not a parliament that sought to remodel society or upset the balance of the orders and stations of people. But it was responsive to the need to display a rational, calculating and positive response to the worst abuses of society, and to remedy them by sound and carefully drafted legislative means. Politics offered the means to effect the necessary remedies; and political action was what O'Connell, for his part, welcomed. Emancipation was to him an example of what might be achieved for Ireland: 'political' in contrast to 'social' changes which might break to pieces the framework of society'.[1] And since Ireland was now in a position to send Catholic as well as Protestant representatives to Westminster, there was good reason to believe that O'Connell could build upon Emancipation and, as one of his ablest lieutenants put it, diffuse the spirit of Emancipation

> into every department of state. . . . It must be worked into the essence and being of the Government. It must be found everywhere—at the desks of office; on the bench of justice; at the green tables in the courts in the boxes of the jury, and of the sheriff; in the treasury, the custom-house, and the Castle; nay, it must appear in the village school room and in the policeman's barrack.[2]

This was an ambitious—indeed, as it turned out, over-ambitious—programme, but it summed up an important aspect of Irish politics as they had by now developed under the Union. This was that the advance of the Irish Catholic was, in one sense, an example of the growth of confessionalism in Ireland, and yet it could reasonably be presented as the advance also of the great cause of reform, democracy and improvement as Irish O'Connellite and Whig M.P.s pressed for the removal of abuses that by any standards—except Irish Tory standards—needed remedying. Irish Tories were caught on the wrong foot; and it cannot be said that their rabidly anti-papist outpourings, their crudity of outlook, their certainty that the Protestant religion, liberty and reason were inseparable, recommended their ideology to reforming or progressive opinion. Yet this would be to do Irish Toryism a great disservice, for it was genuinely convinced that it stood for all that was best in the British constitution as against the fanaticism of Rome. The problem was that its vehemence of expression seemed to belie its belief that it stood for freedom against slavery; and while its principal supporters (landlords, the clergy of the Established Church, a large part of the bar, and the ordinary Protestant farmer or shopkeeper or, for that matter, labourer) provided a cross-section of society and comprised talented and educated people, it tended to be let down by its close association with the Orange Order, which by 1835 numbered about 1,500 members, mainly in the north of Ireland.[3] Orange lodges were social as well as political clubs; they were no more violent or disorderly than Catholic societies such as the Ribbonmen, but they fell under the censorious gaze of British Whig and Radical groups, and were regarded as the source of nearly all sectarian mischief in Ireland. With friends like the Orangemen, Irish Tories hardly needed enemies. They were handicapped too by the state of British politics, for the decade after 1830 was a period of almost unrivalled Whig power in Britain; and British Whigs were even more dangerous to Irish Tories than O'Connellites, since they were in a position to use the machinery of government to reform Protestantism out of existence.

The new style in Irish politics (which could not have been dreamed of in 1800 or even 1828) was shown in the passing of the British and Irish parliamentary reform bills in 1832. O'Connell dismayed Irish Protestant Tories and vindicated all their worst fears when he followed up his Emancipation victory by demanding the repeal of the Union and the restoration of the Irish parliament. Such a parliament would, of course, bear a very different character from the aristocratic and narrowly based assembly that was dissolved in 1800. It is true that Tories could take comfort from the lack of enthusiasm for Repeal in the country, and in parliament, which had no intention of allowing another pillar of the constitution to fall alongside that which had collapsed in 1829. However, they saw yet again the astute political tactics of their great opponent: his ability to maintain a broad political attack, to set himself a goal, and yet not allow it to stand in the way of lesser but equally valuable and popular advances. O'Connell spoke in favour of parliamentary reform, and lined up with the Whigs, now in government, on this issue. In December 1831 he wrote privately that 'I turned the attention of the rest of the country [Ireland] from the overpowering question of Repeal to the suitable one of Reform.'[4] This gained him credit with the Radicals at Westminster. And although he professed himself greatly disappointed with the Irish Reform Act (which allocated only five extra seats to Ireland and did not restore the vote to the forty-shilling freeholders), he was gratified with the move to the Whig and Radical side in Ireland in the first general election to be held after the act, when some thirty-eight M.P.s returned were declared Repealers, and of the other forty non-Tories (who were called Whigs, reformers or Radicals) at least five were pledged to press for Repeal if the British government did not address itself to a more equal administration of justice and a more satisfactory distribution of jobs in state and local government offices. This was, however, by no means a great 'national' victory for the Liberator; nevertheless, to the disgust of his enemies, he swaggered about the House of Commons, making signs to and talking ostentatiously with his followers. His followers were not men of low social status: they comprised landed gentry, lawyers and prosperous merchants, and included thirteen Protestants. Nevertheless, they were regarded by Tories as socially unacceptable; and even English Whig society was nervous of receiving the man of whom Lord Melbourne remarked that 'after one has had O'Connell' as a house guest 'one may have anybody'.[5]

When Earl Grey's Whig administration took office in November 1830, it was confronted with the problem of establishing what Grey called the 'juste milieu' in a country in which he saw 'the high Protestants on the one hand contending for the re-establishment of an odious and expensive power, and the leaders of the Catholics on the other aiming at nothing less than the total subversion of the Protestant establishment and the repeal of the Union'.[6] The Whigs sought their 'juste milieu' by undertaking some legislative measures that might enable Britain to govern Ireland other than through her 'natural' allies, the Protestants; their programme—undertaken at first in a cautious spirit—had the effect of preparing the way for a political alliance with O'Connell, and it was to reveal both the strengths and weaknesses of their policy.

O'Connell's alliance with the Whigs was not altogether unpredictable, however much it may have aroused the alarm and hatred of Protestant Toryism. O'Connell was a leading figure on the British radical stage. He was a member of Brooks's and the Reform Club; his political thought was deeply influenced by contemporary British Radical ideas, and he numbered among his causes the abolition of slavery, a codification of the law, the abolition of flogging in the army, the repeal of the corn laws, the introduction of manhood suffrage, the secret ballot, and annual parliaments. His ability to associate the cause of his followers, and of the Catholic people of Ireland, with the governing party of the 1830s gave him an influence far beyond that of his party in the House of Commons.

This political role, Irish and British, parliamentary and popular, agitational and constitutional, was one that later generations of Irish political leaders found inevitable, and yet cumbersome to operate. So much depended on the shifts and eddies of British political currents; so much on opportunism and tactical responses to realignments in the British political world. And such tactics offered a choice that was at once difficult and yet tempting. For if O'Connell set out to 'test' the Union, then at least that offered a consistent line of action: British governments must be persuaded that they had to create a state in which the Irish Catholic majority became integrated into the constitutional and political system.

The very presence of a Catholic majority in Ireland offered O'Connell another choice: that of repealing the Union and enabling the Irish majority to come into its own. But Repeal frightened Tories in Ireland, and was by no means wholeheartedly endorsed by Irish Whigs, including Catholic Whigs. It was a kind of leap in the dark. And it was bound to be resisted by all British political parties. Repeal, however, offered a means of prising reform out of the British parliament. And while Repeal, O'Connell told his audience in 1830, was preferable, since 'no individual will have his affairs well managed if he leaves them to another',[7] he was prepared to settle for less and therefore to explore the possibilities that might be presumed to lie in an agreement or alliance with the governing

Whig Party. But it still remained to be seen if any new course of British policy would indeed make the Irish Catholics 'West Britons'. O'Connell was disappointed and hurt by anti-Catholic feeling in England, which was on a par with the anti-Scots mania of the eighteenth century; but the circumstances were not exactly the same, since the Scots shared in some degree the British Protestant heritage. O'Connell had a harder task to confront, and he probably made it no easier by such behaviour as 'going out to mass with the largest shamrock that could be had in London'.[8]

Still, the Whigs agreed that something must be done to help reconcile the Irish Catholic to the Union, even if that something might provoke the Irish Protestant, the 'natural' supporter of the British connection, into disaffection. Holland, a member of Grey's cabinet, suggested a line of attack, listing a series of reforms which might be usefully carried out in a number of areas, such as the appointment of lieutenants in the Irish counties, peerages for leading Catholic landlords, grand jury reform and the discontinuation of government grants for the Kildare Place Society (an organisation for promoting education in Ireland, technically non-denominational, but in fact under Protestant control and deeply suspected of proselytising tendencies). He speculated as to whether or not the 'secret consultation of some Catholic bishops' would 'facilitate you in obtaining for the government and for English connection, and withdrawing from O'Connell and the separatists [sic] the co-operation of any large portion of the native and Catholic Irish'.[9]

This strategy produced some Whig legislation for the betterment of Ireland, but legislation that was inhibited by the special conditions prevailing in Ireland, and by the implacable opposition of many Protestants to some at least of the government's proposals. The most inviting target for Whig and Radical reforming attention was the Church of Ireland, a minority church in terms of numbers, but a 'national' church (in its own view) for both historical reasons—since the church claimed a direct line of descent from St Patrick—and reasons of divine truth. The church was also a state church, and so it claimed not only the allegiance of the nation but (equally agreeably) its money. It earned a living from tithes collected from the entire population, the majority of whom were hostile both to its claims and its privileges. The Church of Ireland was not only resented by the Roman Catholics: Protestant Dissenters, especially Presbyterians, set their face against Anglican arrogance, even if Presbyterians did not feel the sense of outrage experienced by Catholics at paying tithes for the upkeep of an 'alien church'. Reforming the Church of Ireland recommended itself to the government on a number of heads: as a rational and progressive measure; as an attack on privilege; as a means of reconciling most Irishmen to the Union; and as a means of satisfying Protestant Dissent. All this would please more of the inhabitants of Ireland, and many of those of England, than it would offend.

The tithe struggle was not prolonged, and it ended in victory for a parliamentary measure of modest ecclesiastical reform in 1832, which enforced a permanent commutation of tithes for money payment. This was followed in 1833 by a measure reforming the Church of Ireland, which had a much larger institutional structure than its members required: four archbishops and eighteen bishops with deans and chapters and some 1,400 parochial clergy were administering to the needs of 800,000 people, barely one-tenth of the whole population. In 1831 O'Connell called for the 'nation' to resume control of the temporal possessions of the Church of Ireland; but the government contented itself with a pragmatic reform measure reducing the number of bishoprics (by suppressing ten sees when their existing occupants vacated them) and scaling down the revenues of the remaining twelve. Bishops and benefices of £2,000 a year and upwards were to be taxed on a graduated scale.[10]

The political context of these measures, however, revealed the dilemma of governing Ireland in such a way as to satisfy the wishes and prejudices of all, or even most, or even some, of her people. Protestant reaction in Ireland, and (though to a lesser extent) in England was one of outrage that such rough hands should be laid on the Lord's anointed. But the question was one which affected not only sacred matters; it had temporal implications of the greatest importance. The Protestant objection was based upon the argument that, as the Act of Union merged the Churches of England and Ireland, then to weaken this keystone of the Union was to threaten the whole edifice. The *Dublin University Magazine* warned that the Churches of England and Ireland were like 'Siamese youths: the death of the one will be soon followed by the death of the other'.[11] The response of the Catholic majority was equally significant. O'Connell had spoken of 'recovering' the Church of Ireland's temporal possessions for the 'nation'; the Whig measure, however, fell far short of any such victory, for Lord Stanley, the architect of the legislation, had a deep respect for the idea of a state-established church and had no intention of destroying it. Stanley spoke of the need to make a 'successful resistance' to the Catholic leaders, in which the government would be 'supported by all reasonable Protestants of both countries, and unopposed, if not assisted, by a considerable portion of the Catholics themselves who are desirous of preserving the union of both countries'.[12]

The difficulty lay, as in 1828–9, in the popular agitation inspired by what from a governmental point of view was a rational and sensible piece of legislation. The agitation against tithes in the years 1830–33 had taken the form of intimidation and even violence over much of the country, so much so that it was called the 'tithe war'. Repealers in and out of parliament contributed to the general disturbance by their immoderate language, and in 1832 Stanley described conditions in Ireland as scarcely creditable in the nineteenth century.[13] The Whig government was reluctant to adopt extra coercive measures and, in particular, disliked the idea of handing additional powers to a magistracy avowedly Protestant and Tory in composition. Holland declared that he preferred what he called 'illegal acts of vigour' by soldiers in keeping the peace to 'insurrection acts and arms bills'. By 1833, however, the government was compelled to introduce coercive legislation, which soon proved effective in controlling, if not eliminating, disorder. But here again the idea of 'satisfying Ireland' was undermined by the very measures that were designed to promote it.

Coercive legislation was a brake on legitimate political action; and the tendency of government ministers to dislike O'Connell and his supporters and to dismiss them as 'poor, pitiful swaggering cowards'[14] was hardly an obvious way to set about binding Irish Catholics to the Union. Then there was the problem of perception. It might appear to government a reasonable assumption that ecclesiastical reform could run in harness with coercive legislation, the one as it were balancing the other. But such 'even-handedness' was described by Catholic representatives as 'base, brutal and bloody'. And Protestant Tories, who dismissed coercion as only halfhearted, considered reform as all too dangerous. In July 1834 the *Dublin University Magazine* declared that Protestants were emigrating from Ireland in such large numbers that the country could not afford such an exhausting drain much longer; yet the Protestants were the very portion of the population which was 'all on the side of England, and of property, and of law'. They were men 'orderly, steady, industrious, loyal and religious' who 'as a body, had no superiors in their class of any nation in the world'. The government was busily conceding to 'clamour, turbulence, and threats'. For all these reasons 'the Protestants of Ireland are leaving the homes of their fathers for the land of strangers'.[15] It was a Whig, who was soon to resign from the government in dissatisfaction with its policies, who perhaps best summed up the central paradox of reforming Ireland for the sake of strengthening the Union. Sir James Graham pointed out that

> So long as the Union continues, the Protestant religion is the religion of the majority. [i.e. of the whole British people]. Therefore a more straightforward course would have been a measure for dissolving the Union, and for establishing the Catholic religion in Ireland.[16]

This was true as far as it went; but it was, of course, politically impossible in 1834, and would almost certainly have had the effect of pitching Ireland into civil war. Fortunately for Ireland, the British government and public were in no mood to accede to O'Connell's demand in 1834 for repeal of the Union; when O'Connell tested British resolve in April, his call for Repeal was overwhelmingly defeated by 523 votes to 38. More significant was the fact that, for all his claims to be the leader of the Irish 'nation', he could only count upon a minority of the Irish M.P.s (early in the 1833 session a meeting at his house to discuss a Whig coercion bill attracted only twenty-six members), and he had to acknowledge that the country as a whole was apathetic about the Repeal question. If the Union was in danger, that danger lay in a dissatisfaction with the character and temperament of British administration, and its failure to put Protestantism firmly in its place, rather than a broader constitutional grievance. Or, rather, the constitutional grievance could only take hold if a series of Catholic causes were linked with it, in much the same way as they had been associated with Emancipation before 1828. But there was no sign of this in 1834, and within a year the wheels of politics had turned in such a way as to place relations between O'Connell, Ireland and the British government on a new and different footing, and one that promised well for the Union as a permanent fixture.

In 1834 Grey's ministry broke up; and Sir Robert Peel's spell in office disposed O'Connell more favourably towards the Whigs (now under the leadership of Viscount Melbourne), for if he failed to support them, he might find himself faced with a sterner opponent. Grey had never enjoyed cordial relations with the Irish Whigs, who had in 1831 proposed various reforms for Ireland, only to be told that Grey would not discuss in detail any Irish bills in preparation. Grey also rejected their appeal for the disbandment of the (exclusively Protestant) yeomanry force, and warned them that to press the government too far might result in the prospect of a less friendly cabinet. Irish Whigs were disappointed by the 1832 Reform Act, which failed to fulfil their hopes for the restoration of the forty-shilling freehold voter and a considerably larger Irish representation.[17] When Grey was replaced by Melbourne in July 1834, they, like O'Connell, gravitated towards a new political alignment in the House of Commons. In March 1835 an informal agreement, the 'Lichfield House Compact', was reached and a combination of Whigs, Radicals and O'Connellites forced Peel to resign, enabling the reappointment of Melbourne. O'Connell, now more closely associated with parliamentary rather than mass politics, was prepared to suspend his Repeal organisation if the new ministry amended the Irish police reform bill, reformed the Irish corporations, and appropriated the surplus revenues of the Irish establishment for charitable purposes. Lord John Russell, the newly appointed Home Secretary, let it be known that the government would at least pledge itself to the last demand, and O'Connell indicated a willingness to serve under the new administration. But the leader of Catholic Ireland was not so easily absorbed into the inner sanctums of the British political system. A number of Whigs expressed their aversion to such a move, and Young, Melbourne's confidential secretary, spoke of the impossibility of making such a 'scoundrel' into a Privy Councillor.[18]

Nevertheless, while O'Connell was not a member of the government, and could only influence rather than help to direct its policy, the next six years of Whig government expressed something of a new spirit in the working of the Union. The chief alteration was not so much the legislation passed for Ireland by the government—

though this included another tithe bill and an Irish poor law—but in the spirit and style of the heart of the Irish administration in Dublin Castle. The Castle itself was the supreme symbol of the tradition of Protestant superiority and privilege; now, under the inspiration of two successive Lords Lieutenant, Lord Mulgrave and Viscount Ebrington, the Castle began to adapt itself to the Catholic majority's oft-frustrated expectations. Thomas Drummond, Mulgrave's Under-Secretary, was the instrument of the new approach, and his unflinching assault on the Orange Order in particular won him much admiration and support: the spectacle of the police and their spies being employed *against* a Protestant organisation was indeed novel. Drummond was strongly backed by Viscount Morpeth, Chief Secretary from 1835 to 1841, and the whole purpose of the administration was to demonstrate that, given fair play and reasonable redress of grievances, the goodwill of the bulk of the Irish people could be enlisted for the Union. This policy was easier to work in the administrative than in the legislative spheres, for while bills for municipal reform, poor law, police reform, tithe settlement, even railways, ran into parliamentary opposition, especially in the Lords, there was nothing to stop the government bestowing official posts on Catholics and liberal Protestants. Six judges of liberal views, three of them Catholics, were placed on the bench. Catholics were appointed as stipendiary magistrates, police inspectors and legal officials. This opened the government to the charge of jobbery. But there was good reason to believe that what might be called 'national' feeling in Ireland was not nearly as strong as O'Connell claimed; and Irish Whigs, many of them aspiring Catholic gentry and middle-class professional people, were (to say the least) pragmatic in their attitude to 'national' causes, especially when social and career prospects were at stake.

This must not be taken as an adverse reflection upon the bulk of the Catholic middle classes in Ireland, whose gratifying progress was now apparently being facilitated by a sympathetic British government. An aspiring and formerly degraded people needed such signs of progress—needed them, it is at least arguable, much more than it needed repeal of the Union. There was also the useful side-effect of reform, in that it provoked strident Protestant opposition; and it was ever the way that one side's deliverance in Ireland was, automatically, the other side's damnation. If Catholics were advanced, it must be at the expense of Protestants, or rather of

Episcopalians, since Presbyterians too had their doubts about Episcopalian pretensions. Nowhere was this more evident than in the Whigs' decision to reform the municipal corporations in Ireland, an institution that could hardly be defended on any grounds save those of Protestant security (and not even defensible on those grounds in the eyes of all Protestants). At the time of the Act of Union there were 117 corporate boroughs of varying size: some were cities, like Dublin; others hardly existed except as legal entities. After the Union the reduction of the Irish representation consequent upon the dissolution of the Irish parliament meant that a number of these boroughs disappeared; and subsequently the 1832 Irish Reform Act extinguished the corporations' right to any say in the electoral process, taking away the power of the smaller corporations directly to elect members of parliament. By thus separating the municipal from the electoral functions of these corporations, the Reform Act rendered them less obvious defences against the political encroachments of Catholics.[19] Thus the corporations were deprived of one of their chief justifications for maintaining them unreformed; and in their unreformed condition they appeared to be simply the bastion of sectarian Protestant jobbery and privilege. The corporations performed few local services anyway, and most of them were in debt. The Whig government, therefore, could tackle the abuses of the system without appearing to undermine the constitution of the whole kingdom; and since they had already reformed Welsh and English corporations, Ireland was the next obvious target.

Yet this reform, so obviously needed that a strong group in the Conservative opposition in parliament felt able to support moderate reform, turned out to be a protracted and even bitter political controversy. This revealed both the strength and the weakness of the new Whig spirit of closer union. Its strength was shown in the energetic and purposeful way in which the government set about the business, with a group of thirteen young liberal barristers let loose in the Augean stables, providing recommendations on which, in 1835, the government based its municipal reform bill. The bill had first of all to endure a six-session parliamentary ordeal, with amendments by the Lords, confusion and dispute between the two houses, and the spectacle of the British Conservatives and Irish Tories at odds over the issue, with Irish Tories feeling that Peel had not offered a stout enough resistance to the measure. The long-drawn-out and rancorous arguments; the uncertain response of the

Tories; their charges of apostasy against Peel; the fact that the debate was conducted entirely on sectarian principles, without manifesting any real concern for the efficiency or otherwise of local services and administration; the exhaustion and unhappiness of the government—all were a poor recommendation for the policy of reforming Ireland. Reforming Ireland could be an unprofitable parliamentary game; and the municipal reform act which was the eventual outcome was a compromise measure, passed in 1840 when the government was so debilitated that it had no choice but to compromise or suffer defeat. Moreover, the act itself differed from the English model, in that it did not grant the municipal franchise to all ratepayers, but confined it to the £10 householders; and it restricted the powers of the corporations and new municipal councils set up under the act. One very significant omission was control of the police, which remained with Dublin Castle. And the sheriff was to be nominated by the Lord Lieutenant, not elected by the council. The municipal corporations, thanks to the restricted franchise, were still not handed over completely to the liberal and Catholic interest; but they were nearly handed over. And so municipal reform in Ireland had again that special characteristic which was to render many reform measures so controversial in Ireland under the Union: it had a constitutional aspect, in that it was held to be a weakening of the Protestant Tory interest, and therefore of the Union itself.[20]

This was even seen in another Whig measure, the establishment of a systematic poor law in Ireland. Ireland was not regarded as a poor country at the beginning of its political union with Great Britain. Its fertile soil, its mild climate and the quality and range of its agricultural products suggested a country which could not only feed itself but could also export considerable quantities of food to a Britain struggling to defeat the French. And then there was emigration, which produced sizeable Irish settlements in Scotland and north-western England, and which provided opportunities for Irishmen to leave poverty behind or, if not poverty-stricken, simply to better themselves. But soon visitors noticed significant changes in the Irish countryside: the presence of large numbers of very poor tillers of the soil, and the inability of industry to expand sufficiently fast to absorb and maintain the surplus population. The condition of the poor in Ireland was a subject for native Irish discussion long before the Whigs turned their gaze in that direction.

The Dublin Society between 1801 and 1832 collected and published statistics on Ireland, county by county; and in a fact-collecting age the poor emerged as a significant statistic, and the means of alleviating their condition as a subject for debate. The income and expenditure of the poor was estimated, and means were sought to bring these into line. But there was no poor law as such in Ireland, though the Irish parliament in 1772 had passed a Mendicity Act, setting up bodies to erect workhouses in every county and county of a city, but financed only by charity. These institutions were clearly inadequate to meet the needs of a large poverty-stricken proportion of the population; but the idea that the beggar was, quite simply, a permanent feature of Irish social life was widely accepted, and no comprehensive provision was made for the Irish poor.[21] Nor did O'Connell, for his part, believe that any provision should be made.

The purpose of statute law regarding poverty and paupers in the early nineteenth century was to discourage poverty, not to cure it. No cure was possible, given the general reluctance to embark on social engineering—and, in any case, the lack of means to do so. In England a new, uniform, centralised law was passed, with the workhouse and the workhouse test as its operative basis. The principle behind the English act was that the able-bodied person would be refused poor relief; if he had no means to support himself or his family, he would no longer receive outdoor relief from the parish, but must remove himself and his dependants to the work-house. To encourage him to improve his lot as quickly as possible, conditions in the workhouse were made worse than conditions of the lowest-paid worker outside; a man would therefore be strongly motivated to find employment rather than remain a permanent burden on the rates. Parishes were grouped together to form a 'union' which provided the workhouse and other necessary services.

The Irish Poor Law Commission presented its first report in 1835. It differed from its English counterpart in that it sought to prevent destitution, not merely to alleviate it; and it suggested remedies, including reclamation of waste lands, and a general plan of economic development. The commissioners were influenced by contemporary thinking on how any poor relief scheme should be financed, accepting that the state should not become directly involved in providing outdoor relief. But their general idea, that the government should intervene to prevent poverty in Ireland, ran counter to the current economic thinking, which envisaged no such positive state role. The government proceeded to set up an inquiry which it had good reason to believe would arrive at the conclusion it already wished to reach. An English Poor Law Commissioner, George Nicholls, made a speedy nine-week tour of Ireland beginning in August 1836, and what he saw directed him towards the conclusion he had already formulated: that a deterrent workhouse system was essential 'as a first step towards effecting an improvement in the character, habits and social conditions of the people'. This would restore good order and peace to the country and assist that influx of capital which Ireland so badly needed to provide employment for her population. Nicholls did not expect immediate improvement in the condition of Ireland as a result of the implementation of his proposals; and he did warn that, in the event of famine, no poor law could prove adequate. His scheme was accepted by the government, and a bill, introduced in 1837, became law in 1838, instituting a division of the country into poor law districts, each with a workhouse under a board of guardians, and with the levying of a poor rate to be paid, half by the landlords, half by the tenants.[22]

Ireland's parliamentary representatives were divided in their reaction to the government's poor law policy. Many Irish Tories resented its high-handed approach to the problem, and in particular its dismissal of the advice proffered to it by the Irish Poor Law Commission. Irish Tories, Whigs and Repealers were found amongst the opponents of the bill, revealing that a deep and non-party division of opinion existed on this issue. The whole episode illustrated the government's reforming style, its determination to distinguish between what it called the 'real' wants to Ireland and the 'wishes' of Ireland, which were 'transitory and intemperate'.[23] This suggested a somewhat peremptory approach to Irish issues. Yet, on the other hand, the attempt to satisfy the 'wishes' of Ireland might drag a reforming government down into the intricacies of Irish party and sectarian politics; and this was illustrated not by the division on the government's bill, which cut across party lines, but in the disagreeable circumstances surrounding the creation of the boards of guardians. These were elected, not appointed; and

naturally they reflected the composition of the religious denominations in the administrative districts, with Catholics controlling the
poor law guardians and responsible for dispensaries, fever hospitals
and workhouses in most counties outside Ulster. Protestants,
especially in the south, recognised another sign of the general
advancement of the majority party in the institutions of administration in Ireland after Emancipation.[24]

If the poor law question eventually crash-landed in the middle of
Irish political controversy, the education question never really took
off from this context. Schools were bound to be at the centre of
Irish political and religious debate, since schools, especially those
established by Protestant evangelical groups, were a danger area:
young minds could be won over by zealots, and perhaps never
recovered. When the Whig government sought to establish a
national system of education in 1831, it was inevitable that it should
attract the suspicious attention of the competing religions in
Ireland. The Kildare Place Society, an ostensibly non-denominational body, was in receipt of an annual grant since 1815 for its
schools system; but the society had fallen largely under Protestant
management and was now competed against by the Christian
Brothers, founded by Edmund Rice of Waterford and approved by
a bull of Pope Pius VII. In September 1831 the government
transferred its grant to a new body, the Commissioners of National
Education, and a month later Edward Stanley, Chief Secretary for
Ireland, announced his intention of creating a system of education
free from sectarianism or prosletysing. But the Church of Ireland
had always been suspicious of any proposal which would deprive it
of the opportunity to propagate religion, and it stood aloof from the
new system. The Presbyterians considered the scheme and pressed
the government to change the rules under which schools could
receive grants from the National Education Board.[25] The plan was
gradually but inexorably modified to accommodate the wishes of
the churches, and the national education system lost its character as
a 'mixed' one and became in effect sectarian in organisation. These
wishes may have been, in Lord John Russell's words, 'transitory
and intemperate', but clearly they rose above whatever 'real wants'
the government identified in Ireland; and the episode revealed again
that the special conditions of Ireland were stony ground for the
rational reformer in London.

This controversy illustrated important aspects of Irish politics as they were developing in the post-Emancipation period. O'Connell's alliance with the Whigs brought him some dividends, especially in the style of administration in Dublin Castle; but he could not bend the government to his will; and a government which set its mind on a programme of legislative initiatives—whether in education reform or the inauguration of a comprehensive poor law—could get its way. This was especially apparent in another attempt by the Whigs to tackle the tithe question, when the government's bills in 1835 and 1836, involving appropriation of surplus church revenues, passed the Commons with O'Connell's support, only to be rejected by the Lords. O'Connell realised that he must compromise; and Russell entered into negotiations with Peel. The result was a bill, proposed by Russell in 1838 and supported by Peel and O'Connell, which commuted tithe to a rent-charge, scaled down in amount, payable by landlords, who could recover the sums from tenants, who in turn could recover it from sub-tenants. To mitigate the impact of these charges, measures were drafted excluding the poorest classes of tenants from payment, and all arrears in tithe from 1834 to 1837 were written off. This measure did not abolish tithes, and indeed was greatly resented by liberals from the north of Ireland, inspired by Presbyterian dislike of the whole institution, who called for total abolition. But it revealed that when British politicians worked together, they could consider and reform, however modestly, a felt abuse in Ireland. But, of course, they could not do so to the entire satisfaction of the majority of the people there, nor, in the case of tithe, to the satisfaction of a considerable and influential minority, the Presbyterians of Ulster. As always, then, British policy was received policy, in the sense that no Irish political group had the final say in its drafting and implementation, however much they might strive to influence its shape. And this could introduce a sense of helplessness, resentment and betrayal on the part of the various groups in Ireland, ever anxious about their future and their relative position towards each other.

Yet it was important for a British government at least to try to hold some sort of balance between the suspicious and at times opposing forces in Ireland—however much this might offend Irish Tories, who saw themselves and their Protestant supporters as the natural friends of the British connection. The 'naturalness' of this friendship was now being so seriously called into question that, on the Poor Law Commission for example, the Tory *Dublin University Magazine* fulminated against the pretensions of the Englishman Nicholls in deciding policy for Ireland on the basis of a self-confessed ignorance of the country. Parliament, Dublin Castle, the educational system, even the boards of guardians for workhouses, were now no longer automatic Protestant preserves. Tithes were maintained, but were still the target of (in this case) Presbyterian abuse and resentment. But the question remained whether or not the Roman Catholic could become a friend, if not to Irish Protestants, then at least to the Union. He might after all make a contented West Briton. But this possibility—regarded as always doubtful by the Irish Protestant—was shaken by O'Connell's decision in 1838 to acknowledge that the Whig government was no longer secure, and to explore the possibility of reviving the Repeal agitation, which he had abandoned in 1835.

Repeal was 'loyal' as well as 'national'. O'Connell always stressed hs veneration of the British monarchy, and especially of the new queen, Victoria, who came to the throne in 1837. This is not as surprising as it might seem, for it was simply the revival in modern guise of the Confederate Catholic concept of the mid-seventeenth century and the Jacobite tradition of the late seventeenth and early eighteenth century: 'For God, King and Country'. The parish priest of Ballingarry spoke in February 1843 of 'the heartfelt and loyal homage which Irishmen will render to their Queen, the third estate of an independent Irish Parliament';[26] and on attending a meeting at Clondalkin in April, O'Connell was met by a band playing 'God Save the Queen'.[27] O'Connell had no notion of restoring a Gaelic Ireland, although he was a native speaker and used the language where necessary in his mass meetings. But he had every intention of restoring Ireland to the 'Irish', by which, again like his forebears, he meant the Catholics. This would not involve separation—at least not in the foreseeable future—but it would involve the majority managing important domestic matters for themselves, and it would end the necessity for the majority to go to the Westminster parliament and seek to cajole a frequently unsympathetic Protestant institution to listen to the Catholic and redress his grievances. It would also restore the Irish parliament as an instrument of majority power; and any benefit to the United

Kingdom that might follow an easing of the role of Ireland in British political life would be offset by the danger of serious civil strife in Ireland, as Presbyterians and Episcopalians sank their differences in a common defence against Catholic power. And these non-Catholic groups had arguments against Repeal other than those dating from the seventeenth century (not that the seventeenth-century arguments were in any way unconvincing). Those in the north of the country could point to an important regional variation in the Irish economy and demonstrate that the north, with the development of its linen industry after 1830, and its ancillary textile engineering industry now developing in turn, needed the support of British capital which Repeal could only frighten away. Against this was the fact that British competition hindered technological advance in Ulster. But then again, Britain had the necessary technological knowledge to revolutionise production, and, on balance, it seemed that Repeal could only do more harm than good. In any case, it was not designed to benefit the Ulster linen industry; and matters seemed best left alone, irrespective of the regional disadvantages that arose from union with a country whose government would not introduce protective and promotional legislation on behalf of the Ulster economy.[28]

Repeal, according to the chief liberal newspaper in Ulster, the *Northern Whig*, was a 'Dublin question'. In April 1840 O'Connell set up a Repeal Association, ready for the occasion to launch a campaign if occasion there might be; but this only involved him in further controversy with the northern Whigs, whose Ulster Constitutional Society, founded to obtain equal rights for Ireland within the United Kingdom while also incorporating the beneficial system of imperial legislation, rejected O'Connell's overtures on the grounds that the Repeal idea only served to divide Irish Whigs and weaken their influence in Great Britain as well as at home. Liberals were not entirely altruistic in this approach to the Repeal issue; they were also only too aware of their vulnerability should Repeal create a Tory threat to their votes and seats in Ulster. O'Connell sought to conciliate Ulster liberals by attending a political dinner in their honour, a dinner described as a 'reform' not a 'Repeal' occasion. But only a handful of Ulster liberals attended, and O'Connell was obliged to answer questions from a deputation of those leading Whigs who were anxious to explain that they were not Repealers.[29]

There were three grave dangers facing the revival of Repeal, two of them Irish and one British. The Irish difficulties lay in the nature of Irish politics and society in 1840. The mutually suspicious religious groups, Presbyterian, Anglican and Catholic, made a kind of shifting pattern; and at times that pattern could settle in one form, and then in another. Presbyterian and Catholic could see eye to eye over tithes (though there were Presbyterians, like Henry Cooke, a minister of Killyleagh, County Down, who interpreted any attack on the Anglican Church as an attack on the Reformed churches in general). Catholic and Anglican could combine in their doubts about Nicholls and his poor law investigation. All three groups had doubts about national education, but here again Presbyterians were divided amongst themselves over whether or not to support the scheme. But this relatively fluid state of Irish politics—as fluid as the state of Irish politics ever permitted—could be transformed by a Repeal agitation, especially one accompanied by O'Connellite speeches with their emotional references to 'Saxon and Protestant' wrongs. Then there was the question of whether or not Catholic Ireland could be aroused to lend its wholehearted support to a new Repeal agitation; the experience of the Repeal campaign of the early 1830s hardly seemed a good omen for its chances. The British problem was equally formidable. Great Britain had conceded Emancipation partly because the opposition to it had gradually weakened over the decades, and partly because the method adopted—that of devising a special oath for Catholic M.P.s which, however personally offensive to individuals, could nevertheless be taken with a reasonably clear conscience—was a very British compromise, reconciling as it did the Protestant nature of the British constitution with a means of allowing non-Protestants access to parliament. But Repeal was capable of no such constitutional fudge; it was a dismemberment of the Union, and however troublesome or unsatisfactory that Union might be to large sections of British political and public opinion, yet they could not imagine its dissolution, or even its modification: it seemed an indisputable fact of life, part of the settled order of things—a logical and inevitable outcome of British political history. Its removal was, simply, unthinkable, precisely because no one in Britain thought very much about it at all.

There appeared not much reason to believe that many people in Ireland in 1840 thought very much about the Union, or about ending it either. If O'Connell's influence can be measured in monetary terms, then it showed a steady decline, with the money collected to maintain O'Connell's position falling from £26,065 in 1831–2 to £8,685 in 1841, a shortfall in funding which helped to account for O'Connell's difficulties in the general election of 1841.[30] O'Connell's Repeal Association won only 18 seats, fewer than half the number held in 1832–3, as against 47 Whigs and 40 Tories. O'Connell himself lost Dublin City. Sir Robert Peel and a Conservative government came to power, and Peel's reputation among O'Connellites was as black as O'Connell could paint it. Nevertheless, within a short time Irish Tories found themselves as much at odds with their British brethren as they had been with the Whigs; for the government, despite representations from Irish Tories to modify the national system of education in favour of the Church of Ireland by means of a separate state grant to the Church Education Society, decided to preserve the existing system. Once again there were mutterings among Irish Tories about the need to form a separate party in the Commons to defend Irish interests, but again this came to nothing, and Tories fell back upon their self-description as 'the English party in Ireland'.[31]

They had, it must be said, but little choice in the matter; for there were once again dangerous signs that Catholic power was on the march, using the same fearful tactics of the Emancipation campaign: mass meetings and violent denunciations of the status quo. O'Connell's personal style, his promise that Repeal was imminent, his millennial speeches, inspired support for his cause throughout the country and seemed to promise insurrection. He was elected Lord Mayor of Dublin in November 1841, a sign of the times; and in 1843 he initiated in Dublin Corporation a debate on Repeal, in which he was opposed by an Irish Tory barrister, Isaac Butt. O'Connell stressed that Repeal would maintain the constitutional link between Great Britain and Ireland, and he urged Protestants to recognise where their true interests lay. But Protestants stayed at home; there was not the degree of sympathy that had been felt even by some Protestants for Emancipation. The working-class Protestants of Dublin, suffering from hardship in the 1840s, did not put their trust in Repeal as a remedy; on the contrary, they responded with a commitment to the religious politics of the Rev. Tresham Gregg, whose denunciations of popery struck a responsive chord in people whose forefathers were numbered among the victors of 1690, but who were now suffering municipal reform, the loss of control of many of the city's important institutions, such as the police and judiciary, and the spectacle of the Catholic local vote swamping that of Protestants with the £10 householder franchise.[32]

O'Connell's oratory was not comforting to such people, nor to Protestants in general. He reminded his audiences of Cromwellian days, of fire, slaughter, the killing of innocents. But no longer: for 'We were a paltry remnant in Cromwell's time. We are nine millions now.'[33] It was just because Catholics were, if not nine millions, then certainly nearly seven millions at a time when the population of England and Wales was estimated at less than fourteen millions, that Repeal was seen by Protestants as the beginning of the end, not only in Ireland but in Great Britain as well. A parliament of papists would stop at nothing to reverse the verdict of history and crown O'Connell king of Catholic Ireland. But among O'Connell's followers there were those who declared that Ireland was not, and could not happily be, merely Catholic. The Repeal movement, by 1843 an internationally admired pheno-menon, attracted the attention of young, able and idealistic mem-bers of the Protestant as well as the Catholic educated middle classes, few in number but strong in enthusiasm: Charles Gavan Duffy, a Catholic journalist, and originally a hater of Protestants but now equipped with a broader outlook; John Mitchel, of Presbyterian and United Irish radical background; William Smith O'Brien, of Gaelic descent and Protestant landlord credentials; John Blake Dillion, a Catholic graduate of Trinity College, Dublin; and the leader and inspiration of the group, Thomas Davis, whose mixed Welsh, English and Irish blood made him in truth what he always claimed to be—a real Irishman. These young men were nicknamed 'Young Ireland'—a title they disliked, but one which was appropriate to their age, their idealism, and their literary aspirations.

Davis and his associates were not political separatists, or even much interested in constitution-making at all. They were cultural nationalists, reacting as much against O'Connell's sectarian nation-alism, and his eighteenth-century political morality, as against English rule in Ireland. Davis was particularly anxious to prevent a Catholic ascendancy replacing the Protestant variety, so much so that O'Connell regarded him as one possessed by a 'Protestant monomania'.[34] He thought such an ascendancy could be averted by channelling the waters of Irish life into cultural rather than political streams.

It was clear to Davis and his followers, as it was to most people in Ireland, that mass politics, as practised by O'Connell, meant that Protestants must be a permanent minority and therefore at the risk of overthrow or assimilation by the majority. O'Connell had no doubt that, deprived of the political support of Britain, this essentially political minority would, as he put it ominously, 'sink' into the nation.[35] This was why even Presbyterians, who nourished no special affection for Anglicans in Ireland, witnessed the junction of two leading lights of their church, Henry Cooke and Henry Montgomery, whose disagreements on matters theological as well as political was hitherto deep. 'Look at Belfast', Cooke challenged Repealers in 1841, 'and be a Repealer, if you can.'[36] Davis appreciated the benefits of a domestic legislature, but he hoped above all to inspire Irishmen with thoughts of beautiful, lofty things; and to this end he proposed that the religious divisions of Ireland be broken down, by drawing his fellow-countrymen's attention to their splendid past and using that to create a more generous sense of nationality for the future.

Davis hoped to do this by revealing to Irishmen that the real enemy of their peace and harmony was England—England, who by her treachery and policy had been the persecutor of Ireland and the manufacturer of Irish political differences. He hoped also to show that the Irish nation was a pluralist one, that the Irish people came from mixed stock, and that their nationality was like that of the Geraldines. The Geraldines first came to Ireland as conquerors, but 'not long our air they breathed' before they were fully assimilated into 'Irish thoughts', which no Englishman could 'by law and force and bribe' deprive them of. The Saxon and Norman colonists were 'melted down into the Irish'; and the Wexford rebels of 1798, though their blood was 'for the most part English and Welsh, though mixed with the Danish and Gaelic, yet they are Irish in thought and feeling'. Thus he pleaded for 'the Milesian, the Dane, the Norman, the Welshman, the Scotchman, and the Saxon' to 'combine, regardless of their blood'.[37]

This element of pleading in Davis's work is significant. Davis was sensitive to the sectarianism of Ireland's past, and he was not blind to its destructive impact; he could not like the Gaelic poetry of the

seventeenth century, because it was racially and religiously offensive. He had therefore to stress that Ireland was a melting-pot of
races, out of which grew the Irish people. This was justifiable
enough in fact; but the point was that it was religious identity,
which in turn was linked to political identity, that was the real
centre of Ireland's discord. And when Davis sought to lower the
barriers between the religious groups in the Ireland of his day, he
was confronted with the opposition of the Catholic Church, and
then that of O'Connell, on the vexed question of education. In 1845
the Conservative government sought to provide university education in such a way as to reconcile the Catholic Church to a state-
endowed system. The government proposed a sum of £100,000 for
the establishment of Queen's Colleges at Galway, Cork and Belfast,
where no religious tests would apply and where chairs of theology
would be endowed by private benefactors. Some members of the
hierarchy were in favour, if additional safeguards were made, but
the formidable Archbishop MacHale of Tuam set his face against
the scheme. O'Connell, though less unhappy with the plan, felt that
he must support the archbishop and the other doubting bishops,
who had, after all, supported him in his political campaigns. Davis
could not but react strongly to the kind of language used to
denounce what to him was an essential part of creating a real Irish
nation; words like 'revolting' and 'abominable' were provocative.
Furthermore, in May 1845 at a meeting of the Repeal Association
O'Connell denounced the bill. Davis, in his anger, let slip a small
grain of Protestant sentiment when he described one of his
opponents in the dispute as 'my very Catholic friend'. He was
immediately accused by O'Connell, in most brutal terms, of
'sneering' at Catholics. It was a lesson to the young man that 'Old
Ireland' was not quite as he liked to imagine it, and that it would
take more than poetry, painting and the revival of Irish names to
break Ireland's religious and political past and reformulate it for the
future benefit of the country.[38]

The Young Irelanders wanted to fuse the Irish people into one
nation; or rather, as they would have put it, to demonstrate to the
people of Ireland that, racially, they were already fused, and that,
politically, they could acknowledge that fusion by looking to their
rich and golden past (or at least to that part of the past that lay
buried in antiquity and predated the religious battles of the

sixteenth century onwards). But he also wanted to show that England was the cause of Ireland's woes, and that England was still the enemy of Irish culture; his anger at the textbooks used in the National Schools was provoked by the fact that these were exclusively in English, and also because they omitted any works that were of patriotic significance, not only to Irish children but to any children. Sir Walter Scott's 'Breathes there a man with soul so dead', for example, was regarded as dangerously exciting. This reflected Davis's dislike of what he called modernisation: 'modern Anglicanism, i.e. Utilitarianism . . . Yankeeism, Englishism, which measures prosperity by exchangeable value, measures duty by gain, and limits desire to clothes, food, and respectability'. This 'damned thing' had been brought to Ireland by English politicians, of whatever party, and it must be checked. Ireland must be restored to her real destiny, as the spiritual and artistic light in a material modern world. This was a theme which was to recur throughout the modern history of Ireland, and was one, apparently, reconcilable with the mass emigration of Ireland's young and able-bodied. And to make it more reconcilable with the harsh facts of Irish economic life, it was essential to blame England for everything; and Davis did blame her for everything. It was necessary, therefore, to erect a brazen wall against the enemy; and this wall was a cultural one: the Gaelic language and literature would be a barrier to anglicisation. Moreover, the Irish language was one specially adapted to the thoughts and minds of the Irish people, 'mingled inseparably with their history and their soul'. And so 'Ireland must be unsaxonised before it can be pure and strong'.[39]

Davis's dislike of racial language within Ireland, and his willing use of it when he came to describe Anglo-Irish relations, was no more than the inconsistency of the zealot who was ready to use any weapon to plead his cause, and whose view of Irish history was, to say the least, partial. What Davis felt he must do was to give Irish society confidence and unity, the kind of confidence and unity of the society that was, for example, portrayed in the novels of his contemporary, Charles Dickens—a society which, whatever its disparities of wealth and social status, was recognisably and indisputably a unique national phenomenon. But what was Ireland becoming? The Irishman who had any cultural pretensions was invariably drawn to England 'as tributaries of England's ambition:

novelist, reviewer, or poet, such an Irishman is expected to provide entertainment and intellectual stimulation on all fronts, but to have no will of his own'. Nationality was 'the only remedy, since the sons of a province . . . never are or were sucked into an imperial metropolis but as captives in mind and body'.[40] Ireland, in such circumstances, would become simply a province, no longer a nation. She must be a nation once again.

This idea of making Ireland a nation once again drew the Young Irelanders into politics. This was perhaps inevitable. Indeed, their cultural ambitions were, after all, political in the real sense of the term, deeply involved with the fashioning and creating of an Irish sense of nationality. And the movement was active in all sorts of ways: founding a newspaper, the *Nation*, to propagate the gospel of nationality, attending Repeal meetings, criticising O'Connell for his tactics, his style, his sectarian rhetoric. They had already become embroiled in the education controversy; and they criticised O'Connell for considering the idea of a federal Ireland within the United Kingdom, an idea put forward by a northern Protestant landlord, William Sharman Crawford, as an alternative to simple Repeal. Davis speculated that O'Connell really wanted to drive Young Ireland out of the Repeal movement, so troubled was he at their disagreement with him on important points of principle; but the truth was that it was exceedingly difficult for O'Connell, so long the undisputed leader of the 'Irish nation', to accept criticism from a younger generation whose purity of mind seemed to set them up as self-appointed keepers of the national conscience. And then O'Connell was a leading British, as well as Irish, political figure. It cannot have been pleasing to him when, in Young Ireland's denunciation of the federal idea, Charles Gavan Duffy warned that any such settlement must lead the Irish governing classes 'still to turn their eyes to London as the scene of their ambition' and to follow 'English manners, feelings, and prejudices and establish a centre of action apart from their native country';[41] O'Connell had, after all, achieved much by establishing just such a centre of action. In 1845 Young Ireland accused him of betraying the memory of the Dungannon Clubs of the Volunteer era by allowing five Irish M.P.s to accept posts as junior ministers in a Whig government. It was hard to take such emotive language from young men who had been children when O'Connell began his long trek to political power and influence on behalf of his Catholic people.

O'Connell might have taken his young critics to task on any number of grounds; he choose to discipline them on the issue of the use or abjuration of force as a means of attaining national independence. O'Connell sincerely detested violence, though his Protestant critics were justified in seeing his 'monster meetings' as a form of coercion, or at least of the threat of coercion. They were at bottom, however, a demonstration of strength and solidarity, a means of defying the government of the day, and O'Connell was always careful to tell his audience to disperse and go home peacefully, and to call for cheers for the soldiers detailed to police his meetings. His wish to avoid bloodshed was tested in 1843 when he announced, and then cancelled, a meeting at Clontarf, deciding at the last moment not to risk a confrontation with the government, which had banned his meeting, and which, as Sir Robert Peel put it, was prepared to endure even civil war rather than let O'Connell continue on his path of challenging the Union with Great Britain. Young Ireland fully supported O'Connell, declaring that only evil and ruin could follow violence. They stood for national education, Repeal reading-rooms, a national newspaper, not conspiracies and war. Yet their poetry rang with warlike and bellicose phrases; and they did not fear to speak of '98. To speak was, indeed, not to act; but they could stand accused of encouraging others to act, by suggestion if not by direct exhortation.

The death of Thomas Davis in September 1845 deprived Young Ireland of their most talented and also their most level-headed leader. In November 1845 John Mitchel, a lapsed Ulster Presbyterian and a thorough anglophobe, wrote an article in the *Nation* describing appropriate tactics for ambushing troops; when O'Connell protested, Mitchel assured him that there was no need for his concern, since Ireland's regeneration could be achieved through moral force; but, he added, only if there were any attempt to destroy the organs of moral force, the free press and free speech, would there be a need to call for 'such terrible methods of resistance'. Non-violence, then, was qualified; moral force, then, was conditional. So O'Connell took it, and in July 1846 he choose to make this issue the occasion for a break with Young Ireland, demanding from the association an unqualified statement that no political objective justified the use of force. Repeal could be achieved by the same means as Emancipation had been achieved, through moral and political pressure alone. The controversy continued, with William Smith O'Brien pointing out that the constitution of 1782 could not have been won without the threat of force, though he admitted that any appeal to arms at present would be madness. Religion surfaced yet again, as it had with Davis's clash with O'Connell over education. Now it was John Mitchel's turn to offend, by declaring that he, a Protestant and a 'Saxon Irishman from the North', and his kind were essential for the salvation of the nation, including the Catholic part of the nation. To drive Protestants out of the Repeal movement by 'needless tests' would perpetuate the degradation of Catholic and Protestant alike. Thomas Francis Meagher brought the matter to a head by declaring that he regarded the sword as a 'sacred weapon', and when O'Connell insisted that he quit the meeting, the supporters of Young Ireland departed, leaving 'Old Ireland' in command.

Force was both an occasion and a cause for O'Connell; but as well as the question of principle, O'Connell was impatient of the general theme underlying Young Ireland attacks on his leadership: the theme that the art of politics, as O'Connell understood and practised it, was not 'manly', but handing over Ireland to 'our old, relentless, hereditary enemy, bound hand and foot'.[42] O'Connell had, after all, achieved much for his people through the art of unmanly politics, and he was always careful to keep open the door for any future co-operation with the Whig Party, should circumstances permit. He was still certain that the Union, while not the answer to Ireland's ills, could at least provide some intermediate remedies; and at any rate it was preferable to bloody and fruitless revolution. His very policy of agitation, of political pressure at Westminster and at home, of seeking sympathy and support from radical organisations in Great Britain, of gaining the respect and admiration of the continent, drew attention to Irish grievances more successfully and consistently than at any time since the Act of Union. His prestige as a prominent figure on the British political stage could not be ignored by any British politician of whatever complexion; and even Sir Robert Peel, who checked him so decisively at Clontarf, and then put him in prison for conspiring to intimidate the government, acknowledged that the skills of politics must be applied to Ireland as a necessary means of preventing the Agitator's agitation from reviving and returning to plague the United Kingdom. As Nassau Senior put it, when the Tories paid all attention to the Irish Protestants, 'Ireland became the stronghold of

Toryism'. But now the Irish Catholics had become 'a nation':

> . . . and no party can satisfactorily govern Ireland which does
> not receive the support, we would not say of the whole, nor
> even of a majority of the Catholics, but of a minority sufficient
> to enable it to give to Catholics a fair share of its patronage.
> Ireland can never be contented while to be a Catholic is a badge
> of exclusion.[43]

Irish Catholics were British subjects; but they were regarded as
British subjects with a difference, not primarily because of their
nationality, which was, after all, shared by Protestants, but because
of their religion and their history of disloyalty, which marked them
out from the generality of British citizens. Nonconformists shared
the same distinction, but suffered from it to a lesser degree, partly
because they were less alien to the religious definition of Britishness, partly because they had a troublesome, but not such a dangerous, past to live down. Yet live it down they must, and they found
themselves under-represented in certain walks of British life,
especially as commissioned officers in the army.

The question which had confronted British politicians when they
turned their attention to Irish matters was one of defining their
attitude to a set of people whose religion, and therefore politics,
seemed to place them beyond the normal conventions of British
political life. It was ironic, of course, that when Ireland had its own
parliament in the eighteenth century, it was the British government
which, in the last decades of that century, pressed redress of
Catholic grievances on a reluctant Protestant nation. Now that
Britain had taken the Catholics under her own roof—or at least into
the lean-to outside the door—she hesitated to grant that which she
had urged upon the Irish parliament from the safer distance of
London. A British government had also to reconsider what its
attitude would be to the Anglican minority in Ireland, which did
share Britain's established religion. This minority in 1800 lost the
power of determining its own political fate; now it must remain ever
watchful of Westminster's attitude and policies. A Whig government had shown that it was prepared to take controversial and
unpopular measures (unpopular, that is, in Protestant Ireland)
against the more extreme Protestant organisations such as the
Orange Order, and that it was ready to harangue Irish landlords on
their duty to their tenants.

But the real test of the Union, as far as British politics was concerned, was the victory of Sir Robert Peel and the Conservatives in 1841. Peel's reputation in Ireland was black, at least in O'Connell's eyes. His administrative record when he was Chief Secretary for Ireland was one of soundness and probity; but he had strongly opposed Catholic Emancipation, not on grounds of religious bigotry, but simply because he believed that the British constitution was a Protestant one and that its character was not reconcilable with Catholic representation in parliament. His determination to maintain the Union was demonstrated when he faced O'Connell down over the Clontarf meeting in October 1843. But Peel was no inflexible opponent of reasonable claims for reform; on the contrary, he perceived that in dealing with Ireland, more than any other political problem, the wise statesman required a sense of timing, the need to appreciate 'what thing should be done, and what time it should be done, and in what mode'.[44] Moreover, the obverse of Peel's opposition to repeal of the Union was defence of the Union through legislative means: the need to make the Union a constitutional reality, not merely a convenient (or inconvenient) formality. He appreciated that although Catholics enjoyed nominal equality, they were not reaping any practical advantage from the removal of their legal disabilities. Peel could not and would not do deals, in the Whig manner, with O'Connell; what he choose to do was to confine the 'Agitator' and then seek means to redress the grievances that he believed lay behind and fuelled the agitation.

Peel's administration began, it is true, tardily in its Irish remedial legislation; but most British administrations began thus. It also began by encountering what was another common phenomenon of British and Irish politics: the demand by one group or other that Westminster pay special attention to its particular supplication. The first Irish issue that Peel had to encounter was the demand from Irish Tories that the government show its colours by making a state grant to the Church Education Society, thus strengthening it against, or at least alongside, the National School system. The supporters of the National School Board strongly objected, with one of their number arguing that the national system 'offered the only means of friendly intercourse between the government and the great mass of the people in Ireland . . . and the only means by which the rising generation of the poorer classes, Protestant and Catholic, can be purged of sectarian bile'.[45] There was also the possibility, the Chief Secretary for Ireland pointed out, that if the Anglicans were supported by the state, the Presbyterians too would demand a separate grant, and the national system would in consequence become a Catholic one, and all at the state's expense. The government was persuaded to stand firm against its Irish Tory wing, partly because to do otherwise would be to open a controversy in Ireland, partly because it believed that to damage the present system would undermine the possibility of Catholic confidence in the government. And the existing arrangement had an important advantage in that it placed Catholic children under what was after all a system devised by a Protestant state.

The education controversy revealed the difficulties involved in seeking to reconcile Catholics to the Union. Peel's government found itself attacked by Irish Tories, who complained bitterly about his failure to support the Church of Ireland. They had other grievances as well, in particular Peel's failure to work the patronage network in their favour. They were able to express their displeasure early in 1843, when at a by-election in Dublin University the Tories put forward their own candidate, George Hamilton, a strong supporter of the Church Education Society, and obliged the government candidate to withdraw. There was even talk in Tory circles of the formation of an Irish party in parliament 'distinct from politics and associated only upon subjects leaving open the welfare and prosperity of our country'.[46]

To conciliate one section of Irish opinion might be—indeed, probably would be—to arouse the resentment of another. This was not abnormal in politics, for vested interests were almost certain to collide with each other. But since Ireland did not elect her own government, these interests were obliged to watch carefully and jealously the doings of the government across the water; and what seemed perfectly reasonable in Westminster could look most unreasonable to the affected parties in Ireland. If Ireland, however, had been in a position to elect her own government, it seems certain that these vested interests would have collided in a much more dramatic and even violent form; but whatever the vexations inflicted upon the political and religious groups in Ireland by a British government intent on steering some kind of middle course between Irish factions, the very presence of that government at least assured that tensions, though frequently heightened by the British, could also be contained by them. British public and parliamentary opinion found itself inevitably involved in Irish matters, especially in the excitement of Peel's confrontation with O'Connell in 1843; and in 1844 Peel revealed the radical nature of his Irish intentions when he wrote to Heytesbury:

> The cry . . . has been for a century past, and I doubt not now 'The Protestants are the friends of the British connexion, reliance can be placed on them.' . . . All this means 'continue to use the monopoly of favour and confidence, which before 1829 the law secured to us. Consider the members of the Church as the garrison of Ireland and govern Ireland on the garrison principle.' The answer is that the system is unjust, is dangerous, but above all is utterly impracticable.[47]

Unjust and dangerous it may have been; but whether it was impracticable or not had still to be proved—at least to Irish Protestant Tories and, what was equally if not more important, to large sections of British opinion. The gap between Peel's goal and its achievement was illustrated in one of the most important and exhaustive debates on Ireland held in the House of Commons since the Union. In February 1844 parliament discussed the state of Ireland for nine days, and the diarist Charles Greville described the debate as marking the 'starting-point of a new Catholic question'. He noted that

> It is impossible not to be struck with the very remarkable change in the tone and temper in which the Irish discussion was then carried on, and still more with the altered state of opinion which now prevails in society on this topic. It is difficult to meet with any one in or out of Parliament who does not admit that *something must be done*, and the whole of the minority of 226, with no inconsiderable portion of the majority . . . not only avowed this conviction, but appeared . . . impressed with the necessity of laying the foundation of a real and permanent union between the two countries.

There was, however, a qualifying phrase which Greville added and which was of considerable significance for the failure or success of this new determination to cement the Union: for, as Greville put it, there was 'much difference of opinion . . . as to . . . what the people of England could be brought to consent, and what the people of Ireland would be content to receive'.[48] This was an important difference in perception, and was the natural consequence of Union politics, which necessitated one country's public opinion deciding how another country's public opinion was to be moulded, satisfied and appeased. It was a view that deeply modified and affected the policy not only of Peel but also of some of his successors as they turned their attention to making a 'real and permanent union between the two countries'.

The centre of Peel's reform policy was, inevitably, religion. Peel believed that the Catholic priesthood was the mainstay of the Repeal agitation, and, as he explained to his cabinet colleagues, his purpose was to secure Ireland to Britain and detach what he called the 'considerable portion of the respectable and influential Roman Catholic population' from O'Connell's cause. Now, he argued, was the 'crisis in the affairs of Ireland which must be taken at the flood'.[49] He mentioned franchise reform, municipal reform, and a commission on landlord–tenant relations, but the first item in his policy was the conciliation of the Catholic clergy. This, however, he must achieve without placing the established Church of Ireland in jeopardy, for, apart from matters of conscience, to do so would risk the unity of his cabinet, and incur especially the displeasure of Willam Ewart Gladstone.

The question of conciliating the Catholic clergy raised the problem of education once again. For if the clergy were educated in a more liberal environment, instead of the context which at present produced 'fifty spiritual firebrands', then a new outlook could be created among this most influential body of men. But the difficulty of working a policy of conciliation in Ireland was revealed in the government's first two reform measures: a registration bill which included a £5 freehold franchise in the counties, and a Charitable Bequests Bill which proposed a bequests board of thirteen, of which five were to be Catholics, to administer charitable donations and act as trustees for property which could be used to maintain Catholic clergy or places of worship in Ireland. The registration bill was opposed by Irish Whigs, who urged their English counterparts to vote against it, and it was postponed and then dropped. The Charitable Bequests Bill incurred the wrath of Archbishop MacHale, who declared that any Catholic who served on the new board would be a traitor to his church, and O'Connell, who warned in most exaggerated language that all Catholic charities would fall within the 'greedy grasp' of the board. MacHale and O'Connell were motivated by the same desire, which was simply to frustrate the government's intention to divide Catholic opinion and win it over by conciliation. Conciliation was all very well up to a point: but that point was reached and passed when it threatened the very power base of the Liberator and the hierarchy. It might then be rather too much of a good thing, and MacHale thundered against the bill as an attempt to associate Catholics 'with the old and inveterate enemies of our faith . . . dependent on the crown, fearful of its displeasure, and fawning on its caresses'. It was the old veto controversy in a new form; it was even worse, as MacHale drew a dark picture of the Catholic members of the board suffering infection with the 'perverse opinions' of their 'new companions'.[50]

Here, then, in a rather rowdy form, was the difference in perception between English policy and Irish Catholic response that Greville alluded to. Peel was indeed alarmed by the possibility of the 'spread of popery' in alliance with the 'democratic feelings and institutions', which he regarded as offering a 'very formidable combination against the peace of Ireland, and the maintenance of cordial union with this country'.[51] Democracy, or at least populism, and religion were strange bedfellows in early nineteenth-century Europe; but bedfellows they were in Ireland, and they must needs be parted asunder if the Union was to become a stable political arrangement. This, of course, was exactly what O'Connell and MacHale feared most of all. Each gained much from this odd alliance: the church, influence; O'Connell, power. When Peel subdued O'Connell at Clontarf, and then inflicted a mild but debilitating imprisonment upon him, he judged the time ripe for conciliation; but in Ireland the manoeuvre looked rather too obvious.

The government felt it had identified the central problem of binding Ireland to Great Britain under the Union: what Sir James Graham, the minister with chief responsibility for Ireland, called the 'severance of the religion of the people from all connection with the State'. To end this severance was the government's purpose; but in Ireland that purpose was denounced by the Repeal press as 'the first essay of Her Majesty's Ministers to place the Catholic clergy under the control of the State'.[52] It all depended from which angle the matter was viewed. And there was, of course, yet another point of view as well, that of Irish Protestants, who saw their 'own' Conservative government seeking to conciliate those who were ever the British monarchy's enemies, and their own. Irish Protestants had no doubt that government policy would replace Protestantism with Catholicism throughout Ireland.

Conciliation, then, was a hard road to travel. How difficult it was became apparent when the House of Lords decided to reverse the verdict on O'Connell and order his release; O'Connell was met with a triumphal parade through Dublin and a joyous reception by the Catholic clergy. Peel's government was now all the more anxious for its Charitable Bequests Bill to succeed, for if it failed, it would demonstrate that Irish Catholic pressure of the more extreme type could frustrate the cabinet and deprive it of any momentum created by its victory over O'Connell in 1843. Peel therefore made every effort to meet the objections of the Catholic clergy, and he sought especially to conciliate those of the bishops who did not adopt MacHale's extreme position: the Archbishops of Armagh and Dublin and the Bishop of Killaloe were asked to serve on the bequests board and agreed to do so, despite much hostility from the nationally-minded press. In the end the government gained a victory, thanks mainly to the willingness of the minority of bishops who accepted the bill and stood out against formidable pressure. But in Ireland the controversy continued beyond the passing of the act, with O'Connell stating his case against it, and with accusations flung about that the British government and the Vatican were in conspiracy against Irish nationalist politics and especially the Repeal movement. The government consoled itself with the reflection that it had on its side the 'seriously religious Roman Catholics' as against those who were 'merely the adherents of O'Connell'. But this was a self-defeating claim: the 'mere adherents of O'Connell' comprised most of the Catholic clergy, and the Catholic O'Connellite following was, as yet, unreconciled to the new British policy of conciliation.[53]

Catholic opinion in Ireland had divided on Peel's Charitable Bequests Bill and had become engaged in a prolonged controversy. Now it was the turn of British opinion to raise the alarm. In 1845 Peel sought to augment the annual government grant to Maynooth College (established for the training of Catholic priests), which he was convinced was too small to meet present needs. In 1841 and 1842 the bishops themselves had approached the government on this matter. Now, however, it was Peel and his cabinet who took the initiative, with the Lord Lieutenant involving himself in discussions with representatives of Catholic opinion. At the beginning of the 1845 session the government introduced a bill raising the annual grant from about £9,000 to £26,000 and giving £30,000 for capital expenditure. Peel defended the measure on pragmatic grounds: since the state already paid a grant, then parliament had approved the principle, and an increased grant was a commonsense response to Maynooth's financial difficulties. It was, he urged, 'perfectly compatible to hold steadfast the professions of our own faith without wavering, and at the same time to improve the education and elevate the character of those who—do what you will—pass this measure or reject it—will continue to be the spiritual guardians and religious instructors of millions of your fellow-countrymen'.[54]

But were Irish Catholics the 'fellow-countrymen' of the Protestant British? Here was the nub of the matter. Within a short time Peel was deluged with protest and petitions from the religious public of England. A central anti-Maynooth committee was established at Exeter Hall on 18 March 1845 to fight the public endowment of popery. Some, like John Bright, opposed the grant because they objected to any measure that tended to set up a state church of whatever denomination; others simply feared idolatry and superstition, as they called it. The government carried the day, thanks to a combination of Whigs and liberal Conservatives. Of the 37 Irish Tory M.P.s who divided on the bill, 10 supported and 27 opposed it. Significantly, the excitement in England was far greater than that in Ireland, where the bill failed to arouse much public interest. The leaders of Presbyterian opinion, Cooke and Montgomery, supported the grant. And many Protestants no doubt considered a Catholic Church with reason to be grateful to the state as preferable to a Catholic Church without any such reason. O'Connell, for his part, welcomed the bill, though characteristically he claimed the credit for its passing. But he also acknowledged that the Conservatives were set upon achieving 'justice for Ireland'—a phrase which was later to become the property of W. E. Gladstone and his Liberal Party.

The Maynooth College Act was a major achievement for Peelite Irish policy, not least because of the manner of its passing: Peel had risked much public and parliamentary unpopularity, yet had adhered to his purpose. There was now, on the face of it, a real possibility of a new construction which could be built upon the foundations of the Act of Union. Previously the various factions and groups in Ireland had existed in watchful contemplation, and in times of danger had found themselves ranged against one another on the great issue of Repeal or the Union. Now, if Catholics could be won over to the Union (and since Protestants were hardly likely to make a sudden dash for Repeal, not even for the pleasure of surprising and discomfiting their enemy), then a new set of boundaries (though still boundaries) might be constructed in Irish politics. Within these, Catholics might accept the Union as permanent, and thus deprive Irish politics of that basic constitutional controversy. And while politics would still be contentious, and religions still no doubt at odds with one another, they would be separated from the long-standing fundamental connection between politics, religion and the constitution. The state's existence, in short, would no longer be a matter of controversy, its legitimacy no longer in doubt. New political alignments might follow in Ireland, or, more realistically, old ones would become compatible with each other.

This, however, could not be achieved in a few pieces of legislation, however important and successful. It was probably too ambitious: for Catholics had in the Emancipation and Repeal campaigns experienced the sense of power, authority and self-will that majority status afforded them in Ireland. It was an experience that was to revive, and survive the vicissitudes of political fortune. They were as self-conscious of their majority position as Protestants were of their minority status. Each had attained their respective status within a relatively short time. The volatile and deep changes in Irish politics that had occurred between the 1820s and the 1840s could hardly be extinguished by Peel's government, for within those two decades Irish Protestants had lost their eighteenth-century inheritance as the political nation of Ireland; and Irish Catholics had assumed their inheritance not only as the political nation but as the Irish nation at large. Protestants might still cling to local positions of privilege, but this could not hide the changed, and changing, times. And Irish Presbyterians watched and waited, not unhappy with the downfall of Anglican pride, but as concerned as any member of the Established Church for their future in an Ireland run by the majority.

There were, in any case, limitations upon even a vigorous and determined administration like Peel's. These limitations revealed the constraints that were imposed on a British government by the prevailing opinion of the day. They were clearly exhibited in two of the government's most significant failures: its land and education policies. The problem of Irish poverty, the unsettled state of rural Ireland, with its secret societies and lawless pockets of agrarian terrorism, had long attracted the nervous fascination of British public and politicians, who, however, had done little but seek to control it by coercion, or dismiss it as beyond remedy, an endemic characteristic of Irish lower life.

Secret societies directed violence as much against farmers (most of whom were Catholics) as against landlords; and indeed, in early nineteenth-century Ireland it was as hard to contemplate terrorising landlords as it was in England, for they were men of immense prestige and power, much more formidable targets than the farmer. Nevertheless, when it came to devising remedies, it was relations between landlord and tenant that inevitably came under scrutiny, and that were regarded as the starting-point for any reform. In 1843 Peel's government established the Devon Commission, which produced facts and figures explaining the extent and depth of rural poverty in Ireland—about which it was agreed that something must be done, but about which no government was as yet in a position to do anything. The commission reported in 1845, having interviewed some 1,100 witnesses and collected a mass of material. But the very extent of its revelations overwhelmed any possibility of remedial legislation: the greater the problem, the more timid the response (a phenomenon not unusual where administrators and reformers meet). The commission recommended that tenants receive compensation for any improvements of their tenancies; it suggested loans for improvements, and exhorted landlords to fix fair rents. The government made a tentative beginning with a bill for compensation for improvements, but it inevitably encountered objections that any such action by the state was unwarrantable interference with the rights of property. Whigs and Tories alike were unhappy about any intervention, and in Ireland Tories disliked the measure, while more radical elements declared that it was but a minor palliative. The bill got as far as a select committee of the House of Commons, but was then postponed to the following year.[55] By then events had overtaken it.

The year 1845 saw another, and more exasperating, check upon the government: the 'godless colleges', which had caused dissension between O'Connell and Young Ireland, exposed the difficulty of pleasing all elements in Ireland on contentious matters of faith and morals. Each group in Ireland, Catholics, Anglicans and Presbyterians, were so used to the idea that their people must be educated in such a way as to secure them in their religion, and advance them in their status, that the idea of a non-sectarian institution, without provision for any specific religious instruction, was to them all equally an abomination. The Presbyterians, for example, desired what Heytesbury called a 'Presbyterian Maynooth'. As soon as the bill to establish the colleges was introduced into parliament it became the object of a public controversy. Objections tumbled upon it from all directions, and the Catholic hierarchy warned that Catholics could not attend the lectures on history, logic, metaphysics, moral philosophy, geology or anatomy without exposing their faith and morals to imminent danger, unless a Catholic professor were appointed for each of those classes. This, in all honesty, left very little that Catholics *could* attend; but the bishops' behaviour can be explained both in terms of bargaining, with the church staking its claim from the beginning for negotiation on the final shape of the bill, and the church's genuine fear of education as a means of dislodging Catholics from their faith. The problem was compounded by the fact that, as Baron Stockmar, the confidant of Prince Albert put it, Peel was a Protestant minister who could not quite escape from his Protestant skin.[56] The bill in the end reached the statute book, and not all bishops opposed it. But Archbishop MacHale had his way, and his influence was felt both in Rome and Ireland, where papal rescripts of 1847 and 1848 drew attention to the dangerous character of the colleges (which were opened in 1849). Catholics were thus suffered to attend under the burden of their church's displeasure. Presbyterians fared rather better, for the university college at Belfast offered them at last an educational institution in their own country, instead of Scotland, as hitherto. But Episcopalians retained possession of their old-established college in Dublin, ensconced in the nation's largest city, and its most prestigious institution, while both Catholics and Presbyterians remained firmly located in the provinces.

The college controversy raised a deeper question, one that Baron Stockmar perceived: could a Protestant state, governed by a Protestant Prime Minister, escape from its skin sufficiently so as to accommodate itself to a predominantly Catholic people? And if it did, could it keep the affection of Episcopalians and Presbyterians? For the problem of British–Irish integration was not racial or even, except in the loosest sense of the word, ethnic. National identity in the British Isles was hard to define and impossible to reduce to a central core. Except, that is, in one respect: that of religion, where the kind of anti-popery suspicion deeply embedded in English thinking could be aroused to vehement life, as Peel discovered over his Maynooth College Bill, and as Lord John Russell was to rediscover, purposely and for political reasons, in the controversy over 'papal aggression' in 1851, when the papacy proposed the re-establishment of the Roman Catholic diocesan system in England.

This was the central problem, and one of vital importance in the history of the British Isles. Peel, for all his efforts, was a Protestant Prime Minister charged with governing a Protestant state and nation which nevertheless contained a large, self-conscious, and at times aggressive Roman Catholic wedge. There can be no doubt that his sincere and sustained efforts to make the Union a real political marriage, instead of a convenient political expedient (which it in origin was), made it easier for a Catholic in Ireland to be a quiet, unostentatious Unionist. O'Connell was still a major political figure in 1845, as he had been in 1841; but he was no further on than he had been in 1841, and his followers still did not encompass the Catholics as a whole. Nor were the bishops uniformly hostile or suspicious of Peel's conciliatory policy, and some of them resented the intemperate language of MacHale.

But if Peel could take comfort in this aspect of his administration, he could hardly be satisfied with the impact he had made on those Irish people who saw their loyalty as the mainstay—the only mainstay—of the British connection. By 1845 Irish Protestant Tories were thoroughly disenchanted with Peel, denouncing his policy as one of 'soothing syrup and sugar plums' such as 'the surrender of the Established Church', a church which Tories regarded as a more important bulwark of the Union than landlords or political parties. Tories showed their displeasure in their apathetic attitude towards registering to vote; they were inclined to retreat into their local habitations and sustain their power through their own organisations, of which the most prominent was the Orange Order—now, in the north, formally reconstituted with the Earl of Enniskillen in the chair.[57] The government was uncertain about proclaiming Orange meetings, since the outcome of prosecutions would depend upon juries, which might not convict. If the Earl of Enniskillen were dismissed from his post as Deputy Lieutenant of Fermanagh, then most of the Protestant J.P.s in the north might resign; but if he were left untouched by the government, then Catholics could complain of partiality. Yet if the government pressed the Protestants too far, Protestant Tories might carry out their threat of shunning English parties and coalescing as an independent party to defend their own interests. Small wonder, then that in 1845 Peel, far from taking satisfaction from his Irish policy, declared that the condition of Ireland seemed to 'preclude honest and impartial government'.[58]

Peel's gloomy contemplation of his administration's Irish policy was not shared by one of the shrewdest politicians and thinkers of his age, Count Camillo Cavour, the maker of Italian unification. In July 1844 Cavour published an article on 'Ireland: Its Present and its Future' in the *Bibliotecha Universelle de Genève*, written when the Repeal agitation was at its height. Cavour, while acknowledging the 'eight centuries' of English oppression of Ireland, nonetheless regarded the Union as 'an event at which humanity must rejoice'. He praised the Whigs in the 1830s, and the Conservatives under Peel, who sought to remedy the social and economic ills of Ireland. He believed that repeal of the Union would be disastrous to Ireland, and the harbinger of civil war. He urged English politicians to continue what he called the work of regeneration in Ireland, a 'measured and prudent march' indeed, but a march nonetheless. And he asked, by way of a conclusion, whether these progressive reforms would succeed in 'completely fusing the sentiments and the interests of [Ireland] with those of Britain'. These, Cavour decided, were 'grave questions which only the future can resolve'.[59] They were no less grave after 1845 when the British government was faced with the spectacle of famine in Ireland.

The Land and its Nemesis, 1845–9

WHEN Count Cavour analysed the Irish problem in 1844, he diagnosed its main elements as the 'religious and social organisation of the country', its defective agrarian system, the division between landlord and tenant, the demands made upon the people by the Anglican clergy, and the abominations of a servile war of peasant secret societies.[1] He focused his attention on the question of the land, arguing that 'the improvement of the relations established by law between the proprietors and the tenants, between the minority who possess and the majority who cultivate, is one of the most difficult problems that the legislator can undertake'; but he did not doubt that a British government 'enlightened, strong and impartial, can by degrees effect great improvements'.[2]

Cavour, in referring to a 'defective' agrarian system, touched upon an issue which, in the early years of the Union, began to force its attention on the British government: the poverty of large sections of the people of rural Ireland, the visitation of famine, albeit on a more limited scale than later, and the tendency of areas of the country to fall into disorder, with peasant secret societies organising and directing violence and murder against landlords, farmers and the forces of law and order. These secret societies had been a part of Irish rural life long before the Union: they adopted titles—Whiteboys, Shanavests, Hearts of Steel, Hearts of Oak, and many others. Their organisation and purpose differed according to local conditions and local problems. In one place they would oppose the extension of pasture farming, which was inspired by the fact that pasture land was exempt from the exaction of tithes for the upkeep of the Church of Ireland; in another they would refuse to pay the taxation levied on local people for the upkeep of roads. Sometimes they assumed a sectarian form, as in the case of the

Defenders at the end of the eighteenth century; on occasion such organisations also included Anglican, Presbyterian and Catholic in a common front against what they regarded as unjust action by landlords, farmers or the Catholic Church as well as the Church of Ireland. What was important about them, generally, was that they fostered the idea of a group in society which could make its own 'laws', enforce them—often with cruel punishments—and for considerable periods of time establish a kind of local power or authority which the law, especially in its primitive eighteenth-century form, found difficult to suppress. Secret societies frightened respectable people, of whatever political or religious belief; and Daniel O'Connell stressed that one of the advantages of his Catholic Association was that it could, he alleged, control and even undermine outbreaks of rural combination and disorder.[3] Certainly the role played by those two main societies at the time of the 1798 rebellion, the Defenders and the Orange Order, indicated that such organisations, however local or particularist, could be mobilised in the interests of a wider cause: could be politicised, used for the promotion or the suppression of an ideology, and—with arms—could offer a threat not only to individuals but to the stability of the state itself.

The tendency of rural people, sometimes in co-operation with urban elements as well, to fall back upon secret societies, either from motives of fear or respect, and to regard them as a kind of alternative to the state, creating and enforcing their own version of law and order, was what shocked most English observers of early nineteenth-century Ireland. Agrarian outrages were an inescapable part of every administration's agenda. Soldiers and secret societies in some areas, such as Cork in the 1820s, fought what amounted almost to a small war; and English observers looked with amazement as well as disgust on a society where 'faction fighting', the trailing of one's coat, the invitation of a group of families to another group to come and fight, at an appointed time and with the assistance of strong drink, seemed so at odds with any concept of what rural society ought to be like.[4] Not even the presence of Luddites in England, with their machine-breaking and their occasional attacks on local manufacturers, could match the horrid fascination of the brutality and disorder of certain regions of the Irish countryside. Contrary to later belief, the landed gentry were not the chief targets for agrarian terrorism in Ireland; they could still defend themselves and could if necessary call upon the assistance of the magistracy and the army. Isolated farmers, Catholic or Protestant, suffered most, and could not so readily find the means to repulse threats or actual violence to their lives and property.

By 1830 it was clear that Britain had taken upon herself a responsibility which she hardly knew how to discharge: that of maintaining law and order in a society, large parts of which appeared to be susceptible to the lure of secret organisations, with their own rituals, their own codes of conduct, their own law-enforcement methods; even urban society was not immune, as the formation of the Ribbon society and its activities after 1820 indicated. The Ribbonmen were particularly strong among the Dublin Catholic artisans and working class; and although they appear to have spent much of their time falling out over money and personal differences, they were an organisation which could muster over a thousand men at a meeting.[5] Improved law and order measures were the obvious response, and by the 1840s an efficient, armed police force and more effective coercion legislation appeared to be gaining the upper hand. But the dislike of British officials for the crude and alarming nature of rural society in Ireland could not divert attention from what might be regarded as a more serious aspect of the case: the poverty and backwardness of the country-side. In particular there was concern for what was coming to be identified as the central problem of that society: the inability of the rural population to break out of the cycle of land subdivision, with plots of land becoming ever smaller as landlords, farmers, labourers and cottiers pursued subdivision as a means of providing for a growing population which made increasing demands on the land.

It is difficult to estimate both the actual population of Ireland in the early nineteenth century and the reasons for its rapid rise. Although censuses were taken in 1821, 1831 and 1841, their reliability was suspect: enumerators faced difficulties, meeting downright hostility in the pursuit of their task; adequate information about parish or townland boundaries was lacking; and it was easy to miss seasonal labourers and beggars. But it is clear that the population of Ireland was increasing: one estimate puts the real figure as 7.2 million in 1821, 7.9 million in 1831, and 8.4 million in 1841.[6] This population growth varied from region to region, with Ulster, the greatest growth area in the early eighteenth century, dropping behind Connacht in the period 1791–1821. And within the provinces there were, of course, local differences. But what was both paradoxical and ominous in these variations was that in more fertile and settled areas population growth increased least; in bogland, woodland and less fertile land it increased most. Population increase was to some extent modified by emigration to Britain and America and by mortality, but this did not reverse the population trend, which always remained on the increase. And the part of the country where population continued to rise, and where distress was most frequently forcing its attention on the state, was the west of Ireland: between 1815 and 1845 the clamour of distress came from Donegal, Kerry, Clare, Galway, west Cork, and Mayo, especially west Mayo.[7]

The reasons for the increase in the population of Ireland, especially among the poorer classes in the western areas, are complex: answers to this question invariably include high fertility, the use of the potato as a cheap and simple food, and early marriage.[8] This argument has yet to be resolved; but more important was the question of what an increasing population would live on, how it would survive, in a country that did not enjoy the economic diversity, and especially the growth of industry, which might be expected to absorb its surplus population. Another, equally important question was what the government would or could do to cope with the importunate pleas that fell upon its ears with such troublesome regularity.

The north of Ireland enjoyed its own regional economic development. In 1839 thirty-five linen-spinning mills employed some 7,758 workers, most of them in mills in Belfast or close by in such places as Banbridge, Larne and Carrickfergus. The linen industry moved from water power to steam power and continued to grow and prosper. It spread into the periphery of Ulster and even into parts of Louth, Longford, Mayo, Sligo and Roscommon. The woollen industry also offered employment. The two industries occupied both men and women, and in the rural areas offered the opportunity for work in the home. Domestic industry of this kind was on the retreat by 1841; nevertheless, it offered what Ireland lacked—cash income, which freed men and women from dependence on the land, from the constraints imposed by land availability, and from the fear of scarcity. For one of the chief problems facing the poorer classes in rural Ireland was not so much unemployment as under-employment: the summer months were especially difficult, when the labourer had neither enough work nor potatoes nor money to purchase other food. Money could be raised by loans, but loans had to be repaid, and the labourer was obliged to pledge the results of his labour, mainly to farmers; and if he could not get credit, then he must beg. Fortunately, alms-giving was quite generous in pre-famine Ireland. But the lack of money to buy food was a problem made worse by poor communications throughout the most remote and impoverished parts of the country.[9]

Shortage and distress occurred, then, long before the great disaster of 1845–7: in 1816–17, 1822, 1826 and 1831. On each occasion the distress was worst in the west of Ireland; but it was coped with adequately, partly through the efforts of the government, which shipped oats, corn and biscuit to the affected areas, and made funds available for harbours and fishery development or public works schemes. New roads were built, and government inspectors appointed to oversee fever hospitals and general health matters. Money was spent on infirmaries far in excess of funds spent in Great Britain. The political culture of the time encouraged philanthropy, and charitable organisations in England were founded to help the Irish poor, whose plight was highlighted by writers such as Walter Scott, Gustave de Beaumont, J. G. Kohl and Alexis de Tocqueville. Above all, Irish landlords were exhorted to do their duty by the Irish poor; and many of them did so, spending substantial sums of money to help distressed areas.[10] But in the years before the Great Famine questions were being asked, not only about landlords' attitudes to their tenants and the Irish poor, but about the whole system of land tenure in Ireland, about the very basis of the Irish rural social and economic structure.

The Irish land system was the despair of any rational commentator on economic problems in Ireland in the early nineteenth century. Unfavourable comparisons with England abounded; for in Ireland, it seemed, there were none of the comfortable hamlets, the sturdy yeomen, the easy intercourse between landlord and tenant, that were regarded as the norm in English society. Instead there was what could only be described as a ramshackle system: landlords living beyond their means; farmers dividing and subdividing land unreasonably, with smaller and smaller holdings parcelled out, sometimes between members of one family; labourers living at subsistence level; tenants falling into arrears; agrarian violence, at times of a ferocious kind; evictions; disorder. By 1844 responsibility for some 1,322 properties with a combined annual rental of nearly £1 million was vested in the Courts of Chancery and Exchequer because of unmanageable debts on the part of the landlords.[11] Landlords were not, of course, solely—perhaps not even mainly—to blame for this alarming scene; their efforts to check subdivision were often opposed by tenants, whose conservatism matched only that of their landlords. For the central fact of the Irish land system was that, for many groups of farmers and labourers, the existing arrangements enabled them to meet their necessities and their requirements. For the medium-sized farmer, subdivision of land enabled him to provide for his family by subletting his land into smaller parcels: sons and daughters could be given a plot of land, sometimes of as little as two or four acres, to provide for them on their marriage. Labourers lived a hard and meagre existence; yet they too could obtain that existence with ease, simply by building a cabin and planting potatoes, and by working for the means of life instead of for cash wages. This in turn suited the convenience of the Irish famer, who could secure labour on his farm without the necessity of making money payment. By the 1840s the practice of subdivision was regarded with disfavour in economic thinking;[12] but by then the practices of generations were hard to reverse.

Reversing this practice, however, required beginning somewhere; and since landlords were at the top of the social pyramid, and since it was their behaviour, in particular, that seemed to contrast most markedly with that of their energetic and innovative English counterparts, it was inevitable that, even before the catastrophe of the Great Famine, British fact-finders and official advisers should find Irish landlords remarkably deficient in the virtues essential to a well-run and satisfying landed society. As one witness, a farmer, put it to the Devon Commission, set up in 1843 to inquire into the Irish land problem, 'It is just like horses; if they are badly handled, they will not pull well—and the people all seem to be badly harnessed. It seems to me to commence with the landlords.'[13]

It seemed to various other observers, both private and official, that the bad handling commenced with the landlords: their relationship with their tenants was what held civilised societies together;

and if they were unsatisfactory, then the blame must be laid where it belonged. But it was easy enough to lay the blame for the landholding system, with its lack of improvement and development, on the landlords; it was more difficult to devise a remedy for the malady. The difficulty was revealed in the Devon Commission's recommendations, published in 1845, about ways in which legislation might act benignly upon the Irish land system. The commission produced many documents and much evidence, and interviewed 1,100 witnesses in the course of its deliberations. But it could hardly do more than uncover the size and scope of the problem. Moreover, it found fault with one of the most protective (to tenants) customs in Ireland: that of the so-called 'Ulster custom'. The Ulster custom was the most marked distinguishing feature of the north of Ireland, and it consisted of the right of the tenant to sell the 'interest' in his holding when he handed his farm tenancy over to a new incoming tenant. This custom was based upon the belief that the tenant possessed some kind of interest in the soil, which arose from the fact that he, and not the landlord, was responsible for its cultivation and development. This did not amount to a claim on the tenant's part that he could deprive the landlord of his right to terminate a lease if he, the landlord, wished to do so; but it provided for a set of securities that enabled the tenant to make good his belief, or claim, that he had an interest in the soil and that this gave him certain benefits. These benefits could be computed in cash: when a tenant left his farm, he was entitled to claim a sum of money from the incoming tenant, which recognised that the new tenant had bought the right to a quiet and untrammelled occupation of the farm. The landlord retained the right to approve of the purchase and the purchaser; but to interfere with the purchase of tenant right, or the right of the present tenant to ask his best price and make his bargain with the incoming occupant, was regarded as high-handed and unjustified.

Tenant right generally carried with it some further privileges and benefits for the tenant. The custom usually involved a claim that the tenant had the right to a continuous occupancy of the farm at a reasonable rent. The landlord could, of course, terminate the lease if he wished, but he was expected in such cases to compensate the tenant for his 'interest' in the land. The rent had to be paid; and there was no 'fixity of tenure' in the sense of an unconditional occupancy of the farm. A 'fair rent' was a variable and uncertain principle, and a frequent cause of dispute, since the size of the rent would affect the value of the tenant right if a tenant were to sell up and move out. Moreover, the whole set of arrangements was a matter not of law but of custom and practice, and was therefore not underwritten by any legal guarantee. Its origin is disputed, but it probably arose from the preference given to a sitting tenant at the end of a lease to continue in his occupancy at a higher rent; if, however, he took the alternative option and chose to leave, then he could sell his 'goodwill' to the purchaser, thus giving the purchaser a clear, undisturbed occupancy of the farm—a token of goodwill and of a settled tenancy. This custom—found most commonly in Ulster, and especially in Counties Antrim, Down and Derry, and in some southern and western counties in a attenuated form—was generally regarded as contributing to good landlord–tenant relations and therefore to social stability.

If the legalisation of the Ulster custom was quite beyond the recommendation of the Devon Commission, then at least the commission's report bore fruit in one respect, in that its most radical proposal became the subject of legislation in 1845. A land bill was introduced by Lord Stanley providing for the appointment of a commissioner of improvements, to whom a tenant could apply for a decision about any improvements he proposed to make: if they were approved, the tenant, on eviction within a certain period, was to be entitled to compensation for three classes of improvement: building, fencing and drainage. The Repeal Association denounced the measure as a 'miserable, transitory instalment of that right delusively promised'; the landlords objected to the idea of any right of the tenant to compensation at all.[14] The parliamentary opposition was so strong that Stanley was compelled to withdraw the bill. The Devon Commission made other suggestions, among them the foundation of agricultural schools, easier loans to landlords, the fixing of fair rents by landlords, and the desirability of landlords getting to know their tenants better. And in the autumn of 1845 Devon himself sent Peel a list of bills which he had prepared to improve the Irish land system, none of which would arouse party feelings.[15] These bills were never acted upon, for the famine overtook events; indeed, it required the scale of the Great Famine to enable the government to act upon the kind of opinion that had been forming in official circles for some time and which was succinctly expressed by Lord Clarendon:

> The landlords are the real obstacle to improvement, and their condition generally is deporable. As a body they are insolvent. Many of them lack the first necessities of life, and, though still exercising the rights of property, they can perform none of its duties.[16]

Nevertheless, when famine occurred, it was to the landlords that the British government looked for a major effort at coping with the disaster.

The Irish rural problem was not unique. In the western Highlands of Scotland too harvest failure, such as that of 1836–7, brought many people to the brink of starvation; here too there was what can properly be called a 'peasant society', with the overwhelming majority of the inhabitants depending to a significant extent on small holdings and tiny patches of land for subsistence. This population was to experience the potato blight of 1846–7 and suffer from its consequences, since the potato was central to its diet. And this area, like much of Ireland, was confronted with a crucial and alarming fact: its population growth, while not in itself a cause of social destitution, was in a kind of imbalance with its resources and its employment possibilities.[17] There were simply no alternatives for the people except the precarious existence available to them from their subsistence on their simple diet and their small patches of land; none, that is, except emigration. Between 1815 and 1845 over a million inhabitants left Ireland; and one of the remedies frequently suggested for the Irish rural problem was state-assisted emigration rather than workhouse relief.[18] But emigration in itself, while possibly a palliative, was not a cure, since the fundamental problem—that of a society in which most people did not have the money to buy alternative means of subsistence if their staple crop failed—remained untouched. What the inhabitants of peasant Ireland needed was greater employment opportunities, which mere emigration could not provide.

The potato blight of 1845–6 was caused by the fungal disease *phytophthora infestans*, which makes its first appearance in the form of black spots on the leaves, with a whitish mould on the undersurface, which contains the spores; these are conveyed to other plants by wind, rain and insects. For germination to occur, moisture is necessary; and Ireland, like the west of Scotland, would naturally suffer if the blight ever appeared there. Its appearance was not new in 1846: a disease of a similar kind was reported in northern Germany in 1830, in parts of the Hebrides in the 1830s, and on the Atlantic coast of North America in 1842. But the outbreak that caused the widespread failure of the potato crop in Ireland in 1845–6 was a disaster on a much larger scale, and it was compounded by the fact that the fungus could lie dormant during the winter, only to return again and again. Thus a new potato crop, planted alongside the slightly infected old potatoes, could become infected when climatic conditions were favourable. Since there was no known chemical remedy, the disease could flourish unchecked and with great rapidity. It was not just the first failure in 1845 that caused the catastrophe, but its repetition in subsequent years; indeed, as late as 1854 the blight was as serious in the western Highlands of Scotland as it had been in 1846.[19] In Ireland the first attack of the blight in 1845 was not as serious as that of 1846. The absence of blight in 1847 occasioned false optimism, but the blight returned in 1848 and destroyed the summer crop yet again, and conditions were as bad as they had been in 1846. By the end of 1849 the worst of the Irish famine, at least, was over.

The complete failure of an indigenous food crop was bound to cause social disaster on an unprecedented scale; the words of one Scottish observer apply equally to Ireland: 'society now smitten at its base'.[20] Between 1845 and 1851 at least 800,000 people (approximately one-tenth of the population) died from hunger and disease. Those hardest hit were the class of people whose numbers had risen rapidly in the decades before the famine: the agricultural labouring classes, whose decline as a proportion of the rural population began and remained unchecked. The famine hit these people hardest because their means of livelihood was that of the penniless entrepreneur: the labourer rented his subsistence in the form of a cabin and a potato patch and paid for them through his work. Cottiers, like labourers, were always engaged in a gamble with existence, depending for their survival on their potato patch. This dependence was fragile; after 1830, as the number of cottiers rose, the cottier was obliged to take a declining quality of land, and was frequently forced to eat a poor-quality type of potato known as a 'lumper' ('Just try it for six months and you'll never want another,' a commission of inquiry into the Irish poor was told in 1836).[21]

The unprecedented scale of deaths in the famine, which truly earned its epithet 'great', was not only due to starvation; disease too struck the starved and weakened people whose means of existence had been destroyed by the blight. The chief diseases which flourished during the famine years were typhus and what was known as 'relapsing fever'. These were not themselves caused by a poor diet, but thrived when conditions of severe destitution were present. Moreover, such diseases were easily transmitted to towns and cities invaded by the destitute from the countryside; famine deaths were not confined to the rural poor alone, but hit the middle and upper classes as well. Medical provision and institutions for the poor did, of course, exist in Ireland; but the county infirmaries, fever hospitals and dispensaries (supported by private subscription) were overwhelmed by the scale of the disaster, and their doctors and medical attendants were themselves susceptible to the diseases which famine brought in its wake. In 1846 a government minister told the House of Commons that 'With respect to the danger of approaching fever, which unhappily generally follows a period of scarcity in Ireland, the Poor Law Commissioners have made the most ample provision.'[22] But in fact many areas did not possess hospital provision of any kind; the system lacked co-ordination to enable it to cope with the emergency; and the dispensaries were incapable of coping with thousands of fever patients scattered over many square miles of countryside. Overcrowding in the workhouses caused the spread of fever; and, in addition, some of them were brought to bankruptcy through the unexpected rush of inmates. Prisons too became places of death; in Castlebar the mortality was 'fully forty per cent' and included the Catholic chaplain, the deputy governor, deputy matron and a turnkey.[23]

Small wonder, then, that contemporaries watched with horror as society itself seemed in a kind of process of dissolution. When the sick were refused admission to the already over-full hospitals, their friends would often bring them in carts at night and deposit them at the door or nearby, in the hope that the staff would admit them.[24] The fear of infection caused people whose custom was never to refuse food and shelter to a stranger to turn away even near neighbours. Fear of contracting fever through contact with the bodies of the dead (caused by the transfer of lice, though this was not known at the time) caused people to discontinue traditional burial ceremonies. Bodies lay for days in cabins which the survivors had deserted. There was even a public outcry against the making of new burial grounds, in case the dead should be the means of killing the living. Many bodies were buried without coffins; many more were found lying on the roadside, often with no means of identification.[25]

Such a catastrophe might, in an earlier age, have been assigned to the judgment of God and regarded simply as divine punishment for some dreadful sin committed by the people. But the Great Famine was different, not only because of its scale, but because of its implications for the government of Ireland under the Union. The image of coffinless bodies consigned without dignity to famine pits, thirty or more at a time, has endured.

Charles Gavan Duffy's verdict, 'a fearful murder committed on the mass of the people',[26] has been answered in cool historical terms: that early Victorian government was not in the business of providing state support on any considerable scale, and certainly not enough to cope with the Irish famine; the age of *laissez-faire* was not the age of the welfare state. And the usual response to famine before 1845 was for charitable action to meet social adversity: private individuals were expected to dig into their pockets to alleviate public distress.

Nevertheless, it would be misleading to imply that the state saw itself as simply neutral or non-interventionist in its essential character; *laissez-faire* was an aspiration rather than a reality, and the government was in fact aware of its need to play some sort of role in mitigating the disaster whose gravity was conveyed to it from its Irish officials in Dublin Castle. The problem lay in defining exactly what role it should endeavour to play. Since the previous decade had seen a gradual state disenchantment with the whole Irish landholding system, and especially with the landlords themselves, it was believed that landlords should now find their own way out of the predicament that their non-progressive estate management methods had got them into. Thus Irish landlords must bear the main burden of relief; they alone could restore Irish society to a healthy condition.

Internal alleviation of famine, however, was bedevilled in all sorts of ways. Many landlords did their best to provide relief, and some endured great financial hardship in so doing. Others refused altogether to subscribe to famine relief schemes. Some held that they were already contributing sufficient funds through the rates

which financed the new workhouses created by the Irish Poor Law
Act. Lord Sligo has been cited as an example of a landlord who
chose the harsh path of eviction, which he certainly did; but, like all
western landlords, he was obliged to cope with a part of the country
where famine hit hardest. By the beginning of 1848 he owed nearly
£1,650 to the Westport Board of Guardians, of which he was
chairman, a debt which he discharged by borrowing. He received
only a fraction of his nominal rental. This, added to his already
existing encumbrances, placed him, in his own view, under 'the
necessity of ejecting or being ejected'. It was a cruel necessity. In
the whole of Ireland a minimum of some 48,740 families were
permanently dispossessed between 1849 and 1854, amounting to a
total of almost a quarter of a million people.[27]

Private charity became a contentious issue through the allegation
that Protestant clergymen were seizing the opportunity to exchange
relief for Catholic conversion to Protestantism. Certainly some
more zealous members of the Church of Ireland sought to take
advantage of the disaster to convert those in need—of spiritual as
well as material support, as they would have said: the Lord's
'chastening rod' was being applied to Ireland.[28] Such individuals
were not truly representative of the Church of Ireland, but their
activities were tolerated by some bishops and other clergy in the
dioceses and parishes; in other cases proselytisers met with strong
opposition. Methodists and Presbyterians alike showed interest in
the missions, which were most successful in the west of Ireland, and
certainly won over some converts; but what was regarded as the
Lord's will by the missions was, not surprisingly, deeply resented
by the Catholic clergy and seen as a manifestation of Protestant
guile. Against this must be set the instances of Protestant clergy
administering food, alongside Catholic priests who attended the
dying. In 1847 forty Protestant clergy died from famine fever,
sufficient testimony to their selfless care for the distressed.
Nevertheless, the sectarian war-cry could catch fire even in the
midst of famine, and allegations of 'souperism' hindered relief
efforts and often caused a breakdown in co-operation between the
different churches. The famine exposed Ireland's lack of general
social cohesion and exposed the resentment and suspicion that lay
not far below the surface.[29]

There was also the human frailty of local and government officials
when they came to devise means to combat the famine and its

consequences. The government's agents in Ireland simply did not expect the blight of 1845, which was not serious by comparison with what came after, to repeat itself in 1846; they assumed that the potato crop of 1846 would be sufficient to feed the population. The officials of the Board of Health took the decline in fever noticed in the summer of 1846 as evidence that the worst was over; here again their confident forecasts were mistaken. Moreover, while the relief institutions looked sound on paper, they proved badly wanting in practice, especially, again, since no one expected them to be subject to such intolerable demand; and while it is easy with hindsight to 'predict' what was about to happen, contemporaries would have been obliged to foresee the extent of the disaster and ask the Treasury to build hospitals and provide remedy for those who were not yet sick. Medical knowledge about the reasons for the spread of disease was inadequate; wholesale treatment of the population would have required a massive and even dictatorial response, compulsorily enforced. As one Irish physician put it, 'we cannot be suddenly wise'.[30]

But it was the British government's attitude which was to come under the closest scrutiny by posterity. And not only by posterity; there were contemporaries in the House of Commons who pleaded for a massive injection of official funds for famine relief.[31] Ireland did in fact receive more state aid than Scotland. The entire amount advanced by government towards the relief of the Irish famine was £7,132,268, of which £3,754,739 was, however, to be repaid within ten years; the rest was a free grant. Of the sum lent, a large part was remitted between 1847 and 1852; in 1853 the total loan was remitted by Gladstone, in consideration of Ireland's assuming the burden of income tax.[32] Large sums were raised through private charity in Great Britain, where the British Association raised £434,251 to bring succour to the 'remote districts' of both Scotland and Ireland. Queen Victoria's personal appeal for relief for Ireland and Scotland raised a further £170,000. The total sum was distributed in the proportion of five-sixths to Ireland and one-sixth to the Scottish Highlands.[33]

Sir Robert Peel, like many British ministers responsible for the government of Ireland, regarded that country with a mixture of scepticism and, paradoxically, a sense of duty (but hardly ever with intimacy). Thus, while he declared that all reports, including those about famine, from his executive in Dublin needed critical scrutiny because 'a haze of exaggeration covered Dublin Castle like a fog', he was aware that as early as October 1845 he was facing a major crisis in Ireland.[34] His measures harked back to the remedies he and others had adopted in earlier Irish famines: the state would act as a kind of enabling agency, setting up a relief commission which included representatives of the army, police and coastguard, the Poor Law Commission and the Castle, which would in turn stimulate local effort and local relief works. He went further than contemporary orthodoxy dictated and set up food depots stocked with secretly purchased Indian meal. Some £185,000 was spent on the government's food scheme, of which £135,000 was recovered in sales of the food by local committees or to private customers.[35] These measures were largely successful, but they were overtaken by the worsening crisis, and the fall of Peel's government in the summer of 1846 coincided with the second, more devastating outbreak of the potato blight. Peel's government fell as a result of his long-meditated decision to repeal the corn laws, and the subsequent split in the Conservative Party. A combination of protectionist Tories, Whigs and Radicals turned him out of office, to be replaced in July by a Whig government under Lord John Russell.

The guiding hand so far in the government's response to the Irish famine was that of Sir Charles Trevelyan, Assistant Secretary to the Treasury. Trevelyan harboured ambiguous attitudes towards Ireland, as he did towards Scotland. The peoples of both countries were, in his view, Celts, members of an inferior and indolent race, who might yet be saved for civilisation through the lessons of famine and prolonged intercourse with the more advanced Anglo-Saxon society. Yet he also declared that 'the people must not, *under any circumstances*, be allowed to starve';[36] and his organising ability and energy surmounted the limited resources of his staff and underpinned the tribute made to Peel by the *Freeman's Journal*: 'No man died of famine during his administration.'

But Trevelyan was determined to ensure that state intervention would not undermine the principle that the government's purpose was to help local effort, not supplant it. Nevertheless, the state found itself going much further in the case of Ireland than it did in Scotland, and it became an administrator of a huge famine relief operation. Soup kitchens were opened in the spring of 1847; and in June a separate Irish Poor Law Commission was set up and put in charge of further assistance under the Poor Relief (Ireland) Act, which empowered boards of guardians to grant outdoor relief to the aged, infirm and sick poor, and to poor widows with two or more dependent children. It also empowered Poor Law Commissioners to permit boards to give food to the able-bodied poor for limited periods, though excluding persons holding more than a quarter-acre of land. The new government also continued the policy of state support for public works, commenced under Peel, with road works and drainage schemes undertaken in order to provide the labouring population with money to buy food. But this encountered two main difficulties. Firstly, the failure of the potato crop caused the price of food to rise sharply. Secondly, while the demand by people for work meant that by the spring of 1847 some 750,000 were employed under the scheme, by no means all of these were the deserving poor, since large farmers or their sons were encouraged by landlords to go on the public works and thus earn enough money to pay their rents. Some who were most deserving of relief were not strong enough to undertake the hard work involved. The enormous cost of the exercise (£4,848,235) was hardly commensurate with the results; and the chief reason lay not with the principle of such public work schemes but with the unexpectedly large numbers of people who flocked to them for relief.[37]

The move by so many labourers, and indeed farmers and their sons, to the public works further dislocated Irish rural society; and there was an increase in agrarian crime as labourers reneged on pledges to pay for conacre land which had yielded only diseased potatoes. There were attacks on ships off the west coast of Ireland; crops were stolen from the fields. But there was no breakdown of law and order, such as the government feared. The worsening state of the country after 1846 produced apathy, not social—let alone political—rebellion. And in September 1848 Trevelyan wrote to Stephen Spring Rice:

> The poorest and most ignorant Irish peasant must, I think, by this time, have become sensible of the advantage of belonging to a powerful community like that of the United Kingdom, the establishments and pecuniary resources of which are at all times ready to be employed for his benefit. At any rate, the repeal of the Union will not be seriously demanded while so large a proportion of the Irish people are receiving union wages and eating union meal.[38]

This is a verdict which posterity has been inclined to contest; and claims have been made that the whole episode of the famine was a kind of British-generated holocaust, a deliberate effort by the British government to allow Ireland to starve. One recent historian has contrasted the British government's expenditure, a few years after the famine, of £69.3 million 'on an utterly futile adventure in the Crimea' with its failure to spend such a sum on famine relief in Ireland, even half of which 'would have saved hundreds and thousands of lives'.[39] This ignores the fact that to the British, and indeed French and Turkish governments, the Crimean War was by no means a 'futile adventure', but a completely necessary use of force against Russian diplomatic ambitions. It also raises the question of how far the British government could exceed the limits which it wished to impose upon itself in its famine relief measures. The government did exceed these limits, to the extent that it accepted in 1847 that a high proportion of the Irish population must be fed without charge and without entering the workhouse. The failure of the government to provide enough food for its depots was exacerbated by the fact that the autumn and winter of 1846–7 saw considerable food shortages throughout Europe, and the government feared that to export inordinate quantities of food to Ireland might provoke a shortage in another part of the United Kingdom.[40] Quantities of food began to arrive from February 1847 onwards; from 1 September 1846 until 1 July 1847 wheat imports were five times as great as the exports, and the import of Indian corn and meal was three times as large as the total export of cereals.[41]

And yet there was the feeling, not without foundation, that an Irish famine was different from an English one, had there been such an event; that the British government failed to respond to the plea made by the Tory *Dublin University Magazine* to send her ships and her men to Ireland to show to Ireland and the world a truly generous and concerned spirit. This case is unproved and unprovable; but the claims of the Irish famine on the state in 1846 were regarded as so large that the Highland famine was not allowed to make an equal drain on the public purse. There was no specifically anti-Irish feeling behind government policy, though there was a sense that indeed this disaster, like its Scottish equivalent, had been brought by the people upon themselves as a result of their backward way of life. However, aganist this must be set the awareness that the government's duty was to save life, and not to adopt a policy of detachment: there was never at any time an acceptance, or even a suggestion, that the Irish or the Scots should be left to starve. There was never any idea that this would provide a kind of dreadful solution to the Irish or Scottish rural questions, even though it was believed that the famines would indeed prepare the way for a more workable and sensible economic system in the Highlands of Scotland and the west of Ireland.

The experience of the famine, both then and later, became inextricably linked with the question of the Union and its reality, even its viability. As we have seen, Sir Charles Trevelyan had expressed the belief that union wages and union meal would make Unionists out of the most ignorant Irish peasant; but in less than a year's time Lord Palmerston expressed his astonishment that the Irish elections had 'gone in favour of Repeal candidates; and this just after two or three millions of Irish have been saved from famine and pestilence by money which if the Union had not existed, their own parliament would never have been able to raise. This is not natural.'[42] This vote for Repeal had little to do with sympathy for famine victims; it was a measure of O'Connell's ongoing electoral and political organisation. But it was the last success of the O'Connellite movement that had maintained itself in Irish and British politics since the 1820s. The famine destroyed the Repeal movement, and indeed Irish political life, for a few years at least. This was a sign perhaps that O'Connell was not the dominating figure, nor his organisation the deep-rooted and permanent one, that they appeared to be. O'Connell himself was ill, and in March 1847 he set out for Rome, dying in Genoa in May. It is doubtful if he could have done much to help his country in the terrible few years that still lay ahead; but it is clear that he believed that if any relief was to be provided, then the government, in co-operation with the landlords of Ireland, should provide the means of financing it—that the twin bulwarks of the Union must show that indeed they could rescue Ireland from misery.[43]

This was not a belief shared by O'Connell's most persistent critics, the Young Irelanders. The death of O'Connell and the collapse of the Repeal movement left the way open for other, bolder spirits, with the foundation of the Irish Confederation in January 1847. But it was not clear just how bold they would prove themselves to be. Young Ireland had addressed itself to the land question, arguing that the landed aristocracy should be preserved, if their loyalty to the nation were assured. Davis argued for the establishment of an Irish yeoman class, in possession of small estates, on the model of Norway, mainly because of his hatred of the cities and towns, with their sickly and mean-looking populations.[44] But he had no specific plan of how to bring this about. Charles Gavan Duffy hoped that the landlords' own suffering in the famine would make them more 'nationally' minded. This was not as fanciful as it sounded. The landlords, politically adrift since Peel's apostasy on the corn laws and the break-up of the Conservative Party, were uneasy about the government's response to the famine and its initial determination to make Irish property come to the aid of Irish poverty. This policy resulted in the economic ruin of many of their number and increased the encumbrance of landed property in Ireland. A meeting of peers, gentry and M.P.s of all political parties held in Dublin in January 1847 pressed the government to change its policy on the famine relief question. But this gathering, like a further meeting in May, failed to come up with firm and immediate remedies; it could only hint at what might be done if only men would work together for the common good.[45]

The Young Ireland movement was now faced with a dilemma: landlords—Ireland's natural political leaders, and a class for whom the Young Irelanders still had a considerable, if possibly misguided, faith—could not help Ireland in her hour of need. But the great majority of Young Irelanders were not fiery revolutionaries, bent on leading a starving peasantry in the manner of the great French Revolution of 1789; and in the autumn of 1847 and the spring of 1848 they followed the propensity of many Irish political movements—they split. In October 1847 John Mitchel called on tenants to withhold agricultural produce for their own consumption. In December he appealed to the Irish peasants to arm themselves in defiance of the government. But Charles Gavan Duffy immediately prohibited Mitchel from using the pages of the *Nation* to call for insurrection, whereupon Mitchel resigned from the Irish Confederation policy committee and urged the use of arms to resist eviction. But when the Confederation met to debate the crisis in February 1848, Mitchel confessed that he did not as yet advocate the use of force in Ireland's 'broken and divided condition'. He simply did not rule it out absolutely. He said to the people 'arm, arm', not 'agitate, agitate', as the Confederates did; yet he denied any intention of 'leading out a starving peasantry to be mown down in open fields by regular troops'. He then made his position even more complicated by declaring darkly that there were 'far worse things going on around us than bloodshed'. William Smith O'Brien moved a resolution committing Young Ireland to constitutional action and the 'force of opinion', whereupon Mitchel, John Martin and Thomas Devin Reilly, representing the 'physical force' minority within the movement, withdrew from the Irish Confederation, and Mitchel founded his own newspaper, the *United Irishman*, to propagate his beliefs. But what were his beliefs? In the *United Irishman* he declared that the people must await attack and avoid shedding the first blood.[46] Thomas Francis Meagher, who was wont to sing of the virtues of the sword, explained that, like O'Connell, his object was not to draw blood from the government, but to prevent it from being drawn from the people. The whole tenor of the Young Ireland 'physical force' group was defensive; no one as yet wanted to take the initiative.

Political splits and the battle of the newspaper press were hardly likely to help the starving people of Ireland; a rebellion would almost certainly prove even less efficacious. The likely outcome was more divisions (and no doubt more newspapers). But events abroad prompted some of the Young Irelanders into drastic, if futile, action. In Paris, three weeks after the Confederation debate on the use of force, a revolution overthrew the monarchy; and the spectacle of liberals, socialists, republicans, middle and lower classes, all combining in one great wave of popular protest to overthrow King Louis Philippe and establish a popular government was enough to inspire the weakest heart. Republicans and Confederates alike in Ireland met to hail this new dawn, as their political ancestors had greeted that of 1789.

In this kind of revolutionary ferment—a ferment of the few, for the mass of the Irish people were indifferent or engaged in the grim business of survival—anything seemed possible. The idea of a republic was resurrected, for the memory of 1789 triggered off memories of 1798 and 1803. Mitchel denounced the previous objectives of Young Ireland, which had demanded only the restoration of the Irish parliament on College Green. Now, he declared, the demand must be for a republic, 'one and indivisible'. And now a levelling social spirit manifested itself: Mitchel asserted that the 'life of a labouring man is exactly equal to the life of one nobleman, neither more nor less'. The tenant right question was now being defined as one which could only be resolved, as James Fintan Lalor put it, by rooting the peasantry 'like rocks to the soil of the land'.[47]

But there was an air of philosophical debate, even about these stirring war-cries. No one had yet defined the 'peasantry' that was to be 'rooted' in the soil: was this peasantry to include well-to-do tenant farmers, or the poor labourers, who were now fleeing from the land in large numbers for fear of hunger and death? And was force to be initiated by the Young Irelanders, or should they follow Smith O'Brien's advice and wait upon British provocation to arouse a general resistance? The Young Irelanders might have debated this point for ever, had not the government indeed taken the initiative. Mitchel was arraigned on a charge of treason and transported. Duffy, Meagher, Michael Doheny and Thomas D'Arcy McGee were arrested, *habeus corpus* suspended, and membership of the Confederation Club declared sufficient grounds for arrest. The remaining Confederates, led by Smith O'Brien, decided they had no choice but to strike at once. Their chances of success were few: there was no popular desire for an uprising—indeed, there was no popular desire for any political action—and the Catholic Church was hostile. In July 1848 O'Brien, Terence Bellew McManus, James Stephens and about forty Confederates engaged the Irish Constabulary at Boolagh Commons, near Ballingarry, Co. Tipperary, in what became known to posterity as the 'battle of the Widow McCormack's cabbage patch'. In August Smith O'Brien was arrested and transported, his request to be hanged, drawn and quartered for treason being refused by the bench. Meagher, McManus and Doheny followed him to Van Diemen's Land. In September 1849 there was a brief sequel, when at the instigation of Lalor an unsuccessful attack was made on Cappoquin police barracks.

Later generations were to look on 1848 as an inspiration—or at least later generations of revolutionaries, however few in number, were to so regard it. But no general conclusion regarding the state of public opinion on the Union, and the British government's attitude to the famine, can be based upon the events of 1848. In 1849 Queen Victoria visited Ireland amid a display of popular enthusiasm. This may not have been deep; nor should it be taken as evidence that Ireland was devoid of grievances. But the public response to the royal visit was as deep, or as shallow, as any other political opinion in Ireland in the wake of the famine. Ireland was politically directionless, and politically safe, as far as anti-Union feeling was concerned.

But it was in social and economic terms that the real importance of the famine lies. The famine reduced the proportion of the labouring classes in rural Ireland, which in the previous decades had comprised two-thirds of the population, outnumbering the tenant and independent farmers by four to one: by 1900 farmers outnumbered labourers, and the gap between them in social status was larger. This was partly because of the consolidation in farm holdings. One farm in four disappeared between 1845 and 1851, with the decline confined to holdings of less than fifteen acres. The average size of a farm increased; by 1851 51 per cent of farms were more than fifteen acres, while the proportion of holdings under five acres fell from 24 per cent in 1845 to 15 per cent in 1851.[48] This left the tenant farmer as the largest class in Ireland, though not yet a 'class' in any sense that would imply solidarity or sense of common purpose. Indeed, even when that class began to develop such characteristics, these varied from region to region, depending on the economic and social gradations and differentiations within the broad category 'tenant farmers'. The cottiers and labourers, whose number fell by 40 per cent during the following sixty years, were the only 'peasants' properly so-called; their role as founders and members of agrarian secret societies was now sharply curtailed, and despite the fact that landlords in certain areas of the country continued to carry out evictions, agrarian crime decreased markedly. Landlords also moved against middlemen, who had paid a fixed rent on a long lease, and who were responsible for much of the practice of subdivision of land before the famine; both they and their sub-tenants were removed, for example in the Kilrush Union in County Clare.[49] The famine greatly accelerated the trend, already evident, for the rearing of livestock to replace tillage; and this, with the decline in the labour force, the rise in wages, and the international trends towards higher prices for livestock products, now became the main business of the Irish farmer, except in the west of Ireland.[50] That area, which had borne the worst of the famine, was, oddly enough, the area which returned to the potato crop most quickly and generally. Finally, the famine greatly accelerated another development which contemporaries hardly noticed: the massive and sustained decline in the Irish language.

This would imply that the chief changes of the famine were indeed economic rather than psychological; genuine and lasting folk memory of the great hunger was found, not among the leaders of nationalist Ireland, but among the poorer farmers and labourers, and especially the emigrant, that archetypal figure of the famine. Yet even the impact of famine on emigration must not be exaggerated. The rush to flee the country was, of course, an increase in demographic movement, and a dramatic one; but still an increase, not a new development. Landlords and philanthropic societies had actively assisted emigration before 1845; and travel between Ireland, Great Britain and America was cheap and readily available. The famine increased this trend, and shifted its geographical origin, which had lain mainly in Ulster, to the south and west. The image of the 'coffin-ships', however, was new: passengers in the famine emigration were of the poorest and most destitute kind, and they brought diseases, especially typhus, with them.[51] European emigrant ships fared much better because their passengers had not suffered the destitution or exposure to infectious diseases that emigrants from Ireland experienced. This emigration, both to Britain and America, has been taken as a major development in a particularly virulent kind of Irish nationalism, which harboured a deep and bitter sense of anti-Britishness. But at the time this was not a factor in British–Irish relations, and would not become so for more than a decade. Even then, its importance must be carefully assessed. No country was less concerned about its emigrant population than Ireland; indeed, that very sense of isolation from the homeland which bred a sentimental and backward-looking nationalism was increased by the fact that the Irish abroad were regarded by the Irish at home as very much abroad, and by the fact that the Irish, of all emigrant peoples, showed the least tendency to return home[52] (though they might sing of it often enough). The Irish in Britain and America were to add a new element to nationalism, and, more importantly, much money to its coffers. But they were nonetheless marginal to the experience of Ireland, even though they were central to the total Irish experience.

The famine did not mark the beginning of the end of the Union; nor was it taken by anyone as signifying that the Union had failed, though criticism was made of government policy, and Young Ireland raised its futile revolt. Nor were the landlords as yet seen as the great oppressors of their country; rather they were, more accurately, exposed as the sufferers (in a very different way) of the consequences of the pre-famine agrarian system and the post-famine consequences of that system. In 1849 the government passed an Encumbered Estates Act for the purpose of enabling financially embarrassed landlords to sell up. It allowed every creditor, except the petitioner who was forcing the sale (and even him, if he obtained the leave of the court), to bid for the encumbered property and to become its owner with an indefeasible title. Owners of land could themselves apply to the court to sell their estates. When the sale was completed, the court was to distribute the purchase money among the various claimants, pay the residue to the vendor, and grant the new proprietor a clear and legal title to the land.[53]

The purpose of this act was to introduce into Ireland a new kind of landlord who would make an economic success of the land system, and who would introduce new and enlightened personnel as well as new methods—for English and Scottish farmers would, it was hoped, accompany the landlords and demonstrate their farming abilities in an Irish context. Between 1849 and 1857 over 3,000 estates were sold under the act; but of the 7,200 purchasers, only about 300 came from Great Britain, and there was no general input of capital from England and Scotland (the British purchasers contributed less than £3 million out of the £20 million purchase money). Moreover, the bulk of land in Ireland was still owned by the old landed families: the famine did not produce a new set of entrepreneurial landlords. In this respect at least the famine changed society, and yet left it familiar enough.

The famine left its deepest mark on the poorest members of society, who were of no immediate political significance, but whose memories ran deep. The traditional beliefs and customs of the rural labourers, now diminished and still diminishing in numbers, who held to what may be called (in an admittedly ambiguous phrase) the folk ways of Ireland, began to disappear with the people who lived by them. This decline was noticed in the 1820s and 1830s, as wakes, traditional festivals and magic beliefs were being undermined by a society in search of progress and advancement and open to modern and commercial pressures.[54] The death of so many people, particularly the elderly, the rapid emigration of so many more, especially the young, accelerated the disappearance of a real 'hidden Ireland'. That Ireland was now rapidly replaced by the Ireland of the tenant farmer, an increasingly dominating influence on the style and attitudes of the countryside (and therefore of the social, political and religious life of the nation as a whole), with his solid house, orthodox religious beliefs (purged of any troublesome pagan or deviant notions), unshifting conservative outlook, and that most dynamic of all desires in any society—the desire to better himself, and to ensure that he went on bettering himself. Such people were likely to give their children an education, unlike the labourers, who were mainly illiterate. Such people were likely to listen to their clergy, whose views and values they shared, and whose approval would be a sign that they were getting on in this world as well as the next one. 'Modern' Ireland was in the process of being born; 'traditional' Ireland, when it was resurrected in the 1890s, would bear little resemblance to the real traditions of the poor and weak who died or emigrated as a result of the Great Famine. Their fate might be a useful item in later nationalist propaganda, though not as much as might be expected, for few wanted to restore the Ireland that modern and modernising Ireland was—it seemed—far better without.

The census of 1851 revealed that most Irish people still lived on the land (83 per cent); that the families of the 570,338 tenant farmers enumerated by the census officials comprised over half the rural population; that the majority of the rest were landless labourers; and that the landlords, some 10,000 in number, owned most of the land, numbering among their ranks such figures as the Duke of Leinster, with 73,000 acres in Kildare and Meath, and the Marquis of Downshire, with 115,000 acres in five counties. In 1851 47.8 per cent of farms were over fifteen acres; by 1861 some 40 per cent of the land was held in farms of a hundred acres or more. This process of consolidation of holdings slowed down after 1851, but it was never reversed. For those tenants who held the farms of less than fifteen acres, which comprised one-half of the total, farming was still a precarious and uncertain business, liable to raise alarming memories of the famine. Landlords were themselves more inclined to take a closer interest in balancing their books than they had done before the famine: estate management and a tighter rein were essential. In a clash of interests, tenant and landlord would find little room for manoeuvre.[55]

The famine did not destroy, or even undermine, the Union; it might even be suggested that it stabilised it, by debilitating the Repeal movement and Young Ireland, thus leaving the way open for

Irish politics to be based upon other, less divisive issues. It did, however, establish a historiography of its own, in both England and Ireland, where writers as diverse as Cecil Woodham Smith and the I.R.A. leader Ernie O'Malley shared a common view of the famine as a kind of deliberate act of genocide. This view has been refuted by most modern Irish historians, who see the Russell government as unable to free itself from the economic orthodoxy of the day. The genocide theory[56] is utterly without historical justification. The British government was determined to save as many of the people as it reasonably could—though not at too high a cost. From mid-1847 it was convinced that it had done enough for Ireland, and left the Irish Poor Law Commission to cope. And it did see Ireland not as an integral but (like Scotland) as a rather remote and certainly different part of the United Kingdom: as a backward land, set in unprofitable and obscurantist ways of life and thought. Once the famine was (officially) over, then England could get on with the ordinary business of government, leaving the Encumbered Estates Court to encourage free trade in land. In this sense the famine revealed that the United Kingdom was a political convenience rather than a genuine political concept. But this was not necessarily a weakness. For if the Union, by 1850, was not based upon a consensus about 'common citizenship', then it could at least rest upon acquiescence. And the tenant farmers, now consolidating their holdings and emerging as the key group in the Irish country-side, next to the landlords, had other preoccupations than the tragedy of the famine (the most savage indictment of which was left to the Ulster Presbyterian Young Irelander, John Mitchel). In a loose and diverse political association such as the United Kingdom was (and continued to be) acquiescence was as good a political cement as any. Indeed, few political systems, encompassing a variety of peoples and religions and economies, could claim foundations half as secure.

Political Diversity, Religious Division, 1850–69

THE two decades after the famine were, for the most part, an era of fragmentation in political terms. The Repeal Association disintegrated. Liberals and Conservatives held the centre of the stage; but it seemed as if the stage had no real centre to hold. A whole variety of parties and groups emerged, some campaigning on the issue of the land, and especially tenant right; some concerned to promote the interests of their particular social or religious constituency. Landlords regained their confidence, finding that they could still win seats, even a majority of them, in a largely Catholic electorate. They were challenged by the Irish Tenant League, founded in 1850 to seek redress of agrarian grievances on the basis of co-operation between north and south, and to build up the unity of tenant farmers in the cause of gaining official, legal recognition of the 'Ulster custom'. But it seemed impossible to establish any kind of clear direction; and it was not until the end of the 1860s that the emergence of Fenianism as a threat to both Britain and British rule in Ireland concentrated political minds and helped Gladstone to convince the British public that the time was right for his first Irish adventure.

But these were decades also when the nations of the British Isles were awakened to a new recognition of the competitive nature of their various religions. The first sign of religious enthusiasm appeared, oddly enough, in England, with Lord John Russell's campaign against 'papal aggression'—the restoration of the Roman Catholic diocesan system in Great Britain. Ireland did not suffer the same depth of feeling on this issue, but she was soon to experience the impact of new religious perceptions. Catholics and Anglicans, Presbyterians and Methodists, were caught up in a new sense of religiosity, one notable for its central belief that Catholicism and Protestantism were deadly enemies, sworn foes, defenders of the right against the wrong, of truth against error. This religious fervour was not, of course, a constant factor in Irish life; other, more material and secular preoccupations intervened. But the churches began to sink their roots deeply into Irish social as well as religious life. They sought to keep their congregations apart. They saw themselves as necessarily involved in political life, the better to organise their separate development and the interests of their own people.

This pattern was to emerge by 1870; but it was by no means clear in 1850 that it would. For the first sign of revival in Irish politics after the famine was one aimed at identifying what might broadly be defined as class rather than religious interests as a basis of political organisation. Ireland took the first important step forward into something like political modernity with the passing of the Irish Franchise Act of 1850, which settled the franchise upon the occupant of property to the poor law valuation of £12 in the counties and £8 in the boroughs. Within three years 88.7 per cent of the electorate was registered on the new franchise, with the poorer sections of the old electorate firmly excluded.[1] This virtually new electorate might have been expected to create new political possibilities, and for a while it seemed it would, with the foundation of the 'League of North and South' and its efforts to exert pressure on Westminster for the legalisation of Ulster tenant right.

Tenant farmers in Ulster had more to lose than elsewhere from the agricultural depression which followed the famine. They felt especially threatened as a result of their belief that the landlords were taking advantage of the reduced price at which a tenant could sell his tenant right in order to curtail and circumscribe the operation of the Ulster custom on their estates. There was also the fear that tenant right would be compromised in legal terms as well as economic, since the attempt to legalise tenant right in 1847 in a bill introduced by an Ulster landlord (who had once been a supporter of O'Connell), William Sharman Crawford, was rejected. Moreover, tenant right seemed to be caught between two forces: parliament had rejected Crawford's measure, but an attempt in 1848 by the Irish Chief Secretary, Sir William Somerville, to grant a limited measure of tenant right included the consent of the landlord as a necessary condition for the tenant to recover compensation for improvements. Sharman Crawford feared that Somerville's bill, however well-meaning, might undermine the Ulster custom; but as it was a general step in the right direction, Crawford and his supporters did not oppose it. The bill's failure revealed again the slender chances for improvement of tenant right through legal means, and its contents spelt out the assumptions held by those in government about landed property rights.[2]

Such setbacks were sufficient to persuade Crawford and a Liberal Ulster journalist, James MacKnight, to found the Ulster Tenant Right Association in May 1847, in which Presbyterian ministers and tenant farmers found common cause. Farmers gained moral support, and the clergy were able to claim that security for the tenant would reduce the incidence of agrarian crime of that type which all too often disfigured the face of (Catholic) Ireland.

The Ulster Association was characteristic of Irish politics after the fall of O'Connellism: it was local, parochial, and limited in its aims. But it at least began a process which developed quickly, for it persuaded three political journalists to seek to build a new, broader movement for the advance and protection of tenant right in Ireland as a whole. Charles Gavan Duffy, first editor of the *Nation*, had been the principal exponent of Young Ireland's efforts to use exclusively legal means to advance nationalism and the national cause; he had, in his own words, felt from the age of nine that it was necessary to deliver 'our race from the subjection of Orange Ascendancy'. But he was always a believer in the pragmatic exploitation of opportunities for improving the lot of the Catholic people of Ireland within the British parliamentary system, and he was ever on the lookout for opportunities to foster political consciousness among what he called 'the ranks'.[3]

The famine seemed to Duffy to offer a chance of combining landlord and tenant to defend the best interests of Ireland; and as early as 1847 he was hoping to create a contingent of Irish M.P.s dedicated to famine relief and repeal of the Union, pledged against taking office, and quite independent of English parties.[4] This came to nothing; but a few years later Duffy, Frederick Lucas (an English convert to Catholicism and editor of the *Tablet*) and John Gray, Protestant proprietor of the nationally-minded *Freeman's Journal*, considered the idea of a 'political society' of social and religious leaders of Ireland to provide organisation and direction for the rural population, which would do for them what O'Connell had done for the self-respect of the Catholic people in his great campaigning days. But this new land movement would be an association of 'North and South', acting together for the rights of farmers; and the *Nation* called for the consolidation of tenant societies already in existence. The influential Archbishop MacHale of Tuam supported the idea of an organisation for land reform. In October 1849 Duffy convened a national conference in Dublin, 'fit to speak for all Ireland'; and from this impetus, it was hoped, local tenant right leagues and associations could break out of their parochialism and work together for the common good, and thereby make the land question a 'national' question.[5]

This idea was crystallised in August 1850, when a tenant right conference met in Dublin and founded the Irish Tenant League. The League adopted as its policy the legalisation of the Ulster custom and its extension throughout the country. A tenants' charter was drawn up, demanding that all land should be valued, that the tenant must not be disturbed in his holding as long as he paid the valued rent; and that tenants' property and improvements be held sacred, with the tenant left free to sell them. But the difficulty in creating a 'national' movement appeared even before the conference convened, and was to be exacerbated soon after the Tenant League was inaugurated. It was attacked by the Irish Democratic Association, a body composed of Irish writers and journalists of nationalist outlook, whose newspaper, the *Irishman*, criticised the League for its lack of republicanism. Landlords were hostile to it. And Protestants in general were suspicious of Dublin's role in the movement, for Duffy himself acknowledged that his agrarian policy was

> a design wisely subordinated to the facts of our constitution but necessarily expanding itself till it fills up the entire breadth—the purpose of making Ireland a free, prosperous and honoured nation. . . . We cannot win our rights by a blow, but *we must win them in detail*.[6]

This was to ignore a warning of the *Londonderry Sentinel* of 28 March 1850 that

> The alliance we require is one whose sole and exclusive object should be to establish the right of the tenant-farmers. Everything political or religious must be absolutely excluded.

'National' ambitions were a threat to a really national, pan-Irish movement. At a by-election in Limerick in December 1850 the Tenant Right candidate made a Repeal speech; he was repudiated by non-Repealers in the League, and he lost the contest. In 1852 Tenant Right candidates performed poorly in the north of Ireland. Duffy won the seat at New Ross, County Wexford, by 82 out of 113 votes, on his own admission with strong local clerical support. Only one Tenant Right candidate was returned in Ulster, and even the doyen of the cause, William Sharman Crawford, was defeated in County Down. But as the excitement over papal pretensions died down and the objectives of the League became better appreciated, Tenant Right candidates began to make progress. In 1852 they comprised some forty of the newly elected members pledged to stand in independent opposition to the government if it did not take up the principles of Crawford's bill of 1847. And all this despite the appearance on the Irish electoral scene in August 1851 of a Catholic Defence Association, under Archbishop Paul Cullen's patronage, which supported the idea of Irish M.P.s at Westminster acting in defence of what were specifically termed 'Catholic' grievances.[7]

The Tenant League began to consolidate its parliamentary activities. It allied with the 'Irish Brigade'—M.P.s who were broadly of the same mind on the need to promote Irish issues in Westminster—and in August 1852 a conference was held in Dublin which included members of the Brigade and the League, as well as lay and ecclesiastic dignitaries. A resolution was passed adopting the policy of independent opposition in parliament; but, again, few Ulster supporters attended. Moreover, many of the independent members were pledged also to disestablishing the Church of Ireland. This revealed a weakness in the League, and in Irish political organisation generally. It had a Catholic aspect, even though it was not at all exclusively Catholic in character; yet it was suspected by Archbishop Cullen, who disliked Duffy's role in the movement, since he feared that Duffy was tainted with dangerous radical attitudes, survivals of his Young Ireland days. Cullen, while he feared an 'Irish Mazzini', did not care for the English, whom he described as 'worse than Turks'.[8] But he worked hard to restrain priestly support of the Tenant League and to warn his flock to beware of candidates hostile to the church. In October 1854 Duffy accused Cullen of deliberately undermining the Tenant League's efforts, thereby incurring the wrath of the archbishop, who returned from

Rome in the spring of 1855 determined to 'free Irish Catholicism' from all Young Ireland influence 'of which the spirit is so evident in the *Nation*'.[9]

These difficulties troubled the Tenant League. But its representatives were overshadowed by their lack of parliamentary experience. On the face of it, Westminster politics were well suited to the plan laid down by the Irish party of 'independent opposition', since the break-up of the Conservative Party after Peel's repeal of the corn laws in 1847 threw parliamentary politics into that state of flux and uncertainty so brilliantly delineated by Walter Bagehot in his study of the English constitution in 1866. With weak party discipline, personal political followings, and a highly unstable party system, conditions for a skilful deployment of parliamentary tactics were certainly present, if only they could be exploited by the Irish party.

The difficulty lay in the party's failure to use the room afforded it by these conditions in parliament. It was over-cautious in its refusal to support Lord Derby's administration, which was prepared to make concessions on the tenant bill issue, and its members joined with the Whigs, Radicals and Peelites to bring Derby's government down in December 1852. But this display of strength proved to be a costly one: for the government which replaced Derby's, that of Lord Aberdeen, was a coalition which proved too attractive to some of the Irish members, whose pledge of independence did not survive the lure of office. John Sadleir's and William Keogh's acceptance of office was a blow to the party's prestige; but more significant was the party's inability to make itself a distinctive part of the British political system. It could not render its support indispensable to any British party, and so it could not find or create a role in parliamentary politics where it might exert pressure and bargain for concessions.[10]

The fate of the 'Irish Brigade'—which finally disappeared as an effective political entity in 1859, and perhaps never really appeared as an effective political force at any period of its life—was instructive for the position of Ireland within the Union in more general terms. Irish political parties—whether Liberal, Conservative, Tenant League or 'Irish Brigade'—found it hard to establish themselves in an easy role in British politics. When they disagreed profoundly with their English colleagues—as the Irish Tories did with Peel over the handling of Irish policy in the 1840s—they were faced with the

stark choice of self-destruction in downright opposition, or learning to live with the vicissitudes of political life, nursing their
grievances and hoping that the wheel would turn and place them in
a more advantageous position. As one of them wrote darkly in
1853, 'Without political influence and power, any class is treated as
a cypher, and Ireland is treated as a mere political convenience for
England.'[11] The Liberals fared rather better in one sense, in that the
presence of their party in government for reasonably long periods
of time at least enabled them to bask in the glow of official
patronage; but otherwise they were nothing more than the most
westerly outpost of the British Liberal Party. In short, the Tories
could not afford to rebel against the English parliamentary system,
and the Liberals felt no need to. And the fate of 'independent
opposition' was a sufficient lesson to both, had they been inclined
to alter their tactics. A mass support was needed, to enable an Irish
political leader to hold his followers up to dangerous public
obloquy if they disputed the party's discipline, but the independent Irish party had neither support nor discipline. In this respect it
seemed that Irish politicians after O'Connell would fulfil the same
role as Scottish politicians and simply act as some sort of geographical expression of political representation. This seemed to be borne
out by the fate of the National Association in 1864, an organisation
strongly supported by Archbishop Cullen to campaign for denominational education, land reform, and the disestablishment of the
Church of Ireland. The Association might be described as tradition-
ally Irish, in that it was divided in its aims, personnel and ideas, and
it made but a poor showing in the general election of 1865.
Moreover, it enjoyed no parasitical link with a British political
party, and could not even offer to aspiring politicians the best
prospect an Irishman could envisage—the high road to political
patronage. On a broader stage, it offered no prospect of advancing
Catholic interests in the form of state action for redress of
grievance.[12]

Irish Conservatives in the 1850s could at least take comfort from
the fact that, if they occasionally felt frustrated by their inability to
get a hearing in Westminster, they nevertheless possessed considerable local political influence—and this despite the franchise reform
of 1850, which, Lord Sligo declared, actually benefited the landlords, since it made elections once again 'a matter for landlords'
agents . . . which will prevent priests from having a word to say'.[13]

The return of 48 'popular' candidates in 1852 was something of a blow; but the landlords recovered, using a combination of political influence and a genuine identity of their interests with those of the tenants, based on the common experience of living in rural society. In 1852 no fewer than 68 out of Ireland's 104 M.P.s were from the landed interest. And the Conservative part of that interest won 46 seats in 1857, 55 in 1859, and 47 in 1865. This in part reflected their fight back after 1852, when they reorganised their political machinery by founding the Central Conservative Society in 1853 to consolidate Irish Conservatism and provide some means of bringing pressure to bear on their English party.[14]

Yet despite the Conservative rally, and the débâcle of the Catholic National Association, there were grievances in Catholic Ireland that Conservative and Liberal Ireland might yet ignore at their peril. The comparison with Scotland could not be pushed too far; for one of the central distinctions between the two countries was that, whereas Scotland had its established majority church, the Presbyterian Church, strong and deep-rooted (despite its schisms), the Church of Ireland remained a state church based on a minority of the population. This elicited Presbyterian as much as Catholic disfavour; but the Catholic case was the stronger, since Irish Presbyterians too were the church of a minority. Scottish landlords were no better and no worse than their Irish counterparts; but Irish landlords, while still firmly rooted in Irish politics and society, were beginning to feel the first breaths of a later criticism that would convince British statesmen, as well as Irish nationalists, that they were not true members of the Irish nation. A historicist argument was in the process of being concocted, one founded perhaps by James Fintan Lalor, that the landlords were, or should be, excluded from the club of Irishness. 'Ireland her own—', declared Lalor rhetorically, 'Ireland her own and all therein, from the soil to the sky. The soil of Ireland for the people of Ireland, to have and hold from God alone who gave it.' And to achieve this ideal state it was necessary to repeal 'not the Union but the conquest'.[15] Landlords could claim with justification that those among their number who were improving or modernising landlords, seeking to replace smallholders with larger tenants, were resisted, while those landlords who stood still and did nothing were criticised.

All this was, however, of no political relevance in the Ireland of the 1850s. Tenant right was a bargaining-counter, representing a rational conflict of interests between landlord and tenant, one which involved the Presbyterian farmer of Ulster as well as the Catholic farmer of Munster; and no Ulster farmer (and few, if any, elsewhere) denied the right of the landlord to exist, to hold what *he* had from the soil to the sky, and to play his role in politics that his social and economic position entitled him to. In any event, the prosperity of rural Ireland was increasing, even though its fragility in the less fortunate areas, such as the west, could be dangerously demonstrated, as in 1861, when a wet season once again brought hardship. As far as Britain was concerned, the very fact that Irish political parties of all hues and complexions were kept at arm's length was a happy arrangement; and it seemed safe for Westminster to ignore or belittle what was, after all, Ireland's favourite occupation—the pursuit of the grievance.

The question was whether this sense of grievance was more effectively advanced through political organisation for political goals, or whether it was best asserted through the means of an internal 'Irishisation' policy. This latter was the kind of approach favoured by Archbishop Cullen, who wanted Catholics advanced at all levels, and to whom the Catholic Whig—making his way in the world and gaining the benefits of patronage and place—was Ireland's brightest hope. Self-government was a doubtful prospect, not least because it was tainted, in Cullen's eyes, with the godless republicanism of the Young Irelanders, disciples of the unspeakable Mazzini. This did not mean that Cullen and those who thought as he did were not 'patriotic'; it was simply that, whereas O'Connell saw repeal of the Union and the return of domestic Irish politics as the best way forward for his people, Cullen and the Catholic Whigs—the bulk of the Catholic electorate—saw other and more immediately promising means of advancing their cause. The means to do so would be pressure from Ireland which would push a Westminster government into action, even against its will. And so Ireland could enjoy the benefits of not having self-government—a realistic notion, since the politics of the 1850s and early 1860s were devoid of any prospect of a revival of O'Connellism.[16]

This concept of Irish politics was anathema to the vast majority of the Protestant people of Ireland. Tenant right was an exception, of course; but tenant right too lost its appeal when it took on, as it did in the early 1850s, a distinctly Catholic line. It was not for

Presbyterians to use historicist arguments to advance their cause, for they too might in the event suffer from the accusation that, while everyone who lived in Ireland was equally Irish (as the more liberal-minded nationalists like Gavan Duffy claimed), some were more equal than others. Some were indeed descendants of those who had come, if not with the conquest, then certainly with the seventeenth-century overthrow of Catholic Ireland. The sectarian aspect of Irish life, though it must not be exaggerated, surfaced from time to time. It was prominent in a County Mayo election in 1852, when, in the excitement generated by the Ecclesiastical Titles Act, the campaign took on a religious mantle. The Church of Ireland's congregation was denounced as 'aliens in blood, language and religion'.[17] The Conservative Club of Mayo retaliated by demanding to know how candidates stood on the Protestant character of the British parliament, the claims of popish supremacy, and the payment of Romish priests.

The middle decades of the century were an era of religious enthusiasm on all sides. Within Protestantism, it was the Presbyterians who took the initiative in the great religious revival of 1859, which sought to bring God and an awareness of His presence to the Irish people in a simple, direct, evangelical fashion. Men and women could be 'saved', if they 'accepted' the Lord, and the man or woman thus saved was transformed into a Christian. This revival began in the Sixmilewater valley in County Antrim, but it was part of a wider movement which originated in North America and touched other parts of the British Isles. And whether in Ireland, Wales or the United States, it was characterised by religious fervour, a deep concern to convert souls to God's love, and a meeting of Episcopalian and Presbyterian, together with other non-Catholic denominations, in a united Protestant 'crusade'. It was part, too, of a desire to rediscover a lost golden age, to return to the simple piety of the past: to that of the seventeenth century, when the people 'who had been careless and ungodly, became truly religious—delighting in all the ordinances of the Gospel and glorifying their great God and Saviour by their exemplary lives'.[18] It was also the result of hard work and effort by individual ministers of religion who were anxious about the 'formality' and 'indifference' of Irish religious practice, and about the evils of sin and especially intemperance. Like all such movements, it experienced a dramatic rise and decline: after its spectacular zenith attendances at meetings dropped; there was no formal religious structure to act as a permanent institution; there was no doctrine to give the movement coherence.

And yet, though the tide receded, it left behind it certain enduring marks. The claims made by its strongest adherents included the erosion of sin, the growth of Sunday schools, even the conversion of Roman Catholics, who became noted for their 'cleanliness and decency of appearance'. Catholics who experienced such conversion found that their children did not beg, and that they never fell into the ways of crime, for the Word of God worked powerfully in 'the enemy's camp', despite the efforts of the priesthood to frustrate it.[19] Its chief critic, the Rev. Isaac Nelson, dismissed the 'year of grace' as the 'year of delusion', filled with fantasies and divisive in its effects, with its firm conviction that those who were 'saved' were to be separated from those who were not.[20] But, however justified these criticisms, the revival did bring many Protestants together in a sense of common religious experience. It was noted that when the mission spread to Belfast, it was supported by Presbyterian, Episcopalian and Methodist church leaders, thus creating 'fraternal sympathy and united action'.[21] It also created a whole multitude of 'gospel halls', small religious groups banded together by the idea of faith and salvation, and playing a central role in the religious and social life of Protestant Ulster: salvation crossed denominational boundaries.[22] This, of course, provoked those, like Henry Montgomery, who took exception to Henry Cooke's idea that 'there was not one sin recorded in heaven's book against him'.[23] But the idea of man absolved of sin was a dynamic one—and dynamic in political as well as religious terms. The Manichean idea of black and white, of sin and salvation, touched the whole Protestant people, and it also influenced their relations with Roman Catholics, now seen more and more as wilfully blind to the grace of God. (This could also work the other way, as Roman Catholics, for their part, referred to 'black Protestants'.)[24] The belief that God was not far away from the world (and especially Ulster) was a potent one; the idea that Protestantism and the defence of the Word were inextricably bound up with the freedom of Ulster was politically explosive. The Bible and the defence of Irish Protestantism, especially its Ulster variety, were inseparable.

Catholicism experienced a similar girding of the loins, though with a stronger institutional bedrock. This had its roots in earlier decades, and was a kind of Irish 'counter-reformation', with its purpose of attacking (in a religious sense) and winning back the ground lost to Protestant missionaries in the 1830s and 1840s. This grew apace after the famine. In 1835 there was one priest to every 3,000 Catholics (the Irish Established Church, with fewer numbers, had a ratio of one to 408 of the faithful). By 1870 the ratio in the Catholic Church was one to 1,476. The regular clergy increased from 200 in 1835 to 420, and nuns rose most rapidly, from 120 in 1800 to 3,719. Similarly, there was an increase in the number of schools, hospitals and orphanages run by sisters, and in education the Christian Brothers were prominent in safeguarding Catholic children from proselytising societies—for which purpose they had been granted a speedy brief of approbation by Pius VII in 1821.[25]

This great increase in religious activity was watched with anxiety on both sides. Two Protestant clergymen wrote in 1826 that the Christian Brothers' schools were 'most intolerant and mischievous', 'poisoned receptacles'. In 1831 an M.P. called them 'exclusive', while another accused them of developing 'superstition'.[26] The religious rivalry of the post-famine era stirred up mutual resentment. The danger to Catholics was social as well as spiritual, for Protestantism was still very much the religion of those who had their way to make in the world, and who did so most successfully. Protestantism might be despised as a religion, but it could be envied as a passport to social and public advancement. Soon Ireland was on her way to a peaceful but fundamental revolution, some of it brought about by local initiative (schools, a Catholic university) and some by the British parliament (disestablishment of the Church of Ireland, Catholic chaplaincies in the public service). Cullen and his partisans quite simply knew that the Catholic belonged in Ireland, and that Ireland belonged to the Catholic. If this was not 'nationalism' in a formal political sense, if it contradicted indeed everything that Young Ireland stood for, then it was nevertheless a most potent force for political mobilisation. The outward and visible sign of the Ireland of the future was the building of new churches, Victorian Gothic in style, a style that almost became synonymous with Roman Catholicism in Ireland and expressed its essential character: solid, large, enduring, and above all respectable.

It was perhaps foreshadowed too in small but significant occasions, such as Cardinal Cullen's appearance in his robes and red hat at the Lord Mayor of Dublin's banquet, when, the *Catholic Directory* noted with satisfaction '"a prince of the church" whom the penal code was designed to annihilate' ascended the dias 'next to the Lord Lieutenant, having on his arm Lady Rachel Butler, sister to Earl Russell, and chatting pleasantly with Lady Abercorn, in a room which was once the very temple of Protestant ascendancy'.[27]

The potential for religious change to divide Ireland into two distinct groups of people must not be overestimated. Presbyterians and Episcopalians still thought of themselves as possessing much that was different in both religious and social terms; and Ulster in particular was dotted with small sects, each certain that it knew the way, the truth and the light—and that no one else did. But when danger threatened, they could easily find common cause, as they did in 1841 when the rivals, Henry Cooke and Henry Montgomery, stood side by side against O'Connell. And one of the central principles of the Protestant idea was that Protestantism stood for liberty. Henry Cooke declared in 1841 that Presbyterians were republicans 'if by republican it is meant that Presbyterians are in favour of popular rights and liberties'. The British government was 'the only perfect republican government this world ever saw', since it stood for liberty—as it had done in 1689 and 1690.[28] In Belfast in the 1850s there was as strong anti-popery feeling among Presbyterians as among Episcopalians; in 1857, 1864 and 1868 there were sectarian riots. The period saw also the expansion in the number of Orange lodges. Belfast Liberals admitted the difficulty of their position in the 1860s, when one of their number lamented the migration into the Conservative fold of Presbyterian voters, arguing that the only remedy might be to 'stand a Presbyterian, who might bring sufficient of his co-religionists out of the opposite camp'.[29] This brought a blast of criticism from the *Belfast Newsletter*, which asked on 3 July 1865: 'What have the Presbyterians of Belfast and Ulster in common with the Roman Catholics?'—a question it had already answered to its own satisfaction when it declared that

> The Protestant alliance is the true political alliance in Ireland: that Presbyterian, Episcopalian and Methodist, as they love one common Bible, and equally hold the grand principles of religion, have a kind of brotherhood which ought not to be

severed in the day of trial. A doctrine more insulting was never propounded than that the Presbyterians should go to the poll side by side with the Roman Catholics. For how would Roman Catholics vote? In nine cases out of ten as the priests direct.[30]

Liberals managed to recover from the disaster of the 1865 general election, when they lost both Belfast seats to the Conservatives. They created an Ulster Liberal Registration Society to attend to the electoral register, which they had neglected, and to provide a rallying-point for all Ulster Liberals 'among all classes in town and country'. Lord Charlemont was the Society's chairman, and among its supporters were the Earl of Antrim, Lord Dufferin and Lord John Hay. The middle-class and non-Catholic nature of Ulster Liberalism still contrasted with the bulk of its supporters in Belfast, who were Catholics.[31] And although the party made a better showing in the general election of 1868, with a victory for their candidate, Thomas McClure, it was not as clear-cut a triumph for Liberalism as it appeared. McClure's success was owed in some degree to the Liberal ability to make the necessary compromises with the circumstances of Ulster political life. The most important change was a split between the Conservative Party and the Orange Order. William Johnston, who led a famous procession in 1867 to protest against the Party Processions Acts of 1850 and 1860 banning political marches (including Orange marches), was able to enlist the newly enfranchised Protestant artisan voters. These voters were Orange, but resentful of the Tory oligarchy that ran the town of Belfast. Johnston combined his role as something of a Protestant martyr (he had been jailed for his illegal parade) with a general anti-establishment reputation and a sound Protestantism—potent forces in Ulster politics. The combination of Tory split and populist appeal was shrewdly exploited by the Liberals. Their candidate, McClure, was chosen because he was a Presbyterian who would win the confidence of 'his own religious community'. At the same time he spoke of his desire to unite Protestant and Catholic under the Liberal banner.[32] Johnston and McClure stood side by side against two Tory Episcopalians. Lord Dufferin in 1867 referred discreetly to the fact that, while he was 'no friend of the Orange Society', yet 'Orangemen were loyal, orderly and respectable', and he called for the repeal of the Party Processions Acts. All these preparations paid off, and political expediency was vindicated in the election victory of 1868. But it was a popular victory in a sectarian mould. As the Catholic newspaper press put it, 'There may be reasons for exceptional and unnatural policy. These, however, are transient as well as unsafe influences. They cannot be relied upon for good; for no good can come out of such an evil combination.' Certainly the fragility of the alliance was demonstrated in 1872 when serious rioting broke out on 15 August, the feast of the Assumption of the Blessed Virgin. The reason was the 'provocation' offered by Catholic efforts to mount a procession equal in size and ostentation to that of the Orange Order on its annual Twelfth of July parade. This attempt to emulate the Orange parade, and to march armed with banners bearing religious and political slogans, revealed a new spirit among Ulster Catholics, and a determination to assert their right to parade. It also revealed the determination of Protestants to check such triumphal displays of Catholic consciousness.[33] And it was symptomatic of the new, or at least reinvigorated, sectarianism of Irish life in the two decades after the famine.

The 1861 official census of Ireland put beyond any remaining doubt the realisation that Catholics—despite the ravages of the famine and emigration—were the firm and undisputable majority in Ireland, comprising some three-quarters of the population, and forming a minority only in certain defined areas in the north-eastern part of Ulster. But how was this demographic fact to be translated into political action? Where was the Catholic Church to begin the process of creating the state within a state, and prodding a reluctant and somnolent Westminster into creating Irish policies that would realise the hopes of Catholic Ireland under the Union? Catholic, Anglican and Dissenter might belabour each other in a polemical literature whose length and capacity for scriptural quotation must still astonish the reader; but all this was no more than a battle of the books unless it were to attract attention from British political parties. Herein lay the weakness of the Cullenite theory of the Union, one demonstrated in the inability of Conservatives and Liberals to establish a firm and constant foothold in the respective English parties. For Union politics to work—or to work in favour of Catholic (and perhaps also Dissenter)—Westminster had to be convinced that it must pay attention to Ireland. But Westminster did not want to pay attention to Ireland. It was, paradoxically, the activities of a secret society dedicated to the overthrow of British rule in Ireland that prepared the indifferent British parliament and public for remedial measures, and for what W. E. Gladstone described as 'the government of Ireland by Irish ideas' (Irish meaning Catholic).

There was no particular reason, in Ireland itself, for the founding of the Fenian Brotherhood in 1858, apart from the disgust felt by more advanced and idealistic nationalists at what they regarded as the corruption and futility of Irish politicians at Westminster. But in an international context the times were indeed exciting. Britain had suffered a *frisson* at the spectacle of the apparent near-loss of her Indian empire under the onslaught of mutinous sepoys; Anglo-French tension was high, with even the possibility of war between the two powers. Moreover, the Irish emigrants in America had by now begun the process by which they became more Irish than the Irish who stayed at home—and more prone to blame England for the fact that they, the emigrants, had not. As it happened, many of the men of 1848, of a Young Ireland background and outlook, had fled to America, where they found an outlet for their political activities (and they had no other visible activities): John Mitchel, who came to America via penal servitude in Van Diemen's Land; and Thomas Francis Meagher and Terence Bellew McManus, who had escaped and arrived in the United States before Mitchel. There they met other members of the Irish Confederation who had challenged O'Connell in the 1840s; and there too they found a suitable place for operations, since their brand of Irish patriotism had the advantage of giving the Irish emigrant both a sense of pride and identity and a means of political organisation in American politics and, within a short time, in the Irish regiments serving in the American Civil War.[34]

But the question remained whether or not this kind of nationalism could be launched in Ireland; and here the difficulties were indeed formidable, for whereas the surviving Young Irelanders were held in some reverence, they could hardly hope to make a political impact in the country at large. But they laid the foundation for a second generation of enthusiasts, men such as Thomas Clarke Luby and John O'Leary. These men were the kind of people who, while hardly suitable for the ordinariness of political life, were educated, literate, talented and restive—and above all imbued with the optimism of youth or young manhood. They were educated in

the university of revolutionaries and ideologies—the Paris of 1848
—and two of its graduates, James Stephens and John O'Mahony,
saw themselves as potential liberators of Ireland. Ireland, if not
ready for liberation, was in many respects at least ready for political
activity beyond that practised by Archbishop Cullen, the Catholic
Whigs and the tenant farmers. It was a country which, in the city
and the town, and even the small town, was producing a set of
literate, newspaper-reading, self-educated young men. History and
literature and politics were, since the days of Young Ireland, never
very far apart in Ireland; and discussion groups, with a tendency to
attack the established view of older Ireland, were at least the nucleus
of a new kind of politics, or of a kind of politics not seen since the
days of Thomas Davis. One such group was the Phoenix Society of
Skibbereen, County Cork, which devoted itself to social and
recreational activities, and also indulged in discussion—which in
Ireland usually meant political discussion. This society was adorned
by Jeremiah O'Donovan Rossa, whose father had worked a small
farm near Rosscarbery, but whose mother and family emigrated on
the death of the partriarch, leaving the young Jeremiah behind. He
worked as a clerk, but married a girl with some property in 1853
and set up a hardware business in Skibbereen. Here he encountered
James Stephens when the latter was making his celebrated perambu-
lation of parts of Ireland in 1856–7. The growth of a kind of lower
middle class in certain parts of Ireland—artisans, clerks and shopkeepers—facilitated the Phoenix Society type of organisation, with
its ability to offer fraternal association and some political excitement as well. The leadership of such young men was provided by
activists like Stephens and Rossa, and other equally talented
journalistic and literary men such as Charles J. Kickham and
Thomas Clarke Luby.[35]

Fenianism was, in one sense, a connecting link that bound
together the 1798 rebellion, the Young Ireland revolutionary
gesture of 1848, and, in the future, 1916. Yet it was firmly Victorian
in its methods, aims and style. Not all Fenian leaders were out-and-
out republicans: John O'Leary was never certain if the organisations' title, I.R.B., stood for Irish Republican Brotherhood or Irish
Revolutionary Brotherhood. Two of its most prominent figures,
O'Leary himself and C. J. Kickham, were willing to live under the
British crown, provided Ireland were granted self-government.[36]

The Fenians were somewhat public conspirators, founding a newspaper to advance their cause and spending much of their time
rebutting their critics, most notably those from within the Roman
Catholic Church. Their rhetorical style was heavily marked by the
declamatory devices favoured by Victorian writers, whether English or Irish. They offered too a kind of social club for those who
were on the lookout for status and spare-time occupation. Their
typical membership—clerks, publicans, shopkeepers, shoemakers,
tailors, workers in the building trade, and soldiers in the British
army—were men who could be stirred into a simple patriotism,
reflecting their resentment at those who looked down upon them,
their religion and their country. Not surprisingly, Fenianism
flourished among the Irish emigrants in Britain, unsure of their
role, doubtful of their status, and resentful of those who (as was
often the case) resented them. To be a Fenian, in Ireland and in
Britain, was to be somebody: it enabled one to endow oneself with
a feeling of importance and belonging, to become a regarded local
figure, to enjoy a sense of solidarity with those of similar class and
background. There were farmers in the Fenian ranks; but rural
Fenianism, though not negligible, was unimportant in shaping the
organisation's character, and it drew its main rural support from the
lower orders, labourers and cottiers. Stephens had no doubt that the
Fenians recruited from marginal men; and he, for his part, launched
a verbal onslaught against the 'hostility of the aristocracy, the
apathy of the farmers, the pig-headedness of the bourgeoisie'.
Kickham, who wrote a popular and sentimental novel about the
rural small man, also attacked graziers who had turned the land over
to grass for a quick profit. 'Those men of bullocks' were 'about the
worst men in Ireland who had no sympathy for the people'.[37]

Fenians were, however, well disposed towards a group of people
who, they believed, had played a noble and far too often forgotten
role in the Irish struggle and the Irish revolutionary tradition: the
Presbyterians of Ulster. They had formed the backbone of the
United Irishmen in Antrim and Down in 1798. The Fenians
reminded Catholics that they had 'not even the courage to complain
of their wrongs till Presbyterian Ulster roused them from their
despair'.[38] But, while Presbyterian radicalism was by no means
exhausted, it no longer looked to revolution to achieve its ends.
Presbyterians were still a closely knit, self-consciously different

kind of Irishmen. They entertained strong feelings about the Episcopalians, especially their Episcopalian landlords; but they were now involved in advancing their cause through education and commerce—and all under the benign gaze of the Lord, whose favour was borne out in the fact that many Presbyterians were, according to their historian James Seaton Reid, supplanting the aristocracy in their 'baronial halls'.[39] Moreover, Presbyterians stood for respectability, or at least the desire to attain it; Fenians were a low, and possibly disorderly, class of people, with whom no self-respecting Presybterian should have any truck. The convulsion of 1798 was not forgotten; but it was now so far away, in time but also in circumstance, that Presbyterians could take pride in the exploits of their ancestors, without any fear that they would thereby generate some historical memory that would arouse the emulation of the present generation.

Fenianism made no immediate impact on Irish politics in the first few years of its existence. British politics seemed to be working against any possibility of characterising the Union as a failure and Irish self-government as the only alternative. In 1858 Lord Palmerston resigned, and a Tory government under Lord Derby took office. Derby had never been particularly sensitive to Catholic demands; but Benjamin Disraeli was anxious to make overtures in order to explore the possibilities of a Tory–Catholic alliance—a natural enough arrangement, on the face of it. Concessions were made on a series of small but significant Catholic issues, such as the place of Catholic chaplains in the army. In a general election in May 1859 the Irish Conservatives won fifty-five seats, with considerable co-operation between Tories and independents, and with much Catholic support. The international crisis which seemed to threaten war between the United Kingdom and France in 1859–60 (and thus perhaps invite a rebellious manifestation in Ireland) passed; and Fenianism remained an organisation with no immediate expectations, but with an appeal to those who remained attracted to its fraternal atmosphere, its advanced political ideas, and its emotional potential.[40]

This emotional appeal was demonstrated in one of the most striking political events in mid-Victorian Ireland: the funeral of Terence Bellew McManus, a rebel of 1848 who died in exile in New York. This coup was originally an Irish-American plan; no one in

Ireland was involved. But a group in Ireland—the National Brotherhood of St Patrick, a literary/political-cum-radical organisation founded in the 1850s to celebrate the national day with flags, music and banquets—announced its willingness to co-operate with the ceremonial reinterment of the dead hero. A McManus Committee was formed to co-ordinate the transatlantic organisation, and the funeral was duly held on 10 November 1861, in circumstances which vindicated the tactics of its originators. It attracted thousands in Cork and Dublin, and T. C. Luby, in his graveside oration, referred to the Fenian hope that McManus's example would give 'us faith and stern resolve to do the work for which McManus died'.[41] The Irish Constabulary dismissed the affair as merely a pious gesture for a man of 1848. And no doubt many of those who turned out on the day did so out of curiosity or a desire to participate in a gala occasion. Certainly the attendance at the laying of the foundation stone of a new building for the Catholic University at Drumcondra attracted an equally impressive demonstration.[42] But the point remained that a nationalist occasion could be an impressive and even spectacular one. This did not imply that the audience at the McManus funeral were all republicans, let alone potential rebels; rather, McManus and his like were admired for their role as glorious failures. The successful achievement of Fenianism's stated objective—the creation of a liberal nationalist non-sectarian Ireland by military means—would no doubt have offended the opinions of many of those who turned out to see McManus dead but who would not have followed McManus living. But the idea of honouring a rebel figure within measuring distance of his act of defiance, which did not happen after the '98 rising or Emmet's rebellion of 1803, was a new phenomenon, and one to be repeated in future generations.

The McManus funeral brought Fenianism into conflict with the Catholic Church, or at least with Archbishop Cullen, ever vigilant in his watch for godless revolutionaries. Cullen was anxious, not that his priests should stay out of politics, but that they should only enter political activity in a manner of which he could approve. The Fenian newspaper, the *Irish People*, through Kickham's pen declared that the Fenians only demanded for the people what was the people's by right: the right to act according to their own judgment in all matters of wordly concern. Catholic members of the brotherhood were not taking sides against their faith, but, on the contrary, were sincerely attached to their church. The idea that Fenians were enemies of the church was a 'vile calumny'. There was much justification in this defence; for while the bishops were suspicious of the Fenians, the priesthood was less solid. Many priests were hostile to English rule in all its arrogance and insensitivity (as they saw it), and some were covert, others overt, Fenian sympathisers.[43]

But the running battle with the bishops was certainly a problem for the Fenians, as their frequent assurances in the *Irish People* that they were not godless republicans illustrated. The fact, however, that Fenianism was in a kind of natural opposition to authority (which in Ireland meant priests and policemen) gave it a certain appeal among its younger adherents; for priests and policemen assumed that deference to their authority was the natural order of things. But while this refractory attitude towards established authority went down well with the urban young, Fenians looked with less certainty for a foothold in what was still a central Irish political issue—the land question.

It was once thought that the weakness of Fenianism was that it had nothing to say on the land question; but, on the contrary, its problems arose from the fact that it had much—too much—to say, and that what it said was unwelcome to many influential rural groups in Ireland. The difficulty was that Fenianism was an organisation of the lower social orders in the towns, led by the middle classes; and the rural equivalent of its urban following were the Ribbon lodges of Connacht, Cavan, Longford and Westmeath in particular. It was true that Fenians described any attempt at bettering the condition of Ireland without freedom as putting the cart before the horse. But at least they knew there was a cart; and they launched attacks in the *Irish People* on the farmers, both for their apathy towards nationalism and for their greed. Labourers and the sons of peasants were acclaimed as the salt of the earth. 'The land for the people' was an exciting slogan which could be used to good effect. But this raised difficulties for the Fenians; for who were the people? The aristocracy and gentry were natural targets; but the restoration of the land to the people might upset not only the gentry but the stronger and middling farmers as well. The return of exiles would, the *Irish People* declared, enable the homecomers to 'raise new homesteads on the grass-covered sites of the cabins of their murdered kindred'.[44] This was a rhetorical line which, when decoded, might well disturb the slumbers of farmers who had taken the opportunity to consolidate their holdings after the famine exodus of 1847–9. When it came to the land, then, Fenianism suffered from the same difficulty as it did over religion: it sought to unite all Irishmen, but could only divide them, since all Irishmen did not share the same social status, political or religious beliefs, or economic prospects.

That Fenianism was indeed a far from national movement was shown in its patchy organisation: strongest in Munster and Leinster, reasonably good in Connacht, weak in Ulster.[45] It was also an organisation which, again despite its national semblance and mode of expression, suffered from the besetting sin (if sin it was) of Irish life and politics—its excessive localism. Fenians in particular areas were prone to regard their territory as a kind of feudal fief. The leadership was frequently at odds, with Stephens proving a most difficult and at times dictatorial head, yet without the real power needed to co-ordinate local Fenian circles into an effective force. Moreover, a central organisation would be all the more easy for Dublin Castle to penetrate, and so again Fenianism suffered the worst of both worlds: it was centralised enough to be broken up by police agents, yet not centralised enough to be effectively coordinated. Fenians were in any case rather open conspirators, and their tendency to talk about their plans rendered them open to infiltration. But international events, which had let them down in 1859–60, suddenly seemed to take a turn for the better. The outbreak of the American Civil War in April 1861 offered what appeared to be a golden opportunity for the cause.

If Fenianism needed an army, the Federals seemed able not only to provide one, but to provide it as a battle-hardened force. Irish regiments were engaged in the war's bloodiest conflicts; they were imbued with a sense of solidarity, and their Irishness was reinforced with their regimental identity, their green flags, shamrocks and harps. And there was also the possibility, which at one stage seemed very real, that Britain would become involved in the war on the Southern side. Britain did not become involved; but the end of the Civil War saw the return of a hundred or so experienced soldiers to Ireland: not enough to beat the crown forces, but enough to make plans for a rising move forward; for Fenians must (by their own token) strike soon or never. But the vast majority of the Irish people did not want a rebellion, however much they professed to admire those that had taken place in the past. Once again a potential Fenian advantage proved in the event to be a disadvantage. In September 1865 the Dublin Castle authorities at last suppressed the *Irish People* and arrested Kickham, Luby and O'Leary. Stephens escaped, but, despite urgings from other Fenian leaders, he procrastinated over staging a rebellion. The government had time to make its preparations, order the removal of potentially disaffected regiments of the British army from Ireland, cancel the militia exercises of 1866 and 1867 (which might inadvertently place arms in Fenian sympathisers' hands) and seize weapons.[46] 'Soon or never' turned out to be 'somewhere in between'; and the Fenian rising of 1867 was a weak, unco-ordinated and at times farcical affair, easily suppressed by an efficient combination of military and police forces, the suspension of *habeas corpus*, and the arrest of scores of Fenians.

An abortive rising, however, was not proof that Fenianism was now erased from the political life of Ireland. On the contrary, the inevitable aftermath of rebellion—rumour, fear of further violence, fear of instability—all kept the British government and large sections of the Irish and British public in a state of alarm. This was fed by the unprecedented spectacle of Irish revolutionary activity in Great Britain itself, with an abortive Fenian raid on Chester Castle in February 1867 and the shooting of a policeman in Manchester in September 1867 in a Fenian rescue attempt. The subsequent trial of five men, and the execution of three of them, fuelled interest in Fenianism both in Ireland and among the Irish in Britain. The defiant and manly bearing of the 'noble-hearted three' was reported in the Irish newspaper press, their speeches from the dock were published and widely read, and seemed to emphasise the contrast between Irish gallantry and cowardly English vengeance. Irish certainty about this contrast was perhaps shaken by the attempted escape of a Fenian from Clerkenwell prison on 13 December 1867, when the blowing up of part of the prison wall brought death and injury to numerous people living nearby. But once again the Irish sense of self-righteousness was restored when the furious response of British public opinion provoked a closing of ranks against Ireland's overbearing neighbour.[47]

All this would seem to imply that the 1860s were marked by a widespread and popular surge of Irish republicanism. But instead it saw the revival, after a long period in the doldrums, of Irish political life. Fenianism shocked Britain out of political apathy on Irish affairs; and its suppression enabled Irish politicians, wary of the danger of being too closely associated with violent means, to emerge and combine national fervour (which the Fenians had undoubtedly aroused) with practical politics (which the Fenians hoped to destroy). Even while Fenianism was moving towards its doubtful climax Cardinal Cullen had launched his National Association for the redress of Catholic grievances and tenant right reform. These objectives, together with legislation to disestablish the Church of Ireland, were to be the policy planks of the Association, which pledged itself to a new form of 'independent opposition' until these demands were met. The Association made little impact in the general election of 1865, winning only three seats.[48] But just at the point where Irish political impotence in the Union parliament seemed to be demonstrated yet again the British Liberal Party was being transformed, mainly by Gladstone and John Bright, into the party of the Celtic fringe. The Liberal Party was moving decisively towards its role as the party of Welsh Nonconformists, Irish Presbyterians, Scottish Presbyterians and Irish Roman Catholics, all in alliance with English Dissenters. This combined Dissent was vulnerable and open to an English Conservative counter-attack on understandable nationalist grounds. But the mobilisation of the Celtic fringe against the Tory English heartland offered new prospects to the marginal Britons. The whole British Isles was about to experience popular if not yet truly democratic politics; and Ireland under the Union could participate in this enterprise.

If she were to do so successfully, then it appeared in 1868 that Irish Liberals were the party to provide the necessary leadership and tactics. They had always had the advantage of feeding off political patronage in the first half of the century; now they had the possibility of picking up votes in a changing British political context, where Liberalism at the centre was offering political reform to the regions. Ireland had one other means of attracting attention when it came to catching the eye of English Liberalism. Fenianism was still a live issue, with the process of trials, sentences, passionate defence, and all the theatre that patriotism aroused. But this in the end only fuelled Catholic democratic politics, for the Fenian, once safely elevated to martyr status—as were the 'Manchester Martyrs', whose memory was kept alive until they were replaced by the 1916 rebels—could be admired but would not interfere with the serious business of getting concessions from England. All this could take place within the context of the Union; indeed, reform of felt abuses could take place within no other political context. The Fenians gave Ireland priority over Wales and Scotland, for they predisposed the British public to wake up to Irish Catholic demands.

Fenianism, which in life had divided Irish Catholics, united them in death—or at least in that twilight zone reserved for failed but popular rebels. The Manchester Martyrs opened the way for reconciliation between the Catholic hierarchy and Fenians, with the saying of masses for the souls of dead Fenians. This did not imply clerical endorsement of Fenianism, but it amounted to an acknowledgment that, as the *Dublin Review* put it, there was 'a difference . . . between the Fenian society and the Italian Carbonari'.[49] The difference was that Fenianism was now accommodated into the Irish Catholic tradition; and the launching of an amnesty movement for Fenian prisoners in November 1868 by Isaac Butt, a Protestant lawyer (and former Conservative) who had defended Fenians on trial, gathered clerical as well as public support. Some clergy were able to draw a distinction between support for the amnesty movement and support for violence, a distinction difficult to make when Fenianism was a real military threat, but easy to make now that it was no longer so. Leading constitutional nationalists, like A. M. Sullivan of the *Nation*, had long approved of physical force in principle, while losing no time in denying its practicability. Sullivan published some verses written by his brother, T. D. Sullivan, which under the title 'God Save Ireland' (the cry of the Manchester Martyrs from the dock) became the anthem of nationalist Ireland until after independence in 1922.

Fenianism was now becoming respectable; a fact shown by the election of a Fenian prisoner, Jeremiah O'Donovan Rossa, for Tipperary in November 1869, and the defeat of his Catholic Whig opponent. The poll was low, and the unsuccessful candidate, D. C. Heron, regained his seat in February 1870 following Rossa's exclusion from parliament as a convicted felon. The R.I.C. submitted alarming, and alarmist, reports of the circumstances of Rossa's election, which, remarked a chief superintendent, 'has produced an extraordinary reaction in favour of Fenianism all over the country'. Another report listed the names of Catholic clergy who had 'recently by letters or speeches appeared before the public more or less in support of Fenianism or Agrarian outrage'. A Resident Magistrate warned that 'the Fenian organisation never was so perfect as at present'.

These reports must be treated with caution; they failed to notice that Catholic Ireland could respond to a convicted patriot and yet remain firmly political. Isaac Butt's amnesty movement was designed to control and manage, as much as to express, such attitudes. A police inspector reported that Butt disapproved of displays such as were made at various amnesty meetings, and recommended instead the adoption of petitions to be 'quietly signed' and presented to Her Majesty on behalf of the prisoners, whereas John Nolan (secretary of the committee) advocated 'agitations and demonstrations of that kind'.[50] Catholic and nationalist Ireland entered a new phase of popular politics in the United Kingdom as a constitutional system tempered by association with patriots and martyrs. It was a curious combination; but Catholic and nationalist politics in the last decades of the nineteenth century were indeed curious: a hybrid of sentiments and aspirations often apparently at odds with each other, and yet reconcilable—if handled with the right degree of political skill.

The first person to exercise that skill was not an Irish politician at all, but an English one, who was, however, set on establishing his reputation as the friend of Celtic Britain: William Ewart Gladstone. Gladstone was motivated as much by British or English as by Irish considerations. Ireland was a weakness, a problem, an irritant for Britain, 'a preoccupation, not an interest'. His policy was devised from an English perspective: 'to endeavour to draw a line between the Fenians and the people of Ireland and to make the people of Ireland indisposed to cross it'.[51] This would require not the abandonment or even modification of the Union, but the adoption of the policy of giving to Ireland, or fostering there, local institutions and conditions that would bind her all the more firmly to the British connection. This would involve, in short, land reform and the disestablishment of the Church of Ireland. The new interest in Ireland produced the unusual spectacle of British political parties vying with each other to conciliate Catholic Ireland. Disraeli, never one to miss an opportunity, was first in the field. When he became Prime Minister in February 1868 he conceded a charter to the Catholic University in Dublin. But this offer, made in a debate on the state of Ireland in the House of Commons, was bettered by

Gladstone, who declared that the Church of Ireland 'as a state church' must cease to exist. In March 1868 he gave notice of a series of resolutions in the house for the disestablishment of the Irish Church. On 3 April he carried by a majority of 56 a motion that the house should go into committee on his resolutions. The resolutions were subsequently carried by large majorities. Disraeli decided to appeal to the country, and in the election of November 1868 Gladstone won a majority of 112 in favour of Disestablishment. The government at once resigned, and Gladstone became Prime Minister with the task of framing his proposals and guiding them through parliament.

This was not the beginning of the end of the Union; that was not considered even remotely possible in 1868. But Irish Anglicans regarded Disestablishment as a serious compromise of the principles upon which the Union had been constructed. The Church of Ireland had been united, in theory at least, with the Church of England; and the Protestant establishment thus cemented was regarded as one of the critical bonds of the Union, making explicit its Protestant character as an essential part of the British constitution. Gladstone was now bent on recognising a central fact about that church and that Union: that it was based on the shaky foundations of Protestantism in Ireland, and that it could hardly survive the growing self-consciousness of the Catholic majority, three-quarters of the Irish population, that they were indeed not only the majority but perhaps even exclusively identifiable as 'the Irish people'. If Catholic Irish grievances were redressed, then Catholic adherence to the Union would be secured, through the means of Catholic support for existing institutions and political parties. It was at least a policy, though one which might run into trouble, both from those groups in England who resented its invasion of Protestantism and church property rights, and from Irish Protestants who, while not threatened with the Repeal politics of O'Connell's era, nonetheless resented the advancement of the Roman Catholic and the spectacle of Catholic triumphalism and Protestant defeat.

Gladstone pressed on with his proposals. These were that the Church of Ireland should become, from 1 January 1871, a voluntary body, its property (in land, buildings and tithes to the value of some £600,000 a year) confiscated and vested in a body of 'Commissioners for Irish Church Temporalities' which would provide for the life interests of the clergy, subordinates and other ecclesiastical officials of the church. Provision would also be made for Presbyterian ministers in receipt of the *regium donum*; and a sum of money would be paid to Maynooth in lieu of the annual grant. The remaining church property was to be applied, at parliamentary discretion, for the benefit of the people of Ireland, but not for the endowment of any form of religion. Gladstone, under pressure from Catholics, Presbyterians, and the radical John Bright, abandoned his original concession to the Church of Ireland of allowing it to keep its glebe-houses and some of their 'immediately annexed lands'; his reduced offer under this head gave him bargaining room when his bill encountered opposition in the Lords. But, in any case, no British politician of any stature wanted the question of the church left open. A settlement was needed, and a settlement was made; and Gladstone could take comfort in the reflection that his Irish church policy had united his party.[52]

Defenders of the Church of Ireland saw it all differently. To them the bill was an outrage, its passing a betrayal. It was more than sacrilege, for it was an assault on the Union itself, since a United Church of Great Britain and Ireland was an integral part of the Act of Union. English defenders of the Irish Church, led by Disraeli, were lukewarm; they could not deny that the whole Irish church establishment needed reform, and the church's position had been weakened by a sustained pamphlet attack made upon it, in both Britain and Ireland, since the 1850s. The general feeling outside the ranks of the Church of Ireland's closest defenders was that justice had been done. But the Church of Ireland's defenders, concentrating as they did on the constitutional aspect of their case—that Disestablishment threatened 'the Protestant Constitution of the Empire' and ignored 'one of the fundamental principles of the Act of Union'—struck a response among some Presbyterians. At a meeting in the Ulster Hall, Belfast, on 29 April 1869 Presbyterians passed resolutions deploring Gladstone's proposals as a 'concession to turbulence and disorder' and to the 'turbulent and disorderly portion of the Irish': 'Protestantism is at stake in this country.'[53]

Most Presbyterians were more concerned with their own church's position and the question of the *regium donum*; they were not sorry to see 'prelacy' brought down. But for Catholics there was a more particular lesson to be drawn from the disestablishment of the Church of Ireland. The belief held in Catholic quarters was that the Protestants had been undermined, and undermined by their natural 'defenders', the British parliament and government. This provoked consternation in Protestant circles, for it implied that the Catholics were indeed the majority, not only in a numerical but in a political sense as well: intelligence, talent, loyalty, the natural attributes of Protestants (in their own eyes at least) were to stand as nothing in comparison with mere numbers backed up by political pressure. Ireland, it seemed, might be given up to new masters. But it would not be given up without a fight. Irish Anglicans rallied to their church as never before. It provided a kind of national institution, a focus for all their hopes and fears in the last quarter of the nineteenth century, a means of political and social as well as religious organisation. It still held to what one of its historians called a 'divine mission' backed by its 'historic claims', and one which the Irish people might come in time to recognise.[54]

Gladstone, of course, intended no such extravagant interpretation of his policy, and certainly no such far-reaching consequences. He wanted to adjust, not change, social relations in Ireland; he wanted to adjust one aspect of the Union, not alter its terms nor call into question its existence. He seemed to have succeeded, for one Catholic clergyman spoke of him as the Joshua of the Irish Catholics, who would be to the Catholics what Joshua had been to the Israelites: 'the leader of the people' who would take them towards 'liberty'.[55] Gladstone had built his Irish Church Act upon the momentum created in 1868, when in the general election in Ireland Liberals, largely Catholic in their electoral support, won 66 out of 105 seats—seats won on the basis of a promise by candidates to support Gladstonian Liberalism. Gladstone also gathered his following in Ireland from the Presbyterians of Ulster, winning Londonderry City and Newry from the Conservatives.[56] After seventy years, famine and Fenians notwithstanding, the Union was secure.

The year 1868 was the year when Catholic (and Presbyterian) Ireland, like Nonconformist Wales, decided that its political future lay with Gladstonian Liberalism, with its peculiar brand of Celtic empathy and reforming policy that kept Gladstone the darling of the Celtic fringe—or bits of it at least. But its permanence depended on many factors: upon the ability of the British parliament and public to attend to the needs of Ireland; upon the Irish Catholic majority's decision about where its best interests lay or could be served; upon the kind of patriotic sentiment inspired by the Fenians, who, while ill-supported when they were a real threat to the peace, nevertheless had planted some seeds of Irish national sentiment, which flourished all the better when the Fenians were safely dispersed. Above all, it depended on whether or not Catholic self-consciousness, fed by Gladstone's first excursion into his notion that Ireland needed to be governed by 'Irish ideas', would be content to remain within the Liberal political fold or strike out for itself. And this in turn depended on how Irish Liberals played their political cards, for they were, until 1868, a party almost without an ideology (though endowed with the excellent political cement of patronage in an era of British Liberal ascendancy between 1832 and 1841 and from 1847 to 1868). The future of Ireland within the Union depended upon the direction in which Irish Catholic aspirations would go, and the response of the British people and state to these aspirations. It also depended, though this was not yet obvious, on the reaction of Presbyterian Ireland and Episcopalian Ireland to the new and altering political conditions of the British Isles as a whole. When Gladstone embarked on his newly contrived policy of governing Ireland by 'Irish ideas', his strategy would be applied to an Ireland in which 'the most apparent characteristic of . . . Christians was their fear of each other'.[57]

The Shaping of Irish Politics (1): The Making of Irish Nationalism, 1870–91

G LADSTONE'S disestablishment of the Church of Ireland was, as he himself put it, 'but one of a group of questions': there was also 'the land of Ireland' and 'the education of Ireland'; and these constituted 'the many branches from one trunk, and that trunk is the tree of what is called the Protestant ascendancy'.[1] Gladstone's declared aim was to lay the axe to the root of that tree. There can be no doubt that his Disestablishment policy was popular with the Liberal Party, and indeed with the electorate in Great Britain at large. But land was a more troublesome matter, for it raised the question of property rights, their sacrosanctity or otherwise, and was likely therefore to provoke at least some unease in the Liberal ranks. Yet no one could doubt that land reform would be a popular policy in Ireland, not only with Catholic middle class opinion, which was strongly behind it, and with the farmers, who would benefit from it, but also with Protestant tenant farmers, whose religious or political doubts about Catholics did not extend to a refusal to identify where their own best economic interests lay. Tenant right had, after all, been one of the recurring themes in Irish politics since the Great Famine; now it was revived and directed by two leading political figures in Ireland: Isaac Butt, Irish Conservative now turned moderate Conservative/nationalist, a man with a new career to map out as well as a genuine concern for his country; and John Gray, owner of the *Freeman's Journal*, a figure typical of the patriotic Protestant nationalism founded by Young Ireland in the 1840s.

When it came to the drafting of a bill, however, the problems of reconciling Irish demands with British responses were clearly seen. Gladstone's Irish Church Act had at least broken the ground in property rights, and their disturbance, for it contained some small modifications of the terms on which tenants who lived on church property held their tenancy: they were given the option of buying their holdings, raising three-quarters of the purchase money on mortgage at 4 per cent. Now Gladstone sought to find legislative form for a further interference with tenancy, but in a way that was politically practicable. The classic tenant demand for the 'Three Fs' —fair rent, fixity of tenure and free sale—was much too ambitious for both Gladstone and his cabinet. But there was another way: to avoid any major invasion of property rights and to seek instead to legalise custom. Gladstone's Land Act of 1870 therefore gave the 'Ulster custom' the sanction of law wherever that custom existed; where it did not exist, then any such similar practices were also given legal support. The tenant had the right therefore to sell his interest in his holding, and to obtain appropriate compensation for any improvements he had made in his holding; and he would be less likely to suffer eviction, since if he were evicted (and he could be, of course), he would be entitled to a reasonable degree of compensation. Where the Ulster custom was not acknowledged, a tenant was given compensation for improvements on giving up his farm; and if he were evicted, his landlord would be liable to compensate him for 'disturbance'. Gladstone's hope was that the bill would be acceptable not only to Irish but also to British opinion; and he was careful to stress that it did not establish a precedent for the United Kingdom as a whole. He also played on notions of a dispossessed 'Celtic' race and the justice of restoring its ancient lawful rights. Finally, he hoped that by reducing the main causes of friction between landlord and tenant, by ending what he called 'wanton' eviction and 'demands for *unjust* augmentations of rent', he would therefore help fashion in Ireland what already existed in England: good landlord–tenant relations, social stability, and willing incorporation within the United Kingdom.[2]

Gladstone's act did discourage 'wanton' evictions,[3] but it did not thereby discourage evictions that were, in the eyes of the landlord, not wanton but desirable and necessary (and there were good reasons for evictions as well as bad ones, for not all tenants were models of perfection). The act was disappointing to all classes of tenant farmers, even though the landlords called it a daring and even over-ambitious measure. Ulster tenants who enjoyed their long-established custom would hardly be over-enthusiastic for the legislation of what they already held of right. Moreover, in a dispute between landlord and tenant, the burden of proof was put upon the tenant, who must now convince a court that his tenancy was indeed subject to the custom, and that the right he sought to establish at law was part of that custom. This could prove to be a lengthy and expensive procedure, and the landlord, with his superior financial resources, would almost certainly find litigation easier than the tenant. But, whatever its drawbacks, the 1870 Land Act was major piece of legislation, embodying a right of compensation for disturbance, and securing Irish tenant farmers in rights which no British government would have dreamed of granting to English farmers. It was characteristic of British reform: it was a search for the middle way, and it was able to cloak its radicalism in a comfortable conservative style and language.

Gladstone hoped to sweeten his land legislation with two more measures: state support for an Irish railway system, either by purchase or by sponsorship; and the freeing of what Gladstone defined as 'purely political offenders' from among the Fenian prisoners housed in British and Irish jails.[4] But although the Land Act gave the tenants some of what they wanted, it disappointed expectations about the 'Three Fs' and only whetted the appetite for more; and the Catholic bishops placed themselves in the forefront of the demand for 'more'. The government began to hear alarming reports, no doubt exaggerated but nonetheless disturbing, of a recrudescence of Fenianism and Fenian sympathy, and Gladstone was obliged to frame coercive measures to restore stability; land reform and coercion thus went hand in hand. Gladstone's final Irish measure of his church, land and education trilogy was, necessarily, slowed down, not only by pressure of business elsewhere, but by the fact that the subject was, as Gladstone himself acknowledged, 'a difficult and probably a dangerous one for the government'.[5] The difficulties and the dangers lay in the nature of contemporary Catholicism as much as in the problems any British party would face in drafting education measures, which were always likely to upset vested interests. Ultramontane feeling in the Vatican was provocative to any Protestant country; the resentment which it occasioned was, of course, equally provocative to any Catholic country. And Victorians were obsessed with the role of education in forming and moulding men's minds on all sorts of controversial subjects, especially the relationship between science and religion.

Gladstone's approach was therefore cautious. He would not offer any financial concessions to the bishops, who had hoped to negotiate cash from the government on the hierarchy's own terms—a plan which the Liberal Party, with its Nonconformist roots, could hardly be expected to like. Gladstone turned instead to the existing framework, as he had done over the land question. He proposed the replacement of the Queen's College system by a new and enlarged University of Dublin, with the foundations in Cork, Galway and Belfast and the Catholic University in Dublin as affiliated institutions. This would provide a kind of 'neutral' university, and would be preferable to the totally unacceptable idea of a concurrent endowment for the Catholic University in Dublin (the Queen's Colleges were largely ignored by Catholics). To overcome Catholic doubts, no chairs of history, theology or philosophy were to be founded. This plan was consistent with Gladstone's belief, almost universally shared in Great Britain, that state endowment or support was not the best principle of organisation; and certainly state support for denominational purposes had, after all, been rejected in the general disestablishment and disendowment of religion in Ireland, a proposal which the Catholic bishops heartily endorsed in 1869, but found less acceptable in 1873. Irish Liberals, acting on Catholic advice, voted against the bill, or abstained, as did some English Liberals, and it was defeated on its second reading in March 1873 by three votes. Gladstone resigned, only to be put back in office by Disraeli, and a general election was held in 1874—an election which in Ireland was to offer a public test of the effect on public opinion, and especially Catholic opinion, of three years of laying the axe to the tree of the Protestant ascendancy.[6]

It was ironic that Gladstone's desire to lay his axe to this tree should have occasioned the foundation of a political party that was in 1874 to demonstrate that Liberal Ireland, if not yet overthrown, was confronted with a serious challenge to its existence. The disestablishment of the Church of Ireland was a piece of legislation which, with the benefit of hindsight, appears not only inevitable, but wholly consistent with natural justice; but to Irish Protestant Conservatives it was the destruction of what they liked to call the 'national church'. In truth, such people, especially landlords, had resented the call to support that church in the past, especially when it seemed to require them to empty their pockets on its behalf; but human nature is nothing if not inconsistent. And now that the church was cast down, it seemed all the more attractive and indeed necessary to Protestant Ireland. Now a land act was in contemplation, and some Irish Protestants fell back upon a sentiment that was ultimately self-destructive but which was at least temporarily satisfying: that of showing the British government, which had made their church a 'bauble in the battle of party',[7] that its closest allies in Ireland were prepared to assert themselves. If England was so lacking in care and understanding for all that was best in Ireland, ought not England to be given a lesson? Conservatism was a long-established supporter of the Union, and although no one proposed to break that Union, the time now seemed ripe for a return to an older notion, floated by Sharman Crawford in the 1840s, of some kind of modification of the Union on the basis of a federal reorganisation of the United Kingdom. This might have the added advantage of allowing Protestant Ireland to give Catholic Ireland the leadership that it so badly needed, that is Protestant and landlord leadership. Isaac Butt, who played the leading role in the making of the new party—called the Home Government Association—was a typical member of the Irish Protestant middle class: the son of a clergyman and a graduate of Trinity College, Dublin. Butt had already made his name public property in his defence of Fenian prisoners. His political thinking contained elements of orange (or true blue) as well as his newly acquired green. He believed that in 'home government' there lay a real possibility of reconciling Ireland's rights and needs with the Union. Ireland could claim that she was not innovating in her call for a domestic parliament, since she had enjoyed such an institution in the eighteenth century; the Irish parliament would have a House of Lords; and he reminded his audience that the Irish parliament would consist of the 'Queen, Lords and Commons of Ireland', while there would also be a central British parliament in which Ireland, England and Scotland would be represented. The Irish parliament would legislate for Ireland, except in 'those matters which the Federal Constitution might specifically reserve to the Imperial Assembly'. The Lord Lieutenant would remain as the queen's representative; he would, however, act on the advice of Irish ministers responsible to the Irish parliament. Ireland would still send M.P.s to the imperial parliament to vote on imperial questions, and she would be taxed from the centre and would contribute to the national debt, the civil list of the crown, the army and navy, foreign ambassadors and civil establishments. However, taxes raised from each member of the federal United Kingdom should be assessed according to their means. There would be no change in the existing franchise. Yet all this modern machinery of government was meant to assist an ancient nation to recover its rights and its destiny after 'centuries of misery and humiliation' and show to the world what pious, uncorrupt Ireland might offer in a sceptical modern age. To those who pointed out the dangers of Ireland's religious dissensions, Butt replied that they should take note of the fact that these were the responsibility of England, who had fostered them in such a way as to make Protestants 'anti-Irish'. If Ireland were a nation, then, like Germany, she would mould together different creeds; it was only when 'religious ascendancy' was admitted that differences of creed could become a source of national strife.[8]

This plea for an Irish centre ground seemed to get off to a good start. At a meeting held in Bilton's Hotel, Dublin, in May 1870, Butt's proposals resulted in the appointment of a committee to further the cause of home government; it contained twenty-eight Protestant Conservatives, ten Liberals, seventeen constitutional nationalists, and six Fenians or Fenian associates: the religious breakdown was thirty-five Protestants and twenty-five Catholics. But within a short time the Irish Protestant Conservative element was diminished; by October 1870 Butt admitted that Catholics were a small majority on the committee—and Liberals outnumbered Conservatives by three to two.[9]

There would always have been difficulties in keeping together Irish Protestant Conservatives, Liberals, Catholics and Fenians in a good cause; for once the shock of Disestablishment began to wear off, and once Conservatives began to rally to their poor church *as a church*, then Protestant enthusiasm might be expected to wane. But there was not only the problem of keeping Conservatives up to the mark; a greater difficulty lay in attracting public support for a rather over-sophisticated scheme of home government in a country which had other, more immediate aims: Catholic aims, farmers' aims. When Major Laurence Knox, a Conservative, and editor and proprietor of the *Irish Times*, offered himself as a Home Rule candidate in a by-election in May 1870, he lost, as did a similar candidate, E. R. King Harman, in August. But in a by-election in County Meath in January 1871 the Home Rule candidate, John

Martin, contested the seat against a Gladstonian chosen by the Catholic clergy, the Hon. George J. Plunkett. This was a strong tenant farmer constituency, and the farmers who had votes showed their disappointment with Gladstone's Land Act by staying away in numbers, and yet returning Martin to parliament by 1,140 to 684 votes.[10]

Butt, for his part, had earlier written in support of what he called the 'Celtic race' in a pamphlet published in 1866, arguing that 'it is impossible for any interest in the country to flourish while the tenant farmers are miserable and discontented' and suggesting that fixity of tenure was the only remedy.[11] He had also established his credentials in his able defence of Fenians and in his role in the amnesty movement on their behalf. He thus revealed that he could ride several horses at once—horses which, however, might ultimately want to go in different directions. But he gained a success of a kind when Cardinal Cullen's Catholic Union, launched in 1872 to defend Catholic interests in Ireland and abroad, failed to influence Gladstone's education bill in 1873. If Catholic interests were to be defended, then it was becoming increasingly clear that they might most ably be defended in the Home Rule Party rather than in the Irish section of the Liberal Party, and certainly not in Cullen's abortive political enterprise.

As the Home Rulers continued to test their strength in by-elections, certain patterns began to emerge in Irish politics as a whole. Cullen's political failure was not at all a sign that the older divisions of Irish society were on the wane; on the contrary, the appeal of Home Rule lay in its growing association with the grievances of the Catholics of Ireland. In a by-election in Galway in February 1872 clerical support for the successful Home Rule candidate—a Catholic landlord, J. P. Nolan—was very much in evidence; the contest resulted in a petition lodged against Nolan, which prompted the judge who tried the case to denounce clerical interference and the Catholic Church in general, bringing a storm of protest—and the reluctant criticism of Butt—upon his head. In the same month in Kerry the local bishop opposed the Home Ruler, fearing that Butt's Irish parliament would be run by an unholy combination of Protestant landlords and godless Fenians; but many of his clergy supported the Home Rule candidate, and it was clear that Home Rule could attract popular acclaim, including that of non-voters, as Repeal had attracted them in O'Connell's time.[12]

The general election of 1874 made explicit what these by-elections suggested: that Home Rule could catch fire if it were associated with popular demands (especially tenant right), popular notions of the Irish/Catholic past, ideas of the 'ancient race' and its wrongs, and protest against 'Saxon laws'.[13] The general atmosphere of anglophobia sat uneasily with Butt's modest proposal for a federal United Kingdom; but what was happening was that Irish politics were reviving, and the federal idea was becoming accommodated to their necessities and realities. In particular it was becoming accommodated to the undercurrent of Catholic grievance which had won Gladstone his prominent position in Irish Catholic imagery and propaganda, and which was now fairly on its way to destroy that position in the minds of the Catholic electorate.

And yet there were complications and reservations. Not all the Home Rule M.P.s elected in 1874 (some sixty) were avid nationalists; many were Liberals who saw the way the trends were going, and who had participated in Butt's reorganisation of the Home Government Association as the Home Rule League in November 1873. The Fenian John Barry wrote to Butt immediately after the 1874 election expressing disappointment at the calibre of the majority of the men returned.[14] And the party was divided between M.P.s who had been earlier converts to Home Rule (and the idea of parliamentary 'independence') and those who had been Liberals and perhaps still were Liberals at heart. Then there was the continuing presence of the Liberals in Ulster constituencies, mainly Protestants (with only a few Presbyterians and no Catholics among those elected) and relying primarily on Catholic and Presbyterian votes. In the 1874 election (the first held under the secret ballot) the Liberals performed well, winning both seats in County Londonderry, one in Down, and nearly taking seats in Antrim and Donegal; they won three borough seats as well. No Home Rule candidate was returned in Ulster outside Cavan. And Irish Conservatives were not driven from the field; they won thirty-three seats.

The Home Rulers, despite their successes in 1874, seemed uncertain of the best tactics to pursue; indeed, they appeared almost unprepared for the parliamentary session which opened in March 1874. Their own divided counsels were revealed in their resolution at a meeting held in Dublin at which they committed themselves to forming 'a separate and distinct party in the House of Commons', while also 'making all reasonable concessions to the opinions of each other'. Butt's first speech as leader of his group was less than rousing: 'He did not at present ask the house to concede Home Rule to Ireland. That question remained to be discussed, and perhaps to be discussed for many years.'[15] The Conservatives were in such an overwhelming majority in the Commons that at least Butt did not face the difficulty of the independent Irish party of the 1850s, of defection to government offices. And he was careful to press for other reforms as well as Home Rule, especially tenant right and education; but such concessions as the Conservatives made were too late for the Home Rulers to claim the credit, and Butt's inability to make any impression on parliament brought criticism from a more radical, and less scrupulous, section of his party, of which Joseph Gillis Biggar and Charles Stewart Parnell became the leading advocates. This faction used tactics which were as infuriating to British politicians as they were eye-catching to the Irish electorate, and to the Home Rule Confederation of Great Britain, which was in many ways more extreme in its nationalism than the Irish in Ireland. The practice of delaying to the point of disruption the business of the House of Commons was the tactical ploy of the Biggar–Parnell faction; and the use of rebellious language in parliament was its style. When Sir Michael Hicks Beach claimed that the Fenians were the 'Manchester murderers', Parnell retorted that 'I do not believe, and never shall believe, that any murder was committed at Manchester.' This language won Parnell much popularity with the Irish political organisation in Great Britain, and he became president of the Home Rule Confederation of Great Britain in 1877. It also attracted the support of the Fenian Brotherhood, now resigned to awaiting the decision of the 'Irish people' before attempting another round with Britain, and willing to throw its support behind the tactics of constitutional Fenianism. Parnell led the new men in the party, men who were young, enterprising, and untrammelled by the Whig tradition that hung round the shoulders of Isaac Butt's less radically-minded followers. He was clearly ambitious and willing to make concessions to the sentiments of the Irish Republican Brotherhood, Irish-Americans and other marginalised groups of people. But the party as a whole still lacked deep and wide popular appeal, the kind of mass appeal that had brought O'Connell to victory in 1829; and it lacked charismatic leadership, which, again, was necessary in a country where 'mass' politics could make headway with those who did not have a vote but had a voice and even a physical presence (i.e. their fists). And the party, though not vulnerable to a Liberal counter-attack, had to bear in mind that a wily politician like Gladstone (who paid his first visit to Ireland in 1877) might yet have some surprises in store.

What made the difference, what transformed the political land-scape of Ireland, was the agricultural crisis which began in 1878 and led to the 'land war' of 1879–82. But what was equally important was the mood which this crisis engendered among important sections of the Irish tenant farming class—the most numerous, significant and (after 1849) homogeneous part of the population of Ireland. This homogeneity must not be exaggerated: there were small farmers and large ones, there were those who lived in comfort and experienced growing prosperity and those to whom an agricul-tural depression would mean disaster. These were the people who, apart from their experience in voting in general elections, had for the twenty years since the famine their own organisations and meetings, their own opportunity to think and act politically, using that expression in its widest sense. Tenant right associations were well established, well organised, and widespread throughout the country. What was needed was leadership, propaganda and organisa-tion on a nationwide scale. The agricultural depression produced these and forged an alliance with the Home Rule Party, thus creating a mass movement which gave the parliamentary party both its mass base and its role until the end of the First World War.

The agricultural depression of 1878 was, of course, a British and European phenomenon, but it fell upon an Ireland where the chief emotion and preoccupation in the countryside can be summed up in one word: insecurity.[16] Landlords did not live at permanent (or even temporary) war with their tenants; tenants had no doubt that landlordism would continue to exist. Nevertheless, tenants per-ceived that their interests and those of the landlord were often at variance, with tenants pressing for some further protection for their rights, and landlords, naturally enough, looking to defend their privileges (for landlordism in Ireland still afforded privileges). This meant that landlord and tenant were occasionally at odds; but there was a bond between them in that they shared doubts not only about their respective positions in a country which had experienced a gradual rise in tenant prosperity, but also about the permanence of even this very recent and still *relative* prosperity.

Tenant farmers were caught up not so much in a crisis of rising expectations as one of rising frustrations. They believed now that the famine was not an act of God but a conspiracy of landlords. They did not see why they should stand by in 1879 as they had done in 1847 and endure the worst effects of an agricultural catastrophe.

Hence the popular explosion that occurred in the west of Ireland in 1879. This area, and especially County Mayo, where the Land League originated, was one of the least prosperous in Ireland. It was here that landlord–tenant relations broke down—or were broken down—in the spring and summer of 1879 as new ideas and new prospects excited the tenantry. The tenant had little to lose, and perhaps much to gain, by taking on the landlord. And this area contained a high proportion of politically active, radically-minded people: newspaper editors, Fenians, M.P.s and organisers of tenant defence associations. Men such as John O'Connor Power, Matt Harris and James Daly (editor of the *Connaught Telegraph*) were experienced politically and were no respecters of persons. They were joined by Michael Davitt, a Mayo man whose family had been evicted in 1851 and who had been brought up in Lancashire from the age of six; by 1879 he had long been hardened to imprisonment and harassment for his subversive beliefs. It was Davitt who sought to give radical nationalism a new impetus by welding the open and secret wings of nationalist politics—in particular to create an active alliance between Fenianism, Irish-American politics, and the Home Rulers who followed Parnell's more vigorous leadership.[17]

Davitt joined with John Devoy, a prominent Irish-American Fenian, in deciding to break out of the dead hand of moribund republican politics and offer his support to Parnell as the rising star of the Home Rule Party. In October 1878 Devoy offered Parnell Fenian support on certain conditions: federalism would be dropped in favour of a simple call for self-government; there would be a vigorous agitation for peasant proprietorship; purely Catholic issues would be avoided; and the Irish Parliamentary Party would act in a vigorous and disciplined way at Westminster. This was as far as the 'New Departure' went; but it was given a firm push in the direction of agrarianism by Davitt, who attached himself to the land agitation after it was launched at Irishtown, County Mayo, in April

1879. Davitt did not attend this inaugural meeting, but he kept himself informed of its proceedings. The meeting called for the best solution to the crisis in the short term—a reduction of rents. This was a modest enough demand, and fell very far short of an attack on landlordism itself, and it was pitched to attract the maximum amount of support from tenant farmers wherever they might be, including Ulster. In August 1879 a more ambitious future for rural Ireland was projected when a meeting in Castlebar resulted in the foundation of the National Land League of Mayo with the call for 'the land for the people'. Such a demand was more likely to prove divisive: it might frighten off the large farmers; it would certainly incur the close scrutiny of the Catholic clergy and bishops; it might prove an obstacle to the co-operation of the Protestant farmers of Ireland and especially Ulster. But it became Davitt's slogan and the focus of his effort; it became also part of the Home Rule Party's political apparatus, and indeed the main plank of its platform next to, and sometimes above, self-government.

In October 1879 the Irish National Land League was founded in Dublin with Parnell as president. Parnell had hesitated; he was uncertain of the depth and nature of what might turn out to be a revolutionary movement. But he knew in the end that he could do no other than place himself at the head of an organisation whose founding fathers he would, were he prime minister of a Home Rule government in Dublin, lock up.[18] At least he could console himself with the thought that an Ireland in which landlord–tenant conflict was resolved would be an Ireland where a natural aristocracy and gentry could take their place in society.

Parnell's speeches to the Land League and to the public were a mixture of agrarian radicalism and urgent advice to remain within the law. At Tipperary on 21 September 1879 he declared that 'It is quite useless for us to mince matters. The land of this country cannot be cultivated unless the people of the country own it.' If the occupiers of the land could be made into its owners 'at a reasonable and fair valuation', they 'would be able to improve and develop their farms to such an extent that they would be able to pay by instalments the purchase price of their farms'. If landlords were to decide during the coming winter that the right of being a landlord was 'an undesirable thing', then 'when they are desirous of selling' they 'will be glad enough to facilitate the obtaining by purchase of the farms by the tenants who occupy them (*cheers*)'. But, continued

Parnell, the tenants must not look to parliament for this; they must rely upon themselves. They must stand together and insist upon a reasonable reduction of rent, and where they failed to get a reasonable reduction, they must pay no rent at all. This Parnell described as 'extreme'; yet he offered his 'no rent' call in reply to a cry from his audience of 'shoot them'. In Mayo on 24 November he congratulated the tenants 'upon your attitude today—calm, determined, self-reliant, and within the law (*cheers*). In this way we shall teach our rulers that although they may violate the constitution, although they may rush into illegal acts, we are not going to be induced to follow them (No, no! *and loud cheering*).' He approved of their action in paying no rents and in keeping a firm grip on their homesteads, but warned them again 'with all the little power or force that I may possess to maintain the attitude that you have maintained up to the present . . . and not to allow any provocation to draw you away from your duty (*cries of* Never!). Even if your leaders are torn from your midst, let them go—others will take their place.'[19]

The strength of the Land League lay in the varied and variable tactics and responses which it could use to gather in the support of the Irish tenant farmer. It operated within the framework of the United Kingdom, and it was in a position to dare the British government to use extensive coercion against it; but extensive, or at any rate persistent, coercion was exactly what a British government could use only at the risk of undermining its own moral authority to govern the country. At the same time the League could fall back upon the rural habit of self-organisation, with a whole range of coercive penalties to enforce conformity amongst the local population: at worst, intimidation or even violence; at best, the exposure of those who would not bow to the popular view. It was inspired and led by Catholics, and it could draw upon ideas of the 'Irish people' and its struggle to reverse not the Union but the conquest; but at the same time it offered tangible benefits for all tenant farmers, and could hope to gain the sympathy, if not the actual support, of the Protestant farmers in the north. It was in the beginning a movement whose followers were on the poorer side of rural life (though its early and formative meetings included farmers on horseback); but the opportunities it offered could embrace the support of more of the Catholics fortunate enough to possess a horse, and a fair number of acres to boot. At its most powerful it could aspire to form a kind of alternative government, at least in the sense of creating and maintaining a large body of farmers who could defy the law with impunity, draw up a plan for their campaign against landlordism, and operate it effectively.

The League's slogan 'the land for the people' was in a sense a socially conservative one—that of the farmer becoming the owner of his land. Michael Davitt's call for land nationalisation was ignored. The transfer of ownership should be attained by buying out—rather than chasing out—the landlords; the vagueness of the time-scale involved was a strength rather than a weakness, for who could resist the promise 'before many years you'll own your own lands'? Davitt complained that peasant proprietorship was 'simply landlordism in another form';[20] but that was its main attraction: to supplant one set of large landowners with a set of medium and smaller landowners. The lack of a 'communistic' element in the League enabled Catholic priests to join and support it; it also reassured those bankers, shopkeepers and the like that this was no general attack on property rights, no attempt to wipe the slate clean of all debts. Its nationalistic overtones, its call for the land to be given back to its 'real' owners, attracted money from the Irish-Americans; yet it also appealed to tender British consciences (especially Liberal consciences), with their doubts about the whole history of the English in Ireland, and especially their notion of a dispossessed 'Celtic' race. But above all it was exciting, daring, and contained within itself the seeds of a much larger enterprise, which Parnell identified, and sought to exploit and foster, when he declared at Cork in October 1880: 'We are determined to take the power of governing Ireland out of the hands of the English parliament and transfer it to the hands of our own people.'[21] This, however, harboured its own special contradiction; for if the League was indeed to be the vehicle of a larger assault on the Union, then it would hardly attract, let alone keep, the goodwill of the Protestant tenant farmers of Ulster, whose ambitions did not lie in that direction, and whose dispute with their landlords was in no way connected with the presence, or absence, of British power in Ireland. Still, the League did manage to get a hearing in the north, even though it was tenant farmer societies, rather than the Land League, that formed the solid basis of farmer organisation there.

And it also got a foothold in Catholic rural areas, again without as yet provoking the strong sense of Protestant territorial solidarity that usually produced counter-meetings and clashes.

The Land League could claim great success in the first years of its life. It had grown in extent and in popular support. It enjoyed the sympathy of the Catholic clergy, and the church was now able to provide an organisational infrastructure, as it had in the time of O'Connell. And it had forced a change on the Home Rule Party, still essentially led by the Buttite group (under the control of the party's new leader, William Shaw, a Protestant barrister) but now, after the general election of March–April 1880, invaded by an influx of new men: nineteen of the twenty-one new Nationalist M.P.s were supporters of Parnell. Matters came to a head when, at a meeting of the party in Dublin in May 1880, Parnell successfully challenged Shaw for the leadership and won by 23 votes to 18. A majority of those who had opposed Parnell refused to follow him, but there was no attempt to create an alternative party which might have seriously weakened the Home Rule movement. The dissidents scattered, some becoming Liberals, some independents, but none were destined to enjoy a prolonged political existence. The party was smaller in its parliamentary representation for a time, but it was now equipped to follow the vigorous, combative leadership of Parnell. Its formidable leader was prepared to take maximum advantage from the developing predicament in rural Ireland—and, equally importantly, from the developing shape of politics at Westminster.

In September 1880 Parnell declared that 'The measure of the land bill next session will be the measure of your activity and energy this winter.'[22] This statement showed that the agrarian agitation was now linked indissolubly with the parliamentary party; it also attracted more radical nationalists, especially those Fenians now seeking a constitutional (or semi-constitutional) outlet for their moribund activities. But Parnell's speech bears closer reading than this; for in it Parnell presupposed, and indeed predicted, that there would be a land bill 'next session'. He did so because the election of March–April 1880 had been won by Gladstone and his Liberal Party; and Gladstone was, if not the Old Testament figure of 1868 leading the Irish people to the promised land, still a political figure from whom much more than coercion might be expected. The government gave earnest of its approach when the Queen's Speech on 20 May announced that the long-standing coercion measures, due to lapse on 1 June 1880, would not be renewed. Gladstone's Land Act of 1870, however disappointing, had indicated that here was a politician who would take an interest in landlord–tenant relations. This interest was not as fervent as the Land League liked to believe; when Gladstone took office, a royal commission, appointed under his predecessor, was already at work examining landlord–tenant relations, and Gladstone appointed another one to examine the working of his 1870 Land Act. But he was obliged to act sooner than he would have liked, and in June 1880 the government introduced the Compensation for Disturbance (Ireland) Bill to protect tenants in arrears from eviction. When the Lords rejected the measure, Gladstone let it drop. And the disturbed state of Ireland convinced him, reluctantly, that the government must introduce new coercion legislation. This did little to improve the state of the country; and indeed Parnell's call in Ennis in September 1880 for the League to boycott, rather than shoot, anyone who 'transgressed' the League's 'unwritten code of laws'[23] created another level of League control over rural society and was followed by the creation of 'Land League courts'. The government's response was the arrest and detention without trial of those 'reasonably suspected' of incitement or participation in any act of violence or intimidation 'tending to interfere with or disturb the maintenance of law and order'. But as well as this extraordinary legislation, the government moved towards a new measure of agrarian reform, thereby demonstrating to the League that it had achieved a considerable success.

The League needed a measure of success. It was, on the face of it, a united and powerful organisation, extending itself into the richer provinces of Leinster and Munster, and even establishing a foothold in Ulster. But it was a hybrid. There was little room in it for the labourers, a class that had declined since the famine and which in 1871 constituted only some 13.8 per cent of the total population, and by 1881 only 9.1 per cent. Labourers could, because of their declining numbers, command better wages; this gave them less cause to complain, and, because of their decrease, less opportunity to do so. They were left largely outside the Land League's doors, despite calls from time to time for their interests to be consulted.[24] More serious, however, was the contrast between the interests of the small farmers of the west and the more prosperous men who had come belatedly into the movement and who were now threatening to stamp their character upon it. When Gladstone's Land Act finally appeared in August 1881, it offered the substance of the 'Three Fs': an independent commission was established to determine equitable rents in disputed cases; tenants paying such rents would be secure from eviction; and the tenant was given the right to sell his interest in his holding with only a minimal reference to his landlord. This measure, together with the return of better seasons in the early 1880s, was important in easing tenants over the hard times they had endured since 1878; but it did little to resolve the problem of tenants on what were fundamentally uneconomic holdings. Parnell was able to turn an awkward situation to his advantage by pointing out (quite rightly) that the act did nothing for leaseholders, nor did it help tenants who were in arrears with their rent. At the same time he called for a series of 'test cases' in the new land courts to assess how effective the act might be. This was interpreted by the Chief Secretary for Ireland, W. E. Forster, as an attack upon the whole act; he believed that if Parnell were removed from the scene, the tenants would give the act a fair chance.[25]

Parnell's arrest in October 1881 was the best thing that could have happened to him at the time. He was in danger from two sides: from tenants who might accept the act, find it useful, and abandon the agitation which had made the Home Rule Party into a major political force; and from the Fenians and Irish-Americans who hoped (without foundation) that the agitation might be turned into another round of the war between Ireland and England. Once safely in jail, Parnell was able to avoid the difficulty caused by the fact that the more prosperous farmers, now an increasingly influential force in the Land League, would not condone a 'rent strike', and neither would the Catholic clergy. He also appeared to be the victim of 'coercion', thus satisfying the radical nationalists who had worked with him since 1878. Parnell's absence caused a crisis in the League, for with the removal of central direction it began to lose its co-ordination and lapse into factionalism. The high moral tone of the League was difficult to maintain as the agitation absorbed local vendettas, violent criminal activity and attempted murder with firearms. It was clearly in the interests of Parnell and Gladstone to find a way forward, and they reached agreement in April 1882 when Parnell was released from prison and the Land Act was amended to protect tenants in arrears.

Parnell was anxious to assert political control. The Land League had run its course as far as he was concerned. He used it to form the 'National League', combining part of the Land League's name and also its nationwide branches, built around his leadership and in close alliance with the Catholic Church, whose active support would soon be demonstrated in elections. This enabled him to distance himself further from violence, which he had always sought to restrain (while at the same time appearing to sympathise with its causes). His leadership of the Land League had nonetheless made him vulnerable to the charge that, if he did not himself use force, he was not averse to profiting from other people's use of it. What enabled him to face and ultimately dismiss this charge was the murder in Phoenix Park on 6 May 1882 of the new Chief Secretary, Lord Frederick Cavendish, and his permanent Under-Secretary at Dublin Castle, T. H. Burke, by the 'Invincibles', a hitherto unknown terrorist group. Parnell denounced the crime with the utmost vehemence (and sincerity). Attempts subsequently to associate his name with it, through forged letters published in the *Times*, came to nothing. Thus did Parnell escape from the suspicion that, whatever the horror of this particular crime, he had in fact dabbled in the politics of the Fenians and law-breakers in his rise to power, and had certainly behaved in a manner unusual in a parliamentarian. The Phoenix Park murders also enabled him to denounce the coercion act which inevitably followed the outrage, thus keeping him still the focus of hope among more radical nationalists who, however, drew the line at murder.[26] Moreover, the Land Act of 1881, which was by now producing a general reduction in rents, was, at least on the face of it, attributable to Parnell.

Parnell's new National League was one wing of his strength. The other was the pledge, introduced in 1884, which committed candidates, if elected, to vote with the Irish Parliamentary Party on all occasions when the majority decided that the party should act in unison. This strengthening of party discipline came at a time when franchise reform was about to change the face of British politics generally. The Franchise Act of 1884 and the Redistribution Act of 1885 resulted in an increase in the size of the electorate from 4.4 per cent to 16 per cent of the population and brought about a reduction in the representation of the boroughs. In Ireland the result was to give the vote to small farmers and landless labourers, thus augmenting, but not significantly changing, the rural, tenant farmer base of the party's electoral support.[27] To this support was added that of the Catholic Church, now happy (at present) to entrust the party with the advance of that cause dearest to its heart: education. But it would be misleading to see the nationalist movement as the consequence merely of opportunists and pragmatists jumping on the bandwagon of Home Rule. If the older nationalist picture of a risen people needs much qualification, then it would be equally a guying of the Home Rule movement to dismiss it as the result of selfish calculation or as an organisation which had to make its way *against* popular indifference or apathy.

The Home Rule movement's experience in the Land League years was vital to its success in the 1880s. For whatever the varied social mix of the Land League; however much its aims were qualified by its composition; however much the wealthier farmers came to use it for their own ends; whatever the role of local considerations and vendettas; however much shopkeepers saw it as way of increasing their profits (all of which is only to say that it was composed of human beings and not spiritual entities)—in spite of all these extenuating features, the League was a powerful and energising experience for the generation which lived through the land war. Irish Catholics were as divided in their outlook and interest as any other kind of people; but the League involved tenants, labourers, priests, publicans, journalists, cranks, in a kind of communal experience, in the making of a myth. That is to say that these diverse elements were collectively responsible for the creation of a sense of the 'people' versus the 'landlords', the 'people' against the state. The tiller of the soil 'had the first claim on it'; landlords were 'as much foreigners today as their forefathers were 300 years ago'; they were the 'heirs of confiscation'. Anyone who supported the League went down in history as patriotic; anyone who sought to discredit it could expect little political future in Ireland.[28] And the aims of the League were linked through its experience to that same cause that O'Connell had managed to promote in the Repeal years: a cause which had at its heart the notion that the Union was not the best political arrangement for Ireland; that, on the contrary, it might be and probably was the worst; and that some measure of 'freedom' was bound to benefit the nation—now defined as non-landlord, and possibly non-Protestant as well.

For here was another strand of nationalism that the land war influenced. The Land League and the National League that replaced it could offer real benefits to the Protestant farmer, but found it difficult to reconcile this with the notion that the League—both Leagues—expressed the collective experience of the Catholic people of Ireland, their collective historical fate, and their only possible remedies, namely the overthrow of landlord power and the renegotiation of the Act of Union—and possibly its destruction.

'Destruction' might seem a strong term to use, in the light of Parnell's own essentially conservative political ideas (which were based on a mistaken notion of the working of Grattan's Parliament. But the reason is that the Catholic people of Ireland were ambitious for power—power of a social as well as political kind. The fact that the party could rely on home-based financial donations for its cause (after the Land League agitation had died down, and after the National League had been instituted)[29] showed that something had happened in Ireland that might be called a revolution of the mind. That revolution was the conviction that, whatever the immediate attraction (or lack of attraction) of Home Rule, the Catholic people of Ireland saw the Nationalist Party as the way in which their ambitions, goals and desires could best be advanced. Their hopes and fears, their hostilities, their apathies—all alike found a voice in the Irish Parliamentary Party. They might not always regard Home Rule as the main political concern of the day; but neither would they operate for long outside its political world. As Archbishop Walsh put it, in a speech at Blackrock College in November 1885,

> Politics now simply mean food and clothes and decent houses for Irishmen and women at home; they mean the three great corporal works of mercy; they mean the protection of the weak against the strong, and the soil of Ireland for the Irish race rather than for a select gang of strangers and spoilers.[30]

For better or for worse, for richer or poorer, the Home Rule Party was synonymous with nationalist Ireland, even though the party's social composition was not representative of the farmers, its main source of support. This is to say that image and idea are as important in politics as the pragmatic calculation of political gains and losses, and also to acknowledge that farmers are not, perhaps anywhere, the class of people likely to take an active part in politics, because they have other more pressing and unavoidable duties in working on their farms.

And so 'the land for the people' took on another meaning. It now meant the land in a political sense: Home Rule, freedom, self-government, or whatever shorthand slogan sufficed. But this contradicted the policy organised and approved of by the Catholic Church since the 1850s, for the church had found the United Kingdom a reasonable context in which to advance the best interests of its people, and had even regarded the British empire as a wider world ripe for the spread of the Catholic faith. The Catholic Church was, after all, a colonising institution. Now Parnell had to overcome clerical suspicion of his religion, his movement and his Home Rule ambitions. Michael Davitt had already made the necessary overtures when he declared at a Land League meeting in Irishtown in May 1880 that the League was not a communist movement, for 'Ireland was essentially a Christian country'.[31] Parnell, as a Protestant, had to pick his steps more warily, and he showed himself willing to oppose measures that the church disliked (such as the non-Catholic university system),[32] while admitting the clergy to their share in selecting candidates for the parliamentary party (the thirty-two conventions held in connection with the 1885 election averaged 150 laymen and fifty priests each). Parnell and the church began to exchange compliments. Parnell referred to the 'union of priests and people' which 'has been cemented afresh . . . never to be broken'.[33] He dismissed as preposterous any claim that Protestants would suffer in a Home Rule Ireland; he pointed out that he himself was perfectly content to live in the midst of a Catholic people.[34] In 1886 the four Catholic archbishops met in Dublin to prepare for a forthcoming national synod and declared that Home Rule alone could 'satisfy the wants and needs of the Irish people'.[35] As always, the hierarchy was showing a lively appreciation of the trend of public opinion; and thus Parnell found a formula in which the Catholic Church would lend its support to his political movement, while he, for his part, would give the church its proper position in Irish nationalist politics as a kind of consultant, whose advice would always be solicited and, if politically possible, taken. No Irish nationalist leader, from Parnell to de Valera and beyond, could afford to do less.

Parnellism operated in an Irish political context where the ability to negotiate and act as a broker between various groups and institutions was an essential part of the practice of politics. On the one hand he committed himself to operate within the British parliamentary and constitutional context; yet on the other hand he did this while associated with agrarian agitation. He spoke of the battle of Celt and Saxon; yet he conducted his war over the dispatch box and played a leading role—as did his colleagues—in the day-to-day business of the House of Commons, speaking and voting on a wide range of British domestic, foreign and imperial issues. His party was no 'alien force' in the British parliament, but a significant part of its life: Irish members were at home in the best club in Europe, in the smoking-rooms as well as on the floor of the house.[36] It is hardly surprising that the experience of operating at so many, and varied, political levels should at times come near to exhausting Parnell; and it is interesting to speculate on how long even he could have kept in tandem the different factions in Ireland, the Anglo-Irish relationship, the tactical moves in the House of Commons, the need to speak in Great Britain and the United States of America, as well as Ireland. But he was, by 1884, operating in a British political environment that seemed to be developing to his advantage. Ireland was emerging from some five years of agitation and violence; these had been as vexing for the government as they had been for the police and soldiers who tried to maintain the government's law and order in Ireland. No one in Britain—least of all Gladstone—wanted to meet the Irish Party's demand for Home Rule; yet the endless round of coercion and conciliation, of conciliation that failed and coercion that could not succeed, seemed to urge that some means of breaking out of the cycle, of removing the Irish anomaly from the British political centre, must be found. Ireland was becoming an expensive business, in terms of parliamentary time, British prestige and British legislation. By 1885 this seemed to be accepted as much by the Conservative as by the Liberal Party.

Or, at least, there were hints from some Conservatives that this might be so, and that the alternative—a modest measure of self-government for Ireland—might be the lesser of the evils involved in maintaining the Union. Gladstone, for his part, was moving towards the same conclusion, on grounds not only of justice for Ireland, but of justice for England as well. For he was aware of the international dimensions of what was now regarded as the 'Irish question', and he believed that the Union would be strengthened by some measure which the British political parties could agree upon and which would meet the Irish Party's demand for Home Rule and elicit from it an acceptable assurance that such a settlement would end the quarrel of centuries. His concern for the future of the Liberal Party—so evident in his Disestablishment policy of 1869—was no doubt a factor as well; but it was less important than his own personal political creed—most notably his belief that there came, at key moments in a statesman's career, an opportunity to capture public opinion, to mould it and direct it, and all towards some great and even good end. Ireland, he was coming to convince himself, was just one of those opportunities, if only the moment could be grasped.[37] But his political sense also urged prudence; it would be preferable, he thought, for the Conservatives to take up the policy of an Irish legislative settlement and enact it with the full parliamentary support of the Liberals. This was not as unlikely as it seemed, if the hints and nudges, coming from Tories like Lord Randolph Churchill and Lord Carnarvon, were anything to go by.

As it turned out, they were nothing to go by. The Conservatives defeated the government in the House of Commons and took office in June 1885, pending a general election delayed by the changes in the franchise under the 1884 act. Their first Irish measure was the dropping of coercion and the introduction of a land purchase measure, the 'Ashbourne Act', which provided for the advance to a tenant of the sum necessary to purchase his holding, repayable over a period of years at the rate of 4 per cent per annum. Inspired by the political overtures coming from Carnarvon in particular, Parnell asked Gladstone for his bid on the Home Rule issue. Gladstone, although moving in this direction, would not be drawn. Parnell then threw his support behind the Conservatives and called upon the Irish voters in Great Britain to vote Tory in the coming general election. There is disagreement about how much difference this made to the election; but there could be no doubt about the significance of the result, which saw the return of 335 Liberals, 249 Conservatives, and 86 Home Rulers. Parnell could keep either party out of office, but he could only put the Liberals in. While this was being digested there came the astonishing revelation, made by his son Herbert, that Gladstone had been converted to the policy of Home Rule for Ireland.

The possibility of devolving some power, administrative if not political, had been canvassed before 1885, not least by Joseph Chamberlain. He had favoured the creation of local democratic authorities in Ireland; in 1874 he spoke out for devolution, provided that the imperial link were maintained; in 1885 he advocated a 'Central Board' for Ireland which 'will only be the Metropolitan Board of Works on a larger and more important scale'. But his opposition to Home Rule was important, not only because it helped destroy Gladstone's hopes of getting it through the Commons, but because it expressed the attitude of many in Britain who came down on the Unionist side of the fence in 1886. Chamberlain opposed Home Rule because he believed it threatened to end the Union: an Irish parliament, with an Irish executive, was self-government of a very different order to the kind of local bodies he had envisaged; and such a concession would isolate and give special priority to a solution of the Irish problem, rather than including Ireland as part of Chamberlain's desired 'federal' or 'home rule' all-round rearrangement of the United Kingdom constitution.[38] And the other sticking-point was, the kind of men who would rule Ireland under Home Rule. If agitation and threat had helped bring Parnell to power in Ireland, its lessons, or apparent lessons, were not lost on many in England: they saw crypto-Fenians, agrarian terrorists and violent nationalists as clearly unfit to rule Ireland. And while the Catholic Church was not, of course, pro-Fenian or pro-terror, nevertheless it had an Irish past to live down, and its ambitions were, in the eyes of many Protestants in Great Britain, unreasonable:[39] had not the prospect of state support for Maynooth brought the wrath of many upon the head of Sir Robert Peel? Suspicion of Irish nationalists and their ways was hard to overcome; even that stalwart radical, John Bright, failed to overcome it, and made strong speeches against Home Rule and in favour of the Protestant minority of Ireland.[40] It was possible to be a radical, to believe in land purchase, to believe even in justice for Ireland, and yet oppose Home Rule. Conservatives were joined by a section of Gladstone's own party, including Bright and Chamberlain, in the division lobbies on 8 June, and the Home Rule Bill was defeated by 343 votes to 313.

Gladstone's bill was complex and, almost certainly, unworkable. The chief problem for Gladstone lay in deciding how the division between 'imperial' matters—those affecting the whole United Kingdom—and purely local Irish concerns should be made. Irish representatives had an interest in the general imperial topics, such as the upkeep of naval and military defence of the United Kingdom. This entitled them to speak and vote with the rest of the representatives of the British people. But if they were in the House of Commons for the purpose of dealing with all business, including purely English, Scottish and Welsh business, then they would have an unfair advantage over these countries, for Irish M.P.s could discuss the affairs of others, while others could not discuss matters of purely Irish interest. Yet if they were removed from the house, then Irish M.P.s could not discuss 'imperial' subjects of interest to themselves. Gladstone's solution, to exclude completely Irish members from Westminster in a 'clean cut', was one of the most controversial aspects of his bill. This might be expected to satisfy British M.P.s tired of Irish quarrels, but the solution smacked of separatism and threatened the unity of the United Kingdom. If the bill was separatist in this arrangement—and Gladstone agreed to reconsider the question—then it was not separatist in its other details, for it affirmed Westminster's sovereignty over Dublin and retained direct control on all matters affecting the crown, peace and war, defence and foreign relations, and it defined very narrowly the fiscal powers of the Irish parliament. But the bill was welcomed almost with rapture in nationalist Ireland. It was more than Parnell had expected; and it was also, he knew, the best he could get in the British political circumstances in which he operated (and there were no other circumstances in which he could, or for that matter wanted to, operate). In July 1886, following the defeat of the Home Rule Bill, Gladstone asked for, and was granted, a dissolution. In the ensuing general election he and his bill suffered a total rejection by the English electorate; the Liberals performed much better in Scotland and Wales; and Ireland confirmed its majority support of Home Rule. But Ireland's will depended upon England's public opinion; and there was now nothing left for Parnell to do but wait upon the turn of events that might once more work to his advantage.

Parnell was perhaps changing in his political style. His private life and his secret liaison with Mrs O'Shea conditioned him to discretion and secrecy; it was, for example, frequently impossible for his own party to know where he was at any given moment. Moreover, he now showed a marked disinclination to get involved again in the hurly-burly of politics in Ireland, or, as he put it, to come into contact with the butt-end of a policeman's musket.[41] This was evident in the 'Plan of Campaign' in 1887 when John Dillon launched a new wave of land agitation. Tenants on a number of estates were encouraged to offer a self-defined 'fair rent' to landlords, and to withhold all rent until this was accepted. The Plan of Campaign, though it took place against a background of agrarian depression as serious as that of 1879–80, failed to move out of the poorer areas of the west. It still presented a frightening spectacle to those landlords who were already finding it hard to make their estates pay; and once again it revealed that Catholicism, land agitation, nationalism and a general assault on the 'foreign garrison' could hold together a sustained land movement. No matter who a landlord was, declared the parish priest of Mountcollins, County Limerick, even if he was 'an angel from heaven, he is a bad man provided he is a landlord'.[42]

The British government once again found itself in the centre of rural agitation, with all the usual difficulties of obtaining convictions in the courts for agrarian-related offences. Sir Michael Hicks Beach, Chief Secretary for Ireland, found the task of defeating the Plan quite beyond his powers, and it was left to Arthur James Balfour, who combined toughness with some useful experience of a lesser version of land problems in the Western Isles. When the R.I.C. opened fire on a hostile crowd in Mitchelstown, County Cork, on 9 September 1887, killing three people, Balfour earned himself the sobriquet 'Bloody' (which he doubtless preferred to that bestowed on the hapless Hicks Beach—'Mickey the Botch').[43] This caught the imagination of British Liberals, who roamed Ireland in search of evidence of cruel repression.[44] Meanwhile Parnell remained 'comparatively inactive'[45] and was frequently absent from the House of Commons. But British Liberals were doing his work for him. It was just as well, for Parnell barely concealed his hostility to the Plan, which continued for a few more years, but lost momentum and only threatened to cause dissension in the parliamentary party.

Parnell disliked both the methods and the objectives of the Plan, assuring its supporters that a Home Rule parliament would more satisfactorily settle the land question. To achieve this he depended upon British politics and British public opinion; and by 1889 events seemed to be working in his favour. The accusation that he had condoned the Phoenix Park murders was shown in court to be false; his enemies were discredited, and their corruption exposed. He was given a 'perfect ovation' at a dinner of the Eighty Club at which various English political luminaries presided; in July he was presented with the freedom of the city of Edinburgh, at which he gave a 'disgustingly moderate speech', calling for the concession to the Irish people of the power to work out their own future, and assuring his audience that this could do no harm, but only good to the United Kingdom and the empire.[46] There seemed every prospect of a Liberal return to office, with Gladstone carrying Home Rule on a wave of popular support.

The feeling that there must indeed be a better way of governing Ireland than mere coercion was present in the Conservative and Unionist Party as well. It was heartening for the government to see Balfour prove his mettle in Ireland, and by 1890 he was clearly closing in on the last pockets of trouble occasioned by the Plan of Campaign. But it would not do simply to confront the British public with Irish repression, and leave the matter there. And Balfour himself was responsible for the beginnings of what later became known as the policy of constructive Unionism when he extended the Ashbourne Act in 1888 by the advance of a further £5 million. It was becoming clear that the policy of land purchase, and the resolution of the Irish land question, however piecemeal and delayed by the vagaries of politics, was now an 'agreed policy' between Liberals and Unionists. Gladstone in 1886 had regarded land reform as of equal weight as the policy of Home Rule. Conservatives could not accept Home Rule, but they were concerned to seek out other means of 'pacifying Ireland'. However, this search brought them no political dividends as the government lost successive by-elections and found its original majority of 188 shrinking to a mere 70.

On 24 December 1889 Captain O'Shea filed a petition for divorce on the grounds of his wife's adultery with Parnell. As the legal proceedings drew near, Liberals began to question members of the parliamentary party about the implications for Parnell's leadership; but the belief was that if the party continued to support its leader, he would be safe. On 18 November 1890 a meeting of the National League in Dublin, with John Redmond presiding, pledged itself to stand by Parnell. A few days later a meeting of Nationalists and Liberals in Leinster Hall, Dublin, followed suit, with T. M. Healy declaring that 'For Ireland and for Irishmen Mr Parnell is less a man than an institution.' John Dillon, in an interview, stated that the priests would not ask the people to abandon the movement if Parnell remained leader of the party.[47]

But there were already signs of a different view among supporters and members of the Liberal Party, and a belief that this was a moral issue and that 'Mr Parnell must go'. John Morley reported to Gladstone on 21 November that the Nonconformists would insist on Parnell's resignation. Gladstone did not ask the party to drop its leader, but he did point out that his leadership of his own party would be rendered impossible, since Gladstone was so closely identified with the presentation of the Irish cause. The Irish Parliamentary Party met on 25 November to consider its position. Its choice was by now plain: it must decide whether it would stand by Parnell, and thus lose the Liberal alliance and a Home Rule Bill, or jettison its leader, retain the hope of Home Rule, but stand open to the charge of dictatorship from Gladstone. Parnell was rejected by the majority of his parliamentary following, and thereupon embarked on his battle for power through an appeal to the people who had acclaimed him as the 'uncrowned King of Ireland'.[48]

Parnell had in the past spoken of the possibility of withdrawing his party from Westminster if he ever felt that the day had come when it—and nationalist Ireland—would be better served if he did so. Now he declared that that time had come. The bulk of his party disagreed, and the sexual and moral aspect of the case came painfully to the fore as the Catholic bishops, who had seen in Parnell a suitable vehicle for their hopes for the church and the people, declared against him. This clerical pressure was resisted in the cities and towns, where Parnellites showed a vehement loyalty to their chief. But in the countryside the clergy could still command obedience, or at least help sway the public against Parnellites, who were denounced as adulterers.[49] The church, moreover, had been gradually pushed into the background and for some time had played a lesser role in the politics of Parnellism; it could use the opportunity to fight back and assert its primacy once again.

It is hardly surprising, then, that Parnell's last struggle should leave scars of the deepest kind; but the deepest scars were those inflicted on the Irish Parliamentary Party, on the constitutional nationalist movement, and on the grand coalition that had been Parnellism: that hybrid of Fenianism, the church, constitutionalists and agrarian radicals which Parnell had contrived to hold in harness and direct towards the winning of Home Rule. In the autumn of 1891, as Parnell struggled for his political existence, he used words and phrases that were still, at bottom, moderate, but which gave the impression that he had despaired of the Liberal alliance and the tactical responses that he had championed for a decade as party leader. He called for an independent Irish party; he warned that if Ireland deviated from the constitutional path 'upon which I have set her', then he would not say that he would 'not accompany her further'.[50] But neither the bulk of his party, nor the Irish nationalist electorate and people, would abandon the path that seemed most likely to lead them to success. And when Parnell died on 6 October 1891, worn out with his struggle to hold power in areas where he had once taken it for granted, he left his party weak, divided, a prey to recriminations, but with the large majority still clinging to his fundamental policy of the Liberal alliance.

And that alliance was still in business. Gladstone returned to office in 1892, and his second Home Rule Bill was supported by a majority in the House of Commons. This bill, unlike its prede-cessor, provided for the retention of Irish M.P.s at Westminster, and was less open to the charge of 'separatism'. But the opposition still denounced it as an attack upon the integrity of the United Kingdom and a surrender to agitation and disloyalty. The bill was rejected by the Lords, and Gladstone accepted his defeat—although both he and his party harboured dark thoughts about the role of the Lords in British parliamentary politics. Gladstone's successor, Lord Rosebery, was, like a growing number of Liberals, anxious about the implications for the party of its close association with Irish Home Rule. He was also concerned about its possible danger for the empire; and he rather inadvisedly announced in 1894 that 'Before Irish Home Rule is conceded by the imperial parliament England, as the predominant member of the partnership of the three kingdoms, will have to be convinced of its justice and equity.'[51] Whatever the embarrassment of this speech (and the even more embarrassing efforts of Rosebery to explain what he really meant), it was the plain truth, as the Home Rulers would realise when, twenty years later, their star seemed in the ascendant once again.

Nationalist politics, then, had taken shape between 1870 and 1891, only to lose that cohesion in the splits and divisions occasioned by the fall of Parnell. Factionalism and localism were left to assert themselves again, as they had done after the Great Famine and the decline of O'Connellism. And yet the Irish political landscape was, in its general features at least, not fundamentally altered. Various groups would compete for power in the wake of the Parnell disaster; but they would work within a context in which Irish nationalism was accepted as the ideology which expressed the history of the Catholic people of Ireland and advocated their hopes. Nationalism would still pay attention to land reform and a settlement of the land question on terms which appealed to the vast bulk of its tenant farmer supporters and adherents. And even when the policy of Home Rule seemed far away and marginal to the aspirations of the Catholic nationalist people, the notion that the Catholic nationalist people were the 'Irish people' or even the 'Irish race', whose destiny might yet be fulfilled, did not die out.

The period 1870–91 was also important for what it did not do; for its omissions as well as its achievements. Nationalism gave the Catholic people of Ireland a political goal or series of goals and a sense of purpose. But nationalists failed to ask themselves what they meant by expressions such as the 'Irish people', the 'Irish nation', or the 'seamless garment' that was Ireland. In particular they found it difficult to reconcile their notions of a dispossessed people with their professed aim to create an Ireland in which the dispossessed and those who (in nationalist ideology) did the dispossessing could live together. They called for reconciliation with Protestant Ulster; yet they spoke of Ulster as an area to be 'invaded' and to be made 'ours'. Only when Parnell was searching desperately for a lifeline in 1891, and had suffered his breach with the Catholic Church, did he declare that

> It is the duty of the majority to leave no stone unturned, no means unused, to conciliate the reasonable or unreasonable prejudices of the minority. . . . Until the religious prejudices of the minority . . . are conciliated . . . Ireland can never enjoy perfect freedom, Ireland can never be united.[52]

But the general assumption of nationalists, including Parnell in his prime, was that Ireland was already united.

All this gave the Protestant population of Ireland, a people who already possessed a lively sense of the lessons of Irish history, a self-recognition and self-realisation that might create an idea of a whole Protestant community. This community would draw its strength from its past religious experience and its present civil and religious liberty, won in the teeth of Catholic power in 1690 and now threatened once again. There were many obstacles to be overcome, many particularist and local interests which must be broken down. But if they could be broken down, then Protestants, especially in the north of Ireland, could be welded into a formidable political force which would press its claims despite all opposition.

The Shaping of Irish Politics (2): The Making of Irish Unionism, 1870–93

WHEN Isaac Butt founded the Home Government Association in 1870, he was able to take advantage of Protestant and Conservative disillusionment with Gladstonian Liberalism and with the British attitude to Ireland generally. This kind of frustration, expressing itself in words (and, much less often, deeds) of political defiance had been seen before. It arose from the conviction that England was wilfully blind to the realities of life in Ireland, and, in particular, to the fact that she needed the full support of her loyal people if she were to maintain the Union and thereby bring to Ireland the benefits of fair and equitable government.

But Conservative disillusionment of this kind tended to be short-lived. And, whatever the irritation that British attitudes and British policy inflicted upon the Protestants of Ireland, they knew that ultimately the Union stood between themselves and the government of those who hated England and wanted Home Rule 'that they may get place and power'. It was possible anyway to rationalise the great betrayal of 1869, for now that the church was free of 'state servitude' it could assume its proper place as the agent of 'educational and moral progress'.[1] By 1874 the *Dublin University Magazine*, the voice of educated Anglo-Ireland, was declaring that the Home Rule agitation was 'as wicked and demoralising as O'Connell's was, and avowedly constructed with the very same end in view—the dismemberment of the Empire'.[2] A few years later Richard Bagwell, the historian of Tudor and Stuart Ireland, declared that the 'Protestant ascendancy was bad', but that it no longer existed. Whereas a parliament in Dublin would mean a Catholic ascendancy, and he asked if there was

any reason to suppose that its yoke would be a light one? Not the slightest. Irish history tells us plainly that wherever those of one religion in Ireland have the power they have oppressed the others. Agrarianism, Nationalism, Ultramontanism are all united against the Protestants, especially against the Protestant landlords. The Union must be maintained as the only possible means of getting fair play for all.

The answer to Irish discontent, Bagwell asserted, was for British Conservatives to 'bring in practical good measures for Ireland, and so take the sting out of the Home Rulers' taunts'.[3]

Between 1870 and the first Home Rule Bill Irish politics became set in the mould of nationalism against Unionism; but there were cross-currents, and the varied and regional nature of Irish Protestantism made it hard to turn that common sense of danger into a permanent political shape. There were landlords and tenants; there were Episcopalians and Presbyterians (and the various other Protestant sects); there was the agrarian south and west and the industrial north-east; there were substantial Protestant groups in Dublin and Cork, not to mention Ulster; there were scattered handfuls of Protestants in Connacht; there were the middle classes, the businessmen of Belfast and the Lagan valley; there were the working classes. These differences could be accentuated by British policy. For if British Liberals or Conservatives were to intervene to adjust the relations between landlord and tenant, then this would encourage a sense of difference between them, whatever their religious common ground—just as, for example, the disestablishment of the Church of Ireland divided the Episcopalian from the Presbyterian. If the major British parties were as adamantly opposed to Home Rule as they appeared to be in 1870, then the Protestants of Ireland could take comfort and could see the Union, as Bagwell saw it, as the best means of reconciling Irishmen of whatever creed. And yet that sense of danger, which past crises had provoked, could prove a formidable rallying-cry, for the triumph of Irish nationalism would indeed be detestable. It remained to be seen whether that fear could provide the basis for a permanent political organisation, one that would survive the differing vested interests of Irish Protestants.

Protestants had no doubt that God found their religion and their whole way of life pleasing; and they were always on the watch for signs and portents. Like Catholics, however, their mental attitudes shifted between the humdrum, the local, and its complete opposite: the communal and the millennial. They were prepared for the Last Battle. But they were also ordinary people who had to get on with their everyday lives. So it is not surprising that the advance of Home Rule candidates in the south of Ireland in the early 1870s made no appreciable impact on Protestant politics, at least in the north of Ireland. This was because the Home Rulers were slow to penetrate the north; but it also arose from the prominence given to the land question, and to the status of Ulster tenant right, and especially to the hopes raised (only to be disappointed) by Gladstone's 1870 Land Act. It was also because of the three-cornered nature of Ulster society, with Presbyterian, Catholic and Anglican occupying a narrow political ground. The two groups of what might be called 'dissenters' (Catholics and Presbyterians) found themselves in the same camp when it came to choosing between the Liberals and the Conservatives. Liberal candidates were exclusively Protestant; but they were preferable to Conservative candidates, also exclusively Protestant. In the rural areas the tenant farmer, especially the Presbyterian tenant farmer, watched carefully over what Thomas MacKnight, the Liberal journalist, described as the equivalent of caste to the Brahmin: 'To an Ulster farmer his Tenant Right was his all.'[4] This offered the chance for Liberals in Ulster to drive a wedge between landlord and tenant and exploit their differences. In the general election of 1868 William Gray, the Liberal candidate in County Monaghan, called for fair rents and fixity of tenure and compensation for improvements. But the question was debated in more general terms, and the central issue in that election was Disestablishment.[5]

Within a few years, however, the tenant right question held a very different place in Ulster politics. Whereas Isaac Butt was concerned lest the tenant right question run away with southern politics altogether, there were in the north few effective leaders, and certainly no one of Butt's stature, and the lack of political organisation on a sufficiently large scale retarded the progress of the cause. Thomas MacKnight attributed this to landlord coercion and the tenants' lack of self-assertion;[6] but opinion needed organisation. There was at least the beginning of organisation in 1869 when the Route Tenants' Defence Association was founded in Ballymoney, County Antrim, and this, together with the Antrim Central Tenant Right Association, provided a focus for tenant opinion, especially when the disappointments of the 1870 Land Act became evident. Its enthusiastic historian, S. C. McElroy, explained how the Route Association sent a deputation to the government to discuss the act's shortcomings and passed resolutions calling upon the government to remedy them. One grievance which especially concerned the Association was the possibility of the landlords 'absorbing by rackrenting, in part or in whole, the tenants' interest, whether purchased, inherited or created'. The Association also called for the market value of the land, in case of eviction, to be made the basis of compensation to the tenant.[7] The tone of the address and the whole style of the meeting which produced the resolutions was, however, far from radical; nor was it inspired by the fear of destitution. The Route Association was an organisation of the reasonably comfortable, calling for the protection of their interests;[8] indeed, their property and respectability were the basis of any influence they hoped to exercise, and they had no desire to confront landlordism as such. MacKnight, for all his Liberal sentiment, was anxious to refute the Conservative allegation that the purpose of the tenant right agitation was to drive out or compromise the landlords: 'Nothing of the kind.'[9]

Such a movement, based only upon the interests of the farmers of County Antrim, and north Antrim at that, could hardly develop into a broader Liberalism in Ulster. Liberalism was closely bound to the sentiments and concerns of the Presbyterians, and it could not break down suspicions between them and Anglicans. MacKnight revealed the predicament when he admitted that

> Of many of those Ulster Tenants it might be said that they looked at political questions very much according to their own interests. Sometimes, though calling themselves Liberals, they had apparently less public spirit than the Orangemen. They considered every question from the point of their own farms. They appeared to think of no other.

MacKnight qualified his criticism by pointing out that such people were far away from the great industrial centres of the United Kingdom. Left to themselves, they gained little sympathy 'except when they could be used as voting machines'.[10] This role, however, gave them political leverage in time of general elections. The Ballot Act of 1872 afforded tenants any protection that they may still have needed from the influence of their landlords. The opportunity of exploiting Ulster politics in the interests of the tenant farmer was not lost on the leaders of the tenant right movement. When in December 1873 it was proposed that a conference be held in Belfast (a 'National Conference', as it was called) on the land question, the circular advertising the meeting declared that 'In view of the general election, the necessity of placing the question in its rightful position is becoming more imperative.' It was hoped that the Belfast meeting, building on earlier gatherings in Dublin and Cork, would 'demonstrate that Ireland is thoroughly united on the great subject of tenant right'. And the hope was expressed that the conference would unite northern and southern farmers, encourage those in the north to help their southern brethren rise to the northeners' level of prosperity, and enable farmers to 'join in the same ardent desire for the welfare of the common country'. At Belfast the Rev. S. Finlay 'impressed upon the people the great necessity of returning to parliament true representatives'.[11]

Tenant right associations were anxious to stress that their movement was not a party one, and that they would support any candidate who sympathised with tenant right. In 1873 the seat in County Tyrone fell vacant with the death of Henry T. Lowry Corry, a member of one of the county's largest landholding families, the Belmores. Following discussion among the leading county landlords, another member of the Belmore family, Captain Henry W. Lowry Corry was selected as a Conservative candidate. But the County Grand Orange Lodge of Tyrone put forward its own candidate, J. W. Ellison Macartney, who declared that he stood for staunch Protestant principles but also lent his support for amendments to the 1870 Land Act. The Orange Order warned that it required 'any candidate who shall come forward and claim their support to pledge himself to support any measure in parliament necessary to legalise Tenant Right on the expiration of leases and to abolish all estate restrictions as to amount of years' rent or otherwise on the sale of farms'. In his election address Lowry Corry pointed out the 'rights and privileges' that tenants on the Belmore estate had 'ever been ungrudgingly granted' and gave his assurance that, if elected, it would be his 'most earnest desire to promote any measure which may tend to advance and secure the interests of the occupying tenants'. Another piece of advice came from one Stuart Knox to Belmore: 'We know your brother would be well received, but undoubtedly the ballot and Land Bill made the people independent.'[12]

Lowry Corry won the seat, despite Macartney's strong challenge, and some observers drew attention to the lessons to be learned from this campaign. The disaffection of the Orange Order was put down to the fact that 'Orangeism has not been fashionable of late years, and the gentry, with very few exceptions, have withdrawn from them. The masses of the Orangemen have felt this deeply.'[13] The Earl of Belmore's land agent also identified the agrarian question as a major difficulty. Just before polling he referred to the consequences of 'several land cases and acts that would better have been left alone for some little time'; these had 'aroused a feeling of democratic antagonism to landlord influences' which 'I hardly expected had taken such deep and decided root'.[14]

The revelations of the County Tyrone by-election were, as the landlord and Conservative interest feared, a sign of the times. In the general election of 1874 contests occurred in all the Ulster counties. Conservative candidates, while standing as always upon Protestant principles and the constitution, again felt obliged to mention the land question. The beleagured Captain Lowry Corry spoke of the need to settle the 'long-vexed question' of the 1870 Land Act, the need to 'make it more perfect in its details, especially as there seems to be some doubt whether it applies to leaseholders whose time has expired'. He declared himself willing to support 'any reasonable amendments of that Act which will secure Tenant Right to occupiers on the fall of leases' and any other amendments 'which may define more accurately the rights of landlords and tenants, and check the litigation which the Act seems to have given rise to'.[15] Nevertheless, on this occasion Macartney topped the poll ahead of his two Conservative rivals. Liberal candidates in particular endorsed the tenant right question and demanded fair rents and free sale. Tenant right associations helped the Liberals' campaign, selecting candidates, assisting with election expenses, and canvassing. Priests as well as Presbyterians attended some Liberal meetings.[16] Even the sceptical Gladstone, no particular admirer of the Ulster Liberals, described the Liberal performance in 1874 (with three victories in County Londonderry and Down and several impressive performances in Antrim and Donegal) as having given 'most striking and most cheering indications'.[17]

The 1874 general election revealed that Conservatives and land-lords could no longer take for granted their dominant place in Ulster rural society and politics. And the land question remained the key political issue in the north, even as the Home Rulers began to make their significant gains in the rest of Ireland. In June 1876 an Antrim Central Tenant Right Association was founded, bringing the various branches within one organisation, and once again offering the northern hand of friendship to the south for the purpose of gaining redress of tenant grievances. It acknowledged the need for 'true parliamentary representation' as indispensable 'to a just and full recognition of agricultural interests'.[18] In February 1878 the Route Association held a 'soiree' in Ballymoney Town Hall, at which the chairman 'strongly blamed the government for indifference to the cry that had arisen from every part of Ireland'. Another speaker described Gladstone, then on a visit to Ireland, as the Irish farmers' friend, and called upon him to divert himself to County Antrim.[19] This mood of unrest and anticipation was expressed in a series of by-elections between 1874 and 1878. In County Donegal the Conservatives retained their seat in 1876, but their candidate was a local Presbyterian who supported tenant right and made strong declarations in favour of land reform.[20] In County Down in May 1878 Viscount Castlereagh won back the seat for the Conservatives, but throughout his election he declared that he would 'always support the just rights of the tenant farmers of Ireland', that he was a strong supporter of the placing of lease-holders 'on the same lines as the tenant from year to year', and that tenants must not allow radicals to sow dissension between tenants and landlords. His campaign cost him £14,000.[21] In December 1878 the Liberals held a seat in County Londonderry, a disappointment for the Conservatives, 'none of whom anticipated such a decisive defeat', and a performance which revived Liberal hopes after the Down defeat.[22] Conservative anxiety over the government's failure to tackle the land question provoked the Marquis of Hamilton into criticising Disraeli for doing nothing at a time when there was 'only one subject that these tenant farmers in the north of Ireland at the present time care about'. He forwarded a letter to Montague Lowry, one of Disraeli's secretaries, written by a County Donegal proprietor warning that the fear of popery, which 'alone kept the Presbyterians loyal, is decreasing; you are now losing them by the hundred, for they now consider the land question the all-important one'. The whole political aspect of the north was 'gradually altering'.[23]

The Irish Conservative dilemma was made more acute by the steady erosion of its power in the south, as well as its jeopardising in the north. In the north there were still Conservative victories to be won, even though they found themselves holding only a minority of the seats in the north in 1880 (eight, against eight Liberals and two Home Rulers). But in the south Conservatives found their representation reduced from the steady returns of the 1850s and 1860s (20, 26, 20) to the figure of 14 in 1868, 12 in 1874, and 7 in 1880. The seven seats won in 1880 disguised the real weakness of southern Conservatism. Of the seven, two were Dublin University seats, the rest were seats in the small boroughs of Bandon and Portarlington, a seat in County Leitrim, and two in County Dublin. The Conservative struggle in the south was not one to win or keep political power in the country (though they still hoped to exercise much influence in the Conservative hierarchy in London). It was to stand up, be counted—and then sit down again. In 1885 Conservative candidates in the south gathered only 31,772 votes, against 231,454 for Home Rule opponents;[24] in the uncontested seats Home Rulers could claim that the unpolled electorate was on their side even more emphatically.

Nevertheless, the 1868 election in Belfast had shown how an astute choice of candidate by the Liberals, and a split in the Tory vote, could spring a surprise, even in the most Conservative of strongholds. At the same time no Protestant candidate, of however independent a kind, would push matters so far as to jeopardise the basis of his support, the Protestant voter, whose deep suspicion of Catholic power never deserted him (however much it might be temporarily suspended). William Johnston was something of a special case, with his gleeful prodding of Tory sensitivities on, for example, the case for 'the interests of labour', combined with his tributes to Orangeism. But J. W. Ellison Macartney, who had wrested a seat from the official Conservative in 1874, and who remained a leading tenant right advocate, was in 1879 thanked by the County Grand Orange Lodge of Fermanagh for his support of 'Protestants in this County' in the last session of parliament and for

drawing attention to attacks on Protestants by Catholics in Conne-
mara. Macartney responded in kind, thanking the lodge for its
resolution.[25]

The touchy side of Ulster society was revealed in the controversy
over the Liberal government's educational policy in 1874. The
opposition of the Catholic Church proved fatal to the scheme (allied
to Gladstone's refusal to contemplate state endowment for a
Catholic university). But, according to MacKnight, a leading light
of Liberalism, the whole scheme dismayed some of the government's 'Ulster friends'—Liberals, and especially Presbyterians, who
were hostile to the bill.[26] S. C. McElroy, strong Gladstonian
though he was, acknowledged in 1879 that the whole education
question was a 'knotty question at any time for the Liberals to deal
with'; he hoped it would be 'thrown' upon the Conservatives, with
Liberals retaining the right of criticism, though in such a way as not
to frustrate the passing of a measure, should it be a 'reasonable
compromise between all conflicting interests'.[27] In the Tyrone by-
election of 1873 the official Conservative candidate was urged to
oppose 'sectarian education',[28] and the issue also surfaced in the
Londonderry City by-election of 1872[29] and the Down election in
1874.[30]

There was another nagging difficulty confronting the non-
sectarian style of politics in Ulster. Liberals had a Catholic
following (whose loyalty they strained in the Belfast election of
1868). But they were insensitive to them and were reluctant to allow
Catholics to play any role in the party. Liberals won eight seats in
the general election of 1880 (with two seats in each of the county
constituencies of Londonderry, Donegal and Monaghan, and one
each in County Armagh and Tyrone); yet this depended to a large
extent not only upon the radical stance made possible by the land
issue, but also by the acquiesence of Catholic voters in non-
Catholic leadership. For while Home Rule associations were
founded in Belfast and Londonderry in 1872, and in Cavan and
Tyrone in 1873, and although their meetings attracted large crowds,
they were not well organised.[31] But it remained to be seen whether
or not the rising tide of Home Rule, or the land question, or
a combination of both, could arouse the northern Catholic to a
new political consciousness, one which involved the rejection of

non-Catholic monopoly of his political leadership. And then there were religious disturbances and troubles on the streets of Belfast: in 1864 on the occasion of the inauguration of the O'Connell monument in Dublin, and again in 1872. These left the north still a place of relative political flexibility in 1878, but a place whose flexibility was due to tactical cross-denominational voting. And this type of voting might be tested both by the challenge of Home Rule and by the efforts of Conservatives to take the edge off land agitation and win back Protestant votes to the landed interest.

The land question was vexatious to Conservatives, offering as it did a chance for Liberals, or any political independent, to adopt a radical pose and steal away valuable tenant farmers' votes. If Ulster was to remain, in part at least, non-Conservative in political representation, then rural Ulster must be held for the alternative party; for in 1880, while the Liberals did well in rural areas, they won only one borough seat, and were clearly a party of the countryside, identified with farmers' grievances, particularly those of Presbyterians.

Farmers' grievances were what made the Land League a formidable organisation in the south and west; but it seemed to have potential for the north as well. At first it failed to make much progress in Ulster, partly because of slower organisation, but also because of a reluctance on the part of Ulster Catholics to become too openly committed to a movement which was closely connected with the Home Rule cause. 'Trouble-making' of that sort, it was felt, was potentially dangerous in an area where Catholics were conscious of their local minority status. In the north the tenant right associations were the chief rural pressure group. But the Land League began to hold meetings in mainly Catholic areas, and found to its satisfaction that Protestant tenant farmers turned up as well. There was no equivalent of the land war in Ulster, and agrarian crime was less evident, except in parts of mid-Ulster; but the distress that gave rise to the Land League was felt across the province, and even large farmers had to draw upon their capital to survive. The value of Ulster tenant right fell, and shopkeepers were affected by the general recession, with less money spent in their shops, less business, and less profit. By March 1880 nearly 20,000 people were receiving poor relief, compared with 16,000 in 1878. Farmers began to demand abatement of rent, and this movement soon became as popular as tenant right.[32] But it was never a campaign on the Land League model; there were few threatening meetings or breaches of the law. Landlord and tenant were still on better terms in Ulster than they had been in the south for some time.

Nevertheless, farmers expected the landlords to do something, and to do it quickly. Some landlords, like the Earl of Erne, were willing to make speedy and generous rebates; others, like the Earl of Charlemont, were not.[33] In the general election of 1880 Conservative candidates were careful to include in their election addresses frequent and pointed references to the need to do something for the farmer: to 'more clearly define' tenant right.[34] In Fermanagh the Conservative candidate made an issue out of Home Rule, but he also referred to the 'cordial relations which have always existed between my family and the tenantry on their estates' and promised to guard the 'vested interests of the occupiers in their holdings'.[35] Such promises to tackle the land question and do something for the tenant were common across Ulster. Liberals, for their part, pressed the tenants' case with vigour; and the general election of 1880 was, Thomas MacKnight noted, 'memorable as being the last one in which the Catholics were mostly united with the Protestant Liberals'[36]—and although this was not the case in all constituencies, it was true in many of them.

The 1880 election made it certain that land reform would soon be the subject of legislation. Tories emerged from the election determined to make the settlement of the land question a pressing political issue; Liberals had outbidden the Conservatives by calling for the 'Three Fs', the arbitration of rents, and the more certain commitment to the idea of peasant proprietorship. But the Land Act of 1881, which began the process of undermining the Land League in the south, also had implications for the north: once it began to take effect, once it (together with the return of better weather and better harvests) took the edge off agrarian radicalism, then it opened up the gap—a gap that had always been there—between the tenant farmers of the north and the south. That gap was widened by the growing identification of the land movement with the Home Rule cause. In the north, as well as the south, Home Rule began to be perceived as a Catholic political option. In a by-election in County Tyrone in September 1881 the Catholic vote, which was

100 per cent Liberal in the general election the previous year, was now split two ways, with the Liberal and Home Rule candidates getting an approximately equal share.[37]

This shift, at first only gradual, in Catholic opinion was paralleled by the landlords' belief that the land question must be settled; for only by a radical piece of legislation could they recover the ground lost in 1880 and interrupt the alarming sight of Protestant and even Orange support for land reform—for reform that was the particular demand of the Land League and the Liberals. And as the bill went through parliament the northern Conservatives showed a different approach from that of their southern brethren, in that, while they opposed details of the legislation that they did not like, they were careful not to throw themselves into a general opposition to the measure. Disraeli, who led a strong English Conservative opposition to the bill, complained that the Ulster Tories had 'sold the pass' and had vitiated Conservative opposition 'not only in the first division but throughout the conduct of the bill'; and another leading English Tory, John Gorst, declared that the Ulster landowners had dragged 'the whole Conservative Party in bondage at their heels' and had expected people 'to subordinate opinions based in actual experience to the crude ideas which they hastily take up as most in accordance with what they imagine to be their own interest'.[38] This difference in perspective, between the English and the Irish Conservative attitude to political problems in Ireland, was important for the relationship between Conservatives, and later for Unionists, in the two countries; for it foreshadowed that difference that provoked Irish Unionists both north and south into making their own arrangements in time of trouble, for fear that their Tory allies across the water might not in the end prove durable or sympathetic or even grateful supporters in the common cause.

The decks were being cleared by landlords for the reassertion of their power in Ulster rural society; and the beneficial effects of the land laws took the edge off Ulster discontent—while not, however, eliminating the land question as an election issue: not until 1909 did it disappear from manifestos and political platforms. The opportunity for landlords to make a comeback was not due to the neglect of the land question by the Orange Order; rather it was because they saw the sense of the Order's advice to meet tenants' demands as far as possible and thus prepare the way for a united Protestant rural front against the assault of Irish nationalism, of which, they believed, the Land League was the vanguard. These shifts and movements were vital to the making of Ulster politics in the 1880s. By the autumn of 1880 Land League branches were established in Down, Armagh, Tyrone and Londonderry as well as Fermanagh. The police feared that this would lead to disturbances, but none occurred. However, on 17 October an inaugural meeting of the League in Armagh was met with an advertisement calling a counter-meeting by the Orange Order, which threatened to drive out or kill the Parnellites. The County Grand Orange Lodge of Fermanagh declared this to be official policy in November 1880, and its members were instructed to drill and acquire arms.[39] Orange and Protestant misgivings were inspired too by the fear that the League was being organised among Protestants, and, more alarming still, that it numbered Protestants among its leadership. Nothing was more hateful to the Protestant than the prospect of 'rotten Prods' going over to the other side.

These realignments—or perhaps return to older alignments—were peculiar to Ulster, with its mixed population, its regional demographic patterns, and the presence of considerable Catholic and Protestant blocs adjacent to each other in areas such as County Armagh. Where Catholics were fewest, as in north Antrim, Presbyterians felt more secure and were less prone to succumb to Orange panic. Elsewhere in Ireland Conservatives could only stand by and watch Home Rulers win the day; these beleaguered Protestants were now forced to rely on their English Conservative allies for support and sustenance. But the Home Rule issue, as it began to replace the land question after 1881, was bound to have profound effects on the north, and push Protestants there into a closer alliance with their co-religionists in the south. The Grand Orange Lodge of Ireland had already pointed the way, when at a meeting held in Dublin on 3 November 1880 it warned brethren about 'a sinister conspiracy having for its immediate object the confiscation of every kind of property and undue interference with legitimate trading, but with the ulterior purpose of uprooting and extinguishing Protestantism and, with it, civil and religious liberty in Ireland'. The perceived purpose of the Land League was to break the last link that held England and Ireland together.[40] The shifting perspectives in the north were revealed following Forster's coercive legislation and the lodgment of Parnell in Kilmainham jail in 1882: this produced a wave of unrest in the south; but in the north of

Ireland Forster enjoyed 'the sympathy of all the loyal population, whether Liberal or Conservative'.[41] More importantly, the decline of the Land League, which did have a following among Protestants in Ulster, and its replacement by the Home Rule Party, began to fulfil the darkest warnings of the Grand Orange Lodge and helped to define more sharply the political frontiers within Ireland, and especially within Ulster.

The Home Rulers' tactics in the north could hardly have served the Grand Orange Lodge of Ireland's predictions better. In September 1883 it was announced that Parnell would speak in County Tyrone. Nationalist confidence had been boosted by the Home Rule victory in the Monaghan by-election of July 1883, where the Catholic Liberal vote collapsed and the victorious candidate, T. M. Healy, won some non-Catholic votes as well, a phenomenon which showed the apparent willingness of farmers still to look for the best pickings from politics. Healy kept Home Rule in the background and concentrated instead on land.[42] But the possibility of Parnell coming to Tyrone aroused apprehension, especially in the wake of the Monaghan victory, which, whatever its qualifications, caused his supporters to raise the cry 'Ulster is ours' and proclaim their ambition to 'carry the war into the very heart of Unionist Ulster'. This provoked the Grand Orange Lodge to look to its defences and confront the 'Nationalist invaders'. The lodge deployed its earlier tactics of holding a counter-demonstration at Nationalist meetings. At Draperstown in August 1883 Michael Davitt declared that 'We are deemed revolutionaries because we have seized Irish landlordism by the throat and forced it to disgorge some of the plunder which it took from the farmer in Ireland in the past.' Nationalist flags and sashes were discouraged, so as not to give offence to Protestants; nevertheless, serious clashes were only prevented by the police. There were disturbances in Clones, Portadown and Armagh, a dangerous confrontation in Londonderry, and trouble also in Newry. Parnell did not, in the event, 'invade' the north; Healy and the more neutral figure of T. P. O'Connor stood in for him and again stressed the agrarian question. But they nonetheless encountered a hostile demonstration in Dungannon.[43]

The stage was set for the kind of political *cause célèbre* which Ulster politics produced from time to time. At Roslea, County Fermanagh, on 16 October 1883 Nationalists organised a demonstration which the Orange Order resolved to oppose, mustering local brethren to defend the north and repulse the Home Rulers as the Repealers had been repulsed years before. Lord Rossmore, a magistrate and Grand Master of the County Grand Lodge of Fermanagh, urged brethren to assemble for the purpose of counter-acting the rebellious party. Revolver shots were fired, and angry defiances were exchanged. Nationalists called upon the government to allow them the right to hold meetings; Orangemen urged that Nationalist demonstrations called by 'rebels' should be suppressed, but loyal meetings permitted. The government sought to find a middle way, and Lord Rossmore was dismissed from the magis-tracy, provoking yet more Orange outrage and further loyalist demonstrations, this time against the government itself. The loyal cause had at last found a martyr in the person of Lord Rossmore (who was later quietly reinstated by the Conservative govern-ment).[44]

The land question was no longer the keystone of Ulster politics; it could not at any rate guarantee to break up or divert political Protestantism, and it could not divert the hostility of the Orange Order in the frontier areas of Ulster. However, where 'national' causes and strength were less strong or threatening—in north Down, in Antrim—there matters were different. Tenant farmers still voted Liberal and held to the self-interested and independent political behaviour they had adopted in the 1870s. But any chance that this might roll back the sectarian tide that was threatening elsewhere in rural Ulster was destroyed by the political revolution of 1885–6, which saw the turning out of three governments in thirteen months, the holding of two general elections in quick succession, and the threat—as it was perceived in Protestant circles—of the dismemberment of the United Kingdom.

The suddenness and shock of Gladstone's conversion to Home Rule is hard to overestimate. As late as 1884 the *Coleraine Constitution*, a tenant right newspaper, was still able to describe the condition of Ulster politics as a crisis for Conservatism, rather than one for Ulster or Irish Protestantism: 'Ulster Toryism has been weighed in the balance and found wanting.'[45] The Conservatives could not command the support of the mass of the Protestant farmers. But this was a misleading assessment of the direction which politics were taking in the north. In January 1884 a Liberal was returned unopposed for County Londonderry, but the candidate, Samuel Walker, was a Protestant Episcopalian, strongly committed against Home Rule 'and all that was understood by Irish National-ism'.[46] When Sir Stafford Northcote, the leader of the British Conservative Party, visited Ulster in October 1883, he found himself embroiled in the growing sectarian atmosphere of the province. Northcote's declared purpose was not to forge an alliance between Conservatives and Orangemen, but to 'infuse a rather more imperial spirit into the party; and to draw them a little away from the disputes among themselves to the great questions which affect the whole empire'. 'Undeveloped Conservatism', he argued, 'needs to be fostered into life.' Great interests were at stake 'equally dear to Catholics and Protestants', and Parnellites were the 'com-mon enemy'.[47] But although Northcote declined an invitation to lay a foundation stone for an Orange hall in Belfast, for fear of alienating 'a good many other friends, and driving them into a corner by parading an *entente cordiale* with the Orange Associa-tion', he found himself, as a stumping politician, obliged to reflect the opinion of his audience, which was, as he himself admitted, not to trust nationalists, not to trust the government, but to organise in their own defence.[48] Orangeism was, after all, 'the backbone of our party in the North of Ireland, and we must not discourage or alienate them'. In view of the attitude of the Home Rule Party, and the 'bribes recently offered in the Land Acts', it would be a 'fatal mistake to reject or throw cold water on their zeal for the constitution'. This led Northcote into some embarrassing and confusing situations, as when, for example, he was obliged to listen to a speech by the Rev. R. R. Kane, an Orangeman, who 'did not believe that the leaven of loyalty in the Roman Catholic community was large'. Northcote consoled himself with the reflection that his presence was 'the sort of use that a lightning-conductor is. It gave comparatively safe means of escape to the electric fluid with which the air was heavily charged. . . . It let off more steam than it generated; and a good deal of zeal was expended in cheering me which would otherwise have gone to breaking heads and discharg-ing revolvers.'[49]

When the Home Rule crisis broke, therefore, the problem of discovering a lightning-conductor became acute. The problem was that a distinctively Ulster Protestant outlook was being forged before 1886, and it was being forged as a kind of 'siege mentality', for those who were aware of the shifts and eddies of Irish and British politics saw that Ulster and Irish Protestantism was under threat from two directions: the nationalist one, seen in the border areas and in the Monaghan by-election; and the British one, that of indifference among Tories no less than Liberals to the growing fears of Irish Protestants. Treason was to be found in various places, not least in the seat of the imperial parliament in London. When the parliamentary reform legislation of 1884–5 was being drafted, Salisbury and Gladstone sought agreement over the redistribution of seats. Salisbury failed to ask for special protection for his Irish Tory allies in the new arrangements. The Redistribution Bill of December 1884 treated Ireland the same as Great Britain, disfranchising boroughs with populations of less than 15,000. Irish Conservatives protested that this cost them a disproportionately large number of seats, and they launched a campaign for the amendment of the bill, even making efforts to create a separate Irish Conservative party in the House of Commons.[50] Then came the Conservative flirtation with federalism as a means of settling the Irish constitutional issue. Fortunately for the Protestants of Ireland, Gladstone not only embraced Home Rule and a Parnellite alliance; he was, it seemed, caught in the act of doing so in a clandestine manner. Now Irish Protestants—or those of them who had been long suspecting a British betrayal of Ireland—could come out and declare themselves as Unionists, opponents of Home Rule, defenders of the Protestant cause, as they had been at the time of Derry, Aughrim, Enniskillen and the Boyne.

But this common cry of defiance and anxiety was one that necessarily had certain local and regional differences, reflecting the different distribution and social and economic background of the Protestant and Unionist people. There was the notable disparity of numbers, with southern Protestants existing as a small minority of the total population of the south, though with a certain class influence that their landlord leadership was able to invoke in the British Conservative Party. There was the strong concentration of Protestants in the north, but one divided into rural and urban groups, with rural classes only recently at odds over the land question. Then there were the various religious denominations, Anglican, Presbyterian, Methodist and an array of smaller sects. And the Ulster Protestant, with his tendency to follow his own line come what may, was an individual not easy to gather into, or keep within, a broad united political front. Northern and southern Unionists experienced different political fortunes when it came to general elections. The southern Unionists fielded candidates in fifty-two constituencies in the south in the general election of December 1885 and failed to win a single seat: the only Unionists in the House of Commons were the unopposed and sitting members for Dublin University.[51] In Ulster in the same election Unionists secured sixteen seats. But this performance was a disappointing one, reflecting the unprepared state of the Protestants. In East Belfast E. S. W. de Cobain, an Orangeman, successfully opposed Sir James Corry, a nominee of the Belfast Conservative Association; and in North Fermanagh William Redmond, brother of the future leader of the Irish Parliamentary Party, won because of poor Protestant organisation and what one Conservative called 'the abstention of many rotten renegade Protestants from voting'—a crude characterisation of Protestant unpreparedness and tenant farmer suspicion of landlord power.[52] Liberal Ulster was reluctant to break with the parent party in Great Britain, until the details of Gladstone's Home Rule Bill, made public in April 1886, provoked their outright opposition. Within a week of the bill's introduction Liberals and Conservatives gathered at a mass meeting in the Ulster Hall, Belfast, to protest against Home Rule. A few weeks later the Ulster Liberals, in a mood of sorrow as much as anger, but convinced that Gladstone was throwing over his most devoted followers by repealing the Union, formed a committee to publicise their objections to the bill; on 4 June 1886 this became the Ulster Liberal Unionist Committee.

There were many reasons for the formation of this united—if not altogether solid—Protestant front against Home Rule. Irish Conservatism had, of course, always been hostile to repeal of the Union, ever since the time of O'Connell; and this threat provided a basic rallying-point for all Protestants in time of danger. There were also, of course, political calculations of a more self-interested kind: landlords who had found their relationship with, and hold over, their tenants weakened by the land question had now the chance to reassert themselves in a common cause. There was the network provided by the Orange Order in Ulster, which had already sounded the alarm over the ambitions of Parnellites and Land Leaguers and had urged a settlement of the land question in the interests of Protestant solidarity (though not everyone approved of the Orange Order, not even in Ulster Protestant ranks). Above all, there was the great industrial city of Belfast, which provided the focus of Ulster Unionism and expressed that curious mixture of progressivism and traditionalism that was the hallmark of Unionism in the north.

The industrialisation of the north-east of Ireland was a regional phenomenon, comparable to that of the north-west of England and the west of Scotland. This process was led by the mechanisation of the linen industry and, after slow beginnings, the related manufacture of textile machinery. Iron, steel, shipbuilding and marine engineering became important in the half-century before 1914. This industrial development depended on cross-channel trade and overseas demand, and was vulnerable to recession anywhere in Great Britain or outside the United Kingdom. Nevertheless, Belfast could, and did, claim with pride that it was the foremost manufacturing and business city of Ireland. It became the chief port in the north, surpassing Londonderry and Newry; it soon surpassed Dublin in handling the largest share of Irish exports, and by 1835 was the leading port of Ireland. Between 1823 and 1896 the city's boundaries expanded, and its population increased eighteen-fold.[53] *Industries of Ireland*, published in 1891, proclaimed Belfast's message to the world:

> This great community presents in the annals of its latter-day advancement an exceptionally forcible illustration of the rapid development of civic and mercantile importance which may, and generally does, result from the efforts of an enterprising and intelligent population. . . . Very few cities of the present age owe more to the splendid public spirit of their residents in all spheres of life, or to the specially high ability of individual citizens who have devoted their energies and capacities to promoting the common welfare of the place and people.[54]

But there was one exceptional aspect of the 'great community' which had significant political as well as social implications: the fact that the vast bulk of Belfast, and indeed Ulster, businessmen were Protestants; and the industrial wealth of the north was in predominantly Protestant hands. This Protestant control of the economic life of the province was shown in the fact that in 1893 only 3 per cent of the Belfast Chamber of Commerce were Catholics. The fusion of business and political interests in the north was vital to the formation of Ulster Unionism. It offered sound economic arguments against Home Rule, for Ulster's prosperity was due to what the Chamber of Commerce called the 'security and protection' offered by the Union to the 'frugality and enterprise' of the people. It offered money to finance anti-Home Rule campaigns. And it posed the picture of a progressive and god-fearing community whose livelihood, as well as lives, were put at risk by the danger of rule by a rural-based, Rome-inspired Irish nationalist movement. It was true that in the province of Ulster as a whole Catholics were in a majority in Donegal, Cavan, Monaghan, Fermanagh and Tyrone. But the Protestants possessed what the Catholics did not: a solid heartland in Belfast; a series of spokes radiating out from the centre of the Belfast core, and radiating back in again to that powerful political (and potentially administrative) base.[55] Catholics in Ulster remained a kind of dispersed people, even a border people, for it always looked as if they were on the outside looking in, rather than (as the Protestants were) on the inside looking out. Parnell's border campaigns and his projected 'invasion' of Ulster only made the same point more effectively.

Within the industrial classes of Belfast, the 'core', there were significant distinctions between Catholics and Protestants. Workers were divided into those who earned high or low wages, and those in skilled and unskilled jobs. Trade unions were themselves divided into skilled and unskilled groups, with each concerned only to look after the interests of its own. Catholics were under-represented in skilled occupations; for example, in 1901, when they formed 24 per cent of the population of Belfast, Catholics occupied only 6 per cent of jobs as shipwrights, 10 per cent as engine and machine workers, 10 per cent as boilermakers, 15 per cent as carpenters, 27 per cent as bricklayers, and 12 per cent as plumbers. They represented one-half of the female linen-spinners, one-third of general labourers, and 41 per cent of dockers. This is not to say that the Protestant working class as a whole was an 'aristocracy of labour', but rather to illustrate that advantages were unequal. For example, the more skilled workers were able to take to trade union activity to maintain their privileged position against any worker. And it was amongst the unskilled working classes that sectarian conflict was most common.[56] In June 1886 a fight which began in the shipyards spread into uncontrollable rioting which killed 32 people and injured 371.[57]

The fear of Home Rule drove businessmen and landlords, tenants, farm labourers and industrial workers into the same political fold. In January 1889 a Mr R. MacGeagh of MacGeagh & MacLaine, flax, tow and yarn spinners of Killyleagh, County Down, wrote from Belfast to Hugh de Fellenberg Montgomery, a prominent local landlord, explaining that 'when the tenant farmers were struggling against a despotic and practically irresponsible landocracy, without representation, or the protection of the ballot', he had supported 'equal justice and fair play'. But now the secret ballot and the land acts had changed his mind; now he thought the landlords were the victims of 'the tenants' greed and dishonesty'; but above all he wanted the whole question settled 'for the peace and prosperity of the country'.[58] Among the churches, Presbyterians, Methodists and Episcopalians alike warned against the perils of Home Rule, the threat to religious freedom, the danger to Protestant and liberal education, the dire implications for their respective minorities, the desperate prospect of rendering life and property insecure. Southern Unionists tended to differ from their northern counterparts in that they sought, and to some extent enlisted, a residue of Catholic support for the Union; but they too could marshal formidable arguments against Home Rule, and their social status afforded them a special position in British Unionist circles.[59] From 1886 the alliance between British Conservatives and Irish Unionists seemed cemented and secure, and it was to remain so as long as Ireland was the key divisive issue in British politics.

For there could be no doubt that the initial Unionist resistance to Home Rule in Ireland depended to a large extent on British support. Colonel E. J. Saunderson, M.P. for North Armagh and the organiser of the Irish Unionists in the House of Commons, spoke of the need 'within the Orange Association' to enrol 'a body of men who would adopt a uniform and be drilled as far as the law would permit'.[60] But there was no organised armed resistance to Home Rule in Ireland in 1885–6, and indeed Saunderson's cautious rider 'as far as the law would permit' revealed the tentative nature of his proposal. This being the case, Irish Unionists had to look to the British parliament to defend them, as indeed in effect it did by rejecting the Home Rule Bill. But Irish Unionists were in no doubt that they needed to organise themselves as a group in the British Unionist Party as a whole in order to keep that party up to the mark; for other preoccupations were only too likely to invade the British political horizon, and then Unionists might have to look to themselves—as, eventually, they did.

This was a dilemma for the Unionists of Ireland, north and south. But they had to confront other difficulties as well. First there was the depressing fact that a small minority of Protestants came out in favour of Home Rule. The hero of Ulster tenant right (at least in his own eyes), S. C. McElroy, explained how the Route Tenants' Defence Association, at a meeting on 27 May 1886, 'sympathised' with Gladstone in his efforts to settle the question of Irish self-government and 'hailed with satisfaction' the possibility of a Liberal reconciliation on the basis of continued Irish representation in the imperial parliament.[61] An Irish Protestant Home Rule Association was formed, numbering some distinguished figures among its members, and with branches in the north and the south. Whatever the numerical inferiority of these Protestant Home Rulers, they offered Nationalists some useful propaganda in Great Britain.[62] Then there was the varied and heterogeneous nature of the Unionist movement as a whole, with its very different perspectives, north and south. At least northern Unionists had a strong constituency to which they might turn if British politics threatened to expose them to danger, whereas southern Unionists had to rely entirely on the force of reason. This caused some southern Unionists to use language that the average Ulster Unionist—or anyone else—might have found difficult to interpret: 'Mr Gladstone has undergone as many transformations as Proteus, as many transmigrations as Indur, as many stages of evolution as a protoplasmic cell.'[63] Irish Unionism as a whole encompassed intellectuals such as W. E. H. Lecky, a former Liberal sympathiser with moderate nationalist aspirations, and still something of a patriot, and the most excitable Orangeman from Portadown. Northern Unionists were more Rome-fixated, offering lurid pictures of the fate that lay in store for helpless Protestants, with the prospect of a repetition of the 1641 massacres. Southern Protestants, though they also feared the Catholic upsurge, liked to believe that the Irish Catholic was fundamentally a decent fellow, led astray by the moonlighters and rogues who rose like scum to the surface of Irish political life.[64]

Yet, even in the north, Unionists had always to offer more than a negative policy; they had to conciliate Protestant labourers as well as tenant farmers, workers as well as employers. They had to beware of tactical voting. But they were able to close ranks against what the *Northern Whig*, the mouthpiece of Ulster Liberal Unionism, called 'not a measure' but 'a revolution', a 'new system of government' which threatened to 'dissolve the community'. Ulster Protestants did not develop a 'nationalism' of their own, simply because they did not need to do so: the whole basis of their creed was a denial that nationalism was a genuine or tenable political belief. It was a sham and a fraud, since there had never been a united Irish nation in the first place. And from the 1880s until the 1912 Home Rule crisis it was possible for both northern and southern Unionists to maintain that loyalty was perfectly compatible with a wider British patriotism. Their claim was that Ireland was divided into 'loyal' and 'disloyal' Ireland. Home Rule would degrade their country to an inferior status 'below that of a colony', the *Northern Whig* warned. It added that 'Englishmen and Scotsmen are not foreigners in Ulster', nor were Ulstermen 'aliens' in Great Britain.[65]

The 'revolution' of 1886 was reflected in the general election of that year. Not only were the battle-lines more clearly drawn than ever before; the number of contested constituencies in Ireland (only 33 compared with 79 in 1885) revealed that a new kind of electoral system was emerging, one in which each side knew its own ground and would not contest ground that was clearly unwinnable. The electoral map told another story. In Ulster Unionists won 15 seats, Liberal Unionists 2, and Nationalists 16. In the rest of Ireland 2 Unionists and 68 Nationalists were elected.[66] This showed that the only Unionist strength lay in Ulster; it also demonstrated that this strength could be hotly contested by Nationalists. Unionists therefore could feel really safe in no part of Ireland. They knew that they had to see to their electoral machinery, their party organisation, their links with the Conservative Party in Great Britain. They knew that they could not relax their vigilance. And, what was even more alarming, they found that they had to sustain their ideology in quieter times, as the threat of Home Rule receded. After the excitement of 1886 this proved difficult, as it did after the scare over the second Home Rule Bill of 1893. Unionism was the direct product of a nationalist threat; if that threat were not sustained, Unionists feared they might lose all. They need not have worried, in that the political lines of Ulster (as of the rest of Ireland) had been drawn and would remain as firm contours right into the last quarter of the next century. But they were not as sure about this as the historian can be with the benefit of hindsight, and they did not feel the sense of security that might be suggested by such a fixed and durable realignment.

They did not feel secure, because the enemy within was not only the disloyal Catholic but also the backsliding Protestant. And the cause of backsliding—the land question—still had some potential to divert attention from the main issue. The Plan of Campaign organisers spared 'no effort' to force the reduction of rent and to abolish landlordism, wrote Thomas MacKnight; and he noted that there was 'undoubtedly some hesitation even among the northern tenant farmers who, as Unionists, had no sympathy with Irish nationalism'. But, MacKnight alleged, the day was saved by a powerful speech delivered by Joseph Chamberlain at Coleraine to the independent-minded tenant farmers. Chamberlain told his audience that the new land bill of 1885 had done much for the leaseholders; he regretted that it had not done more. But he announced that the revision of 'judicial rents' had been agreed to by the government on his suggestion and that of his fellow Liberal Unionists. This is an exaggeration; but Chamberlain struck a shrewd blow at the Nationalist hegemony of the land question as a political slogan. Chamberlain urged his listeners not to support land agitation. 'This is a more excellent way,' one Presbyterian farmer remarked to another. 'Ay, maun,' came the reply, 'sure this is better than the Land League.' In the general election of 1892 Gladstonian candidates said as much as possible about land purchase and as little as possible about Home Rule, but all were defeated.[67] This is not to say that the land issue was dead by then, or that landlord–tenant relations were now established on an entirely easy footing. But at least they were prevented from threatening the Protestant front against Home Rule. The question remained, however, whether this threat might return when Home Rule declined as the issue of the day.

Unionism as a united political front was based upon fear of nationalism: fear of nationalist tyranny, of nationalists supplanting Unionists as the leaders of industrial and economic life in the north, and of nationalists quite simply lording it over their former masters. In 1892, as in 1886, Unionists managed to create a united front, culminating in the Ulster Unionist Convention, a great anti-Home Rule demonstration at the Botanic Gardens, Belfast, on 17 June. Such a convention had been considered since 1886; the idea was taken up again in March 1892 as a Liberal election victory seemed likely, with the imminent possibility of another Home Rule Bill. The Ulster Convention made the usual appeal for unity amongst all classes of Ulster loyalists and encouraged the southern Unionists to organise a convention for themselves.[68] But it was not primarily concerned to distinguish Ulster from the rest of Ireland. Its speakers still referred to their pride in themselves as Irishmen, and still liked to describe Irish nationalists as their deluded fellow-countrymen. The gathering was eminently respectable, and it stressed order, progress and civilisation—all of which Home Rule placed in jeopardy. But the failure of the second Home Rule Bill, the split in the Home Rule Party, the agreeable spectacle of nationalists demonstrating their unfitness to govern themselves, let alone anyone else, all served to lower the temper in Unionist Ireland. In 1895 the chairman of the Unionist Clubs movement admitted that the country was 'worn out with politics'.[69]

Moreover, the land question returned to disrupt Unionist organisation in Ulster. In the early 1890s T. W. Russell, an opponent of Home Rule but a man of liberal temperament, led the movement among Ulster tenant farmers to demand compulsory purchase. This was opposed by landlords like Hugh de Fellenberg Montgomery, who held that landlords had already offered too high reductions of rent, and who argued that buying out the landlords would weaken the Protestant cause. Mutual suspicion between landlord and tenant, therefore, survived the great test of the Home Rule crises—a measure both of the potential of this threat for uniting disparate groups of Protestants and its inability to keep them firmly together once the threat receded.[70]

Irish Unionism, then, emerged from the period of its birth and baptism of fire with both its strengths and weaknesses revealed. It could call upon Protestant traditions, fear of popery, fear of nationalism, and build up an impressive opposition to Home Rule. It could even, it seemed, depend upon the support of a major British political party. Yet its early years had revealed, too, great problems for the movement. Its internal tensions, especially between landlord and tenant, had not been removed, but only temporarily set aside. It had no clear plan of what to do should the British political system no longer work to its advantage. Colonel Saunderson could threaten the use of force; but this, while it showed Unionist determination, was open to counter-attack. If force were to emerge, it could be denounced as dangerous and illegal activity; if it failed to emerge (as so far it had), it could be dismissed as merely a war of words. To paraphrase Patrick Pearse, the Orangeman, with or without a rifle, had not much to recommend him even as far as his own leadership was concerned, for some Ulster Unionists in the House of Commons were at pains to disavow any connection with Orangeism. The armed or unarmed Orangeman, moreover, found little sympathy or support from embarrassed British Conservatives, who doubted (in their calmer moments) how 'loyal' the Ulster Unionists were, and who deprecated any threat of force (Lord Randolph Churchill proving the exception that demonstrated the rule).[71] Ulster Unionists were left with the rather weak alternative put forward by a leading layman in the Irish Presbyterian Church, Thomas Sinclair, who declared in 1892 that 'We will have nothing to do with a Dublin parliament. If it be ever set up, we shall simply ignore its existence.'[72]

Southern Unionists had not even the doubtful choice of threatening to arm and defend themselves. Although they were formally united with their northern brethren through membership of the Irish Unionist Alliance (which had succeeded the Irish Loyal and Patriotic Union in 1891), it was clear that the Ulster Unionists were inclined to follow their own path when it came to resisting Home Rule. The real hope for Irish Unionists, north and south, lay not in a resolution of the Home Rule conflict—the outcome of which no man could foresee but all could fear—but in its falling into abeyance. Yet this offered no permanent security, either: for if Home Rule fell into the political doldrums, as it did after 1893, then it would be hard to keep Irish Protestants up to the mark, hard to convince them indeed that they must stick with Unionism through thick and thin. And since both the northern and southern branches of Unionism were essentially counter-movements, aimed at defending the status quo against the forces of revolution and rapine, their dependence on a wider Irish and British context is hardly surprising.

Irish Unionism and Irish nationalism, as they formulated themselves between 1870 and 1893, bore many resemblances to each other. Both were rooted in deep and genuine historical tradition, based on legend, myth and experience. Both needed a national constitutional crisis to pull them together into a coherent whole. Both found that, without such a focal point, parochialism reasserted itself. Unionism and nationalism were alike too in that they were,

despite assertions to the contrary, genuinely popular and democratic movements, owing much of their power and organisation to
the more open, more public political world that was created
throughout the British Isles after 1868. Both were part of another
British political development: the role of religion in British national
identity. Both were buttressed by their respective churches. Both
adopted exclusive interpretations of what were, on paper at least,
broad and inclusive ideologies. Nationalists called for all Irishmen
to take their rightful place in the nation, yet used tactics and
language that rendered Protestant participation difficult, if not
impossible. Unionists spoke of the central place of liberty, freedom
of conscience and freedom of speech in their movement; yet they
were reluctant to extend this to the Roman Catholic. Nationalists
were, on the face of it, unconcerned about the Protestant's religious
faith—unlike Unionists, who held that the nationalist was in thrall
to Rome and slavery. But this difference was more apparent than
real, for the nationalist refusal to accept diverse traditions meant
that the Protestant tradition was regarded as hardly 'Irish' at all.
Both had significant regional differences which affected their
political outlook: southern nationalists could feel most relaxed,
owing to their local majority status; northern nationalists least
relaxed. Southern Protestants were much more obviously a minority than northern Protestants; but northern Protestants (outside
their obvious strongholds) held an uneasy position midway between the comfortable enjoyment of local majority status and an
uncomfortable consciousness that this might be converted into an
unacceptable minority role.

Neither nationalism nor Unionism attracted all their adherents in
equal degree of commitment. There were fervent followers, middle-
of-the-road supporters, fair-weather friends and occasional con-
formists—and even some dissidents, in the shape of Protestant
Home Rulers and covert Catholic Unionists. But it was hard for
anyone to break out of the fundamental divisions of Irish political
life, however much Protestant and Catholic might share common
ways of life, in the working-class streets of Belfast, in the farms of
County Antrim, in the shop or the public house. And even those
people who were hardly serious practitioners of their religion found
that, in time of crisis, it was the touchstone of their political beliefs;
indeed, it shaped their whole identity. It was even harder for
anyone from either section of the people to enter the minds of the

other, however sincerely he might try: both sides had their notion of what a good Protestant or a good Catholic was like.[73] In time of crisis such slender understanding as existed was exposed to intolerable pressures and melted away. The two decades after the crisis of the second Home Rule Bill in 1893 did not fundamentally alter those conditions of life in Ireland.

Conciliation and Conflict, 1892–1914

THE Parnellite split in 1891 fractured the pattern of Irish politics that had been constructed since 1870. The alliance of the Irish Parliamentary Party, the Roman Catholic Church and constitutional Fenianism in Ireland was damaged and discredited. This is not to say that nationalist politics, or politics of any kind, had been wiped out; nothing could be further from the truth, for nationalism retained its central Catholic character, and still depended on the Liberal Party for the grant of Home Rule. What was different was that one-man power, as T. M. Healy put it, was replaced by the powerlessness caused by the division of the Home Rule Party into three, and then four, segments: T. M. Healy's own group of anti-Parnellites, with its decidedly clerical flavour; John Redmond's Parnellites; John Dillon's following, which opposed Parnell at the split and constituted the bulk of the party; and then in 1897 a breakaway Parnellite faction which disagreed with Redmond on the possibilities of reunion with the anti-Parnellites. This left room only for local initiative. And the strategy of the Liberal alliance, constructed and then denounced by Parnell, was relegated to the background of British politics. With the retirement of Gladstone in March 1894 and his replacement by Rosebery, the Liberal Party lost much of its commitment to the Irish cause: as Rosebery himself put it (in a not altogether happy phrase), 'as there were many roads to Rome, there were many ways to Home Rule'; and he admitted that 'there has been for a long time no enthusiasm for any measure'.[1] Unionist predominance in British politics after 1886 and the powerful Unionist majority in the House of Lords also worked to keep Home Rule at a distance.

The question of the constitution, then, was not in the forefront of British politics; and this suited the British Unionist Party, which had maintained all along that Irish nationalism must not be pandered to when it demanded Home Rule, but could be satisfied, and indeed undermined, if a British government set out on the road to reform, treating Ireland as a part of the United Kingdom. Paradoxically, this meant treating Ireland very differently from the rest of the United Kingdom, for it obliged the party to evolve what was called 'constructive Unionism' and to devise policies that required, above all, state intervention. To deny that Ireland was different meant treating her as an anomaly; but Unionists had already embarked on that road when they extended the operation of the Ashbourne Act in 1885 by the advance of another £5 million for land purchase. In 1886 A. J. Balfour drew up another bill laying aside more money for land purchase, this time some £33 million.

The difficulty, as always, lay in the impact all this had on the British electorate. The parties were wont to make political capital out of the disagreeable fact that what was called 'British taxpayers' money' was being lavished on Ireland, that not particularly grateful recipient of British largesse.[2] The policy of 'killing Home Rule by kindness' involved killing it with money; and when Home Rule was dead as a political issue, it was even harder to convince the Unionist rank and file that they really needed to put themselves out for Ireland. Nevertheless, the Unionist leadership knew that it needed something more than a simple blank refusal on Home Rule; it had to be able to claim that it had an Irish policy, beyond the purely negative. What suited its book, therefore, was a policy which demonstrated that the Unionist Party stood for the Irish Union, would legislate to maintain it, but would not accord it too high a profile in British politics. Hence the Unionist ameliorative legislation in the shape of local government reform in 1892 and state aid for the less prosperous areas of the country, especially in the west of Ireland, which, however, did not prove an intolerable drain on the Treasury. At the same time the Unionists, especially under Balfour's Chief Secretaryship, showed themselves unflinching defenders of the constitution. This combination of firmness combined with constructiveness was about as good an Irish policy as the Unionists could evolve. It also enabled the party to maintain a neat balancing act between the Unionists and nationalists in Ireland, for, after all, the policy of constructive Unionism was supposed to call for equitable treatment for all Irishmen. An example of this policy in action was the 1898 reform of local government (which followed the ineffective 1892 measure). Balfour had incurred a rare all-Ireland outrage when it was revealed in a Financial Relations Report that Ireland had been overtaxed to the tune of £2,740,000 per annum. Balfour appealed to nationalists' goodwill in his reform of local government (which placed most local councils in Ireland firmly in nationalist hands) and to Unionists by his offer of a generous government subsidy of the rates—a measure which Horace Plunkett described as a 'purely English necessity'.[3]

This spectacle of Unionists and nationalists combining in their criticism of British financial arrangements revealed new possibilities in Irish politics in the decades after the Parnell split. It was not, of course, anything more than a temporary junction of forces against the mismanagement of Ireland, a grievance which Unionists could resent just as much as any nationalist. It was not, perhaps, anything more permanent than those occasions in the past when exasperation at British policy decisions produced resentment (as the disestablishment of the Church of Ireland did in 1869) and a Protestant reaction, which quickly evaporated when the mood passed—as pass it must. But it was symptomatic of an era when the weakness of nationalism and the lack of tension in Irish politics seemed to offer new opportunities for new political activity—even for activity that was not political—which would heal the deep divisions amongst the Irish people.

The fragmentation and weakness of the Irish Parliamentary Party discredited both the party and its methods, but it also seemed to some that it created a vacuum in Irish politics—indeed, a kind of vacuum in Irish life that might be filled by other, more fruitful and less divisive activity. In reality it had done nothing of the sort; it had merely driven Irish politics back into particularism and dissent. But for decades Irish writers had been told that politics must precede culture: that creative and artistic endeavour must be bent to political ends, or even suspended until the great political goal of independence had been attained. It was not surprising, then, that the collapse of Irish nationalist unity after 1891 should seem to offer literary men the chance to assert their art, but also to fashion a kind of cultural activity that would draw under its influence people to whom literature and the creative arts were of no importance whatsoever. This might seem, in retrospect, a futile idea: where was the audience for this movement? How could a land of tenant farmers and the like, of priests and Presbyterians, possibly respond to a movement which aimed at teaching them the values and virtues of fine literature?

But the Ireland of the turn of the century was a changing country; it was receptive to new moods and ideas—or at least some of it was. Ireland had evolved a middle class of a sort. Sons of publicans, shopkeepers, small farmers, policemen, civil servants were not, perhaps, anybody's ideal material for a revolution in the public mind; but they were a restless people, on the lookout for some means by which they could proclaim their identity and assert their independence of the dead hand of the Home Rule movement. Catholics were at last making real advances in the world: they had established, or were establishing, a kind of local ascendancy in municipal councils and in poor law guardianships in districts where they constituted a majority. The British parliament was legislating for Ireland on a regular basis; it was a British Unionist who declared that the policy of the government should be to 'obliterate and do away with all class distinctions'.[4]

But change produced insecurity, especially when that change was neither self-willed nor self-achieved, but continued to be paced and controlled and granted by British governments. Ireland in 1900 had formed, or was forming, a political elite, or a potential one, which (if Ireland were not under the Union, or at least had Home Rule) constituted a generation with every reasonable expectation of gaining political power. But the Home Rulers held that power, and the British mediated it, and the educated (or half-educated) Catholics of Ireland felt a double frustration.

This is not to say that, in some mechanistic way, a generation was 'ripe' for political mobilisation; rather, that there was a receptive audience for those who now sought to offer an opportunity to find new ways of expressing their sense of identity. They were both radical and conservative in temperament: radical, in that they disliked the sterile politics of Home Rule; conservative, in that they sought solace in an Ireland that might still be rescued from the levelling and homogenising influence of the modern world—which, in Irish terms, meant English influence. The potential for this mood to be turned into some form of activity, non-political in a narrow sense, but potentially highly political at heart, was demonstrated in the success of the Gaelic Athletic Association, founded in

November 1884 by Michael Cusack, which excluded from membership policemen, soldiers and other people associated with 'Britishness'; and that definition of 'Britishness' was extended to those who played 'foreign games', of which cricket was the most disgusting and extreme. The G.A.A. was essentially a rural movement, and, like all bodies which had a recreational function, it incurred the suspicion of the Catholic Church, ever alert to rivals in the field. But it offered a chance for people to cut a dash in the eyes of their neighbours; and it offered a chance too for its members and organisers to combine politics and athletics as an aspect of the 'perpetual war with England'. The G.A.A. vision of Ireland was of a country 'dotted all over with miniature armies of hurlers, bowlers, jumpers, weight-throwers, merry dancers and joyous singers'.[5] It is not surprising that such a movement, with its political orientation and vision, should attract the early attention of the Irish Republican Brotherhood.

The G.A.A. was, however, a clearly divisive movement with its stigmatising of 'non-Gaels' as unwanted foreign elements. The leaders who sought to tell the people of Ireland that they needed a new outlook after the failure of parliamentary politics had different motives. The dominant figure of what became known as the Irish literary renaissance was William Butler Yeats, whose creative talents and high ambitions for his country marked him out as the champion of a new sense of Irishness and a new and respected place for Ireland in the world. Yeats gathered around him a following whose names read like a portrait gallery of some of the most creative figures in Irish life at the turn of the century: Lady Gregory, George Moore, J. M. Synge. Yet this great line of eminent figures had an ancestry; and that ancestry offers a clue both to the breadth of its vision and to the fundamental reasons for its failure.

The ancestors of the literary renaissance were the rather unlikely figures of Thomas Davis, Sir Samuel Ferguson and Standish James O'Grady. Davis and Ferguson were very dissimilar in their talents, for while Davis was a publicist and a populariser, Ferguson was a scholarly and withdrawn figure. O'Grady was very much in the Davisite mould, with his heroic view of the Irish past and his determination to make it known to all men. But they all had in common their Protestantism, and their pride in their Protestantism; and while they had in one sense forsaken Protestantism as a religion, they had not abandoned their pride in the Protestant Irish tradition, and especially their belief that their people had made, and could again make, a valuable contribution to the life of Ireland. They believed that an Ireland without Protestant talents, and perhaps even Protestant leadership, would be a poorer place. They were non-sectarian; yet they had in their minds strong views about the necessity of saving what could still be saved of the Protestant tradition in Ireland, and in this sense they were self-consciously aware of the danger of the Anglican Protestant opting out of public life. As J. O. Hannay, the rector of Westport, and a talented novelist, put it, while the Roman Catholic Church was obtrusively raw and self-assertive, the Church of Ireland 'has turned its back deliberately, even ostentatiously, on the town. Within the locked gates that led to it the gravel is smoothly raked and the grass on the graves trim and tidy.'[6] This expressed symbolically the withdrawal of Anglicanism from its proper role in modern Ireland.

Hannay, like Sir Samuel Ferguson and the vast bulk of Irish Anglicans, was a Unionist in politics. O'Grady was a kind of eccentric Disraelian romantic Conservative. Davis was also a conservative (with a small 'c'), but with a general sympathy for Irish political aspirations, though deeply suspicious of those aspirations as expressed in the dark Catholic depths of O'Connellism. Yeats, for his part, was broadly in sympathy with the nationalist ideal, and sought to play a part in the celebrations to mark the centenary of the 1798 rising. But Yeats's guiding theme was 'unity': a literary revival would be based upon Ireland, and its writers would explore Irish themes and characteristics; but they would do so in the English language, and with a lively sense of the place of Ireland in the mainstream of European culture. In retrospect, this seems an ambition quite impossible of achievement, but it did not appear so at the time. Yeats was prepared to go down to the market-place, to speak to ordinary people, to publicise the cause, and to tell Irishmen that they deserved respect in the world. He insisted that they had a past, not to hate and despise and quarrel over, but to be proud of. He inspired popular versions of his literary creativity, and he encouraged by his example minor talent as well as major. But the limitations, as well as the extent, of his success were revealed when Yeats gave a lecture to the National Literary Society in Dublin in May 1893. He appealed for an Irish literature free from political rhetoric and insularity and yet unmistakably Irish. The chairman, Fr J. F. Hogan, replied that

> They should pay all possible honour to those who were distinguished in literature in Ireland in the past, especially to those who were faithful to the country (*applause*). Speaking of the important part which literature played in other countries, he said that, when Hungary was making a struggle for national independence, similar to that which they were making in Ireland, they had three literary men who did more, perhaps, for their country than any three generals who led the army to battle (*applause*).[7]

This was not quite what Yeats had in mind, but he bore with it because it was a means of enlisting support for his grand design; the price would be paid later in the riots over the production of Synge's *Playboy of the Western World* in the literary theatre.

What Yeats's literary movement did, in political and social terms, was to set a series of ramps against which Irish nationalist ideas dashed themselves and revealed their underlying character. This was not obvious in the early days of the revival, for the revival did convince many literary observers in England that indeed something exciting was happening in Ireland, and that the nation was not composed of buffoons and agitators. But pride came before a fall; and the fall came in the storms that beset the literary theatre after its foundation in May 1899. The distinctive style of the theatre, its development of a special literary medium, was lost on an audience which could not accept the theatre's exploratory and innovative view of Irish life. For the revival was a kind of fault-line that exposed the depths and nature of nationalist sentiment: Irish nationalism emphasised the piety of the Irish people (as against the impiety of their English masters); the nobility of the Irish peasant (in contrast to the mean and base slum-dwellers of the industrial cities of England); the beauty of the Irish language (in contrast to the cockney slang of the so-called great imperial metropolis, London).[8]

This, in turn, threw light on the Irish Catholic predicament at the turn of the century. When James Joyce wrote of Dublin as the 'centre of paralysis', he hoped to help it break out of that paralysis, by devising an artistic principle, a form of art which would heal a broken culture, or at least encourage it to mend itself. That would play an important part in the process of uncovering a new life (instead of searching for an old one, instead of reinventing a failed past). The Irish must accept themselves, not as a heroic people, but as a small people, who nevertheless deserved their respected place in the world. They needed a 'small light', not a blinding illumination.[9] How was the anglicised, Catholic, educated middle-class man to find a role in the modern world—at least, in his own part of that world, where the dead hand of English rule and Catholic education held him pinioned to his bitter past? Joyce did not answer these questions, but later generations may appreciate their importance. For Joyce wanted to prevent his fellow-countrymen from pursuing the futile roads of excess of heroism and obsession with the past. His modern, democratic style was a breath of fresh air in the Ireland of his day—in a country of old men, and, what was worse, political and religious old men.

Joyce knew his people in a way that Yeats never did and never could; for they were not Yeats's people, however much he plunged into absurd expressions like 'West Briton' to describe anyone who opposed his vision of an Irish culture.[10] But Yeats did tap a reservoir of feeling: that of people of modest means but intellectual aspirations, or at least the aspiration to show that they were a people entitled to respect and position in their country. The most typical figures in these new movements were the schoolteacher, a man possessed of book-learning and usually of strong nationalist inclination, and the clerk, educated (up to a point) and anxious to play a role in political life, a role which both the Irish Parliamentary Party and his own special status as a government official denied him.[11] It was to such people that Douglas Hyde appealed in the Gaelic League, which he helped to found in 1893 with the avowed object of 'de-anglicising Ireland'. And yet Hyde too stood in that same Protestant tradition as Davis, Ferguson, O'Grady and Yeats, and, like them, sought to fight a last rearguard action for his people, the Anglo-Irish as they were now called, who could yet give Ireland the cultural leadership from which democratic politics excluded them.

The Gaelic League was, ostensibly, a non-political movement, and, like the literary movement, it enlisted some Protestant and Unionist interest in its early days. This is not as odd as it might seem; for, after all, Ferguson had been a Unionist (and Davis a conservative), and both had hoped to use culture as a substitute for politics: to set aside politics, with their divisive ways, and encourage all Irishmen of whatever political persuasion to take pride in, and unite on, their common (and distant) past. It remained a delicate issue about when that past ceased to be common—hence the longer ago it was, the better. Hyde disliked both Protestant and Catholic behaviour in the Ireland of his day. The Catholic was, as he put it, 'crawling to social position'; the Protestant was refusing to concern himself with the wrongs of his nation;[12] both needed a vision for the future, which could be culled from a vision of the past. The idea of the Gaelic League was to revive the Irish language, but not only for linguistic reasons: the language would be a vehicle for a cultural remoulding of Ireland, one in which a whole way of life and thought would be re-created. These radical developments would not spring from any antiquarian concern, but would have as their purpose the creation of a modern country, able to take its place among the nations of the world.[13] The cultural revival would create an 'Irish race', a race which would assimilate all exotic elements, including the 'Saxon' population of the north. Hyde was a firm believer in the racial theories prevalent at the end of the nineteenth century, much to the disgust of Eoin Mac Néill, a co-founder of the Gaelic League, but an Ulster Catholic with, perhaps, more realism in his makeup. But the ideas of the southern Protestant Irishman, Hyde, won more acceptance than those of the Catholic Ulsterman, Mac Néill; and the League accordingly attracted those who believed that the Gaelic language was really a Catholic possession, and that the League stood for the reassertion of the Irish Catholic race against its enemies, both without and within. The new Ireland would be 'Gaelic at the core'.[14]

Hyde had not turned his coat. He hoped to set aside the great divisive force, religion, that branded him and his kind as a 'garrison'; instead he would substitute the concept of race, which would include his own people in an Irish identity. His was the response of a Protestant people whose political space was denied to them, since in an age of counting heads the majority in the island of Ireland must have its way, politically and democratically, sooner or later. Both the literary revival and the Gaelic League were, at another level, the last stand of Protestant—or rather of southern

Protestant—Ireland. One leading Church of Ireland Gaelic Leaguer, T. W. Rolleston, wrote in 1905 that Irish politics

> have been like everything else absorbed into the church—everything else but one thing, the Gaelic League. The league represents the last effort of the Irish spirit for national and personal independence. The church began by opposing it—it is now, as usual, doing its utmost to absorb it.[15]

Unfortunately for Rolleston and those who thought like him, the Gaelic League soon went the same way as other organisations. In 1904 the *Church of Ireland Gazette* denounced the League; a year later it advocated a separate Protestant branch, which indeed was founded.[16] In 1906 J. O. Hannay was excluded by the parish priest of Tuam from being elected to the *feis* committee on the grounds that his novels had attacked 'Catholics and Irishmen as such'[17]—in itself a most revealing phrase.

The consequences of these movements were not immediately apparent. But they did inspire a debate about the nature of Irish identity—a debate which the Irish Parliamentary Party would never have bothered to initiate. And that debate inspired the foundation of a new political movement which, like the cultural movements of the day, sought a means of reconciling the divided people of Ireland. The Home Rule Party had been, in fact if not in name, a party for the Catholic, even though the tenant right movement was, of course, by no means a purely Catholic cause. But it was clear that the Catholic Church saw the party as a vehicle for promoting Catholic interests, especially in the educational field; and the party's rhetoric was one based on an essentially Catholic view of Irish history. Now, however, a new idea was floated, one which owed its inspiration to the debate of the 1890s. That movement, later dubbed 'Sinn Féin', was in its inception not a political party at all, but a loose grouping of literary societies, clubs, individuals, journalists, and political strays. Its founder, Arthur Griffith, was himself a journalist and a somewhat eclectic ideologue. He admired the Protestant patriots of the eighteenth century; he wanted to restore the Gaelic language and culture; he wanted a modern industrial state. Griffith, whose policy for Ireland was comprehensively enunciated in 1905, stood for a federation of advanced nationalist groups, with 'the utmost liberty of action'; this action, however, was essentially that of self-help and inner regeneration—hence the name Sinn Féin ('Ourselves'). He admired Belfast as an industrial city and a model for the rest of Ireland, and he had a high regard for the Presbyterian radicals of 1798. Yet a Catholic he was, and a Catholic he remained—as he revealed in his thin-skinned response to Protestant anger at the papal *Ne temere* decree of 1907 (which required from the parents in a mixed marriage an undertaking that the children would be brought up exclusively in the Roman Catholic faith). And this was symptomatic of a contradiction at the heart of his movement.[18]

Sinn Féin stood (allegedly) for all Irishmen, yet only for a particular version of Irish history and politics, the nationalist one. Like the Home Rulers, Griffith asked Protestants to accept the nationalist idea of the past, present and future; indeed, he asked them to accept rather more, in that he believed in economic protectionism, which was alarming to the Protestant business classes of the north. And when Sinn Féin finally decided to test its electoral strength in a by-election in 1908, it did so in a nationalist constituency, not a Unionist one: an obviously sensible decision, provided it was taken for granted—as it was—that no nationalist stood much of a chance of winning Unionist votes. Sinn Féin polled 1,157 votes to the Irish Parliamentary Party's 3,103, a highly respectable performance. But this was due in large part to the fact that its candidate was a former Home Rule M.P. and therefore had a local following. Sinn Féin was short of money, organisation, followers and numbers; and yet in its general political and cultural approach it had something in common with the constructive and exciting movements of the day. Its oppositional role meant that it did not yet have to confront the contradictions that faced any would-be comprehensive movement in Ireland.

But its beginnings, however modest, were part of that general—if only temporary—softening of the rigidity of Irish politics at the turn of the century. For there were other symptoms as well. In particular, recent developments associated with the land question seemed to reveal that an issue which had deeply divided classes as well as religions in Ireland could be settled round a table, on the basis of give and take. This did not seem likely in 1898, when the question was revived in a serious form for the first time since the Plan of Campaign. At first it seemed like a re-run of the agitation that had occasioned the foundation of the Land League in 1879: a distressed west of Ireland, a local agitation, and then a national agitation given organisation and control by a well-managed political leadership—in 1898 the United Irish League, founded by William O'Brien. O'Brien persisted in describing the landlords as foreigners and descendants of Cromwell, as against Redmond's view that they must be welcomed as 'Irishmen . . . men of education and ability'.[19] But the western agitation was not specifically against landlords, but against 'graziers' or 'ranchers', who were more likely to be Catholics (and even members of the priesthood). The United Irish League was not, in the event, the kind of nationwide movement that the Land League had been at its peak; but it did revitalise nationalist politics, and it pushed the Parnellites, under Redmond, and the anti-Parnellites towards a rapprochement, if not yet a reunion. It was not, however, a force that could unite all Irishmen, and any possibility that Irish Parliamentary Party nationalism or United Irish League nationalism might do so was dashed in the wave of an almost hysterical anti-British feeling invoked by the Boer War, which broke out in October 1899. In a sense this recrudesence of 'disloyalism' was only to be expected; the party had not had a good grudge nor the pleasure of a strong sense of self-righteousness at the expense of the British for a very long time; but the virulence of the campaign, the establishment of 'Transvaal committees' in Ireland to mobilise support for the Boers, who were depicted as fellow-sufferers under British domination, was at odds with Redmond's declared and genuine hope that his party might yet do better than Parnell's and reconcile all Irishmen 'in a movement in which all classes and creeds of Irishmen could unite'.[20]

The United Irish League, whatever its shortcomings, showed that a popular cause and a determined leadership could act as a threat to the still estranged factions of parliamentarianism. The final push was given when it became plain to both Redmond and Dillon that the League was not going to go away, that it had established itself firmly in certain areas, and that if it were not to meet with a positive response, then it might threaten the parliamentary party's leadership of nationalist Ireland. It was this which finally drove the warring factions into meeting on 30 January 1900 in the House of Commons to reunite the party. The upshot of some hard and complex bargaining was the election of John Redmond as the leader of the reunited party.[21] However, there remained one piece of unfinished business for the party, and in particular for its leader: the question of its relationship to the United Irish League.

This was to be tested in the as yet great unsolved question of Ireland—the land question. This question was by now coming to be seen for what it really was: not just a question of who owned the land, but of how the land could be best used to promote prosperity. The difficulty was that in Irish nationalist politics it was always hard not to look backwards to the great figures of the past and their actions in order to chart the way forward to the future. The United Irish League had risen on agitation and propaganda; but it was after 1900 an agent of political and electoral organisation, as the police carefully noted.[22] Since the purpose of constitutional nationalist politics was above all to maintain a united front, there was little chance of an imaginative, let alone radical, approach to the Irish land question from that quarter. And indeed, such imaginative thinking as there was came from a rather unexpected source: Protestants and Unionists.

This took two forms. One was an attempt to get down to the economic and organisational difficulties of Irish agriculture and build a spirit of co-operation which would permeate the political and social sphere. Just as the cultural revival would act (it was hoped) as an alternative to political action, transcending it and creating a new and genuinely national spirit, so economic efforts would promote not only scientific agriculture but self-help and a sense of community among all Irishmen. The economic equivalent of W. B. Yeats was Horace Plunkett, a young Protestant and Unionist landlord, who was deeply impressed by the agricultural methods of Denmark. Plunkett founded the Irish Agricultural Organisation Society in 1889. His work was viewed with favour by the government, and the Conservative administration established a Department of Agriculture to further his efforts. Plunkett won support from priest and parson, Catholic and Protestant, northerner and southerner. His slogan was 'Better farming, Better business, Better living',[23] which reflected his desire to promote not only prosperity but self-reliance and self-respect in the Irish countryside.

Plunkett, though a Unionist M.P. for South Dublin, was convinced that his politics need not stand in the way of his patriotism. Indeed, his apparently mundane approach to Irish politics attracted those, like George Russell (AE), who saw in it a kind of primitive Celtic revival, with rural co-operation representing a return to an old Celtic social order, a kind of Celtic communalistic civilisation.

Russell undertook to edit Plunkett's journal, the *Irish Homestead*, from 1905, and he sought to extend the scope of the movement to include the establishment of local libraries as well as modern dairies and marketing boards. The *Irish Homestead* published work produced by literary revival writers, thus neatly making the connection between the two and symbolising the new spirit of co-operation that seemed to be abroad.[24] That spirit was apparent too in the second approach to the land question, again coming from a Protestant and Unionist (and landlord) source. In 1902 an Irish landlord, Captain John Shawe-Taylor, publicly proposed that a conference should be called consisting of representatives of landlord and tenant, to settle their outstanding differences through a process of negotiation. This was not a disinterested call: landlordism in Ireland was losing any economic attraction it might have formerly possessed; and there was always the possible hidden bonus of a settlement of the land question undermining the force of the Home Rule movement—as John Dillon, for his part, feared it would. Landlord control over tenants was, after all, destroyed; local government had been handed over to democratic control; and when in December 1902 a Land Conference met, presided over by Lord Dunraven, agreement was reached which became embodied in a new land act in 1903, passed by the Unionist government and steered through the house by George Wyndham. The act was defective, and had to be revised by the Liberal government in 1909; but it established land purchase as the final solution of the land question.[25]

The question now was whether or not that spirit of co-operation, in rural economic organisation, in the Irish Land Conference, could be extended in the wider sphere. There were—or it seemed there were—all sorts of reasons to believe that such might be the case. One of the leading supporters of the thrust for a settlement of the land question was T. W. Russell, the Unionist M.P. for South Tyrone. Russell's Protestant credentials were impeccable, and they were made even more so by William O'Brien's newspaper, the *Irish People*, describing him as one of the 'bigots of South Tyrone'.[26] But Russell believed firmly that land purchase was the only ultimate solution to the land question; and his advocacy of that cause, together with his firm commitment to the Union, made him the doyen of radical Ulster Liberal Unionists. Ulster tenant farmers were as much concerned about the working out of British land legislation as anyone else. They had found enough satisfaction in this legislation to prevent (what was never likely anyway) their making a common cause with nationalism, or even with the Land League and the United Irish League. But they had their grievances, notably the relative hardship suffered by those who still paid rents, as against those who had concluded purchase agreements with their landlords; and they felt that landlords were dragging their heels, and needed statutory compulsion to sell. These grievances surfaced during periods when Home Rule posed no immediate threat; and the early twentieth century was just such a period. In this climate maverick Unionism could make mischief; and Russellite candidates began to contest by-elections, defeating the official Unionist candidate in East Down in 1902, followed by another victory in North Fermanagh in 1903.[27]

But once again the limits of these remarkable developments were soon exposed. It was hard for a Unionist to appropriate votes from a fellow-Unionist; it was even harder for him if he was openly given Nationalist votes, as Russell was by John Redmond in 1902, for this linked him with what were called 'seditious and treasonable ends'. In these circumstances the last thing that Russell needed was a Home Rule scare; but this was what he got when in 1904 Lord Dunraven and the Under-Secretary at Dublin Castle, Sir Antony MacDonnell, proposed a scheme of devolution which would establish a central Irish council exercising a measure of local autonomy. This form of devolution had been acceptable to Joseph Chamberlain, amongst other leading Unionists, as an alternative to Home Rule. But to the Irish Unionists as a whole it smacked of intrigue, desertion and—that most emotive of loyalist words—'betrayal'. The controversy that ensued revealed the Irish Unionists in their least favourable light, and A. J. Balfour, in particular, was deeply offended at Unionist hounding of George Wyndham in what he dismissed as a 'silly and sordid controversy'.[28] But it enabled the Ulster Unionists, in particular, to achieve two important goals; they reorganised their province-wide machinery and created the Ulster Unionist Council; and they appealed to pan-Protestantism, branding 'Russellism' as the kind of insidious internal threat of which the devolution crisis was an external manifestation. The Ulster Unionist Council, as it was formally called in March 1905, was a democratic body. Its central council consisted of 200 representatives, 100 nominated by local Unionist associations, 50 by the Orange Order, and the remaining 50 divided among M.P.s, peers and *ex-officio* members. The organisation was in fact controlled by a few landowners and professional businessmen, and it represented that juncture of rural and urban forces that helped maintain the unity of Ulster Unionism in a region notorious for its contrary politics.[29]

Contrary politics were not, of course, confined to rural Ulster in the early twentieth century. The breathing-space afforded to Irish politics by the collapse of the Home Rule cause, and its continued frustration, saw the emergence of yet more political renegades, disturbing loyalist slumbers with their populist and iconoclastic rhetoric. Now the threat came from Trades Council candidates, six of whom were returned at the Belfast municipal election of 1897, and with further Labour victories in the parliamentary general election of 1906 and 1910.[30] Equally vexing to Unionism was the challenge of the Belfast Protestant Association, which in 1902 unveiled its charismatic leader, Tom Sloan, a shipyard worker and master of an Orange lodge. Sloan had the temerity to heckle Colonel Saunderson at a Twelfth demonstration, and he later contested a by-election in South Belfast as an independent, defeating the official Unionist candidate by 3,795 to 2,969 votes. His expulsion from the Orange Order prompted him to found the Independent Orange Order in 1903, which offered a combination of anti-nationalism and anti-establishment politics. In the 1906 general election Sloan and an Ulster labour leader, William Wallace, made a pact with the Nationalist political boss of west Belfast, Joseph Devlin, to co-operate on labour issues. Wallace was uneasy about this agreement, but it probably brought about cross-sectarian voting.[31] In the same general election R. G. Glendinning, a Baptist linen manufacturer of Belfast, won the North Antrim seat; and this again was an area where the Independent Orange Order counted its strength and offered a platform for voters who were disillusioned with the performance of their sitting Unionist candidate, William Moore (ironically, a leader of the Unionist anti-devolution scare campaign). The point, however, remained that these challenges to Unionism were most effective when they were made by Unionists, that is by those whose Protestant and constitutional principles were impeccable. Russell, now under the cloud of Nationalist support, found that his candidates fared badly in the general election of 1906; whereas the Presbyterian farmers of North Antrim were offered the choice of an anti-official Unionist who nonetheless was politically sound; moreover, Glendinning had no Nationalist opponent to take the Catholic vote (some of which he must have picked up himself on anti-establishment-Unionist grounds).[32]

All this micro-political behaviour depended on the macro-political context. The general election of 1906 saw the return of a Liberal government to power with a massive parliamentary majority. But this safe majority meant that the Liberals were able to postpone Home Rule as any kind of major political issue; and their candidates were noticeably reticent on the subject when on the stump. And Liberal legislation, though contentious in some respects, was not the kind of threat to the status quo that would harden the political contours of Ireland into the mould of 1886 and 1893. Legislation was passed to improve housing in Ireland, both urban and rural; and the financial provisions of the 1903 Land Act were amended. Wyndham's act had laid it down that the ratepayers should meet any financial shortcomings arising from land purchase, but the Liberal Chief Secretary, Augustine Birrell, sought to persuade the Treasury that they, the ratepayers, could not meet this burden. His bill revised the finances of the land purchase scheme, provided for compulsory purchase orders against reluctant land-lords in the congested western districts, and gave coercive power to the Land Commission for the first time.[33]

Even the government's most controversial (in Unionist eyes) legislation, the Irish Universities Act of 1908, proved a useful, if politically motivated, settlement of the Catholic Church's desire to control university education among its flock. The Royal University was abolished and two new universities established in its place: the National University of Ireland, with colleges at Dublin, Cork and Galway, and the Queen's University of Belfast. This aroused the hostility of Ulster Unionists against what they called a scheme for 'satisfying the monstrous demands of the Roman Hierarchy';[34] but there was some respect for Catholic claims from Sir Edward Carson, now emerging as a rising hope of Irish Unionism, and a man who appreciated the importance of denominational education to Catholic thinking.

But one prospective piece of Liberal legislation revealed the fragility of Irish politics in the period preceding the third Home Rule Bill. In 1907 the government outlined an Irish Council Bill which would give Ireland a partly nominated but mainly elected

council with control over eight departments of the Irish administration, subject to the Lord Lieutenant's veto. Redmond was
originally receptive to the bill, as 'no bar, but a help and a further
advance, to complete Home Rule'; and the ensuing Unionist fury
was, as always, useful ammunition for Nationalist support of
British legislation. But the opposition in the country mounted, and
the cry arose that nothing short of the full measure of Home Rule
would suffice. Redmond opposed the bill at a convention called in
May 1907, and nationalist Ireland affirmed the policy that it had
stood by since the 1880s: no surrender.[35]

This political furore, however, only expressed what observers
noted in the Ireland of the new century: that while much seemed to
have altered, and some things indeed had altered, yet much
remained the same—or at least that deep division between the
people of Ireland remained fundamentally unaltered, in spite of all
that had been attempted by British legislation, constructive Unionism, literary and Gaelic movements, Unionist mavericks, Russell-
ites, trade unionists, and all the rest of them. Ireland, wrote the
French observer Louis Paul-Dubois, was 'full of rancour for the
past, and of distrust for the future, and she cherishes the hope and
ambition of revenge'.[36] This may have been an exaggeration; but
there were signs of the times that augured ill for the future of the
country, should matters ever come again to a Home Rule crisis of a
serious sort.

These symptoms ranged from the private to the public life of the
Irish people. In 1908 the *Ne temere* decree (which had excited
Arthur Griffith into revealing his Catholic heart) provoked a major
storm, as it was held responsible for a Belfast Catholic husband's
abandonment of his Presbyterian wife. At a Presbyterian convention held in Belfast in February 1912 it was declared that

> Under Home Rule . . . the parliament and executive alike are
> certain to be controlled by a majority subject to the direction of
> the *Ne temere* and *Motu proprio* decrees against whose domi-
> nation all safeguards designed for the protection of a Protestant
> minority . . . would be wholly useless.[37]

Making allowance for the kind of menacing rhetoric typical of such
occasions, it yet remained true that the connection between Catholicity and Irishness, and indeed between Catholicity and moral
earnestness, were characteristic of early twentieth-century Ireland.

There was even a proposal, made by some clergy, that darkest Ulster was an appropriate place for missionary conversion.[38] Catholic magazines were published to counter English and non-Catholic publications. D. P. Moran, a leading journalist and Gaelic enthusiast, only said what many thought when he wrote that the Irish nation was *de facto* Catholic, and that Protestants must accept the ideals of the majority. Absorption was therefore necessary, or, failing that, partition, leaving the 'Orangemen and their friends in their north-east corner'.[39]

Partition, then, was first put forward as a solution to the problem of Irish Catholic nationhood by a Gaelic, Catholic and nationalist writer. But at least Moran could always be relied upon for his mordant style and harsh uncompromising honesty. It was harder to see in what direction the official guardians of the Irish nation, the Irish Parliamentary Party, were going. Still paying lip-service to the idea of a single nation, as they had done since 1886, they managed to combine that with a general denunciation of the Protestant role in the tragic nationalist and Catholic past. The mild Sir Horace Plunkett found his creameries an object of nationalist hatred: as the nationalists of Rathkeale put it, 'Every pound of butter made in this creamery must be made on nationalist principles, or it shan't be made at all.'[40] John Dillon was equally forthright: in 1900, when Plunkett was defeated in his Dublin constituency, Dillon exploited the split in Unionist ranks that caused Plunkett's downfall by declaring that

> A vote for Mr Plunkett would mean a vote for Mr Chamberlain and Lord Salisbury, a vote for Dublin Castle, and a vote for Irish landlordism with all its bloody records in the processes of the extermination of the nation.[41]

To be fair, Plunkett compounded his Protestantism when in his book, *Ireland in the New Century*, published in 1904, he included (against his friends' advice) a section on the Roman Catholic Church, in which he stated that the backwardness and unprogressiveness of the Irish Catholics was largely responsible for Ireland's lack of modernisation. This point occupied only four pages of his book; but the strong reaction to it was typical of the thin-skinned and sensitive nature of Catholicism when Protestants revealed their—in this case quite unconscious—native prejudices. [42]

The Irish Parliamentary Party further compromised its national-ism—or vindicated it, depending on the point of view—when it took under its wing a new, northern-based political organisation, the Ancient Order of Hibernians. Ulster Catholics had during the 1880s transferred their political allegiance from the Liberals to the Home Rule Party. But Catholic Ulster was, and remained, a remote outpost of nationalism, a still rather unknown territory, which required 'invasion'. Now, however, Ulster nationalists began to organise for themselves. The focus of their activity was the A.O.H., a combination of friendly society and defender of Ulster Catholic interests. The A.O.H.'s symbols were the exact reverse of those of the Orangemen: King James, the green, shamrocks and Catholic martyrs, as against King William, the orange lily, masonic symbols and the Bible. The A.O.H. was given a vital political role by Joseph Devlin, a man of generous instincts with a lively awareness of the shared poverty of the Belfast working classes, whatever their religious affiliation, but also a born politician who saw his main task as that of mobilising and delivering the Catholic vote. Certainly the northern Catholic needed some input into an essentially southern-run parliamentary movement; and the Home Rulers saw what they could gain from this, even if they did not like the overtly sectarian base of the A.O.H. (covert sectarianism was more acceptable). Redmond, Dillon and Thomas Kettle made the necessary obeisance to the A.O.H.; and Dillon in particular, never a man to refuse an obvious political opportunity, however short-sighted, warmly welcomed the A.O.H. as 'a body of men for whom, I confess, I have the greatest regard'.

The A.O.H. claimed as its price for organising the Ulster nationalist vote a place in the Irish Parliamentary Party's organisa-tion. A.O.H. representation was increased at the party's national convention from 24 in 1903 to 417 in 1909, out of a total of about 2,500–3,000 delegates. The A.O.H. showed its usefulness when in 1913 it came to the aid of William Martin Murphy, then embroiled with the Dublin tram workers' strike, and acted as a new manifesta-tion of 'physical force' nationalism (breaking strikers' heads). It also broke up meetings of William O'Brien's nationalists, the All-for-Ireland League, and turned its attention to Sinn Féin as well. The deployment of members of the A.O.H. as security guards was useful to the Irish Parliamentary Party, but it was hardly a recommendation for conciliation or reasonableness.[43]

Arthur Griffith contemplated the state of Ireland with some alarm when in 1909 he editorialised in his newspaper, *Sinn Féin*, that the guiding light of Irish political life was, and always had been 'Be my brother or I'll kill you'. Men such as William O'Brien, who stood for a settlement by conference of the Home Rule issue rather than an imposed one, or Horace Plunkett were 'either today in retirement or in semi-retirement from public life because the field is closed against them by party prejudice'. 'This', he added, 'is national folly.'[44]

But for the Home Rulers it was national triumph: a triumph which was demonstrated in the political crisis in Great Britain over the reform of the House of Lords in 1911. Redmond let it be known that he would offer the support of the Irish Party to the Liberals only if they agreed that once the Lords' veto was destroyed, then Home Rule would follow immediately. And the policy of reviving the Liberal alliance and making it work as it did—or nearly did—in 1886 was quickly vindicated in the party's fortunes in the general elections of January and December 1910. In January the party suffered some serious reverses, with eleven independent nationalists returned, seven of them followers of the All-for-Ireland League of William O'Brien; but by November it was clear that Redmond could rely on the Liberal pledge to go for the full measure of Home Rule. Redmond and his followers at last found themselves able to resurrect the strategy of Parnellism: to be 'the Dictator of England', as O'Brien put it (he added that this would also make Redmond the 'destroyer of Ireland'). In the second election of 1910 Redmondites performed much better, confident that they were about to break the boom that stood between themselves and Home Rule. And with the Parliament Act of 1911, and the destruction of the Lords' veto, the way was cleared for the triumph of constitutional nationalism.[45]

The introduction of the third Home Rule Bill in April 1912 all but stilled the cacophony of voices that had echoed through Ireland and Irish politics between 1892 and 1910. Now the old battle-lines were redrawn, only this time their redrawing moved them beyond Westminster, beyond the hustings, and into the battlefield of sectarian strife, armed men, and almost certainly civil war. Ulster Unionists had, since the devolution crisis of 1904–5, shown a suspicion of the motives even of their parliamentary supporters, the British Unionist Party. But their efforts to resist Home Rule by force of arms in 1886 and 1893 had been exposed as mere words, words without weapons to back them up. Now the Unionists in Ulster began to prepare themselves for resistance through the foundation of a drilled and disciplined people's army, the Ulster Volunteer Force. But this alone would not have been enough to place them in a favourable position against the Liberals and Home Rulers. They also needed British public and political support; they needed the support of a leader who carried weight in Great Britain as much as in Ireland: for armed resistance—if it came to actual fighting, to the shooting down of British troops on the streets of Ulster—would destroy the Unionists' political case and swing public sympathy, if not behind the Liberal government, then away from loyalists who killed the soldiers of the crown.

The political combination that steered the Ulster Unionists through the dangerous and uncharted seas of armed resistance was the partnership of James Craig and Sir Edward Carson, with the assistance, on the British Unionist side, of Andrew Bonar Law. The Craig–Carson combination has become so enshrined in Unionist hagiography that its unlikely nature hardly attracts comment. For while it is widely appreciated that Carson stood for a broader *Irish* Unionist tradition, and Craig for a more narrowly focused and localised *Ulster* Unionist resistance, it is still not clear why Ulster Unionists, always suspicious of outsiders, should have offered such devoted allegiance to Carson, whose background and outlook were those of the Protestant professional class of Dublin. Carson, moreover, had shown himself on frequent occasions a sympathetic defender of Catholic claims.

The combination of Craig, Carson and Bonar Law was, like all political alliances, dictated by a variety of motives and concerns. Craig was willing to look to the home front, and take care of the administration and organisation of Ulster Unionist resistance; he cared nothing for any other part of Ireland. Bonar Law wished to protect Unionist Ulster, but also to keep his party together on Ireland, for there were British Unionists who, as the crisis deepened, sought a means of escape, perhaps through making a federal Ireland or a federal United Kingdom. Carson wanted to save all Ireland for the Union, but he had a sense of realism, and he knew that he might have to compromise his Unionism if any part of Ireland was to be saved from Home Rule; and that part most likely to be saved was, of course, Unionist Ulster. Carson, once he made his solemn commitment to the Ulster Unionists, was not a man to desert their cause, however much it might in the end differ from his own. All this made the crisis over the Home Rule Bill a complex one; and the various abortive attempts made to reach some sort of compromise were difficult to achieve, not only because compromise in Irish politics was difficult, but also because the contending groups on the Unionist side had different ideas of what compromise meant in the first place.

This difficulty applied also to the Nationalist and Liberal alliance. Redmond had shown himself disposed to take the line of least resistance when it came to dealing with the rank and file of his following in Ireland. He was willling to listen to Dillon's advice that the importance of maintaining nationalist unity was, however short-sighted, preferable to jeopardising that unity for the sake of a rapprochement with northern or southern Unionists. There can be no doubt that he spoke as nationalist Ireland felt. He was aware of the vulnerability of the party's position should the Liberal government explore—as some of its senior cabinet members wished it to explore—the possibility of a compromise based on an exclusion of certain Ulster counties. But here again party politics came into the picture: Asquith knew that his party must tread warily when it came to suggesting compromise, for he had no reason to believe that the opposition would accept any offer he might make; and an offer, once made and refused, would undermine his own party's morale and jeopardise his relations with the Irish Parliamentary Party.[46]

It was easier, therefore, to let the Home Rule Bill proceed on its inevitable way through the House of Commons. The Ulster Unionists had, in their 'Solemn League and Covenant', signed by thousands on 28 September 1912, pledged themselves to resist 'by any means that might be found necessary' the imposition of Home Rule. But they were not as yet armed, and it was possible to dismiss their activities as a gigantic bluff. Carson in January 1913 moved an amendment to the government's bill, striking the whole of Ulster out of its jurisdiction; but this was essentially a tactical move to embarrass the government, for he still hoped to defeat Home Rule altogether. British Unionists stood firmly against Home Rule; but they were split on how far their opposition should go, whether or not they could support rebellion against the government, and with divergent views on what kind of Irish settlement might prove acceptable. Two weeks after the bill was approved by the Commons, in January 1913, it met its expected defeat in the Lords. Now an interval must elapse before it became law under the provisions of the Parliament Act.

But even while the bill was being debated in the Commons it was clear that the crisis was having an effect on nationalist as well as Unionist Ireland. The Home Rulers had always spoken of the possibility, even certainty, of a 'union of hearts', if only England would fulfil her tryst with destiny and grant Ireland the self-government she had sought for so long.[47] But the militancy of Ulster Unionists excited attention among nationalists, who feared that the Liberal government might not keep faith, and who felt an admiration for the men of the north, with their defiant response to a British government (even though that government was engaged in passing a Home Rule Bill).

While nationalists watched and wondered at Unionist militancy Ireland slipped further into the politics of polarisation. This time the cause of labour was at stake. Labour received scant support from either the Irish Parliamentary Party or Sinn Féin; Griffith denounced the prospect of what he called a 'proletarian dictatorship'. It did, however, find a sympathetic hearing in the republican press; and republicanism and labour edged closer in the Dublin strike which began in August 1913. James Larkin organised a strike of the Dublin tram workers and other lower-paid workers; he was joined by James Connolly, who had led the move for the foundation of a separate Irish Labour Party, distinct from that of Great Britain, and had thereby incurred the displeasure of William Wallace, a Belfast delegate and populist leader, who had worried the official Unionists in the 1906 general election. Connolly now moved to Dublin, where he became involved in the bitter dispute between the workers and their (Nationalist) boss, William Martin Murphy. Connolly was a socialist; but his beliefs and writings were heavily overlaid with his own brand of communistic nationalism, for he believed that separation from the capitalist power, England, must precede freedom for the Irish working classes. He had encountered sectarian working-class feeling in the north; but he chose to regard this as a kind of false consciousness, which would be dispersed—or overborne—when the Protestant working classes realised, or were forced to realise, where their true interests lay. Though hard on all capitalists, he was especially hard on Ulster Protestant capitalists; the southern variety seemed to attract less hostility. Connolly's commitment to separatism was sharpened by his observation of the industrial disputes of 1913, particularly the violent clashes between strikers and the police, in which the strikers invariably suffered most. In October 1913 the strikers, under the inspiration of Connolly and Captain J. R. White, an Ulster Protestant nationalist, organised the Irish Citizen Army, to serve, as their motto put it, 'neither King nor Kaiser, but Ireland'. The army was small, hardly more than 200 members, and it was, like the U.V.F., originally armed only with staves; but although its relations with the Home Rulers were uneasy or even hostile, the important point was that here at last was a body of men and women, opposed to the British connection, standing up for the rights of (some) Irishmen. Self-help, organised around militancy and weaponry, was becoming popular in Ireland.[48]

In November 1913 the popularity of arming and drilling was further demonstrated with the founding of the Irish Volunteers, in direct imitation of the U.V.F. The Irish Volunteers' founder, Eoin Mac Néill, was a leading enthusiast of the Gaelic League, and he was joined by two Protestant nationalists, Bulmer Hobson and Roger Casement. Volunteering was slow to develop at first, but by July 1914 the force numbered some 160,000 members. The question remained about what the Volunteers were volunteering for. Certainly they were not formed to fight the Ulster Unionists; nor were they aimed at bringing pressure to bear on the Liberal government, which was, after all, proceeding with Home Rule in the teeth of Unionist opposition. Their aim was more loosely described as 'defending' the rights of Ireland. The Irish Volunteers soon became the object of a struggle for control, or rather two struggles, one overt and one covert. The overt battle was waged by John Redmond, who in June 1914 stated publicly that he must control the Volunteers or take steps that would split the movement. The Provisional Committee of the Volunteers yielded, and Redmond gained formal control of the governing council. The subversive struggle was that of the Irish Republican Brotherhood, attracted to the Volunteers as a militant or potentially militant movement that might be infiltrated and exploited as the G.A.A. and the Gaelic

League had been: not, as yet, with any definite objective, but as an instrument whose value might be proved, and whose day might come.[49]

The U.V.F., which, as Mac Néill put it, 'began' the fashion of forming private armies was a body officered by the gentry and retired army officers; for the purpose of the U.V.F. was to give discipline and order to a Unionism that might easily degenerate into sectarian gangs. Craig defined its purpose as simply 'putting up a good fight' if it came to a crisis.[50] But in March 1914 the general sympathy with the Unionist cause felt among the officer class of the British army was revealed in the Curragh incident or so-called Curragh 'mutiny'. The cabinet had been slow in responding to drilling by private armies: not until the beginning of December 1913 did it decide to issue royal proclamations forbidding the importation of arms. In March 1914 the cabinet began to consider what were to be preventative measures in the event of the outbreak of violence in Ulster. This involved preparing and dispatching a force of troops to the north, as had been done in the case of industrial disputes in Wales; there was no proposal to arrest Unionist leaders (as was rumoured). But in the heightened atmosphere of rumour and counter-rumour, the idea of a 'plot' against Ulster was easily put about, and easily given credence. And certainly Winston Churchill and the Secretary of State for War, Colonel J. E. B. Seely, thought that it would be useful to make a show of strength and 'overawe' Unionist Ulster. In the circumstances the government showed human, if not military, tact in its agreement that officers with Ulster connections would be allowed to 'disappear' for a while. But General Paget, the commander-in-chief in Ireland, mishandled the affair, declaring in an excited speech that the troop movements would put the country in a 'blaze', and giving his officers the option of refusing to participate in operations; the War Office had instructed him to cashier any officer who refused to obey orders. Seely now moved to pacify the leader of the 'mutiny', Brigadier Gough, reiterating that soldiers must obey properly given orders, but adding (on his own initiative) the rider that there was 'no intention whatever' of taking advantage of this to 'crush political opposition to the policy or principles of the Home Rule Bill'. Gough gained a signed assurance from the War Office that this meant that the army would 'not be used under any circumstances to enforce the present Home Rule Bill on Ulster'. The government partly relieved the predicament by securing Seely's resignation, and Asquith himself assumed control of the War Office.[51] But clearly the government had forfeited the moral ground in the question of enforcing Home Rule on Unionists in the north; Asquith's only consolation was that the whole business might possibly swing British opinion against the Ulster Unionists. But the administration was now demoralised and even paralysed, and it proceeded to mishandle gun-running episodes in both the north and the south in April and July 1914. The U.V.F. gun-running at Larne was a successful operation (and one that did not seem to excite the interest of the army, let alone its opposition). At Howth, where the Irish Volunteers followed suit, the army did intervene, but in a chaotic and disastrous fashion, when troops of the King's Own Scottish Borderers, goaded by a crowd, opened fire, killing three people and wounding thirty-eight at Bachelor's Walk in Dublin. The Assistant Commissioner of the Dublin Metropolitan Police, who had asked for military assistance, was selected as the scapegoat and suspended from duty. What was worse was that the government seemed to have accepted the principle that it could do nothing about Ireland's private armies, but must let them go their way, unless they broke the peace. It was a final bankruptcy of the Liberals' Irish policy.[52]

Meanwhile, early in March 1914, Asquith at last offered compromise on the Home Rule Bill: a plebiscite, by counties, on a six-year exclusion. This provision was made in the form of an amending bill, which was, however, promptly altered by the Lords to provide permanent exclusion of the whole nine counties of Ulster. A conference to explore the possibility of a compromise based on special treatment of Unionist Ulster, held at the king's behest at Buckingham Palace on 21–24 July 1914, failed to make progress, foundering on the question of the areas to be excluded. The British Unionists were as yet unable to consider compromise anyway, since, as one of their number put it, 'The fear with our people is as to the effect on our supporters in the country of anything like abandonment of opposition to every sort of Home Rule.'[53] And the southern Irish Unionists were determined that they should not go down in a compromise that saved Ulster but abandoned the Protestants of the south and west. 'The Unionist Party are pledged to fight the battle of the Union,' the Earl of Midleton reminded them in June 1914, 'and its leaders have given many pledges as to safeguards for the provinces outside Ulster.'[54] There was now apparently no other option for the British political parties, the Irish nationalists and Unionists, and their respective volunteer forces, but to confront the fact that the Home Rule Bill would become law, but would not command compliance, and would almost certainly end in bloodshed.

The decades after the fall of Parnell, which had began in an atmosphere of nationalist and Unionist exhaustion, and the release of new ideas and new political developments, had ended in the prospect of imminent civil conflict. The Union had failed to reconcile the religious/political groups in Ireland, and had failed in the end to maintain British authority in the country. Nationalism had not been undermined by the policy of constructive Unionism, by reform, by land acts, or by concessions on Catholic education. As Horace Plunkett put it in June 1891, 'Those who think the "national" spirit sick unto death are, I think, superficial observers.'[55] Nationalism had its low periods; and there were those occasions, in 1903 and 1911, when royal visits to Ireland took place amidst great public interest and excitement. But the idea of Home Rule managed to survive splits, defeats and disappointments. It did so partly because it was expedient for the politicians to keep the party alive, and it suited the various factions in Ireland, from the Catholic Church to republicans, from agrarian radicals to the Catholic urban middle classes, from ideologues to pragmatists, to maintain the cause, for that was the cause that could in the end unite them behind one slogan and under one banner. But there was also Home Rule the idea: the Catholic of Ireland saw the island as his, and the governance of it as the logical outcome of his political progress since Catholic Emancipation, and certainly since 1886. Protestant opposition only added spice to an already attractive prospect.

And yet 1892 had begun with the idea of conciliation, not conflict—conciliation in all sorts of fields, literary, economic, political. But there were two main drawbacks to this mood which were to undermine every attempt made to cross the sectarian divide. One was the fact that some of the most ambitious movements—the literary revival and the Gaelic League—soon became either assimilated to the nationalist idea or rejected by that idea. And in the case of the literary movement there was the additional problem of reaching a public in the north-east of the country that had little interest in, or sympathy with, the romantic ideals of Yeats and Lady Gregory. The socialist movement, which might have been expected to unite the working classes of Ireland, also foundered on the constitutional question; and the most successful mobilisers of the Belfast Protestant working class were men like William Wallace who were sound Protestants and Unionists and who were, in the end, received back into the Unionist ranks.

The second reason for failure is both simpler and yet more complex. It was embodied in the question of where the idea of conciliation was supposed, ultimately, to lead. For conciliation must mean a change in direction for somebody's politics: either Unionists would become less Unionist, or nationalists less national-istic. 'Conciliation' involved the surrender of somebody's position (or at least its partial surrender). Gaelic Leaguers admired Standish O'Grady despite his Unionism, because he was propagating ideas that seemed to contribute to the nationalist idea of the glorious past of pre-conquest Ireland. Unionists liked William O'Brien, but one of them warned him that, nonetheless, he 'did not fully compre-hend . . . the difficulties of the Ulster position':[56] a nationalist who criticised the triumphalism of other nationalists was all right—as far as that went—but it did not go far enough. Even before the resurrection of Home Rule as the central issue of the day, in 1912–14, it was clear that Protestants and Catholics had, at best, only stood on the top of their ramparts and waved their handker-chiefs at each other; perhaps they had even met and shaken hands in no-man's land. But they had failed to find common ground. And the era of conciliation turned out in the end to be no more than one of those long, wary truces that were punctuated by crisis: in 1795–1800, 1828–9, 1841–3, 1886–93, and now 1912–14. And the out-come of this final truce was to be profoundly affected by the Great War that broke out in Europe in August 1914.

The Union Broken,
1914–23

THE outbreak of the Great War offered a last chance for the people of Ireland to sink their political differences in a wider common cause—or so it seemed in the heady days immediately following the British declaration of war on 4 August 1914. John Redmond urged the British government to withdraw its forces from Ireland and leave her defence to her 'armed sons', for which purpose 'armed Nationalist Catholics in the south will be only too glad to join arms with armed Protestant Ulstermen of the North'. And the Foreign Secretary, Sir Edward Grey, described Ireland as 'the one bright spot'.[1]

But the political mutterings behind the scene told a rather different story, or at least a story with a rather different emphasis. J. S. Sanders, an opposition whip and a man in close touch with rank-and-file Unionist opinion, described Redmond's speech as 'eloquent', but commented that it 'did not amount to much', adding that Carson had remarked that if he offered the Ulster Volunteers to the War Office, 'he would only get snubbed for his pains'.[2] Another Unionist wrote bitterly that

> The govt. are now behaving atrociously and trying to get the Home Rule and Welsh Bills—as the Nationalists have told them that Redmond will not be able to hold Ireland, unless he has the Bill. The same old game—'England's difficulty is Ireland's opportunity'.

Certainly Redmond showed determination to press home his claim for the Government of Ireland Bill to be placed on the statute book. When Asquith conceded—adding the rider that an amending bill would be necessary to respond to the Ulster problem—Unionists reacted with fury at what they regarded as the government's 'abominable' behaviour ('They are incapable of honesty or truth'), and the opposition withdrew from the House of Commons—a gesture rendered less effective by the fact that, as one of their number noted, 'everyone else was coming out too'.[3]

When, despite the opposition's anger and dismay, the Home Rule Bill was formally given the royal assent, there were exciting scenes in the House of Commons: a green flag was produced; Redmond responded to a cry 'God save Ireland' with the words 'And God save England too'.[4] And it seemed indeed that Ireland, nationalist and Unionist, would find a common cause in the greater European conflict. The Bachelor's Walk shootings were forgotten as war news filled the press in Ireland, as it did elsewhere in the United Kingdom. Redmond denounced the view that nationalist Ireland had used the crisis to gain an advantage in the Home Rule issue. He declared that the moratorium on Home Rule—that it should not come into operation until after twelve months, or the end of the war, whichever should be later—was not unreasonable; and he added the important comment that

> I would feel myself personally dishonoured if I did not say to my fellow-countrymen as I will say to them here today, and as I will say from the public platform when I go back to Ireland, that it is their duty, and should be their honour, to take their place in the fighting-line in this contest.

Redmond fulfilled this pledge at Woodenbridge, County Wicklow, on 20 September, when he used the opportunity at a review of Irish Volunteers to urge them to fulfil their twofold duty: to defend the shores of Ireland, and to 'account yourselves as men, not only in Ireland itself, but wherever the firing-line extends, in defence of right and freedom and religion in this war'.[5] This speech provoked the first rift in the apparent unanimity of nationalist Ireland's response to the war: the Volunteers split into two factions, with the majority following Redmond's lead, but a minority, led by Eoin Mac Néill, repudiating the idea of Irish participation in a 'foreign war' while 'no National Government which could speak and act for the people of Ireland is allowed to exist'. The breakaway group—who took with them the title 'Irish Volunteers', leaving Redmond's 'National Volunteers'—numbered only about 2,000, rising by 1915 to 11,000. Redmond's following was 170,000 strong.[6]

In retrospect, the 2,000 that remained in Ireland to reserve their strength for a different battle seem to have had the future in their hands; and their exploits, their participation (or the participation of some of them) in the Easter Rising of 1916 assured them a place in history. But there was the other half-million, as the Parnellite Henry Harrison called them: the Irishmen who served in the British army in France, with their own, hardly remembered, history, and their own sacrifice. It would be absurd to claim that every Irishman, Unionist or nationalist, who was in the army or the reserves, or who responded to the call for volunteers for the war effort, fought with political motives in mind. Ireland had always been a fertile recruiting ground for the British army, for reasons unconnected with politics; and not all the anti-army propaganda produced by nationalist organisations, and especially the republican Dungannon Clubs, could alter the attraction of enlistment for men living in poor circumstances, and the attraction of a regular income for the families of enlisted men. Indeed, the British army was in general an apparently permanent part of Irish life in the nineteenth century, and not only for peace-making purposes. Its soldiers led a life in barracks and towns hardly different from that of soldiers anywhere else in the British Isles; they occasionally got drunk, they consorted with prostitutes (of which Dublin, in particular, provided a considerable proportion), and they were as liked or disliked as their comrades were by civilians in Munster as in Manchester.

The war, however, produced a different kind of soldier, in a different kind of army. For these armies, once the regulars and reserves were committed, were people's armies, composed of men who joined together from the same town, the same street, the same office or factory or coal-mine. They were bound to occupy a special place in the public mind; and that public perception of them— favourable or otherwise—would depend, in Irish terms, on how the war related to the Irish predicament.

And at first the war seemed to relate to the Irish predicament in a pattern hoped for by John Redmond. Nationalists organised recruiting meetings. Crowds roamed Dublin waving Union flags. And that ultimate, if distasteful, sign of early First World War patriotism—the attacking and looting of shops allegedly owned by Germans—manifested itself. The King's Own Scottish Borderers, who had unleashed the fusillade at Bachelor's Walk that seemed about to set off civil war in Ireland, were cheered as they left for France.[7] And the sight of men queuing up to enlist as if waiting for admission to a football match was as common in Dublin as it was in cities elsewhere in the United Kingdom. Irish regiments embarked on route marches through the countryside and picked up numerous recruits; some 45 per cent of total Irish enlistments were made between the outbreak of war and the end of April 1915.[8] Clubs were formed to cater for the wives, mothers and children of servicemen; 'comforts' were provided; and when Ireland's first Victoria Cross was won, by an Irish Guardsman, Michael O'Leary, the country responded with a wild enthusiasm—an enthusiasm felt not only in Ireland but in Great Britain as well, for O'Leary seemed to epitomise all that was best in the Irish character: daring, courage, loyalty to his regiment, and a fine typical Irish surname (unlike, say, Pearse).

This change of sentiment, which promised to sweep Redmond into power (eventually) as the first Irish nationalist prime minister, had an impact in Unionist circles as well—or at least in southern Unionist circles. The southern Protestants were at once the war's most enthusiastic supporters, and in the end its greatest casualties (second only to the northern Catholic). Southern Unionists responded to the war as *their* war; the menfolk joined up without question, and those who stayed at home worked tirelessly for the war effort. In these changed circumstances southern Unionists began a process of rapprochement with nationalist Ireland, partly because they felt that the Home Rule Bill, though nothing more than an unimplemented entry in the statute book, had closed a chapter of their political struggle, and partly because they were working with nationalists in recruitment drives, serving with them in the army, and responding in some cases with great emotion to Redmond's plea for Irish unity ('Your speech has united Ireland,' the former Unionist M.P. Bryan Cooper telegraphed Redmond on 5 August; 'I join National Volunteers today, and will urge every Unionist to do same'). And then there was the unforgettable experience of the trenches and of the beaches at Gallipoli; as Bryan Cooper put it,

> The bond of common service and common sacrifice proved so strong and enduring that Catholic and Protestant, Unionist and Nationalist, lived and fought and died side by side like brothers. Little was spoken concerning the points on which we differed, and once we had tacitly agreed to let the past be buried, we found thousands of points on which we agreed. To

an Englishman this no doubt seems natural, for beneath all superficial disagreements the English do possess a nature in common and look on things from the same point of view, but in Ireland up to the present things have been very different.

Not all Unionists shared Cooper's belief that the war rendered a rapprochement with nationalists not only necessary but right; but it could not be denied that the old lines of division had been, or were being, broken down.[9]

This, however, was not the case in the north. That there were some signs of a softening of attitudes could not be denied. For example, Redmond spoke enthusiastically of the Inniskilling Fusiliers being escorted through their own town by combined bodies of Irish and Ulster Volunteers; however, the Catholic Ladies' Society of Ennniskillen insisted that gifts for the troops should go only to Catholic soldiers in the regiment.[10] And then there was the close connection between the Ulster Volunteer Force and the 36th (Ulster) Division, the northern contribution to the new armies. The 36th Division was overwhelmingly Protestant and Unionist in composition, containing only about ten Catholics. Its level of religious observance was high. And before its dilution after 1916 with recruits from other areas of the British Isles it was a force which truly represented Unionist Ulster.[11] This, of course, did not affect the comradeship which was struck up between the division and the 16th (Irish) Division at places like Messines Ridge and Wytschaete Wood;[12] but it was to give a very different emphasis to the Ulster Protestant concept of its finest hour—the Somme, July 1916, when the battle, the casualties, and the thousands of telegrams delivered to homes throughout the province became part of Protestant folklore, and remain so to the present day (with the Somme depicted, not only on Orange banners, but also on loyalist gable walls, to illustrate the 'betrayal' of loyalism by Great Britain).

And then there were politics—Irish politics, which were unable to transcend the battlefield, and which, as in the case of the Ulster Division at the Somme, the battlefield only reinforced. Nationalists and Unionists alike saw the war as an opportunity to vindicate their cause in the eyes of the world, and especially of the British. Redmond believed that blood-sacrifice was necessary for the Irish nation to prove its manhood, to demonstrate that it was worthy of nationhood at all: 'It is heroic deeds entering into their traditions that give life to nations; that is the recompense of those who die to perform them.'[13] Carson was determined that, whatever the outcome of the war, 'We are not going to abate one jot or tittle of our opposition to Home Rule, and when you come back from serving your country you will be just as determined as you will find us at home.' General Richardson, a retired army officer who had commanded the U.V.F. during the Home Rule crisis, urged the Volunteers to recollect 'the events of March last and what the Navy and Army did for Ulster. They came to the help of Ulster in the day of trouble and would come again.' When the war was over, he assured his listeners, 'and their ranks were reinforced by some 12,000 men thoroughly well trained and with vast field experience, they would return to the attack and relegate Home Rule to the devil'.[14]

Nevertheless, the cracks could be papered over; and there was also the prosperity that followed in the wake of the war, as rural Ireland found itself the recipient of profits from selling its rich agricultural produce to Great Britain, and growing fat on the profits of war. But the dissident forces that were gathering in Ireland did not come from the rural areas. The artisan section of the Dublin working class and the middle-class intelligentsia who were involved in the conspiracy that the Irish Republican Brotherhood began to plot in 1915 were not from that class that had formed the main support of the Irish nationalist movement and the Irish Parliamentary Party since the 1880s. They came from the same kind of people—paradoxically—who were busily engaged in joining the British army; the Dublin working men who formed the Irish Citizen Army, and the poet Francis Ledwidge, who served in the British army and would have joined the rising if he could, were typical of the people who became involved in warfare—of whatever kind, for whatever cause. Economic motives did not inspire the men who planned or participated in the Easter Rising; nevertheless Dublin city, almost alone of the large cities in the British Isles, experienced not prosperity but depression during the war, with rising prices for foodstuffs and fuel, and high unemployment. This was to some extent offset by the higher wages which resulted from the shortage of unskilled labour; but it was the Dublin people who began to show signs—felt throughout the south of Ireland by 1915—of war-weariness and disillusionment.[15]

These sentiments were not created by the anti-war propaganda produced by Sinn Féin and other more radical nationalist organisations, even though seditious publications gave plenty of employment for the R.I.C. They were a natural response to the scale of casualties and the unexpected duration of the conflict, and were common throughout the British Isles. But there were special Irish dimensions as well. In particular there was the mutual suspicion between the British military and political establishment and John Redmond, which was seen in the War Office's clumsy handling of the status to be accorded to the 10th and 16th (Irish) Divisions. Redmond wished the Irish regiments which were overwhelmingly Catholic and nationalist in composition to be accorded special recognition, and in particular requested that the 10th and 16th be grouped into a single 'Irish Brigade' for which, he urged, the Irish had a 'historical liking'.[16] This was supported by Asquith but refused by Kitchener. The commander-in-chief of the 16th Irish was General Lawrence W. Parsons, who, while 'an artillery officer of great distinction', was a professional soldier who saw it as part of his profession to despise politicians, and who could not see any special reason why Redmond should regard himself as a kind of unofficial head of the Irish Volunteers now wearing British army uniform. Parsons had prejudices about what constituted an 'officer class', and there were good reasons to believe that he did not include Irish Roman Catholics among that coterie. But it was also a simple reflection of the lack of an officers' training corps in Irish secondary schools, and the consequent lack of Catholic army officers.

Parsons refused the plea made by Redmond and Dillon for a distinct badge for the 16th Division; its distinct identity was not recognised in the way that the 36th (Ulster) Division's was.[17] And when troops from a nationalist background encountered their dreadful baptism of fire at Gallipoli, it was felt that the War Office's official accounts had not given enough credit to the gallantry of the Irish soldiers in his command: 'We felt', wrote Katharine Tynan, 'that their lives had been thrown away and their heroism had gone unrecognised.'[18] This complaint was answered by Sir Ian Hamilton, commander-in-chief at Gallipoli, who acknowledged the importance of the Irish contribution to the campaign; but such slights, however unintended, contributed to the growing disillusionment with the war in nationalist Ireland—a sentiment encouraged by the entry of Sir Edward Carson into the British cabinet in May 1915, which Stephen Gwynn alleged caused a drop in recruiting in Ireland from 6,000 in April/May to 3,000 in May/June.[19] And, despite the common experience of battle, there remained the question of how far Catholics and nationalists 'belonged' in the army and in the war. That they were equally vulnerable to shot and shell could hardly be denied; the Irish Catholic, like Shakespeare's Jew, bled when he was cut. But even Willie Redmond, John Redmond's brother, found himself 'shy and a stranger' in the officers' mess of his regiment. As Stephen Gwynn put it, 'You could not better describe the atmosphere of our mess than by saying that it was a society in which everyone liked and respected Willie Redmond, but one in which he never really was himself. He was only himself with the men.'[20]

These must seem small irritations, when set against the background of the great European and world struggle of 1914–18; and they must not be allowed to obscure the fact that Ireland was in the war from its outbreak to its conclusion, that it provided 170,000 recruits and reservists, (some 41 per cent of the male population between the ages of 10 and 44 in the 1911 census), that many thousands of Irishmen went to work in munitions factories in Great Britain, thus doing essential war work, that thousands of Irish people and the descendants of Irish people in Great Britain joined the army,[21] and that the Irish troops returned in 1919 to a Dublin draped in Union flags and were given a joyous reception (marred only by a few incidents involving Sinn Féiners). But, as Desmond Ryan put it, almost before the shadow of the Great War had passed, the shadow of the little war fell over Ireland.[22] In truth, that little war had never ended; not only were Irish nationalists and Ulster Unionists still firmly ensconced behind the barricades of their beliefs—beliefs which were not in the least altered by what Willie Redmond called the 'suffering' of the trenches[23]—but the militant spirit that had been aroused in the pre-war Home Rule crisis was about to have its consequences for all Ireland, and for Great Britain as well.

The handful of men—Tom Clarke, Seán MacDermott, Joseph Plunkett, Eamonn Ceannt, Thomas MacDonagh, Patrick Pearse and James Connolly (the last two late arrivals, whose names came subsequently to dominate the enterprise)—plotted the rising in a desperate effort to alter the mind of nationalist Ireland and create an opportunity out of the war. They were reacting as much against the politics of John Redmond, and against *all* politicking, as they were against British rule in Ireland. They had to force the issue, and they knew that the issue could only be forced by an uprising, the outcome of which they hoped would be a reawakening of the true spirit of nationalist Ireland. Connolly may have hoped that the fact of a rising would somehow bring out the people; but even that hope deserted him on the morning of the sacrifice—for sacrifice it must now be. Pearse, for his part, was convinced that a blood-sacrifice was necessary, not only for freedom, but to put the heart back into the people; by which he meant, ultimately, the Catholic and 'Gaelic' people of Ireland. Pearse and Connolly exchanged ideas, at least superficially: Pearse became concerned, in a rather incoherent fashion, for the social and economic welfare of the nation; Connolly began to talk of a blood-sacrifice as necessary if the 'Irish race' was ever to recover its 'self-respect' or establish its 'national dignity in the face of a world horrified and scandalised by what must seem to them our national apostasy'.[24]

Eoin Mac Néill, although he was President and Chief of Staff of the Irish Volunteers, was not a member of the I.R.B. and had been excluded from the conspiracy. On hearing rumours that a rising was under consideration, Mac Néill circulated a statement announcing that the existing circumstances did not justify a rising, let alone a blood-sacrifice. But his reservations, and later his outright opposition when the full extent of the planned operation became known to him, only increased the general confusion that surrounded the last desperate week-end before the Easter Rising, when Pearse and his fellow-conspirators deliberately deceived their own Chief of Staff and marched some 1,500 men onto the streets of Dublin to proclaim the establishment of the Irish Republic on the steps of the General Post Office.

Pearse, Connolly, Clarke and the rest were very nearly leaders without followers; their rising was unpopular and unwanted. Yet even while the fighting was in progress there was a certain admiration, not for their cause, but for the way in which the rebels conducted themselves: this was no farcical repetition of 1848 and 1867. The insurgents held out for only a week; but a week is a long time in a rebellion. The rebels surrendered themselves to apparent defeat and perhaps dismissal from the nationalists of Ireland; and it was only when General Maxwell began to shoot the ringleaders that the idea of the blood-sacrifice began to work its desired effect. The rebels, who had already behaved like heroes, and indeed earned the respect of the forces which suppressed them,[25] now began to take on the appearance of martyrs. They were perceived as martyrs not only for Ireland, but for Catholic Ireland, a posture rendered easier by the fact that they died in the faith (at least ostensibly: Tom Clarke took the last rites, although an unbeliever, to maintain a common front with his comrades, as did Connolly, who by this time may have been an atheist). The gap between British comprehension of Ireland and the rebels' comprehension of themselves was of crucial importance. For the British, a piece of condign but limited punishment seemed appropriate; and this extended to the trial and execution, a few months after the rising, of Sir Roger Casement, who, as it happened, had come to Ireland convinced, and hoping to convince others, of the futility of the cause. For the Irish, or at least for a growing number of nationalists, it reawakened memories of Tone, Emmet, the Manchester Martyrs, and all that 'delerium of the brave'. For there can be no doubt that the 1916 rebels had constructed, and were motivated by, a revolutionary ideology. This cannot be attributed in any simplistic way to the impact of the literary and Gaelic revivals; most of the men who marched away in 1916 were almost certainly unaware of Yeats and Hyde. But among the leaders of 1916 were poet-rebels who believed that they were going out to fight the last fight between the Gael and the Gall, and who saw their actions in the heroic context created by the writings of Thomas Davis, Standish O'Grady and a host of followers and imitators. And they gathered under what they believed to be the ancient banners of Ireland—the banners of that very mythology which O'Grady helped to popularise. It was perhaps appropriate that literature should canonise what literature had helped to create; and the Easter Rising was presented in the way that Pearse always envisaged it: an epic tale of heroism, self-sacrifice and, above all, joy—the joy of violent conflict, when the hero is at last face to face with the Saxon foe. What was to British (and Protestant Unionist) opinion a treacherous act, inspired by Germans, was quickly fitted by nationalist Ireland into a heroic mould: one that was ever present in Ireland in the nineteenth century, one that was repeated in popular literature and indeed in the speeches of Home Rulers themselves, and an idea that was refreshed in the decades immediately preceding the rising.[26]

The Easter Rising struck a political/religious response in Catholic Ireland. The piety of the rebels, their reciting of the rosary in the headquarters in the G.P.O., their sheer unworldliness, their sacrifice for what Pearse called 'the people who wept in Gethsemane', all won over a hierarchy which had already expressed its anxiety about the alliance between nationalist Ireland and imperialist Britain. Cardinal Logue had declared that if Irishmen were no longer coming forward to enlist in large numbers, this was because the Irish had been cleared out of their country in the past: it was 'the revenge of time' if the men were not available.[27] Now the hierarchy was in danger of lagging behind the lower clergy, who showed an instinctive (and, as it transpired, politic) transfer of sympathy towards the new nationalism;[28] and it began to fall into line behind the rebels, and even extended its blessing to their blood-sacrifice.

A few days before the rising John Redmond, at a dinner in London, boasted that he could crush all the Sinn Féiners in the hollow of his hand.[29] This was certainly true when he spoke what turned out to be famous last words; but between 1916 and the end of the Great War the position of the Irish Parliamentary Party was relentlessly undermined. And yet there were moments when the downfall of parliamentarianism might have been arrested, when events might have turned out to Redmond's advantage. In May and June 1916 Lloyd George induced Carson and Redmond to accept a settlement based on the immediate implementation of the 1914 Home Rule Act, with the exclusion of the six counties of Armagh, Antrim, Down, Fermanagh, Londonderry and Tyrone. This promised Redmond what he needed most: a Dublin parliament, with himself as prime minister. It also satisfied the majority in the Ulster Unionist Council, which met on 12 June 1916 and unanimously accepted six-counties partition as the basis for discussion with the nationalists and the British government. And it was acceptable even to Sir Edward Carson, who regarded it as essential for the successful prosecution of the war, and who urged the Ulster Unionists to agree on the grounds that any obstructionism would damage Ulster in the eyes of the British public, and Unionists would be left after the war with the 1914 act on the statute book and only the flimsy promise by Asquith of an amending bill. This was a breach of the Ulster Covenant of September 1912, which pledged northern Unionists to resist Home Rule for the whole of Ireland. But when the ship was sinking, then Ulster Unionists felt they had no choice but to man the lifeboats.

The 1916 settlement was a hazardous undertaking. Lloyd George only made his speedy progress because he was able to play upon British as well as Irish Unionist concern about the implications of an unsettled Ireland for the war effort. He worked with great speed, in the hope of presenting the cabinet with an agreement that it would find impossible to resist. But he was vulnerable to the ambiguity of the phrase which applied to partition, that 'at the end of the provisional period Ulster must not, whether she wills it or not, merge in the rest of Ireland'. Carson and Redmond had different understandings about the permanency or otherwise of partition. Yet both desperately needed a settlement, and neither wanted to jeopardise the Lloyd George plan; if ambiguity would save it, then Redmond, for his part, favoured ambiguity. The threat came from southern Unionists, who would be abandoned to the mercies of Irish nationalists, and perhaps Sinn Féiners; and from the support given to southern Unionists by Unionist members of the cabinet, who feared that the whole settlement plan would be construed as a concession to the rebellion of 1916 and would constitute a grave threat to the British war effort.

The Unionist dissidents began to probe the weaknesses of Lloyd George's plan. Gradually they forced Asquith and Lloyd George to retreat. The draft Home Rule Bill was amended to provide that the excluded counties would not be placed under a Dublin parliament against their will; and the nationalists were to be informed that, after an Irish parliament had been established, Irish representation in the British parliament would be reduced, though restored if an amending bill relating to Ulster were brought in. Unionists, still smarting under what they regarded as Lloyd George's duplicity in representing to Carson and Redmond that he had the full backing of the cabinet for his negotiations and his plan, pushed on with their counter-attack. Now they demanded further military and security measures to prevent Irish disaffection from endangering Britain in time of war. Redmond was forced to acknowledge that if he were to persist in his acceptance of a Home Rule parliament, it would be a useless victory, since it would involve permanent partition and a series of humiliating restrictions on the Irish government. On 24 July he bitterly announced that all hope of compromise was over.[30]

But the war continued to work its inexorable influence on British and Irish politics. After the failure of the Somme offensive it was clear that the struggle would be an exhausting and lengthy one; and the question of Ireland fell further into the background as far as British politics was concerned. But if the war was in the foreground, it was essential to impress potential allies—especially the United States of America—with the justice of the cause. In March 1917 the cabinet began once again to cast round for some kind of Irish initiative that would at least give the impression that it meant to settle Ireland. Gradually the alternatives emerged: a new Home Rule Bill, involving the partition of Ireland; or an Irish Convention 'for the purpose of providing a scheme of Irish self-government'.[31]

The Irish Convention began its series of meetings in July 1917; but even as it commenced its deliberations it was clear that the Home Rule Party faced new and alarming developments. Ulster Unionists came to the Convention, but they soon made it clear that they had set their sights on a policy of defending themselves and their own people, and were in no mood to help the Irish Parliamentary Party out of its predicament. This was perhaps only to be expected. But the real challenge to the party's grip on Irish politics came from Sinn Féin, now, after the rising, a party in search of a broader appeal and a more professional organisation. Sinn Féin had been associated, quite mistakenly, with the rising. This might have ensured the organisation's downfall, had the rebels avoided the fate of martyrdom that General Maxwell endowed them with. But Sinn Féin was now in the happy position of being able to claim affinity with the heroic dead, and yet follow a course that would place its adherents firmly in the mainstream of Irish nationalist politics. They scored their first success when a parliamentary vacancy occurred in North Roscommon. Sinn Féin enjoyed the support of a local priest, Fr Michael O'Flanagan, and nationalists in the constituency had been active since the rising. Sinn Féin's decision to endorse the candidature of Count Plunkett was on the face of it an odd one: Plunkett was a wealthy property-owner, a man of letters, an advocate of the Gaelic revival, and an unsuccessful applicant for the post of Under-Secretary at Dublin Castle in 1916. But he was to become a leading figure in Irish politics, mainly because of his son Joseph Mary Plunkett, who had played a leading part in planning the Easter Rising, and who was married on the eve of his execution and died a mystical and pious death. Moreover, Count Plunkett possessed a distinguished appearance, and had to his credit the fact that he was expelled from the Royal Dublin Society because of his family's seditious behaviour. He won the seat, despite his almost non-existent part in his own campaign, on 3 February 1917, with 3,022 votes, a majority of 627 over his Home Rule and independent opponents combined.[32]

The difficulty for Sinn Féin was that it was still a congeries of different groups—Volunteers, Sinn Féiners, the National League (a body formed in the north after Redmond's acceptance of partition in 1916) and individuals such as William O'Brien of the Dublin Trades Council—and, of course, members of the Irish Republican Brotherhood. The Home Rulers had at least the advantage of experience and outward unity. But in April 1917 Sinn Féin itself achieved a measure of unity when the 'Mansion House Committee' was set up for the purpose of co-ordinating the various radical nationalist organisations. In July 1917 the R.I.C. Inspector General reported that 166 Sinn Féin Clubs with a membership of about 11,000 had been noted by the police. A month later the membership had doubled and the number of clubs trebled. Sinn Féin was now associated with the rising even though, as some contemporaries noted, 'the original Sinn Féiners were not in sympathy with the men of Easter Week'.[33]

As Sinn Féin began to advance, Redmond's position weakened. His dilemma was revealed in his post-rising strategy. This was, as he defined it, for his party to maintain its support of the war, but to become 'a regular and active opposition'.[34] What this meant in practice was that Redmond would draw attention to the disparity between the government's professed war aims—to defend the rights of small nations—and its Irish policy. But this would be to do Sinn Féin's propaganda work for it. And there were more effective ways of drawing attention to the apparent hollowness of British war aims, as Sinn Féin demonstrated when it put forward as candidate in the South Longford by-election in May 1917 an I.R.B. member, Joseph McGuinness, with the slogan 'Put him in to get him out' inscribed over a picture of the candidate in prison garb.[35] This highly emotive personification of the victimised hero was soon followed by another symbolic figure: an election candidate wearing Volunteer uniform. This was Eamon de Valera, who successfully contested the East Clare by-election in July 1917; and his style as well as his uniform indicated the link that was being forged between Sinn Féin, advanced nationalists of whatever sort, and the revolutionary idea. De Valera did this by stressing his links with the traditional as well as the new, and especially the close relationship between nationalism—Sinn Féin nationalism—and the Catholic religion. It was in Bruree, he proclaimed, 'listening to the sermons that were given by their patriotic priests . . . that he first learned what an Irishman's duty was. Religion and patriotism were combined.' He and the party he represented were 'sane, reasonable men'; they stood for the 'tricolour . . . and not for the Union Jack'; but while not ruling out the used of force, they must not use it now: 'The robber was stronger than they were at the present moment.' Another Easter Week would be a 'superfluity'; and Sinn Féin were the real inheritors of the mantle of Parnell.[36]

De Valera disavowed the need for war, while leaving the door open, by implication, to a renewal of war should that be feasible. This was the language that the parliamentarians had indeed employed throughout their career, especially during the Boer War; but they had not believed it would ever be feasible, or even desirable, in their lifetime. This language, however, was very different from that of Arthur Griffith's early Sinn Féin, with its emphasis on peaceful protest and non-violent non-cooperation as a means of rendering British rule in Ireland ineffective. But now Sinn Féin was changing as radicals came to the fore. The election of de Valera as the organisation's president in October 1917 signified the new departure. But it is probably true to say that a reasonably generous measure of Home Rule would have satisfied most nationalists; and Sinn Féin had its own problems about the direction of the onward march of its nation. Griffith and his early followers still saw merit in the idea of a dual monarchy; Michael Collins, de Valera, Count Plunkett and Cathal Brugha were republicans. But Sinn Féin showed that it had developed some essential political antennae when it adopted a constitution containing a compromise clause advocated by de Valera: that Sinn Féin aimed at winning for Ireland a republic, and that once that was achieved, the people could decide what particular form of government they wanted. This meant, as he had declared in September 1917, that they could, if they wished, choose a monarchy. Other potentially divisive issues were likewise dealt with. Sinn Féin, it was decided, would not go to Westminster; and it would not be a party of social reform.[37]

Sinn Féin stood between the past and the present. It offered a friendly hand to any parliamentarian supporter or member of the United Irish League who felt that the time had come to climb aboard its new political machine. A *Punch* cartoon of the time illustrated the Sinn Féin party as passengers in a sleek modern limousine, while the Irish Parliamentary Party's lumbering equipage was pulled by a drayhorse. It was an apt symbol. Yet, underneath the bonnet, Sinn Féin's new vehicle contained important elements of the old Home Rule horse-power.

In the early part of 1918 it looked as if the horse-drawn cart still had plenty of staying power. The Irish Parliamentary Party won three by-elections in quick succession; out of a total of eight contested by-elections, Sinn Féin won five, but the Irish Party ran Sinn Féin close in the by-elections in South Longford and East Cavan, with the parliamentarians' candidates emphasising what the party had done for the farmer, and retrieving the Parnellite and Davitt tradition for the Home Rulers. But against this was the fact that the Home Rulers won two of their three victories in Ulster (South Armagh and East Tyrone), where nationalist opinion was slower to move to Sinn Féin, and where the Ancient Order of Hibernans still stood firm for the party, under Devlin's forceful direction. There was also the usual bonus for the Home Rulers that *any* nationalist candidate was anathema to the Ulster Unionists, and parliamentarians could look as green as anybody else.[38]

This at least took the fight to Sinn Féin, whose studied vagueness on politics was, of course, the best route for a party which was on the offensive against a party whose record was now very much under review. Sinn Féin's decision not to join the Irish Convention, however, once again discomfited the parliamentarians. It was not that the Convention was a total failure. On the contrary, it precipitated a breakthrough of a sort, as a section of southern Unionists, led by Lord Midleton and Archbishop John Henry Bernard, found that their southern perspective enabled them at least to exchange ideas with the Home Rulers; and they were also becoming well aware of the vulnerability of their own position in an Ireland that was clearly moving towards some kind of independence, under some kind of nationalist rule, either moderate or extreme. Like the Home Rulers, they too had a vested interest in avoiding the logical consequences of a statement made by Lloyd George in 1917 that the British government would not be a party to imposing nationalist rule on Ulster Unionists, who were as 'alien in blood, in religious faith, in traditions, in outlook from the rest of Ireland as the inhabitants of Fife or Aberdeen'. This meant the partition of Ireland. But the southern Unionists made two significant errors: they did not sufficiently consult their rank-and-file membership; and they never overcame the fundamental hostility felt by their northern counterparts to the idea of any settlement involving compromise with nationalists.[39]

Redmond desperately needed a speedy settlement, and in November 1917 the southern Unionists presented him with a plan for a wide measure of self-government with safeguards for minority interests. The Westminster parliament would continue to impose and collect customs duties; the payment out of the receipts from such duties would constitute the 'imperial contribution'—Ireland's discharge of costs for her share of the general services which membership of the United Kingdom gave her. The Irish government would control internal taxation. A process of bargaining with the Home Rulers now began, and in the end the southern Unionists conceded that customs should also be placed under the control of the Irish parliament. This in turn brought a concession from Redmond, who acknowledged that an Irish parliament would be unlikely to embark on a trade war with Great Britain, and accepted that the retention of customs by the imperial parliament was of great symbolic importance to Unionists.

In 1903 Unionist landlords and nationalist parliamentarians had settled the land question, in its essential features, by 'conference plus business'. Now, under pressure of war, they seemed on the verge of achieving a settlement of the question of Irish self-government. Moreover, the Convention's progress attracted the interest of the British government, and Lloyd George promised that if the southern Unionist scheme were carried by the Convention with 'substantial agreement, i.e. with the opposition of Ulster alone—the P.M. will use his personal influence with his colleagues . . . to accept the report and give it legislative effect'. But the Convention suffered from the loose and at times wayward chairmanship of Sir Horace Plunkett, and despite Lloyd George's encouraging words in January 1918, time was allowed to slip by, and opposition to the scheme was given a chance to organise. The opposition came from dissident southern Unionists, Ulster Unionists and nationalists. The Convention therefore postponed a vote on the scheme, and eventually a modified plan, based on a compromise suggested by Sir Antony MacDonnell, was put forward, reserving customs and excise to the Westminster parliament for the duration of the war and for such time thereafter until the question had been considered and decided upon by the imperial parliament. This was accepted by southern Unionists and Redmondites, but opposed by Ulster Unionists and a mixed bag of doubters which included the Catholic Archbishops of Armagh and Cashel, the Bishops of Raphoe and Down and Connor, the Lords Mayor of Cork and Belfast, and Joseph Devlin. The plan was passed, but by a majority of only four. And although the Convention went on to agree on self-government with special representation for minorities, it was not unanimously accepted, and Ulster Unionist obduracy remained to the end. The combination of Ulstermen and extreme nationalists prevented substantial agreement; but Lloyd George had promised to legislate for Ireland in any event; and the final plan was carried by sixty-six out of eighty-seven members of the Convention.[40] Yet Lloyd George had in the recent past given the Ulster Unionists a promise of no coercion of Ulster which they took as affording them a special position, in that it enabled them to veto any legislation to which they did not agree. It was hardly to be wondered at that, as Stephen Gwynn put it, 'no legislation followed'.[41]

John Redmond died on 6 March 1918. It is hard to resist the conclusion that the Home Rule cause died with him. In the event the war, to which he had fully committed nationalist Ireland, was within a few weeks of his death to destroy the union of hearts that he hoped would be forged in its baptism of fire. In 1918 the German army launched its last great offensive on the western front. The British government was by now desperate for fresh manpower to stem the tide and to persevere with an ever-lengthening conflict. It turned to Ireland as a source which had not been fully exploited because of Ireland's exemption from conscription. The demand for conscription to be applied to the only part of the United Kingdom which had escaped it so far was irresistible. Men in Great Britain between the ages of eighteen and fifty were being called up for military service; the German offensive made it impossible to exempt Ireland any longer. The cabinet was not unanimous in its approach to the crisis, acknowledging the difficulties involved, which might outweigh any advantages. But it made what Winston Churchill called a 'battlefield decision'.[42]

This decision revealed the gap that had by now opened between nationalist Ireland and the British government. Irishmen were at the front; and between April and November 1918 there was a steady stream of recruits to the army, with a monthly average surpassing that of the period between October 1915 and May 1916.[43] But the threat of conscription came when nationalist Ireland was in a defiant and sensitive mood. The funeral of Thomas Ashe, a survivor of the Easter Rising, who died after forced feeding when on hunger-strike, was attended by Michael Collins and by a member of the Catholic hierarchy. Collins declared that the volley of shots fired over the grave of a dead Fenian was 'the only speech which it is proper to make'.[44] Now the anti-conscription campaign developed an almost messianic fervour, as church, people and Sinn Féin combined in a denunciation of its iniquity. The bishops declared that the conscription law was 'no law at all'. Masses of intercession were said, a national novena was launched, and a chapel-gate petition was signed by nationalists after Sunday mass. 'Freemasonry' in the army was denounced (always a useful veil for an attack on Protestant influence),[45] and the Catholic Church in Ireland was declared to be in danger. All this only served to further convince Ulster Unionists, if they needed convincing, that nationalist Ireland was indeed Catholic Ireland, and that Ireland under self-government would be a Catholic state and nation.

The government further discredited the Home Rule tradition through a policy that was meant to make conscription more palatable. A Home Rule Bill would be introduced; but it would not, the government declared, be linked in any way to the conscription issue. Of course, that is precisely how it was linked in the popular mind; and the spectacle of a government which at almost one and the same time was seeking to introduce conscription, suppress an alleged 'German plot' by Sinn Féiners, and introduce a Home Rule Bill illustrated the poverty of British government policy in Ireland in the last phase of the Union.[46]

For most of the United Kingdom the Great War was a unifying experience, even if it did not make 'Britons' out of Scotsmen or Welshmen. Defeat in the war might conceivably had led to serious internal strains, possibly threatening that unity. A victorious nation was likely to be a united nation. Yet, while this was true of Great Britain, Ireland proved the exception. John Redmond had staked his political life, and that of his party, on nationalist Ireland's participation in a successful war, a war which would cement the 'union of hearts' and enable him to enjoy one of the fruits of victory: Home Rule for Ireland. The blood-sacrifice of his people was compromised through that of the rebels of Easter 1916. Tom Kettle, Home Ruler, Catholic Irishman and British soldier, who made his own sacrifice in 1916, spoke resignedly of the future when 'These men will go down in history as heroes and martyrs, and I will go down—if I go down at all—as a bloody British officer.'[47] Unionist Ulster too had made a blood-sacrifice at the Somme and Passchendaele; this strengthened its sense of community and endorsed its claim on British goodwill. Ireland, then, made not one, but three war sacrifices, for what were really different and incompatible war goals. Not even the 'union of hearts' sacrifice, had it prevailed, would have softened Ulster Unionist resistance to Redmondite Home Rule (though it would almost certainly have helped to accommodate southern Irish Unionism). The anvil of war broke the Union of Great Britain and Ireland; it also proved fatal to the political unity of Ireland itself.

That this was the last phase of the Union was made clear—though not apparently to the British government—in the general election which followed the end of the war, and which was held under the new register established by the Representation of the People Act of 1918. The Home Rule Party was by now almost bereft of a policy; its participation in the anti-conscription campaign seemed to deny all its own promises that England would keep faith when all was said and done. Sinn Féin had the advantage of declaring itself all things to all men (or at least most men). It was unhampered by the Irish Labour Party, which, after much heartsearching, resolved not to contest the election, and thus saved Sinn Féin from having to answer tricky questions about its attitude to the working classes in town and countryside. It claimed to be the inheritor of 'true' Irish nationalism, that of Parnell as well as that of Emmet, Tone and the rebels of 1916. It did not advocate violence; but it did not rule it out, should circumstances render it necessary. But these circumstances were not defined.[48]

On the Ulster question, Sinn Féin faced both ways, as indeed nationalists had always done. Ulster Unionists were members of the nation, brothers even—but brothers who must not be allowed to stand in the way of the nation. In July 1917 de Valera had spelt out the consequences of this ambiguity when he declared that he 'did not believe in mincing matters, and if Ulster stood in the way of the attainment of Irish freedom, Ulster should be coerced. Their natural political enemies were Unionists.'[49] There were those who did not even pay lip-service to the idea that Protestants were 'brothers'. In November 1918 a Catholic priest, Fr Thomas Curtayne, told the Killarney branch of the Gaelic League that the League must 'resist . . . reduce, and ultimately . . . destroy the creeping process known as Anglicisation. . . . Every little baby that is born in Ireland can be made either a little Gael or a little West Briton.'[50] Another priest, Fr Michael O'Flanagan, a leading member of Sinn Féin, acknowledged that 'duality' was indeed an essential part of the Irish tradition, and one to be respected.[51] But the most significant point about the Ulster question in the 1918 general election over most of nationalist Ireland was Sinn Féin's failure to articulate any new of more imaginative approach to the most serious obstacle to Irish unity. Indeed, it would be more accurate to say that the question was not an electoral issue at all. The central debate concerned where Sinn Féin stood in the long-standing dispute with England.

It was not altogether clear, however, what precisely Sinn Féin did stand for. Sinn Féin welcomed all 'progressive' nationally-minded people; and this would include Home Rulers, just as the Home Rule Party itself had attracted the support of flexibly-minded Whigs in the 1870s. But it had no clear idea of what kind of self-government the new Ireland would enjoy. This, of course, was also a source of strength to a party which was rising to power on the mistakes and failure of its opponents. It was clear about its tactics: it would not go to that 'House of Shame where Ireland has always been betrayed'.[52] The Bishop of Killaloe favoured abstention from Westminster as the only way 'if we have a particle of self-respect'; the 'leprosy of Anglicisation' was 'the ruin of our national spirit'.[53]

The Home Rulers stood little chance against this tide. Their capacity to renew themselves in each generation was exhausted, and they could only point to their past record, on education, land, and the general advancement of the people. The Sinn Féin victory in the general election of December 1918 was not as impressive as it first appeared. Sinn Féin won 48 per cent of the votes cast in the whole of Ireland; it could certainly not claim to represent the Unionist north. But, of course, it was concerned to claim that it represented a pluralist Ireland, of which the Unionists were a part. At the same time it claimed to speak for a unified monolithic entity which it called 'Ireland'—a completely different concept, and one which had been a long time in the making. And since it won 65 per cent of the seats in the twenty-six counties that subsequently became the Irish Free State, it could and did claim to represent the 'nation'. Unionist Ulster, it was confidently assumed, would come to heel. As for those parts of nationalist Ulster which voted Home Rule and returned five M.P.s from the Irish Parliamentary Party, here again Sinn Féin claimed to represent those who did not vote for it. The Home Rule victories were in any case won following an election pact arranged by the Catholic bishops, who feared that otherwise the nationalist vote would be split in the constituencies. Waterford—the party's only success in the south—was again something of a special case. Here John Redmond's son, William Archer Redmond, was assured of a large personal following, especially in view of the sympathy generated by his father's recent death, and he capitalised on the emotive issue of Irish participation in the war on the side of Belgium and the United States of America. Redmond defined the party's goal as dominion status. Sinn Féin meant 'anarchy and destruction'; it cared nothing for the working classes. Redmond reminded the voters that when de Valera was asked about Labour, he had replied: 'Labour must wait.' The Irish Party's reply was equally emphatic: 'We say Labour will not wait.'[54]

Sinn Féin can hardly be blamed for its·short-term view. Like any party eager to displace its opponents, it was happy to leave any resolution of contradictory policies, half-made promises and contradictory images to a later date. Meanwhile it celebrated its victory, assembled in Dáil Éireann in Dublin, and proclaimed its determination to take Ireland's case to the Versailles Peace Conference, where (it stated) it was assured of a favourable reception. This suited the British government, which could put up with any slight embarrassment Sinn Féin might occasion. Sinn Féin could sit in Dublin, waiting for a British overture as the Hungarians had waited for an Austrian overture in 1867, but with considerably less success.

The Dáil waited, and proceeded to try to give some semblance of reality to its claim to be the 'government' of Ireland. It adopted a general programme of social and economic reform, the 'Democratic Programme', which it was in no mood or position to implement. It sought to create Sinn Féin courts, a shadow bureaucracy, the beginnings of a state. But while it drafted its paper administration there was a new spirit developing among the Volunteers which promised trouble not only for the British but also for Sinn Féin as a democratic political party. This mood saw an aversion to 'politicians' and their ways; and it was a legacy of the growing contempt for parliamentarians, their wheeling and dealing, that the more ascetic and idealistic nationalists had felt since before the Great War. As one republican put it, in a revisionist interpretation of Daniel O'Connell, the Liberator was 'a coward because he called off the Clontarf meeting', and, what was worse, 'he was a politician'.[55]

The Irish Volunteers (now adopting the name 'Irish Republican Army') were still in no condition to launch the kind of general war of independence that many of their number had in mind. They needed arms; and their military weakness in the end proved to be their strength. Raids, attacks on policemen and soldiers, attacks on police barracks, executions of 'spies' and 'informers', gradually developed into a campaign of terror that, despite its restricted scope, placed the British in a military and political dilemma. The Royal Irish Constabulary was a neglected force, its future in a Home Rule Ireland uncertain, its men ill-equipped for counter-insurgency. The army could not be deployed effectively, for if martial law were proclaimed in Ireland, the government would incur criticism and find itself admitting what it was reluctant to concede, namely that it was in a state of war with an enemy in the 'field'.

In these circumstances the cabinet decided to adopt an expedient. The viceroy, Lord French, who narrowly escaped assassination in December 1919, looked instead to the police force for the restoration of order. In January 1920 he took up the suggestion of Walter Long to recruit ex-servicemen to the R.I.C. The government proceeded to overhaul its Irish machinery. Additional legal powers were given to military commanders to carry out searches and arrests. The administration in Dublin Castle, its internal decline a symptom of the crumbling of British rule in Ireland since 1914, was reformed. In July 1920 a new 'Auxiliary Division' was added to the R.I.C., recruited this time mainly from ex-officers and stationed in the most troublesome areas of the country in companies of one hundred men. The Restoration of Order in Ireland Act was passed through parliament in August 1920. This was a formidable response, on the face of it; but it was undermined by its own failure to define the objectives of its military offensive in Ireland, and by the frequently undisciplined and lawless nature of its response. The government's unorthodox law-enforcement measures seemed to indicate that it was prepared to condone in Ireland behaviour which it would never accept anywhere else in the United Kingdom. The I.R.A. campaign was by no means popular, especially in its early days; but it was hard to stand up against it and thus risk one's life, and it was even harder to come out and oppose it when the forces of law and order were, on occasion, taking the law into their own hands—and when the government itself seemed weary and indifferent about the state of Ireland during the troubled years between 1919 and 1921.

The 'War of Independence' was a many-sided struggle. Individual Volunteers showed courage and generosity to their enemies; others revealed a depth of savagery that would have been unthinkable in 1918. Some killed for sectarian reasons, others because they believed they were fighting a tyrannical foe who had held their nation in thrall for eight hundred years. Others fought because they wanted excitement; or because they were unemployed, or belonged to families who wanted to cut a dash locally. But none of them fought to bring about any kind of social revolution. In 1919 and 1920 some kind of social uprising seemed possible as strikes and militant industrial activity surfaced: workers in creameries, breweries and similar establishments struck for better wages and working conditions, and even founded short-lived 'soviets' to operate their premises for themselves. This was inspired by worsening economic conditions and by the growth of pro-Bolshevik views within the Socialist Party of Ireland (eventually causing a split in the organisation as the Bolshevik faction ousted the more moderate leaders such as William O'Brien). Such developments shook Sinn Féin, which feared 'creeping Bolshevism'. It was even more alarmed by the re-emergence of an older form of agitation, agrarian radicalism. But the I.R.A. moved swiftly to suppress this because they were engaged in an unselfish struggle for the freedom of the country; and any attempt to 'cash in on the work of the I.R.A.' by people who 'wanted something for themselves' and did not 'give a damn about the nation' was 'cleaned up'. Irish Labour retreated from its more socialistic modes. By April 1920 Labour in Tipperary had moved away from soviet-style occupations of 1919 to support hunger-striking republican prisoners. In May 1920 the National Union of Railwaymen agreed to a national strike to prevent the carriage of munitions for the crown forces. This enabled the I.R.A. to maintain a common front and create the idea of a nation in arms. Solidarity was put a long way before social reform, let alone revolution.[56]

While these events were unfolding in the south and west of Ireland the north was moving into a crisis of Catholic–Protestant relations worse than any since the 1880s. But the British government's decision to cast around for an Irish policy was not the product of the immediate difficulties in Ireland. It was inspired by the recognition that the formal end of the European war, with the signing of the peace treaties, meant that the Home Rule Act of 1914 would automatically come into operation, unless something were put in its place. It was clear that the 1914 act was no longer relevant to the condition of Ireland; and the government had to acknowledge its promise of special treatment of Unionist Ulster. The coalition government, faced with a weak and ineffective opposition, was able to show a rare unanimity on Ireland. Everyone acknowledged that Home Rule must come; the question was how best to tackle it, given the consequences of the 1918 general election in Ireland. The government examined the options: it would introduce Irish self-government of the traditional Home Rule kind; but this must not coerce Unionist Ulster; and it must not compromise the British in the eyes of the world, and especially of the United States of America.

The government drew up a bill which broke new ground in the long saga of Home Rule bills and acts. Special treatment for Ulster had been considered since 1913; measures had been suggested in 1916 and 1917. But these had always assumed that any excluded area would simply remain an integral part of the United Kingdom. The government's new bill envisaged setting up not one but two parliaments in Ireland: one for 'Southern Ireland', and one for 'Northern Ireland', each endowed with devolutionary powers. In addition, a Council of Ireland would be set up to act as a unifying link for matters of common concern, and perhaps ultimately providing the means for north and south to renegotiate their own reunification. Irish representation would continue at Westminster. Britain would thus avoid any criticism that she was governing nationalists against their will, or that she was giving active support to Ulster in its refusal to unite with the rest of Ireland. No British government wanted the responsibility of permanently partitioning Ireland; but neither could it accept the role (which nationalists cast it in, in fact if not in name) of bending Unionists in the north to the will of nationalist Ireland. Of course, in implementing partition the government was assuming the role of bending nationalists in the north to the will of Ulster Unionism. But the Unionist presence, and nationalist absence, from parliament meant that Ulster Unionists were able to influence the final shape of the bill, both in principle and in detail. In particular, Unionists insisted that the government's Irish Committee's initial plan of a nine-county Northern Ireland must be modified to include only those six counties which the Unionists felt they could control. Even Bonar Law originally plumped for nine counties, for the government was aware of the danger of placing nationalists at too great a disadvantage, and it hoped to establish a much larger, and thus more powerful, minority in the northern state. But the troubles in the south meant that, as Walter Long put it, the government could not afford to disagree fundamentally with both its friends and its critics. And so Ulster Unionists had their way. The bill passed through its various stages and received the royal assent on 23 December 1920.[57] Elections to the new parliaments of Northern Ireland and Southern Ireland were arranged for May 1921. They produced an overwhelming Unionist majority in the north, despite the use of proportional representation in the elections. Once elected, the purpose of the Ulster Unionist government, led by Sir James Craig, was to do its best for its nationalist minority—providing that did not jeopardise the task of building up a Unionist state, preserving its integrity, and keeping the Unionist Party and people together. These developments did not augur well for the Catholic minority, which formed one-third of the population of Northern Ireland. They became the object not only of Unionist suspicion but of violence, as the I.R.A. campaign in the north, retaliatory attacks by Unionists on Catholics, and rioting on a wide and dangerous scale seemed almost to threaten to plunge the province, and the new state carved out of the province, into endless and bloody communal strife.[58]

Nationalists, of course, protested against the desecration of the national territory; but they had nothing to offer the Protestants of the north, except angry rhetoric, war, and a boycott of goods. This boycott, organised by Sinn Féin and fully approved of by Arthur Griffith (his early admiration for the Protestant and his industrial city, Belfast, now quite dissipated), was described by one dissident republican as a tactic which 'denied the whole principle upon which separatists of every generation had claimed for the country independence' and amounted to a 'blind and suicidal contribution to the general hate'.[59] But then, Irish separatists of every generation had never been obliged to face up to the consequences of their wilful blindness to Unionist opinion. And in any event the sectarian character of militant separatist violence, in both south and north, was in its own terrible way an admission of the failure of the republicanism of Tone, Emmet and the founding fathers of the enlightenment in Ireland.

Ulster Unionists gathered their resources to defend themselves against their enemies without and within. But while the north was emerging as a separate state, with a Home Rule parliament, the British government was increasingly unhappy about the consequences of its irregular military and police response to the I.R.A. campaign in the south. The difficulty was not only that the government had no clearly defined military objective in Ireland; it was that the unruly behaviour of members of its forces, especially the new 'Black and Tan' recruits to the R.I.C., were calling in question the morality and legality on which British rule was supposed to be based. A major incident—like the attack by some members of the Auxiliary Division on the main street of Cork city—may have been exaggerated by the republican movement's efficient propaganda bureau; but it was by any standards indefensible, especially by a government which had run a campaign against 'Prussianism' in the Great War and the atrocities it generated. Atrocities were, it must be said, few; but Ireland was still, nominally at least, a part of the United Kingdom, and the British journalists and M.P.s and other public figures who expressed their concern about the government's law and order policy could not see the Irish, Sinn Féiners or otherwise, as a far-away people who could be coerced by militarism and reprisal. The commander-in-chief of the British forces in Ireland, General Sir Nevil Macready, had no liking for the whole Irish political business, and indeed no liking for the Irish people, whom he once described as 'worse than the Boche'. This may have contributed to the pessimistic memoranda which he presented to the cabinet in May 1921, when the general election in Southern Ireland gave Sinn Féin a sweeping victory, though a victory in which intimidation or the threat of it played a part. Macready felt that the army was being damaged by its Irish campaign, in both its morale and its operational effectiveness. Sir Henry Wilson, the Chief of Imperial General Staff, hoped that this would drive the government to 'govern or get out'. But the cabinet had been moving slowly towards the notion that indeed it might, in the end, have to negotiate with representatives of Sinn Féin. The opening of the Northern Ireland parliament on 22 June, at which the king made a sincere appeal for peace, gave the government the chance to put itself right in the eyes of its critics and exert political pressure on Sinn Féin, where military pressure had, it seemed, met with failure.[60]

In retrospect, this decision can appear either long overdue, or an untimely surrender by the British government just at the point when the I.R.A. was, as Michael Collins put it some months later, 'dead beat'.[61] But neither of these views acknowledged the nature of the struggle in which both sides had been engaged. The I.R.A. campaign was confined almost entirely to the province of Munster and the city of Dublin. There was little fighting in the west, that troublesome area of the 1880s and 1890s, and the midlands were almost trouble-free. The north was troubled, but the I.R.A. could not establish itself beyond certain nationalist areas.[62] The I.R.A. was even developing tactics that called for more 'open' warfare, resulting eventually in its disastrous attack on the Custom House, Dublin, on 25 May, when scores of volunteers were captured, many of them in a state of dismay at their officers' folly in having landed them in such a predicament.[63] But this is to miss the point, a point obscured by the application of phrases like 'War of Independence' or 'Anglo-Irish War' to the conflict. The native description 'the troubles' is far more appropriate; for it makes the point that the I.R.A., in its sporadic and at times brutal way, had made the normal government of large parts of the country impossible. They had, as their Chief of Staff put it, 'not beaten the English in spite of their being disciplined, but largely because they were not'.[64] The government had to extricate itself from the embarrassing consequences of its own military response; and the I.R.A. had obliged it to reappraise both the campaign and its objectives—or lack of them. But the I.R.A. and the politicians of Sinn Féin had the same problem. De Valera was anxious that the Dáil should assume responsibility for the actions of an organisation quite out of its control; and this was done in March 1921. But he was anxious about the impact of the troubles of the people; he felt that their burden was heavy. And when the British offered a truce in July 1921, it was certain that it must be accepted, otherwise the whole campaign would lose its direction, its momentum, and the benefit it gained from the image it possessed as the armed cutting-edge of a 'risen people'. Sinn Féin had, after all, been given the status of equal negotiators; and the I.R.A. had gained a truce which left it still in existence should the fighting be renewed.[65]

In reality, however, the British and Irish were not negotiating as equals. The British, by offering a truce and talks, won over to their side those sections of public opinion which had been the government's most vociferous critics in the troubles. The Irish were now at a disadvantage, especially following the British offer in August 1921 of dominion status, with certain safeguards for British defence: this seemed an offer which no reasonable or responsible politician could refuse. It might be an offer which the Irish could not refuse in another, more sinister, sense. For the British had at their disposal superior forces which could now be used with the support of British public opinion. The I.R.A. was still in the field; but the general public was weary of the struggle, in which they were the main casualty. The I.R.A. would find its support diminished if it were to seek to renew the war. This would not, of course, deter some of its commanders from wanting to go another round with British, or with anyone else who stood in the way of the Republic. But they could hardly claim to represent the 'people'.

The Republic was compromised from the beginning; once Sinn Féin accepted negotiations on the basis of the dominion status offer of August 1921, they were committed to accepting less than the Republic—unless, of course, they wanted to break off the talks and renew the fighting. They might, however, outmanoeuvre the government on its weakest point, the partition of Ireland. Here the British cabinet was less sure of its ground. It knew that the British public could be rallied on the issues of the crown, defence and British interests; it was less sure that this would be so if Unionist Ulster proved a hindrance to a settlement.

The Irish delegation had its problems as well. Arthur Griffith and Michael Collins were determined simply to 'do their best for Ireland', which might mean relinquishing the Republic. They were involved in exhausting and complex negotiations, and yet found themselves obliged to account for their actions to the cabinet in Dublin, presided over by de Valera, who believed quite simply that his scheme of Ireland's 'external association' with the British empire, recognising the crown only as head of that empire, but not of Ireland herself, was the perfect compromise between republicanism and imperialism.[66]

Griffith and Collins and their team negotiated as best they could and obtained some concession at the fringe of the British offer of dominion status. They even achieved a modification of the Irish oath of allegiance to the crown. They also managed to place the British government in an awkward position over the Ulster question when in November 1921 the coalition found itself attacked from within by Unionists who believed that the cabinet was about to 'surrender to crime'. But the Irish delegation could not exploit this British discomfiture too far. For if they pressed the partition issue and broke off negotiations, they would be faced with the possibility of a hardline Unionist government that would perhaps abandon the talks and renew the fighting. Lloyd George found that this consideration worked in his favour with his own backbenchers as well: for if the 'diehards' brought him down, they would be forced to face the logic of their own actions and tell the British public that they were not prepared to give the cabinet its chance to explore the possibility that peace could be secured by negotiations. Lloyd George exploited what seemed on the face of it to be his greatest weakness. On 12 November he saw Griffith and told him that Ulster would be offered a choice: either she would come into an all-Ireland parliament, or Lloyd George would confront Sir James Craig with the government's alternative of a frontier rectification, adjusting the boundaries of the state of Northern Ireland. But Lloyd George added that he would do this only if he had Griffith's assurance that Griffith would not afterwards repudiate him and use the Ulster question as an excuse for breaking off the negotiations. Griffith gave Lloyd George a personal written pledge on this. Lloyd George used this pledge in the last hours of the negotiations with dramatic effect, though by then it was less important than it seemed. By the last days of the talks Griffith and Collins were convinced that they had got the best offer they could, and that they must ensure that the Ulster difficulty would not wreck their chances of extorting what Redmond and Parnell had failed to win—an Irish state. A Boundary Commission offered a way out, not only for the British, but for the Irish as well.[67]

The last days, and then hours, of the Anglo-Irish Treaty negotiations were filled with drama: the spectacle of Lloyd George demanding that the Irish delegates sign under the threat of war, 'and war within three days'; the account of Collins signing the document, with suffering in restraint; Collins's own memory of the dark, wet London streets on which he stood, the deed done, thinking 'What have I got for Ireland'?—all these excite the imagination, and are still not free of controversy.[68] There can be no doubt that the Irish signed under duress; but a treaty on the broad lines of the original British offer of August 1921 was the most likely outcome of the protracted negotiations. The longer the talks went on, the more reluctant were Griffith and Collins to lose what they had wrested from the British by breaking them off.

The Treaty was signed on 6 December 1921. It was greeted with joy and acclaim in the British press; but in Ireland the response, at first generally favourable, was quickly embittered by the hostility of those who believed that the delegates had signed away the Republic. These dissidents were given the leadership of de Valera, who, while not a sea-green republican, believed that Griffith and Collins had not exhausted the negotiating process and might yet make a 'grand' treaty on his, and not their, terms.

The Treaty called for a meeting of the members elected for constituencies in 'Southern Ireland' since the passing of the Government of Ireland Act to be summoned, and a Provisional Government of the Irish Free State constituted. Provided that the members of this government signified in writing their acceptance of the Treaty, the British government undertook to transfer to it the machinery of government; and the Treaty was to be submitted to the British parliament and the parliament of Southern Ireland for ratification. The Treaty was debated in the Dáil between 14 December 1921 and 7 January 1922 and was approved by 64 votes to 57. This was an awkward result for the signatories of the Treaty, for its very closeness emphasised the depth of the split in Sinn Féin and deprived Griffith and Collins of a moral advantage. The bitterness of the Dáil debate, the accusations and counter-accusations, the violent emotional tone of the exchange, made (and still make) harrowing reading. The only issue was the Republic; the partition of Ireland played no significant part in the debates. But implicit in the debate was an issue soon to become explicit: the question of whether or not the people and its representatives had 'the right to be wrong'. Ernie O'Malley warned that 'we have never consulted the feelings of the people', to which Cathal Brugha replied ominously (and accurately): 'If so, we never would have fired a shot.'[69]

The controversies surrounding the signing of the Treaty, and the consequences of that event, were soon to move from the debating chamber to civil war. Meanwhile Northern Ireland was experiencing violent conflict in no way alleviated by the signing of the Anglo-Irish Treaty. On the contrary, the prospect, now made more sure, of nationalists' inclusion in a Unionist state provoked not only a determination by the I.R.A. (aided by Michael Collins) to bring the new government to its knees, but a more impressive protest from Catholic teachers in the north who refused to accept their state salaries. Their action involved the Dublin government, which gave financial support to the teachers but found the liability large and increasingly burdensome. By August 1922 the Free State was having serious doubts about the whole exercise; and in November it withdrew its payment of the northern teachers. This left the protesting teachers with financial liabilities, which, however, the Free State declined to meet.[70] It was an acrimonious start to Northern Ireland's existence, and one which further damaged relations between majority and minority there, and between Dublin and Belfast.

Sir James Craig and his cabinet were not inspired by any spirit of malevolence towards the Catholic minority; but they saw as their priority what they called the restoration of order. And this involved not only the use of the army and the police force, but the raising and deployment of the most controversial security force in Northern Ireland's history, the Ulster Special Constabulary. This was first recruited in October 1920, and it was an exclusively Protestant body, based largely upon the old Ulster Volunteer Force of pre-war days. During the truce the British government agreed to suspend not only the army but also the 'B' class of special constabulary to demonstrate good faith to the Sinn Féin delegation. But, as so often, what looked like good faith in one quarter of the British Isles smacked of betrayal in another. Craig was anxious lest vigilante groups should try to usurp what he regarded as the function of the state. But the signing of the Treaty was the signal for renewed I.R.A. activity on the border. Discussions between Craig and Collins in March 1922 failed to bring any improvement in the situation, as shooting, bombing and rioting claimed lives, with the Catholics suffering the greater part of the casualties. A Civil Authorities (Special Powers) Act was rushed through the Northern Ireland parliament in the spring of 1922;[71] now it was used with increasing severity—and increasing effect—to restore law and order in a state which felt itself besieged not only from the south, not only from its recalcitrant minority, but from a British public that might press its government to wash its hands of the whole Irish muddle.

> The fear at the back of my mind [wrote Craig to the editor of the Unionist *Morning Post*] all the time is this, that the British public being unable to discriminate owing to geographical ignorance may begin to think that the North is as bad as the South, in which case they may throw up their hands and say 'Let them go to the devil too.'[72]

Craig was also under some pressure from the British government in security matters. The government was anxious that the draconian powers of the Northern Ireland state should not reflect badly on the British, who were still ultimately responsible for the devolved Northern Ireland state. The British government, in all fairness, was concerned too about the predicament of the Catholic minority. But Craig had one supreme advantage in his dealings with the British: they had no wish to involve themselves in such a way that they would once again be burdened with the direct rule of the north. This consideration lay behind their reluctant acquiescence in the Northern Ireland government's decision to abolish proportional representation in local government elections in September 1922.[73]

The northern minority's difficulty was that, at a crucial time in its history, it lacked adequate representatives to plead its case. Northern Ireland nationalists were divided between, on the one hand, those who still held to the remnant of the Irish Parliamentary Party, whose local leader, Joseph Devlin, was not admitted to any official or high-level discussion, and, on the other hand, the supporters of Sinn Féin. The latter had an advocate in Michael Collins; but his rather hysterical style, and his aid for the I.R.A.'s efforts to undermine the state of Northern Ireland, compromised his position; and in any case his death in August 1922 deprived northern nationalists of even that source of support. The British government was mindful of its responsibilities in the north, and considered an inquiry into the attacks on Catholics;[74] but it was aware of the inexpedience of allowing itself to be manoeuvered into too deep an involvement in the Ulster troubles, for it had its own problems in dealing with the new Provisional Government of the Irish Free State.

That difficulty between Westminster and Dublin arose from the Free State's efforts to draft a constitution which promised to weaken the bonds that held Ireland to the British empire, and from the British government's growing impatience with the failure, as it saw it, of the Free State to move against the anti-Treaty faction of the I.R.A. which, following the Treaty debate in the Dáil, began systematically to prepare itself to defend not only the Republic but also the local power and authority of volunteer units. For there were many commanders who were simply unwilling to concede to politicians, or to anyone else, the prestige that the gun had given them over the past three years. 'Irregulars', as they were now being called, had also other activities besides the purely political, as the catalogue of incidents, including the old rural occupation of cattle-driving, suggested.[75] There were also personal differences, and especially the hostility of Cathal Brugha for Michael Collins. But there was at bottom a division between those in the organisation who were prepared to let politicians make the running and those who took a more simple military view: that the army must stay prepared to renew war throughout the period of the truce that had been concluded with the British in July 1921; and that it had the right to decide to follow its own direction, not that of the politicians, after the signing of the Treaty.[76]

The Irish Free State and the British government were soon in dispute over the draft Irish constitution. This constitution was drafted following an exhaustive examination of constitutions from all over the world; but in the end it bore a more homely—and more republican—look: the oath of allegiance was omitted, and the imperial connection and the place of the king in the constitution were diminished. The British government was determined that the Free State's constitution should conform to the Treaty, and it was sure that it could make the south of Ireland conform. But it feared that it might encounter the same difficulty that threatened its conduct of the Treaty negotiations: that the unrest and trouble in

Northern Ireland would deprive it of the high ground when it came to presenting its case to British and to world public opinion.[77] The British were even more alarmed when the Provisional Government made a last attempt to avoid civil war through an electoral pact with its opponents. On 20 May Collins and de Valera negotiated a pact to cover the elections to the provisional parliament. It was agreed that supporters and opponents of the Treaty would not campaign against each other, but would stand jointly, as Sinn Féin candidates, on a coalition basis, with numbers proportionate to existing strength in the second Dáil. There would also be a coalition executive after the election. Griffith agreed to this only reluctantly; Winston Churchill denounced the proposed election as a 'farce';[78] and British newspapers referred darkly to Michael Collins's 'capitulation' to de Valera. But Lloyd George urged caution. It might become necessary in the end to reconquer Ireland, but 'before that we should make clear to the civilised world that the present position is not our fault'.[79]

The election had at least one merit: it obliged the anti-Treaty group to put their views to the test of electoral approval—or disapproval—a test which was compromised in some degree by the Provisional Government's publication of its constitution on the morning of the election (a device aimed initially at keeping the British, rather than de Valera and his followers, in the dark). The Irish constitution in its final form embodied some concessions from the British. There was no direct oath of allegiance to the king, only an oath of allegiance 'in virtue of the common citizenship of the group of nations forming the British Commonwealth'. The Irish retained a greater than usual share in the nomination and appointment of the Governor-General; and appeal to the Privy Council was allowed only in cases which affected other members of the commonwealth. The crown was still in the constitution; but the constitution represented 'the actual rather than the legal status of the dominions'[80] and could reasonably be described as vindicating Collins's claim that it gave the 'freedom to achieve freedom'.

Collins himself gave the pact a fatal blow when in the election in Cork he urged voters to 'vote for the candidates you think best of'. He got a clear mandate for the Treaty: 58 out of 128 seats, with only 36 going to the anti-Treaty candidates. This election represented, above all, the desire of the mass of the people for a settlement, rather than any great affection for the Treaty. Labour, testing its strength at last, won 17 seats; Farmers 7; and Independents 10. Pro-Treaty candidates polled 239,195 votes; anti-Treaty candidates 132,161 votes; and the other parties 247,082.

The impending civil war could now hardly be averted. The Free State government was still in the agonising position of being vulnerable to the Republican charge that it was acting at British dictation, though it had really gone to the utmost limits consistent with the duty of a government to govern. A crisis nearly came when on 22 June Sir Henry Wilson was assassinated in London by two members of the I.R.A., possibly acting on an order (unrescinded) of Michael Collins. There were cries in Britain for the 'nest of vipers' to be cleared out; the government resolved to press the Free State to act and 'end this state of things'.[81] On 24 June it ordered General Macready to attack the Four Courts, where the Irregulars had established themselves for some months; but Macready was an old hand in Ireland and wisely refused to budge.[82] Two days later, in the Commons, Churchill called upon the Irish government to implement the Treaty or face the consequences; but he remained appropriately vague about what the consequences would be.[83] The Provisional Government was, in any event, facing up to the fact that it must show the will and the military resolve to assert its legal and constitutional authority. The Irregulars provided the occasion when they kidnapped a Free State general as a reprisal for the arrest of some of their comrades. Collins and his military colleagues were now able to overcome their scruples about using force against their old comrades. An ultimatum was issued to the Irregulars who were occupying the Four Courts, requiring their surrender by 4 a.m. on Wednesday 28 June. This ultimatum was ignored, and the civil war began at 4.15 a.m. with the bombardment of the Four Courts by Free State troops.

The civil war was marked by cruelty and bitterness to a degree far greater than might be suggested by the cold statistics of casualties: approximately 4,000 lives lost in all, with government executions of Republicans totalling 77. In comparison with other civil wars in the twentieth century, in states of comparable size and population, this was a modest enough total.[84] And, unlike the 1798 rebellion, there never seemed to be any danger of the country lapsing into a general political and social chaos. There remained a sense of stability, as indeed there had been in the era of the Black and Tan war. But bitterness is not only created by the scale of killing; and Ireland (north and south) exhibited again that characteristic of containing violence within what might be called—in a perhaps unacceptable phrase—an acceptable level, and yet harbouring the most lasting and uncompromising memories of her troubled times. This was partly because of the accusation and counter-accusation, as the Free State supporters reacted angrily to the wholly unjust sneer that the 'old enemy, England' was 'using new weapons lent her, to their shame, by traitors to the Republic'. De Valera accused Collins of acting 'at the bidding of the English'.[85] But the fabric of the state was not, in 1922–3, threatened as it had been in 1798. The Irregulars were, as the I.R.A. had been, an army without banners, but they could enlist no comparable measure of public support, and they incurred the censure of the Catholic Church. And they were fighting against an Irish army that did not feel obliged to account for itself to a critical national and world opinion.

The architects of the Irish Free State, Griffith and Collins, were casualties of the struggle: Collins died in an ambush on 22 August 1922; Griffith had died of a stroke ten days earlier. The new head of state, William T. Cosgrave, presided over a country where the anti-Treaty forces regarded their defeat in May 1923 as merely a cessation of arms, not a final surrender. And the ghosts of 1916 and 1922–3 were to return to haunt not only the Free State's founders, but even its leading political opponent, Eamon de Valera.

Yet the new state was not in such bad shape, after all. The conservatism of the majority of its people was merely dormant in the troubles, and it soon resurfaced at their conclusion. Sinn Féin had associated with agrarian protest only as a means to an end, 'to get these fellows into the Volunteers', as one republican put it.[86] Liam Mellows boasted of the Irregulars relying, as republicans had done in the days of Wolfe Tone, on 'the men of no property';[87] but this only emphasised their weakness, for the anti-Treaty forces were strongest amongst small farmers and labourers—in other words, on men marginal to the existence of the Free State, or indeed any state. The new state, whatever its protest against partition, benefited from the exclusion of the troubled and divided six counties. It based itself upon established institutions of local administration. Above all, while the Free State did not win a romantic affection amongst its people, it did vindicate the claim made by one Irish newspaper that

Ireland is big enough for great things and great movements, but it is too small for Civil War. Civil War means death and destruction. It means the material ruin of the nation and the moral degradation of its people.[88]

The fact that the anti-Treaty forces were confronted with a general election in June 1922 (the 'pact' election) put them at the disadvantage of opposing not only a particular electoral verdict, but the democratic electoral system as such. This was a challenge which neither they nor any of their survivors who sought to influence the course of Irish politics could avoid, and which de Valera, for his part, accepted when he founded his Fianna Fáil party in 1926.

The north was less fortunate. The south experienced deep and lasting political divisions; but its boundaries enclosed a fundamentally homogeneous population, whose tiny Protestant minority made scarcely any impact on the politics, or for that matter the consciousness, of the nation. Northern Ireland was left with a Catholic minority enclosed in a state whose institutions were soon to be constructed for the defence of Ulster Unionism and its people. Labour in the north was vulnerable to Unionist claims that it threatened to split Protestant ranks in the face of danger and was weak on the border question. Labour in the south was, to use de Valera's phrase, 'waiting'. Peadar O'Donnell admitted that 'We had a pretty barren mind, socially; many on the Republican side were against change.'[89] But this is hardly surprising. In Ireland under the Union the social reconstruction or reform instinct always came from Great Britain, with its large, influential and politically and administratively active middle class. Ireland remained, as she had always been, a passive recipient and observer.

The events surrounding the creation of the two states of Ireland deeply influenced their character. The liberal tradition in Irish nationalism, which at least preached the virtues of a pluralist approach to the national question, was weakened as the Free State and the Catholic hierarchy set out to create a homogeneous Gaelic and Catholic nation. Unionists of a liberal disposition in the north (and there were some) were at the mercy of the populist style to which Sir James Craig all too often surrendered himself. Carson's parting advice to his Ulster allies, that they should seek a consensus, while admittedly difficult in the circumstances, was largely ignored.[90] The Union had failed to find or create a settled constitution for the people of Ireland. Large and formidable problems confronted the new states that arose at its extinction, as they embarked upon the experiment of governing for themselves. For as always, in politics, there were winners and losers in the game.

Stability and Strife
in Nineteenth-Century Ireland

THE historian of nineteenth-century Ireland cannot help but notice the odd nature of his choice of period. In chronological terms, it might be said that the century begins, comfortably and logically enough, on 1 January 1801; but before that date the issues and forces that were to dominate the century had already begun to work. In the 1790s the Catholic question was at the forefront of political and public discussion; and that question provoked the Protestant question: the question of what the two main groups of Protestants—the Episcopalians, who still monopolised political power, if not all the means of expressing it; and the Presbyterians, who sought to challenge that monopoly—were to do about the growing confidence and claims of the Catholic political leadership. In the countryside too the familiar landmarks were forming, with a marked rise in agrarian crime and the proliferation of secret societies, which could be harnessed for political ends, and indeed which had, in their crude and frequently violent way, political ends of their own: the defence of land, home, job, religion, family or friend. Catholic political activity, Presbyterian radicalism, agrarian violence, the clash of Orangeman and Defender, were all to collide in the terrible climax of the 1798 rising, or, rather, in the several outbreaks, in Wexford, the west and Ulster, which taken together form what came to be known as 'the '98'. And not only these groups and ideas were formed before 1800: a key element in the history of Ireland, increasingly involved in the 1780s and 1790s, was the British government. This was a government which, under the Younger Pitt, became more concerned about Irish affairs, about the risks and advantages of pressurising the Irish parliament to accept Catholic relief measures, about the possibilities of combining Catholic Emancipation with a union of the two kingdoms. When in 1792 it became known that England supported the Catholic cause, it provoked Catholic self-assertion and Protestant fear, resentment and hostility. The government's decision in 1795 to distance itself from Catholic claims had a dramatic effect on the connection forged between Catholics and the United Irish movement, and led directly to the events of 1798.[1]

Roman Catholics; two main species of Protestants; the British government. These were the groups and institutions which eyed each other with a mixture of suspicion and expectation in the new century, once the Union with Britain was accomplished. And the history of the nineteenth century is the story of the working out of their claims, relationships and policies. It is also, of course, the story of individuals within these broad categories; and of classes, sub-sects and organisations which often fractured what appears at first sight to be monolithic sets of people. Catholic unity was hard to achieve on any issue; the Roman Catholic Church worked as a kind of pressure group, suspicious of any movement that might lead the people astray or compromise their interests (as defined by the church). O'Connell and Parnell stand out as the dominant figures of the age; yet even they had to struggle to hold their movements together, to define common goals, and above all to discover the most effective means of pursuing those goals. Anglican and Presbyterian were often at odds: Presbyterian tenant farmer recognised a clash of interests with Episcopalian landlord. The Belfast working man had little discernible in common with the rural Protestant landlord or tenant; and at times he was involved in serious clashes of interest with the employer, who might be his co-religionist but who still might cut his wages or even deprive him of his livelihood altogether.

Yet for all these divergences of opinion and interest, the two main denominations continued to see themselves as—on crucial occasions, as well as generally—occupying opposite camps and sharing an island which each of them, in effect, claimed rather than shared. The question *To whom does Ireland belong?* was the question posed and answered in one way at the end of the Williamite wars in 1690, and it was asked again as Catholics rose to political self-assertion and Protestants were obliged to consider their position. The Protestant response differed, according not only to region, class and circumstance, but also to individuality: there were those who did not necessarily see conflict, or even an irreconcilable clash of interest, as fundamental to the condition of being Irish. There were political mavericks; there were Protestant

Liberals, like the Rev. J. B. Armour of Ballymoney, whose political nonconformity led him into embracing not only land reform but even Home Rule, and who disliked the Anglican Church and the Conservative landlords as the natural enemies of his people, the Presbyterians of Ulster. There were Catholic Unionists, though their identity was measured individually rather than in any significant or even discernible group. And there were those who hardly cared who was the master, as long as they could plough and go to market. There were also people, in the west of Ireland, who scarcely felt the impact of any state system, and whose way of life crumbled and died in the course of the century, mourned only by Gaelic enthusiasts who misunderstood that way of life almost as much as they professed to admire it.

What these groups would have done, how they would have fared in an Ireland which was not accorded the *pax Britannica* in 1801 is a matter of speculation. But it is hard to disagree with the historian and maker of modern Italy, Count Camillo Cavour, when in 1844 he warned that Repeal would have serious consequences for Ireland. In spite of the regret which O'Connell sometimes expressed, 'no one', Cavour declared, 'thinks of restoring the old Irish constitution. What the Catholic Association [*sic*] desires is the creation of a national parliament on the bases which Catholic Emancipation and the Reform of 1832 have consecrated, in which the Catholic popular element should have an incontestable preponderance.' 'After so many centuries of dependence and submission', he argued, 'the Catholic majority aspires to power and dominance in its turn.' An Irish parliament animated by this spirit and 'subject to the empire of popular demands' would be a bad judge in the cause pleaded by tenants against landlords. 'There is reason to fear that its sentence would be dictated by a spirit of reaction and of vengeance, which may be as fatal to Ireland in the future, as the spirit of oppression and intolerance has been in the past.' As for the Protestants, though but a small minority, they were strong by their wealth, their energy, and their organisation. 'At the first cry of insurrection they would rise in mass, and with the aid of the regular troops, they would unhesitatingly attack the assemblages of Catholics in revolt.'[2]

It is unnecessary to accept the details of Cavour's dire predictions to allow that, in broadest outline, his views deserve at least respect. Cavour went on to argue that the alternative, which he preferred, was that the British government would embark on a programme of reform, social, economic and institutional, which would close the differences between the sects and provide a fair and more just society. He was not certain whether such a programme would succeed 'in radically curing the wounds of Ireland, and in completely fusing the sentiments of that country with those of Britain'. Those were 'brave questions which only the future can resolve'. But he hoped that 'real progress' would compensate Ireland for 'the loss of those brilliant dreams of national independence that she can never realise'.[3] Again the historian must ask a question, this time an obvious one; or rather, he must supply an answer: there were reforms, there was 'progress', but Ireland did, in 1921, seek and achieve a measure of national independence with partition.

This raises the role of the British government in nineteenth-century Ireland. It was, as Cavour noted, in the British interest to promote stability and order through reform; it would save her from the barrage of foreign criticism to which her Irish policy rendered her vulnerable. The problem was, however, that the British government was not always in a position to pursue such a policy wholeheartedly or even sympathetically. There was, after all, a difference between Great Britain and Ireland.

The two countries, it is true, became closer in many respects during the nineteenth century. Communications were improved. The Irish sent representatives to Westminster, thus distinguishing Ireland in a vital respect from analogous countries like Canada. The English language virtually replaced Gaelic. There were no specific Irish institutions that could rival British local and central government models. There was free movement between the countries. English sports were played in Ireland, even if the cricketers were denounced, in rather hyperbolic terms, as fantastic foreigners. Belfast was, in almost all her physical and many of her social aspects, a British industrial city. Irish farmers fed the English market, especially during the Great War. Irishmen joined the British army in large numbers, before and during that war. Ireland was, and remained, a country of the common law. If politics in Ireland were based on religious denominations, so they were in Great Britain as well. And even the parties which, in the House of Commons, were most distinct from the mainstream British parties—the Repeal party and the Irish Parliamentary Party—were in may respects allied to, and a kind of Irish wing of, the Whigs and then the Liberals. Irish Conservatives, for their part, were involved with the British Conservative Party, as were Irish Unionists with the British Unionists, even if their distrust was aroused when the British parties seemed less than sensitive to their local and particularist demands. And Ireland benefited from the extension of British parliamentary and electoral legislation, accompanying the liberal democracy of Britain in the transformation of aristocratic politics to modern democratic politics—and even managing to pick up proportional representation on the way.

And yet there were important differences. The Irish Roman Catholic was regarded as someone not quite, or not at all, within the constitution. His church was ignored by the British state, even at a time, in the late eighteenth and early nineteenth century, when it was well disposed towards the British connection. This made his position rather different from that of the British Nonconformist (with whom he shared many similarities in terms of civil disabilities as a result of the constitutional and religious history of the British Isles). The difference was that no one in Great Britain could doubt that the Nonconformist was a supporter of the British constitution; at least, no one could doubt it from the 1830s, when Nonconformity began to find expression in Whig and then Liberal politics. Welsh Nonconformists, likewise, began to make their way under the umbrella of the Liberal Party and Gladstone's careful canvass of their votes. But the Irish Catholic was suspect, because of his past, and because of the ambitious claims of the Roman Church to which he adhered. Only Gladstone, with his sense of mission and his political prestige, could have made the Catholic political cause a popular one in British Liberal circles, as he did between 1868 and 1893; but even he could not prevent the division of his party, a strong public reaction over much, if not most, of England, and an English nationalist response that denied not only the justice of Home Rule but its very compatibility with the survival of the United Kingdom and its Protestant (and therefore liberal) constitution.

British political parties and the British public had other, more domestic, priorities anyway, as Irish nationalists and Unionists alike found to their cost. British politicians often competed not only in describing enthusiastically what they could 'do for Ireland' (in itself a patronising phrase) but also in exclaiming how absurd it was that their opponents should do so much for Ireland and place the interests of the British second. Even a politician as interested in Irish affairs as Joseph Chamberlain could look for British votes on the grounds that his Liberal opponents were showing excessive favouritism towards the Irish: in the 1893 Home Rule Bill, he pointed out, it had been proposed to give an untrustworthy Ireland autonomy at a cost of £2 million a year to the British taxpayer while leaving virtually untouched the curse of continued Irish representation at Westminster. When Sir Robert Peel made his sincere effort to settle Irish grievances in the 1840s, he was bitterly opposed by members of his own party on the grounds that he was handing over British money to the disloyal and superstitious Roman Church in its seminary at Maynooth.

But there was another, deeper aspect of the Union that made British government of Ireland both a destabilising as well as a stabilising force. The British could and did provide a framework, a constitutional settlement in which the forces of rebellion and sectarian hatred were contained. The Union, for the greater part of the century, seemed to be a permanent fixture, if only because no one could agree about what might replace it in the event of its abrogation, even if the British were to admit of any such eventuality. But the British role in Ireland had other, less steadying consequences. This was seen in 1793–5 when the British government's overt sympathy with the Catholic Emancipation movement raised Catholic hopes and inspired Protestant fears. It happened again when British governments sought to promote the interests of the Roman Catholic, which Protestants regarded as throwing doubt on the British resolve to maintain the Union. To catch the eye of the British state was to raise a local political demand into a major issue; and in Ireland one man's hope was another man's damnation. This became acute when the very question of Ireland's constitution was taken up by Gladstone and the Liberal Party. The revolution of 1886, in both British and Irish politics, caused new fault-lines to emerge, which, however, took their origin in the old divisions of Ireland. Each side prepared for the worst. And Unionist Britain would not give up without a fight, any more than would Unionist Ireland. The period of relative calm which followed the defeat of the second Home Rule Bill in 1893 was succeeded by the tensions and conflict of the third Home Rule Bill. After 1912 each side in Ireland—and they were sides—waited to see what the intentions of the British government would be. When a country did not have a

political existence of its own, when it was engaged in the politics of
a larger and more powerful neighbour, then the intentions and
outlook of that neighbour must be an unsettling and at times even
highly disturbing force.

In this sense Irish politics under the Union were—at least quite
often—the politics of impotence, or of one side's sense of impotence as the other side appeared to have the sympathy of the
government—a government which no Irishman played a major part
in electing. Yet the Union provided at least the possibility of unity
in diversity. When it seemed stable and assured, then indeed the
ground rules of Irish politics seemed to lose some of their rigidity:
literary movements, political dissidents, even labour politics and
tenant right agitation, could cut across the boundaries. Thus the
Union was, at one and the same time, a steadying and yet a
disturbing influence. Colonel Saunderson could describe the Nationalist M.P.s as 'murderers'; yet, when the constitutional question was set aside, he could act with them to persuade the
government to extend to Ireland a rating subsidy that had already
been granted to farmers in Great Britain.[4] Carson was prepared to
go to the lengths of supporting rebellion to save the Union; yet he
spoke up for Irish Catholic rights in educational matters, and
retorted sharply to his own front bench when anti-Irish sentiments
were blurted out.[5] But on the Union there could be no compromise.

This left the question of how far Irishmen could accommodate
their own differences under the Union. It would be wrong, of
course, to suggest that nineteenth-century Ireland was a country in
perpetual strife and crisis. The two rebellions before 1916—those of
1848 and 1867—were complete failures. And there were voices,
from the Young Irelanders to Yeats, which proclaimed the need to
find a common ground for all Irishmen. These movements encountered opposition from nationalists who could not forget that
their movement rested upon Catholic support. The Catholic hierarchy was suspicious of Mazzinian ideas and crypto-Protestantism.
Rightly suspicious, as it happened, for these impulses were inspired
by the southern Protestant need to find cultural leadership where
political leadership was vanishing.

It was difficult for secular or Protestant-inspired ideas to prevail
in a society where religion, even among those who were not regular
church attenders, played such a central part in social as well as

political life. Religion was the means by which people identified themselves and distinguished themselves from each other. Yet, although—or perhaps because—religion was such a point of distinction, each side in the Anglican/Catholic sphere held the same image of the other. This is neatly captured in J. O. Hannay's description of the Catholic Church as raw and self-assertive, obtrusive and aggressive; and in Seán Ó Faoláin's reflection on the formidable barrier of religion, embodied in his native Cork:

> The outward symbol of that barrier is the Catholic church relegated to a remote or back street (cheaper ground, also less likely to attract attention) and the Protestant church plumb in the middle of a town square, or on the hill; and one will note how often the Catholic church is without a spire—that little arrogance forbidden by law. Thus in my native city of Cork the great trident of the spires of the Protestant cathedral dominates the city, all the older Catholic churches are hidden away, and one has a spire.[6]

Methodists, appropriately enough, came somewhere in between. The common Irish Protestant use of the term 'chapel' to describe a Roman Catholic building expressed the dissenting nature of the Catholic Church as an institution; Methodists fared better, in that their buildings were dignified with the name of church. Presbyterians, as befitted a religious group which took its origins from an established kirk in Scotland, grew in pride and confidence in the nineteenth century, and in Ulster constituted a kind of unofficial establishment ('the muscular system in the great body of Evangelical Christendom'),[7] but were also able to claim that the 'old Irish Church was more Presbyterian than Episcopal in its form of government . . . pure in doctrine and Presbyterian in government'.[8]

The Catholic resurgence at the turn of the century deeply affected Anglo-Irish relations for a time, as well as Protestant–Catholic relations in Ireland. A new mood began to emerge, fostered by the Catholic priesthood, who believed that England was a materialistic, immoral and even godless country; that she represented the modern, that she was characterised by drunkenness and evil. This idea, which found its origin in the Pioneer movement for temperance reform inaugurated at the end of the century,[9] bred a new kind of Catholic psyche: ascetic, elitist, self-regarding, and concerned to rescue Ireland, and what was defined as Irish culture, from the thrall of the modern world—which meant, of course, England. Patrick Pearse was its most famous product; Terence MacSwiney, Lord Mayor of Cork, who died on hunger-strike in 1920, was another. Such people staffed the Gaelic League and played a significant role in the Irish Republican Brotherhood and Sinn Féin.[10] Their enemies were not only the English, with their 'masher habits',[11] but also the Home Rulers, who supported the drink trade, were corrupt, were involved in political brokerage, and whose support by the Catholic Church was already under review even before the downfall of parliamentarianism between 1914 and 1918. When, after 1914, British rule was coming to some sort of end, it was clear, at least with the benefit of hindsight, that the Catholic and Protestant groups who built upon the ruins of one administration would lay the foundations of another in a spirit different from that of the best British liberal traditions.

And yet those traditions were not swept away, not even in the revolution of 1916–23. Democratic institutions survived both in the south and in Northern Ireland. The Free State escaped one-party rule, it is true, only because of the divisions of the civil war. This was a high price to pay, and Fianna Fáil, when eventually it arrived on the political scene, began the 'dominant party' system that has lasted until the present day. One-party rule was established in the north. But neither part of Ireland succumbed to military dictatorship; and somehow it never seemed that it would. The long experience of the Union, with its democratic political processes, could not be so easily set aside, even if the need for both north and south to negotiate with their powerful religious vested interests gave the working of Irish democracy a particular flavour.

The Union left another, equally important, legacy in the form of the efforts of British governments to deal with the anomaly that an Ireland integrated with Great Britain created in the first place. Ireland had one overwhelming social and economic problem—land; and to solve or alleviate that problem she needed what Victorian Britain could give her only belatedly. She needed state intervention on a large and consistent scale; she needed interference with property rights in order to enable the problem of an increasing population and decreasing subsistence resources to improve. Ireland did not get this soon enough to save her from the horrors of the Great Famine. And yet it is doubtful if an Irish parliament would have been in a position to do a great deal more than the British government did, though it can certainly be said that an Irish government would have done it with better grace. For there was in British official circles an impatience with what were regarded as a backward people, and a sense that at least the famine would clear such people away and leave Ireland open to the progressive forces upon whose foundation the success of Victorian Britain had been built.

State intervention on a consistent basis was not long delayed. In the late nineteenth century successive British governments sought to bind Ireland to England and create a more settled Irish society. This policy was mediated by the needs of British political parties, their electioneering prospects, and their desire to play to the gallery of the British electorate. But it was nonetheless significant; and its significance lay in the radical and wholly un-British policy of land reform: first Gladstone's attack on the sacrosanctity of property rights, with the gradual improvement of the tenants' position, and then the Conservative drive towards peasant proprietorship. This policy was unsuccessful in its declared object of winning the Irish farmer away from nationalism, since farmers believed that they owed their victory to the Home Rulers and the political supplications of their own priests (mainly from a farming background themselves), not to an open-minded British government. But it did create a solid and politically unadventurous class of landowning farmers of various sizes (as measured by their land), but whose support was essential to anyone with ambitions to establish and govern an Irish state. Much less was done for the labourer, in town, city or countryside; and when in the troubles of 1919–21 the less fortunate sought to do something for themselves, they were quickly put in their place. Land-grabbing, cattle-rustling or industrial strikes were not approved activities as far as Sinn Féin, its courts, and the I.R.A. were concerned. There would be no revolution from below. Sinn Féin built upon this rural conservatism; it succeeded because it managed to convince the farmer that it had no quarrel with him, and that it would do nothing much for Irish society, but that it would do it very well.

All the efforts made by British governments in the last quarter of the nineteenth century could not save the Union. Yet for most of its life the Union, however uneasily it might sit on Ireland and Great Britain, looked secure, especially in the decades following the Great

Famine, when Ireland confronted the reality of her disastrous social and economic predicament. Even after 1870 there were powerful forces on its side. The Liberals regarded Home Rule as a means of strengthening, not dissolving, the United Kingdom. The Unionists presented themselves as the defenders of its integrity. One-quarter of the population of Ireland opposed its modification, let alone its demise. It was the very *strength* of these pro-Union forces that pitched the United Kingdom and Ireland especially into the political crisis that resulted in the rise of new and intransigent anti-Union elements. The return of Home Rule as a central part of the Liberal platform (with promises of a federal reorganisation of the British Isles); the return of British Unionism to its full strength under the leadership of Andrew Bonar Law; the rise of militant Ulster Unionism, led by the dominating figure of Sir Edward Carson—all these essentially pro-Union parties and groups discovered that their desire to settle the future of the Union on their terms, and on their terms only, were not only incompatible, but must perhaps lead to civil war. Redmond, also a pro-Union leader, contributed his share of intransigence by his refusal to contemplate any other solution but the 'union of hearts'—a concept which rang hollow in the bitter confrontation of Catholic and Protestant in Ireland on the eve of the Great War.

The last decades of the Union saw the development of two conflicting ideologies which came to dominate the new Ireland. These were the idea of an Ireland, not free merely, but Gaelic as well; and of an Ulster, not Protestant merely, but free as well; and of a readiness to use violence to achieve these aims and counter-aims. The Home Rule crisis of 1912–14 and the rise of Sinn Féin after 1916 introduced a new instability into Irish politics. Ireland was a nation; Ulster a distinct community: 'Ireland' and 'Ulster' took on new meanings, and were seen as historic entities, fulfilling some kind of pre-ordained destiny. Ulster Unionists did not object to this; for the idea of an Irish nation only fostered their self-fulfilling prophecy that the north must stand up for itself. The Irish Presbyterian people, who supported tenant right and were willing to make informal alliances with Catholics, had no time for an Irish nationalism that seemed to threaten their natural political link with Britain and the British Liberal Party; and there was no place for them, if the truth were told, in a nationalism inspired by the idea put most succinctly by John Mitchel (an Ulster Presbyterian and

Young Irelander-cum-republican) when he explained that his daughter became a Roman Catholic because of her 'sentiment that one cannot be thoroughly Irish without being Catholic'.[12] The British government's attempted solution to the schism in Irish society—Home Rule for both north and south—was at least a recognition that there was here a serious conflict that could not be ignored. But it was a belated recognition, and one that did not provide a solution to the irreconcilable attitudes that produced that conflict.

Yet the violence and crises that marked the end of the Union must not hide the fact that nineteenth-century Ireland was not a society in turmoil. Long periods of ordinariness and quiescence followed the Union of Great Britain and Ireland in 1801. Political crises, political violence, agrarian crime, provocative marches and civil disturbances, all existed to test the will and patience of British administrators. But they did not cause any fundamental disruption in Irish society. Even that most potentially revolutionary move-ment, the Land League, sought (as Michael Davitt feared it would) a fundamentally conservative answer to the question of land in Ireland: the establishment of a tenant farmer landowning (or at least land-purchasing) class. Thus reconstructed by the British govern-ment, Irish rural life assumed its steady and conservative pace. For those who could not find a place in the reconstructed rural Ireland, there was the second great contributor to stability: emigration. Emigration was a particularly important safety valve, in that it provided an opportunity both for those who could find no useful employment (or no employment at all) and for those who simply wanted to better themselves, and for whom the whole English-speaking world, including Great Britain and the British empire, stood open to receive them. It was significant that when the British government stopped emigration, in the war years of 1914–18, it inadvertantly provided a recruiting ground for the Irish Volunteers. Emigration, like the settlement of the land question, did not necessarily make Ireland a more successful or inventive society; but it did make it a more manageable one—at a price.

Religion, though the means by which competing Irish groups identified themselves, and made a mockery out of the idea that there was in nineteenth-century Ireland a 'unity' of the 'nation', was in another respect a stabilising force (given the fact that religious divisions were one of the central mobilising forces in Irish society and politics). Religious communities occasionally collided in traditional marching and fighting areas; but sectarian rioting was virtually unknown in the south, and such manifestations as there were (an occasional attack on a Protestant church when political tensions ran high) were deplored by local church leaders. The reason is that Anglican, Catholic and Dissenter lived such separate existences, secure and confident in the rightness of their systems of belief, happy and fulfilled in their own societies. At least this substituted low-level mistrust and resentment for disastrous friction and violent confrontation. And there were in any event the 'ordinary, everyday compromises' that tempered these 'contending sovereignties': neighbourliness, self-interest and a desire for the quiet life;[13] and such phenomena as the example given by Anthony Trollope in his novel *The Kellys and the O'Kellys* of the Protestant clergyman who 'hated Popery, and . . . carried the feeling to such a length, that he almost hated Papists'[14]—almost, but not quite. Indeed, it was when 'national identity' *was* explored (as in the 1890s) that relations between the sects deteriorated rapidly; for Irish society was too friable to bear a close self-examination, too lacking in confidence to look to tradition or history to find a common ground. Relations also deteriorated, only more seriously, when constitutional matters were raised; for here the survival or otherwise of the major groups was perceived to be at stake, and in such circumstances Anglican and Dissenter rapidly coalesced in a united front against the common foe. But even the last great constitutional crisis of the Union, that of 1912–21, did not overthrow social stability; and its outcome encouraged it, even in the north, for nearly fifty years, for it placed powerful social and religious groups, in both states, in the position of gaining what they wanted from what was (paradoxically) a kind of renewed status quo. The fact that the respective minorities, Protestant in the Free State / Republic, Catholic in Northern Ireland, withdrew into or remained within their own societies, organised around their churches, contributed to a social stability that now seems almost beyond recovery. For this stability a high price was eventually exacted, at least in the north.

The Union did not in the end offer a permanent solution to the constitutional problem of Ireland. It did not remove the Catholic sense of grievance, which was historical as much as practical. By 1900 it might be said that it was hardly practical at all. By then Catholics were making progress in the world. The Catholic Church had its status recognised through the disestablishment of the Church of Ireland and the granting of its dearest wish, Catholic university education. Catholics became more prominent in public life, filling the bulk of the intermediate grades in the civil service and making their way into responsible positions as well. They became J.P.s, they controlled the major part of local government, they controlled poor law guardianships.[15] In vain did Unionists protest that the government was going out of its way to reward sedition and disloyalty. What was even more gratifying to Catholics was precisely this Unionist resentment. Only one position remained to be taken by nationalist Ireland: a Home Rule parliament.

Practical reforms did not offer a political solution, however much social stability they buttressed. Nationalist Ireland had created a grievance culture, in which history was taught, both formally and informally, as the story of a nation coming out of bondage—or, to be more precise, nearly out of it. Britain found that as she 'solved' each problem, the iron law of politics asserted itself again and again: that each problem resolved only created another one, as expectations rose, and as the Catholic majority saw no reason why it should not finally enter into its full inheritance, of which land reform and church reform were but instalments. The Unionist opposition which that assumption provoked in Britain, Ulster and southern Ireland between 1912 and 1914 exposed the hollowness of Catholic claims that Ireland had some intrinsic unity which Home Rule would express, and which could only be discovered 'after Britain'. It also ensured that the end of the Union would be marked not only by conflict between Ireland and Britain, but by a kind of half-suppressed religious war.

The British left Ireland, or most of it, because they could no longer count on the support, co-operation or compliance of enough people to enable them to stay. They had no desire, after 1918, to use the necessary force to remain in Ireland; and such force as they did use, the Black and Tans and the Auxiliaries, only gave rise to public criticism on an unacceptable level. The British attitude had, perhaps, been one that brought the worst of both worlds. Their perception was that, on the whole, it was best to try to be even-handed between the contending groups in Ireland; hence the frequent complaints from Unionists about their tendency to ignore the best interests of the loyal men of Ireland. But they also steeled themselves to hold Ireland, as Sir Robert Peel put it, by force if necessary. When the Liberals took up Home Rule, the Conservatives continued the Peelite policy of opposing any modification of the Union. Yet the Conservatives carried out social and economic policies which, it might be claimed, undermined those very forces in Irish society on which the Union depended, notably the Irish landlords. The determination to maintain British interests, while failing to reconcile nationalists or buttress Unionists, led in the end to the need to offer self-government to two parts of Ireland, as the only means of extricating Britain from the consequences of her own policies.

The Union failed because it did not reconcile Irish diversity with British ambivalence. The symbols of the British state, its flag, its crown, became the very symbols that nationalist Ireland rejected (even when Dubliners flocked to see the sovereign). This was because England was only partially successful in creating a sense of 'Britishness'; for the essence of Britishness was the English experience, widened sufficiently to include the Scots and the Welsh—but not the Irish. Even Irish Unionists, and especially the Ulster Unionists, found it hard to define what kind of Britishness they stood for; in the end they claimed that loyalty was the supreme test, loyalty to the crown (though not necessarily to the government). When Irish Catholics emigrated to Britain, they frequently encountered prejudice on religious and political grounds; and while this must not be exaggerated, it was a symptom of the failure of England to create a homogeneous nation-state. As H. G. Wells put it, 'Britain was not a state. It was an unincorporated people.' Given that this was the case, Britain had to negotiate and balance. This she did, reasonably successfully. Wells hoped that the Great War would produce a 'British nation' at a new level of popular experience and awareness, in which the 'outsiders' would be incorporated. But the war, which forged a workable British identity for the nations of the British 'mainland',[16] only exposed, under stress of war and revolution, the gaps in British political nation-building. And it also made it impossible for the government to maintain its Irish balancing act any longer.

The Union, in the end, did not overcome the sense of difference between Irishmen; nor did it make them into 'Britons'. But it did enable the peoples of Ireland to live with their own differences for a long period of time. When it ended, it was clear that the Irish people could not live together, and so must live apart. Unfortunately their apartness was not complete, for the 1921 settlement left a substantial Catholic minority in the state of Northern Ireland, and a small, politically impotent Protestant minority in the south. It also left social inequalities. But it shaped modern Ireland, in that it underlay so many of what we consider the permanent features of Irish life: the industrial north; the rural settlement; tenant farmer hegemony of power and influence; the formation of Irish political parties; modern Irish literature in the English language; the Gaelic movement; the Gaelic Athletic Association; schools and universities; a poor law and local government; liberal democracy; emigration; the 'Celtic' movement in art, with its discovery of a 'Celtic' style; shamrocks, wolfhounds, harps; Orange and Green lodges, with sashes, tunes and bands; the great revival of the Catholic Church; its massive building programme; the Protestant 'Second Reformation'; its earnest and evangelical character; the ambivalent attitude to violence; the canonisation of violence. Above all, it led to the acceptance of the past as a guide, even a driver, for the future. The experience of Ireland as part of the British United Kingdom meant that the nineteenth century did not end until the Union ended, in 1921. In most respects, however, it did not end even then, but carried forward its legacy of stability and strife to shape the destinies of future generations.

ABBREVIATIONS

B.J.S.	*British Journal of Sociology*
E.H.R.	*English Historical Review*
H.J.	*Historical Journal*
I.E.S.H.	*Irish Economic and Social History*
I.H.S.	*Irish Historical Studies*
J.S.H.	*Journal of Social History*
N.H.I., iv	T. W. Moody and W. E. Vaughan (ed.), *A New History of Ireland*, Vol. IV: *Eighteenth-Century Ireland, 1691–1800* (Oxford 1986)
N.H.I., v	W. E. Vaughan (ed.), *A New History of Ireland*, Vol. V: *Ireland under the Union, I: 1801–70* (Oxford 1989)
P.&P.	*Past and Present*
P.R.I.A.	*Proceedings of the Royal Irish Academy*
P.R.O.N.I.	Public Record Office of Northern Ireland
Q.U.B.	Queen's University, Belfast
S.P.O.I.	State Paper Office of Ireland (Dublin)
T.R.H.S.	*Transactions of the Royal Historical Society*
U.C.C.	University College, Cork
U.C.D.	University College, Dublin

References

Introduction (pp. 1–9)
1. Oliver MacDonagh, *N.H.I.*, v, p. xlviii.
2. Stanley Ayling, *Edmund Burke: His Life and Opinions* (London 1988), 103.
3. William Doyle, *The Ancien Régime* (London 1986), 32.
4. R. B. McDowell, *Ireland in the Age of Imperialism and Revolution, 1760–1800* (Oxford 1979), 687–8.
5. Ibid., 704.
6. R. B. McDowell, *N.H.I.*, iv, 666–7.
7. D. H. Akenson, *Small Differences: Irish Catholics and Irish Protestants, 1815–1922* (Kingston/Montreal 1988), 158 (Appx E).
8. K. T. Hoppen, *Ireland since 1800: Conflict and Conformity* (London 1989), 87.
9. Ibid., 37–8.
10. D. G. Boyce, *Nationalism in Ireland* (London 1982), 97.

Chapter 1: The Union: Prelude and Aftermath, 1798–1808 (pp. 10–33)
1. D. G. Boyce, *Nationalism in Ireland* (London 1982), 123.
2. J. C. Beckett, *N.H.I.*, iv, p. liv.
3. Boyce, op. cit., 124.
4. R. B. McDowell, *N.H.I.*,, iv, 233.
5. R. B. McDowell, *Ireland in the Age of Imperialism and Revolution, 1760–1800*, 155–6.
6. McDowell, *N.H.I.*, iv, 687–8.
7. S. J. Connolly, *Priests and People in Pre-Famine Ireland, 1780–1845* (Dublin 1982), 11, 226; McDowell, *N.H.I.*, iv, 688–9.
8. Connolly, op. cit., 219–36.
9. Ibid., 12.
10. For United Irish activity see Marianne Elliott, *Partners in Revolution: The United Irishmen and France* (New Haven/London 1982), 21–31.
11. John Goddard to Downshire, 2 Sept. 1796 (P.R.O.N.I., D 607/D/149).
12. James McKey to Downshire, 6 Nov. 1797 (ibid., D 607/E/374).
13. Richard Annesley to Downshire, 9 June 1798 (ibid., D 607/F/215). For the religious aspect see Kevin Whelan, 'The Religious Factor in the 1798 Rebellion in County Wexford' in Patrick O'Flanagan, Patrick Ferguson and Kevin Whelan (ed.), *Rural Ireland, 1600–1900: Modernisation and Change* (Cork 1987), 62–85.
14. Lane to Downshire, 24 June 1798 (P.R.O.N.I., D 607/F/272).
15. Elliott, op. cit., 207.

16. William Hartigan (of Dublin) to Downshire, 29 Apr. 1798 (P.R.O.N.I., D 607/F/360).
17. For a summary of the arguments see McDowell, *Ireland in the Age of Imperialism and Revolution*, 685–8.
18. Ibid., 679–85.
19. John Patrickson to Downshire, 1 Jan. 1799 (P.R.O.N.I., D 607/G/1).
20. McDowell, op. cit., 688–91.
21. James Archdale to Downshire, 29 Jan. 1799 (P.R.O.N.I., D 607/G/29).
22. G. C. Bolton, *The Passing of the Irish Act of Union* (London 1966), ch. 5.
23. Patrickson to Downshire, 8 (?) Jan. 1799 (P.R.O.N.I., D 607/G/10).
24. McDowell, *N.H.I.*, iv, 370–3; S. J. Connolly, *N.H.I.*, v, 5–7.
25. Thomas Flanagan, *N.H.I.*, v, 482–7; Boyce, op. cit., 230; Thomas Moore, *Poetical Works* (London 1854), 132–8; Robert Welch, 'Constitution, Language and Politics in Nineteenth-Century Irish Poetry' in Terence Brown and Nicholas Grene (ed.), *Tradition and Influence in Anglo-Irish Poetry* (London 1989), 7–30.
26. Thomas Flanagan, *The Irish Novelists, 1800–1850* (Westport, Conn. 1976), ch. 8; Mary Campbell, *Lady Morgan* (London 1988), ch. 4. For Lady Morgan's discursive footnotes see e.g. Vol. I, 74, 96; Vol. II, 79–82; Vol. III, 37–8 (*The Wild Irish Girl* (London 1806)).
27. Connolly, *N.H.I.*, v, 19–20.
28. Elliott, op. cit., 300–22.
29. Raymond Postgate, *Robert Emmet* (London 1931), 183.
30. R. A. Scott-James, review of Postgate, *Sunday Times*, 3 Apr. 1932.
31. Connolly, *N.H.I.*, v, 18–19
32. W. T. Latimer, *A History of the Irish Presbyterians*, 2nd ed. (Belfast 1902), 393–5. (The yeomanry was in fact a wholly Protestant force.)
33. Hereward Senior, *Orangeism in Ireland and Britain, 1795–1836* (London 1966), 199–200.
34. Latimer, op. cit., 401.
35. Elliot, op. cit., 366–7.
36. Sir Richard Musgrave, *Memoirs of the Different Rebellions in Ireland*, 3rd ed. (Dublin/London 1802), i, pp. ii–xvi; ii, 222–5.
37. James Gordon, *History of the Rebellion in Ireland* (Dublin 1803), xxi, xxxii.
38. Ibid., 355–6.
39. Donal McCartney, 'Writings on Irish History in the Early Nineteenth Century' (M.A. thesis, U.C.D., 1955), 54–64.
40. Gordon, op. cit., 354–6.
41. Dowager Marchioness of Downshire to John Reilly, 9 Apr. 1804 (P.R.O.N.I., D 607/I/25).
42. A. V. Dicey and R. S. Rait, *Thoughts on the Union between England and Scotland* (London 1920), 149–51; P. W. J. Riley, *The Union of England and Scotland* (Manchester 1978), ch. 6.
43. Dicey and Rait, op. cit., 314. But for another view of the Irish see Paul Langford, *A Polite and Commercial People: England, 1727–83* (Oxford 1989), 44, 323–9.

44. Dicey and Rait, op. cit., 303.
45. Ibid., 311–12.
46. Ibid., 259.
47. Lord Hobart to Downshire, 6 Feb., 1801 (P.R.O.N.I., D 607/H/77).
48. Whelan, op. cit., 78–9.
49. P. J. Jupp, *Lord Grenville* (Oxford 1985), 399–401.
50. W. E. H. Lecky, *Leaders of Public Opinion in Ireland*, repr. (London 1912), i, 305–6.
51. Elliott, op. cit., 317; Senior, op. cit., 148–9.
52. Elliott, op. cit., 313.
53. Moore, *Poetical Works*, 141.

Chapter 2: The Catholic Question and Protestant Answers, 1808–29 (pp. 34–57)

1. Henry Grattan, *Speeches*, (London 1842), iv, 57–79.
2. Ibid., 148–9.
3. Fergus O'Ferrall, *Catholic Emancipation: Daniel O'Connell and the Birth of Irish Democracy, 1820–30* (Dublin 1985), 4. Oliver MacDonagh, *The Heriditary Bondsman: Daniel O'Connell, 1775–1829* (London 1988), 117, offers a contemporary description.
4. R. B. McDowell, *Public Opinion and Government Policy in Ireland, 1801–1846* (London 1952), 94.
5. Ibid., 95; MacDonagh, op. cit., 114–15.
6. O'Ferrall, op. cit., 6.
7. Ibid., 7–8.
8. Ibid., 30–7; McDowell, op. cit., 98–9; Charles Chenevix Trench, *The Great Dan: A Biography of Daniel O'Connell* (London 1984), 123–4.
9. *Belfast Monthly Magazine*, Mar. 1811, 232–4.
10. Chenevix Trench, op. cit., 121, 123, 209.
11. MacDonagh, op. cit., 209.
12. Peter Brooke, *Ulster Presbyterianism: The Historical Perspective, 1610–1970* (Dublin 1987), 139–47; S. J. Connolly, *N.H.I.*, v, 77; R. Finlay Holmes, *Henry Cooke* (Belfast 1981), 64–5.
13. G. C. Lewis, *On Local Disturbances in Ireland and on the Irish Church Question* (London 1836), 69–70.
14. O'Ferrall, op. cit., 42–3.
15. Charles Lever, *Charles O'Malley, the Irish Dragoon*, repr. (London 1897), i, 101–7.
16. McDowell, op. cit., 102–3.
17. Ibid., 202.
18. Chenevix Trench, op. cit., 133.
19. MacDonagh, op. cit., 216–22.
20. O'Ferrall, op. cit., 121–33; Thomas Wyse, *Historical Sketch of the Late Catholic Association of Ireland* (London 1829), i, 291–2.
21. McDowell, op. cit., 105.
22. O'Ferrall, op. cit., 137.
23. Ibid., 144–5.

24. David Hempton, *Methodism and Politics in British Society, 1750–1850* (London 1984), 120.
25. O'Ferrall, op. cit., 49–50.
26. E. and A. G. Porritt, *The Unreformed House of Commons*, Vol. II: *Scotland and Ireland* (Cambridge 1909), 291.
27. O'Ferrall, op. cit., 179.
28. Ibid., 181.
29. Chenevix Trench, op. cit., 147.
30. Ibid., 148–9.
31. Ibid., 151–5; MacDonagh, op. cit., 250–3; Bernard Ward, *The Eve of Catholic Emancipation*, (London 1911–13), iii, 225.
32. Chenevix Trench, op. cit., 153–7; O'Ferrall, op. cit., 192–7.
33. McDowell, op. cit., 106.
34. Ibid., 106–8.
35. O'Ferrall, op. cit., 201.
36. Ibid., 201–2.
37. *Annual Register*, lxx (1828) 138–40.
38. Chenevix Trench, op. cit., 159–60; *Annual Register*, lxx (1828), 148.
39. O'Ferrall, op. cit., 240.
40. Daniel O'Connell, *Correspondence*, ed. M. R. O'Connell (Dublin 1974), iii, 134, 345.

Chapter 3: Testing the Union, 1830–45 (pp. 58–97)

1. Charles Chenevix Trench, *The Great Dan: A Biography of Daniel O'Connell* (London 1984), 168.
2. Fergus O'Ferrall, *Catholic Emancipation: Daniel O'Connell and the Birth of Irish Democracy, 1820–30* (Dublin 1985), 264.
3. R. B. McDowell, *Public Opinion and Government Policy in Ireland, 1801–1846* (London 1952), 114–15.
4. Chenevix Trench, op. cit., 212.
5. Ibid., 216.
6. McDowell, op. cit., 142.
7. Ibid., 125.
8. Chenevix Trench, op. cit., 172–3.
9. McDowell, op. cit., 143.
10. Edward Brynn, *The Church of Ireland in the Age of Catholic Emancipation* (New York/London 1982), 252–74.
11. *Dublin University Magazine*, i (Jan. 1833), 9.
12. Brynn, op. cit., 260.
13. McDowell, op. cit., 150.
14. Ibid., 151.
15. *Dublin University Magazine*, iv (July 1834), 1–12.
16. O. J. Brose, *Church and Parliament: The Reshaping of the Church of Ireland, 1826–60* (London 1959), 53.
17. McDowell, op. cit., 155–9.
18. Ibid., 165.
19. Ian D'Alton, *Protestant Society and Politics in Cork, 1812–44* (Cork 1980), 173–4.

20. Ibid., 176–92.
21. R. B. McDowell, *N.H.I.*, iv, 672–9.
22. Helen Burke, *The People and the Poor Law in Nineteenth-Century Ireland* (Dublin 1987), 20–50.
23. McDowell, *Public Opinion*, 203.
24. Chenevix Trench, op. cit., 253.
25. R. Finlay Holmes, *Henry Cooke* (Belfast 1981), 107–8.
26. *Pilot*, 13 Feb. 1843.
27. Ibid., 21 Apr. 1843.
28. Liam Kennedy and Philip Ollerenshaw (ed.), *An Economic History of Ulster, 1820–1940* (Manchester 1985), 62–72, 228–32.
29. McDowell, op. cit., 175–6.
30. Chenevix Trench, op. cit., 249; Oliver MacDonagh, *The Emancipist: Daniel O'Connell, 1830–47* (London 1989), 195–8.
31. McDowell, op. cit., 206–9.
32. Chenevix Trench, op. cit., 271–2.
33. Ibid., 277.
34. Mary Buckley, 'Thomas Davis: A Study in Nationalist Philosophy' (Ph.D. thesis, U.C.C., 1980), 31.
35. Chenevix Trench, op. cit., 286.
36. Holmes, op. cit., 108.
37. D. G. Boyce, *Nationalism in Ireland* (London 1982), 157–8.
38. Ibid., 165–6.
39. Ibid., 155–6.
40. Buckley, op. cit., 78.
41. Boyce, op. cit., 167.
42. Ibid., 165–9; MacDonagh, op. cit., 266–70.
43. Nassau Senior, 'Ireland', *Edinburgh Review*, lxxix (1844), 189–266.
44. McDowell, op. cit., 205.
45. Ibid., 206.
46. Ibid., 209.
47. Donal Kerr, *Peel, Priests and Politics: Sir Robert Peel's Administration and the Roman Catholic Church in Ireland, 1841–46* (Oxford 1982), 128.
48. Ibid., 116.
49. McDowell, op. cit., 212.
50. Ibid., 212–14.
51. Kerr, op. cit., 121.
52. Ibid., 129.
53. Ibid., 197–200, 220.
54. McDowell, op. cit., 220.
55. Ibid., 224–6.
56. Kerr, op. cit., 306.
57. McDowell, op. cit., 226–7.
58. Ibid., 228.
59. W. B. Hodgson (trans.), *Count Cavour on Ireland: Thoughts on Ireland, its Present and its Future* (London 1868), 5, 31, 40, 45, 90, 93, 107.

Chapter 4: The Land and its Nemesis, 1845–9 (pp. 98–123)

1. W. B. Hodgson (trans.), *Count Cavour on Ireland: Thoughts on Ireland, its Present and its Future* (London 1868), 49–56.
2. Ibid., 89–90.
3. Joseph Lee, 'The Ribbonmen' in T. Desmond Williams (ed.), *Secret Societies in Ireland* (Dublin 1973), 26–35; G. C. Lewis, *On Local Disturbances in Ireland and the Irish Church Question* (London 1836), 156–7.
4. R. B. McDowell, *Public Opinion and Government Policy in Ireland, 1801–1846* (London 1952), 59–62.
5. Ibid., 63–5.
6. Joseph Lee, 'On the Accuracy of the Pre-Famine Irish Census' in J. M. Goldstrom and L. A. Clarkson (ed.), *Irish Population, Economy and Society: Essays in honour of the late K. H. Connell* (Oxford 1981), 37–56.
7. Mary E. Daly, *The Famine in Ireland* (Dublin 1986), 9–10, 34–40.
8. For a discussion of these and other points see L. A. Clarkson, 'Irish Population Revisited, 1687–1821' in Goldstrom and Clarkson, op. cit., 13–35; Daly, op. cit., 3–9.
9. Daly, op. cit., 49–51.
10. Ibid., 40–2.
11. Peter Roebuck, 'Landlord Indebtedness in Ulster in the Seventeenth and Eighteenth Centuries' in Goldstrom and Clarkson, op. cit., 135.
12. Daly, op. cit., 27–8; R. Dudley Edwards and T. Desmond Williams (ed.), *The Great Famine: Studies in Irish History, 1845–52* (Dublin 1956), 6–8.
13. Edwards and Williams, op. cit., 10.
14. George O'Brien, *The Economic History of Ireland from the Union to the Famine* (London 1921), 136–7.
15. McDowell, op. cit., 224–6.
16. O'Brien, op. cit., 136.
17. T. M. Devine, *The Great Highland Famine: Hunger, Emigration and the Scottish Highlands in the Nineteenth Century* (Edinburgh 1988), 12–23.
18. David Fitzpatrick, *Irish Emigration, 1801–1921* (Dublin 1984), 3, 14.
19. Devine, op. cit., 36.
20. Ibid., 40.
21. Joel Mokyr, *Why Ireland Starved: A Quantitative and Analytical History of the Irish Economy, 1800–1850* (London 1983), 12.
22. Edwards and Williams, op. cit., 292.
23. Ibid., 296–7.
24. Ibid., 301.
25. Ibid., 302–6.
26. Ibid., vii.
27. Daly, op. cit., 67–8; Cormac Ó Gráda, *Ireland Before and After the Famine: Explorations in Economic History, 1800–1925* (Manchester 1988), 115; J. S. Donnelly, jnr, *N.H.I.*, v, 336–42.
28. Desmond Bowen, *Souperism: Myth or Reality?* (Cork 1978), 17–18.

29. Daly, op. cit., 68.
30. Edwards and Williams, op. cit., 312–15.
31. Ó Gráda, op. cit., 117.
32. Devine, op. cit., 111, 116.
33. Ibid., 116.
34. Daly, op. cit., 68–9.
35. Ibid., 70–1.
36. McDowell, op. cit., 229.
37. Daly, op. cit., 73–85. For a summary and criticism of government relief schemes see O'Brien, op. cit., 246–80.
38. Edwards and Williams, op. cit., 255.
39. Mokyr, op. cit., 292.
40. Daly, op. cit., 72.
41. Edwards and Williams, op. cit., 244.
42. Ibid., 255.
43. McDowell, op. cit., 258.
44. D. G. Boyce, *Nationalism in Ireland* (London 1982), 171.
45. Ibid., 172.
46. Richard Davis, *The Young Ireland Movement* (Dublin 1987), 251.
47. Boyce, op. cit., 173–4.
48. Daly, op. cit., 120.
49. Ibid., 110–12.
50. Ó Gráda, op. cit., 50–1, stresses the importance of the famine in this regard.
51. Edwards and Williams, op. cit., 364–7.
52. Fitzpatrick, op. cit., 5–6.
53. O'Brien, op. cit., 137–8.
54. W. E. Vaughan, *Landlords and Tenants in Ireland, 1848–1904* (Dublin 1984), 5; J. M. Goldstrom, 'Irish Agriculture and the Great Famine' in Goldstrom and Clarkson, op. cit., 155–71; S. J. Connolly, *N.H.I.*, v, 90.
55. Donnelly, *N.H.I.*, v, 343–9.
56. Ó Gráda, op. cit., 78–82, reviews the literature; see also Donnelly, *N.H.I.*, v, 272–85.

Chapter 5: Political Diversity, Religious Division, 1850–69 (pp. 124–153)

1. K. T. Hoppen, *Elections, Politics, and Society in Ireland, 1832–85* (Oxford 1984), 17–18.
2. T. P. O'Neill, 'The Irish Land Question, 1830–50', *Studies*, xliv (1955), 335.
3. D. W. Leonard, 'John Mitchel, Charles Gavan Duffy, and the Legacy of Young Ireland' (Ph.D. thesis, University of Sheffield, 1975), 1–15, 28.
4. Ibid., 32–5.
5. Ibid., 109–10.
6. Ibid., 121; *Nation*, 1 Sept. 1849.
7. Leonard, op. cit., 129, 131–2, 145.
8. Ibid., 162–3.

9. Ibid., 171.
10. J. H. Whyte, *The Independent Irish Party, 1850–59* (Oxford 1958), ch. 11.
11. Hoppen, *Elections, Politics and Society*, 284–5.
12. K. T. Hoppen, *Ireland since 1800: Conflict and Conformity* (London 1989), 113.
13. Liam McNiffe, 'The Politicisation of Leitrim, Sligo and Mayo in the General Election of 1852' (M.A. thesis, St Patrick's College, Maynooth, 1979), 76.
14. Hoppen, *Elections, Politics and Society*, 286–7.
15. J. F. Lalor, *Selected Writings*, ed. Nathaniel Marlowe (Dublin 1918), 84–98; W. Steuart Trench, *Realities of Irish Life*, repr. (London 1966), 120–3, gives a more colourful account.
16. R. V. Comerford, *The Fenians in Context: Irish Politics and Society, 1848–82* (Dublin 1985), 30–2.
17. McNiffe, op. cit., 34–5.
18. R. Finlay Holmes, *Our Irish Presbyterian Heritage* (Belfast 1985), 121.
19. William Gibson, *The Year of Grace* (Belfast 1860), 61.
20. Isaac Nelson, *The Year of Delusion* (Belfast 1859), 24, 175–6.
21. Gibson, op. cit., 380.
22. Peter Brooke, *Ulster Presbyterianism: The Historical Perspective, 1610–1970* (Dublin 1987), 193–4.
23. R. Finlay Holmes, *Henry Cooke* (Belfast 1981), 191–2.
24. D. H. Akenson, *Small Differences: Irish Catholics and Irish Protestants, 1815–1922* (Kingston/Montreal 1988), 143.
25. D. A. Kerr, 'Under the Union Flag: The Catholic Church in Ireland' in *Ireland after the Union*, intro. Lord Blake (London 1989), 37–40.
26. B. M. Coldrey, *Faith and Fatherland: The Christian Brothers and the Development of Irish Nationalism, 1838–1921* (Dublin 1988), 17–21.
27. W. E. Vaughan, *N.H.I.*, v, 737–8.
28. J. L. Porter, *The Life and Times of Henry Cooke* (London 1871), 435.
29. Margaret McCourt, 'Belfast Liberals: The 1865 and 1868 Elections' (M.A. thesis, Q.U.B. 1987), 17.
30. Ibid., 25–6.
31. Ibid., 28–9.
32. Ibid., 30–57; Hoppen, *Elections, Politics and Society*, 316–17; B. M. Walker, *Ulster Politics: The Formative Years, 1868–86* (Belfast 1989), 60–2.
33. McCourt, op. cit., 57–60.
34. Comerford, op. cit., ch. 2.
35. Ibid., 35–42.
36. D. G. Boyce, *Nationalism in Ireland* (London 1982), 176.
37. Ibid., 177–9.
38. Ibid., 178.
39. Ibid.
40. Comerford, op. cit., 55–6.
41. Boyce, op. cit., 183.
42. Comerford, op. cit., 79.

43. Boyce, op. cit., 182.
44. Comerford, op. cit., 115.
45. Ibid., 119.
46. Ibid., 125.
47. Ibid., 147–8.
48. Ibid., 105–7.
49. Boyce, op. cit., 184.
50. S.P.O.I., Fenian Papers, 5065R, 5126R, 5206R, 4902R.
51. H. G. C. Matthew, *Gladstone, 1809–74* (Oxford 1988), 192.
52. Ibid., 191–4.
53. *Authentic Report of the Great Protestant Demonstration at Hills-borough, October 30, 1867* (Belfast 1867), 4; Report of a Meeting of Presbyterians of Belfast, 29 Apr. 1869 (P.R.O.N.I., T 2771/7).
54. Thomas Olden, *The Church of Ireland* (London 1895), 403–4. For Irish Anglicanism after Disestablishment see R. B. McDowell, *The Church of Ireland, 1869–1969* (London 1975), ch. 4.
55. Boyce, op. cit., 186.
56. Comerford, op. cit., 161–3.
57. Vaughan, *N.H.I.*, v, 744.

Chapter 6: The Shaping of Irish Politics (1): The Making of Irish Nationalism, 1870–91 (pp. 154–184)

 1. H. G. C. Matthew, *Gladstone, 1809–74* (Oxford 1988), 147.
 2. Ibid., 195.
 3. R. V. Comerford, *The Fenians in Context: Irish Politics and Society, 1848–82* (Dublin 1985), 180.
 4. Matthew, op. cit., 195–6.
 5. Ibid., 197.
 6. T. W. Moody, 'The Irish University Question of the Nineteenth Century', *History*, xliii (1958), 90–109.
 7. D. G. Boyce, *Nationalism in Ireland* (London 1982), 192.
 8. Isaac Butt, *Irish Federalism: Its Meaning, Its Objects and Its Hopes* (Dublin 1874), passim; John Kendle, *Ireland and the Federal Solution: The Debate over the United Kingdom Constitution, 1870–1921* (Kingston/Montreal 1989), 11–19.
 9. Boyce, op. cit., 194.
10. Comerford, op. cit., 190–2.
11. Isaac Butt, *A Plea for the Celtic Race* (Dublin 1866), 5–7.
12. Comerford, op. cit., 192–4.
13. Boyce, op. cit., 196–7.
14. Ibid., 198.
15. David Thornley, *Isaac Butt and Home Rule* (London 1964), 227.
16. Cormac Ó Gráda, *Ireland Before and After the Famine: Explorations in Economic History, 1800–1925* (Manchester 1988), 132–3.
17. Boyce, op. cit., 206–7.
18. R. B. O'Brien, *The Life of Charles Stewart Parnell, 1846–91*, repr. (London 1910), 407.
19. *Nation*, 27 Sept. 1879; *Freeman's Journal*, 24 Nov. 1879.

20. Boyce, op. cit., 206.
21. Charles Townshend, *Political Violence in Ireland: Government and Resistance since 1848* (Oxford 1983), 111.
22. Ibid., 118.
23. Ibid., 116.
24. Boyce, op. cit., 199–200.
25. Townshend, op. cit., 167.
26. Comerford, op. cit., 242–4.
27. K. T. Hoppen, *Elections, Politics and Society in Ireland, 1832–85* (Oxford 1984), 87–8.
28. Boyce, op. cit., 212–15.
29. Comerford, op. cit., 247.
30. *United Ireland*, 21 Nov. 1885.
31. Boyce, op. cit., 218.
32. *Nation*, 22 Dec. 1877, when Parnell spoke at the Catholic University in Dublin.
33. Boyce, op. cit., 218–19.
34. *Times*, 11 Nov. 1880, in a speech in Dublin; *United Ireland*, 3 July 1886.
35. Boyce, op. cit., 219.
36. W. C. Lubenow, *Parliamentary Politics and the Home Rule Crisis: The British House of Commons in 1886* (Oxford 1988), passim; Alan O'Day, *The English Face of Irish Nationalism: Parnellite Involvement in British Politics, 1880–86* (Dublin 1977), passim.
37. Richard Shannon, 'Gladstone and Home Rule, 1886' in *Ireland after the Union*, intro. Lord Blake (London 1989), 45–59.
38. Roland Quinault, 'Joseph Chamberlain: A Reassessment' in T. R. Gourvish and Alan O'Day (ed.), *Late Victorian Britain, 1867–1900* (London 1988), 79–82.
39. Lubenow, op. cit., 268–9; Kendle, op. cit., 24–8.
40. O'Brien, op. cit., 402–4.
41. Boyce, op. cit., 218.
42. L. M. Geary, *The Plan of Campaign, 1886–91* (Cork 1986), 29.
43. Ibid., ch. 4.
44. Townshend, op. cit., 198–211.
45. O'Brien, op. cit., 416–22.
46. Ibid., 459–61.
47. Ibid., 466–71.
48. Ibid., 472–7.
49. Ibid., 516–19, 535–8.
50. Boyce, op. cit., 222.
51. David Brooks (ed.), *The Destruction of Lord Rosebery* (London 1986), 8–9.
52. Paul Bew, *C. S. Parnell* (Dublin 1980), 128–9.

Chapter 7: The Shaping of Irish Politics (2): The Making of Irish Unionism, 1870–93 (pp. 185–212)

1. *Dublin University Magazine*, lxxxi (June 1873), 631–45; lxxxii (Oct. 1873), 498–506.
2. Ibid., lxxxiii (Apr. 1874), 466–78.
3. Ibid., lxxxix (July 1877), 93–106.
4. Thomas MacKnight, *Ulster As It Is, or Twenty-Eight Years' Experience as an Irish Editor* (London 1896), i, 218.
5. B. M. Walker, 'The Land Question and Elections in Ulster, 1868–86' in Samuel Clark and J. S. Donnelly, jnr (ed.), *Irish Peasants: Violence and Political Unrest, 1780–1914* (Dublin 1988), 233–4.
6. MacKnight, op. cit., i, 210.
7. S. C. McElroy, *The Route Land Crusade: being an Authentic Account of the Efforts made to Advance Land Reform by the Route Tenants' Defence Association* (Coleraine n.d.), 19–20.
8. J. R. B. McMinn, 'The Myth of Route: Liberalism in County Antrim, 1869–1900, *Éire/Ireland*, xvii, 1 (Spring 1982), 143.
9. McElroy, op. cit., 215.
10. MacKnight, op. cit., i, 218–19.
11. McElroy, op. cit., 24–6; Francis Thompson, 'Land and Politics in Ulster, 1868–86' (Ph.D. thesis, Q.U.B., 1982), 245–6.
12. R. W. Lowry to Belmore, 10 Mar. 1873 (P.R.O.N.I., D 3007/P/19); James Greer to Belmore, 12 Mar. 1873 (ibid., D 3007/P/20); Capt. Henry W. Lowry Corry's election address, 15 Mar. 1873 (ibid., D 3007/P/26); Stuart Knox to Belmore, 15 Mar. 1873 (ibid., D 3007/P/27A); James Greer to Belmore, 9 Apr. 1873 (ibid., D 3007/P/117).
13. Earl of Enniskillen to Belmore, 24 Mar. 1873 (ibid., D 3007/P/72).
14. R. C. Brush to Belmore, 5 Apr. 1873, quoted in Walker, op. cit., 239.
15. Printed address from Capt. Henry W. Lowry Corry, Omagh, to the electors of Tyrone, 26 Jan. 1874 (P.R.O.N.I., D 3007/P/135).
16. Walker, op. cit., 240–1.
17. MacKnight, op. cit., i, 296.
18. McElroy, op. cit., 61–2.
19. Ibid., 32.
20. Walker, op. cit., 242.
21. Press cuttings relating to the Down election (P.R.O.N.I., D 3650/1); Walker, op. cit., 242.
22. William Wylie to Lord Waveney, 24 Dec. 1878 (P.R.O.N.I., D 929/HA12/F4/14).
23. Walker, op. cit., 243.
24. K. T. Hoppen, *Elections, Politics and Society in Ireland, 1832–85* (Oxford 1984), 289, 329–30.
25. Minute Book of the County Grand Orange Lodge of Fermanagh, 20 Nov. 1879, 20 May 1880 (P.R.O.N.I., D 1402/1).
26. MacKnight, op. cit., i, 277–80.
27. McElroy to Lord Waveney, 5 Feb. 1879 (P.R.O.N.I., D 929/HA12/F4/14).
28. R. W. Lowry to Belmore, 14 Mar. 1873 (ibid., D 3007/P/19).
29. Thompson, op. cit., 305–13.
30. MacKnight, op. cit., i, 349.

31. Thompson, op. cit., 304, 316–17.
32. Ibid., 374–85; R. W. Kirkpatrick, 'The Origins and Development of the Land War in Mid-Ulster, 1879–85' in F. S. L. Lyons and R. A. J. Hawkins (ed.), *Ireland under the Union: Varieties of Tension: Essays in honour of T. W. Moody* (Oxford 1980), 201–35.
33. Charlemont to Boyle (his agent), 1 [Sept. 1879?] (P.R.O.N.I., D 266/367/1/16); same to same, [spring 1880] (ibid., D 266/367/1/31).
34. Election manifesto of John Leslie, Mar. 1880 (ibid., D 3465/3/27/19).
35. John Madden to Archdale, 24, 26 Mar. 1880 (ibid., D 3465/J/27/8).
36. MacKnight, op. cit., i, 373.
37. Paul Bew and Frank Wright, 'The Agrarian Opposition in Ulster Politics, 1848–87' in Clark and Donnelly, op. cit., 216–17.
38. Francis Thompson, 'Attitudes to Reform: Political Parties in Ulster and the Irish Land Bill of 1881', *I.H.S.*, xxiv, no. 95 (May 1985), 327–40.
39. Thompson, 'Land and Politics in Ulster', 474–8.
40. Minute Book of the County Grand Orange Lodge of Fermanagh, 3 Nov. 1880 (P.R.O.N.I., D 1402/1).
41. MacKnight, op. cit., i, 405–6.
42. Ibid., ii, 34–5; Walker, op. cit., 252; Bew and Wright, op. cit., 218–19.
43. MacKnight, op. cit., ii, 36–42; Bew and Wright, op. cit., 220; John Magee, 'The Monaghan Election of 1883 and the "Invasion of Ulster", *Clogher Record*, viii, 2 (1974), 147–66.
44. MacKnight, op. cit., 43–5; Magee, op. cit., 161–3; Charles Townshend, *Political Violence in Ireland: Government and Resistance since 1848* (Oxford 1983), 183–4.
45. *Coleraine Constitution*, 5 Jan. 1884.
46. MacKnight, op. cit., ii, 47.
47. A. B. Cooke, 'A Conservative Party Leader in Ulster: Sir Stafford Northcote's Diary of a Visit to the Province, October 1883', *P.R.I.A.*, sect. C, no. 4 (1975), 73.
48. Magee, op. cit., 161.
49. Cooke, op. cit., 79–80, 80n.2, 84.
50. Alvin Jackson, *The Ulster Party: Irish Unionists in the House of Commons, 1884–1911* (Oxford 1989), 25–33. For an example of how the new system adversely affected Conservatives in County Armagh see Francis Thompson, 'The Armagh Elections of 1885–6', *Seanchas Ardmhacha*, viii (1977), 379.
51. Patrick Buckland, *Irish Unionism 1: The Anglo-Irish and the New Ireland, 1885–1922* (Dublin 1972), 2–3.
52. Patrick Buckland, *Irish Unionism 2: Ulster Unionism and the Origins of Northern Ireland, 1886–1922* (Dublin 1973), 6; B. M. Walker, *Ulster Politics: The Formative Years, 1868–86* (Belfast 1989), 217.
53. Liam Kennedy and Philip Ollerenshaw (ed.), *An Economic History of Ulster, 1820–1940* (Manchester 1985), 62–101.
54. *Industries of the North One Hundred Years Ago* (Belfast 1986), 35.
55. Kennedy and Ollerenshaw, op. cit., 65–6; W. E. Vaughan, *N.H.I.*, v, 738–40.

56. Henry Patterson, 'Industrial Labour and the Labour Movement, 1820–1914' in Kennedy and Ollerenshaw, op. cit., 167–79.
57. Townshend, op. cit., 185–9.
58. Patrick Buckland (ed.), *Irish Unionism, 1885–1923: A Documentary History* (Belfast 1973), 60–1.
59. Ibid., 75–84.
60. Hoppen, op. cit., 331.
61. McElroy, op. cit., 45.
62. James Loughlin, 'The Irish Protestant Home Rule Association and Nationalist Politics, 1886–93', *I.H.S.*, xxiv, no. 95 (May 1985), 341–60.
63. Patrick Buckland, 'Irish Unionism and the New Ireland', in D. G. Boyce (ed.), *The Revolution in Ireland, 1879–1923* (London/Dublin 1988), 76.
64. Buckland, *Irish Unionism 1*, 13–15.
65. *Northern Whig*, 19, 28 June 1886. For more evidence see James Loughlin, *Gladstone, Home Rule and the Ulster Question, 1882–93* (Dublin 1986), 154–9. For Unionist overtures to the rural labourers see Walker, *Ulster Politics*, 178–9, 222–3.
66. Walker, op. cit., 252–4.
67. MacKnight, op. cit., ii, 204–8, 307.
68. Peter Gibbon, *The Origins of Ulster Unionism: The Formation of Popular Protestant Politics and Ideology in Nineteenth-Century Ireland* (Manchester 1975), 130–6.
69. Ibid., 138.
70. Buckland, *Irish Unionism, 1885–1923: A Documentary History*, 194–201.
71. Jackson, op. cit., 44–5, 126–9.
72. R. Finlay Holmes, *Our Irish Presbyterian Heritage* (Belfast 1985), 136.
73. As Charles Lever's Mickey Free in *Charles O'Malley, the Irish Dragoon*, repr. (London 1897), i, 86, and his 'Tipperary Joe' (W. J. Fitzpatrick, *The Life of Charles Lever* [London 1884?], 14).

Chapter 8: Conciliation and Conflict, 1892–1914 (pp. 213–241)

1. David Brooks (ed.), *The Destruction of Lord Rosebery* (London 1986), 125, 138.
2. D. G. Boyce, *The Irish Question and British Politics, 1868–1986* (London 1988), 36.
3. Andrew Gailey, 'Failure and the Making of the New Ireland' in D. G. Boyce (ed.) *The Revolution in Ireland, 1879–1923* (London/Dublin 1988), 63; Paul Bew, *Conflict and Conciliation in Ireland, 1890–1910* (Oxford 1987), 29–31.
4. Alan O'Day, 'The Irish Problem' in T. R. Gourvish and Alan O'Day (ed.), *Late Victorian Britain, 1867–1900* (London 1988), 240.
5. W. F. Mandle, 'The I.R.B. and the Beginnings of the G.A.A.', *I.H.S.*, xx, no. 80 (Sept. 1977), 424.
6. R. B. McDowell, *The Church of Ireland, 1869–1969* (London 1975), 100–1.

7. D. G. Boyce, 'They Have Got Yeats', *Text and Context*, no. 111 (1988), 42.

8. D. G. Boyce, *Nationalism in Ireland* (London 1982), 233–4.

9. Séamus Heaney, *The Haw Lantern* (London 1987), 6.

10. W. B. Yeats, *Uncollected Prose*, ed. J. P. Frayne (London 1970), i, 266–75.

11. Tom Garvin, 'Priests and Patriots: Irish Separatism and Fear of the Modern, 1890–1914', *I.H.S.*, xxv, no. 97 (May 1986), 73.

12. Boyce, *Revolution in Ireland*, 128.

13. John Hutchinson, *The Dynamics of Cultural Nationalism: The Gaelic Revival and the Creation of the Irish Nation State* (London 1987), ch. 7.

14. Boyce, *Nationalism in Ireland*, 238–9.

15. McDowell, op. cit., 101.

16. Garvin, op. cit., 74.

17. McDowell, op. cit., 101–2.

18. Boyce, *Nationalism in Ireland*, 296.

19. Bew, op. cit., 33, 36.

20. Ibid., 49.

21. Philip Bull, 'The United Irish League and the Reunion of the Irish Parliamentary Party, 1898–1900', *I.H.S.*, xxvi, no. 101 (May 1988), 51–78.

22. Bew, op. cit., 79.

23. Trevor West, *Horace Plunkett: Co-operation and Politics: An Irish Biography* (Gerrards Cross 1986), 3.

24. Ibid., 89–90.

25. Boyce, *Nationalism in Ireland*, 269.

26. Bew, op. cit., 87.

27. Alvin Jackson, 'Irish Unionism and the Russellite Threat, 1894–1906', *I.H.S.*, xxv, no. 100 (Nov. 1987), 376–404; Bew, op. cit., 86–95.

28. Patrick Buckland, *Irish Unionism, 2: Ulster Unionism and the Origins of Northern Ireland, 1886–1922* (Dublin 1973), 43–4; Alvin Jackson, *The Ulster Party: Irish Unionists in the House of Commons, 1884–1911* (Oxford 1989), ch. 6 offers a new interpretation.

29. Buckland, op. cit., 20–1.

30. Ibid., 27–8.

31. Ibid., 28–31.

32. J. R. B. McMinn, 'Liberalism in North Antrim, 1900–1914', *I.H.S.*, xxiii, no. 89 (May 1982), 17–29.

33. Bew, op. cit., 130–3.

34. J. C. Beckett, *The Making of Modern Ireland, 1603–1923* (London 1966), 421–2.

35. Bew, op. cit., 130–3.

36. Boyce *Nationalism in Ireland*, 272.

37. R. Finlay Holmes, *Our Irish Presbyterian Heritage* (Belfast 1985), 136. For Church of Ireland opposition to Home Rule see McDowell, op. cit., 103–5.

38. J. A. Murphy, 'Identity Change in the Republic of Ireland', *Études Irlandaises*, v (1976), 143–58.
39. Boyce, *Revolution in Ireland*, 131.
40. West, op. cit., 30.
41. Ibid., 56.
42. Ibid., 68–76.
43. Boyce, *Nationalism in Ireland*, 275–7.
44. West, op. cit., 116.
45. Bew, op. cit., 194–201.
46. Ibid., 202–11; Boyce, *Irish Question and British Politics*, 48–51.
47. Boyce, *Nationalism in Ireland*, 280–1.
48. Ibid., 301–3; Adrian Pimley, 'The Working-Class Movement and the Irish Revolution, 1896–1923' in Boyce, *Revolution in Ireland*, 194–204.
49. Charles Townshend, *Political Violence in Ireland: Government and Resistance since 1848* (Oxford 1983), 256–61.
50. Josephine Howie, 'Militarising a Society: The Ulster Volunteer Force, 1912–14' in Alan O'Day and Yonah Alexander (ed.), *Ireland's Terrorist Dilemma* (Dordrecht 1986), 211–30.
51. Townshend, op. cit., 266–73.
52. Patricia Jalland, *The Liberals and Ireland: The Ulster Question in British Politics to 1914* (Brighton 1980), 217–29; Boyce, *Irish Question and British Politics*, 52; Townshend, op. cit., 275–6.
53. John Ramsden (ed.), *Real Old Tory Politics: The Political Diaries of Sir Robert Sanders, Lord Bayford, 1900–1935* (London 1984), 79.
54. Memorandum of the Earl of Midleton, 23 June 1914 (Bodl., Selborne Papers, MS 77/115).
55. West, op. cit., 38.
56. Bew, op. cit., 220.

Chapter 9: The Union Broken, 1914–23 (pp. 242–280)
1. D. G. Boyce, *Nationalism in Ireland*, (London 1982), 283.
2. John Ramsden (ed.), *Real Old Tory Politics: The Political Diaries of Sir Robert Sanders, Lord Bayford, 1900–1935* (London 1984), 80.
3. Philip Williamson (ed.), *The Modernisation of Conservative Politics: The Letters and Diaries of William, First Viscount Bridgeman, 1904–1935* (London 1988), 81, 83.
4. Stephen Gwynn, *John Redmond's Last Years* (London 1919), 152.
5. Ibid., 150–1, 154–5.
6. Charles Townshend, *Political Violence in Ireland: Government and Resistance since 1848* (Oxford 1983), 278–9.
7. Patrick Callan, 'Voluntary Recruitment for the British Army in Ireland during the First World War' (Ph.D. thesis, U.C.D., 1984), 50–2.
8. Ibid., 53–4.
9. Patrick Buckland, *Irish Unionism 1: The Anglo-Irish and the New Ireland, 1885–1922* (Dublin 1972), 29–50 (quotation on p. 47).
10. Gwynn, op. cit., 144; Callan, op. cit., 51.
11. Callan, op. cit., ch. 5.

12. Henry Harrison, 'The Other Half Million' in Owen Dudley Edwards and Fergus Pyle (ed.), *1916: The Easter Rising* (London 1968), 51.
13. Boyce, op. cit., 284–5.
14. Gwynn, op. cit., 147, 163.
15. Neil O'Flanagan, 'Dublin City in an Age of War and Revolution, 1914–24' (M.A. thesis, U.C.D., 1985), 12–30, 35–6.
16. Boyce, op. cit., 286.
17. Gwynn, op. cit., 170–4.
18. O'Flanagan, op. cit., 42; Gwynn, op. cit., 195–8.
19. Boyce, op. cit., 286–7.
20. Gwynn, op. cit., 188–9.
21. Callan, op. cit., 358.
22. Ibid., 357.
23. Boyce, op. cit., 287.
24. Townshend, op. cit., 281–5.
25. Harrison, op. cit., 109.
26. Martin Williams, 'Ancient Mythology and Revolutionary Ideology in Ireland, 1878–1916', *H.J.*, xxvi, 2 (1983), 307–28; Boyce, op. cit., 248–9, 263–5, 273–4.
27. Callan, op. cit., 122–4.
28. Ibid., 315–16.
29. Ibid., 218.
30. Buckland, op. cit., 50–82; D. G. Boyce, *The Irish Question and British Politics, 1868–1986* (London 1988), 54–6; Gwynn, op. cit., 231–9; Williamson, op. cit., 100–9, has a very useful insider's view of the crisis.
31. Gwynn, op. cit., 257–8.
32. Michael Laffan, 'The Unification of Sinn Féin in 1917', *I.H.S.*, xvii, no. 67 (Mar. 1971), 358–9.
33. Ibid., 369.
34. Gwynn, op. cit., 243.
35. Townshend, op. cit., 315.
36. Boyce, *Nationalism in Ireland*, 315–16.
37. Ibid., 316–20.
38. F. S. L. Lyons, *John Dillion: A Biography* (London 1968), 434–44.
39. Buckland, op. cit., chs 4–6; for Lloyd George's statement see Gwynn, op. cit., 255.
40. Gwynn, op. cit., 332–3.
41. Ibid., 334.
42. Michael Laffan, *The Partition of Ireland, 1911–25* (Dundalk 1983), 57; Williamson, op. cit., 129, for British reaction.
43. Callan, op. cit., 340–1.
44. Townshend, op. cit., 315–16.
45. Laffan, *Partition of Ireland*, 58–9; D. J. Lucey, 'Cork Public Opinion in the First World War' (M.A. thesis, U.C.C., 1972), 99–110.
46. Boyce, *Irish Question and British Politics*, 58–9.
47. J. B. Lyons, *The Enigma of Tom Kettle: Irish Patriot, Essayist, Poet, British Soldier, 1880–1916* (Dublin 1983), 293.

48. Boyce, *Nationalism in Ireland*, 288–90, 317–20.
49. Paul Bew, *Conflict and Conciliation in Ireland, 1890–1910* (Oxford 1987), 217–18.
50. *Kerry News*, 13 Nov. 1918.
51. Bew, op. cit., 218.
52. *Connaught Telegraph*, 30 Nov. 1918.
53. *Kerry News*, 2 Dec. 1918.
54. Tom Garvin, *The Evolution of Irish Nationalist Politics* (Dublin 1981), 118–19; Boyce, *Nationalism in Ireland*, 289–90; *Munster Express*, 23, 30 Mar. 1918.
55. O'Flanagan, op. cit., 74.
56. Adrian Pimley, 'The Working-Class Movement and the Irish Revolution, 1896–1923' in D. G. Boyce (ed.), *The Revolution in Ireland 1879–1923*, (London/Dublin 1988), 209–11; Paul Bew, 'Sinn Féin, Agrarian Radicalism and the War of Independence, 1919–21', ibid., 232; D. R. O'Connor Lysaght, 'County Tipperary: Class Struggle and National Struggle, 1916–24' in William Nolan and T. G. McGrath (ed.), *Tipperary: History and Society* (Dublin 1985), 401–5; Townshend, op. cit., 322–44.
57. D. G. Boyce, *Englishmen and Irish Troubles: British Public Opinion and the Making of Irish Policy, 1918–22* (London 1972), 108–9.
58. Patrick Buckland, *Irish Unionism, 2: Ulster Unionism and the Origins of Northern Ireland, 1886–1922* (Dublin 1973), 113–26; Patrick Buckland, *The Factory of Grievances: Devolved Government in Northern Ireland, 1921–39* (Dublin 1979), 179–84.
59. Boyce, *Nationalism in Ireland*, 326.
60. Townshend, op. cit., 354–9; Boyce, *Englishmen and Irish Troubles*, 134–41.
61. Boyce, *Englishmen and Irish Troubles*, 140.
62. Michael Hopkinson, *Green Against Green: The Irish Civil War* (Dublin 1988), 10.
63. Richard Bennett, *The Black and Tans* (London 1964) 133–5.
64. Hopkinson, op. cit., 9.
65. Townshend, op. cit., 359.
66. Boyce, *Englishmen and Irish Troubles*, 150–5.
67. Ibid., 156–9.
68. The most vivid account is still Frank Pakenham (Lord Longford), *Peace by Ordeal* (London 1935 and later editions).
69. Hopkinson, op. cit., 15.
70. Clare O'Halloran, *Partition and the Limits of Irish Nationalism* (Dublin 1987), 141–3.
71. Buckland, *Factory of Grievances*, 180–205.
72. Craig to H. A. Gwynne, 8 Sept. 1922 (Bodl., Gwynne MSS).
73. Buckland, *Factory of Grievances*, 231–6.
74. Patrick Buckland, *A History of Northern Ireland* (Dublin 1981), 46–8.
75. Townshend, op. cit., 362.
76. S. M. Lawlor, 'Ireland from Truce to Treaty: War or Peace? July to October 1921', *I.H.S.*, xxii, no. 85 (Mar. 1980), 49–64.

77. Boyce, *Englishmen and Irish Troubles*, 175.
78. Thomas Towey, 'The Reaction of the British Government to the 1922 Collins–de Valera Pact', *I.H.S.*, xxii, no. 85 (Mar. 1980), 65–76.
79. Boyce, *Englishmen and Irish Troubles*, 175.
80. Ibid., 177–8.
81. Ibid., 179.
82. Ronan Fanning, *Independent Ireland* (Dublin 1983), 15.
83. Boyce, *Englishmen and Irish Troubles*, 179.
84. Joseph Lee, *Ireland, 1912–1985* (Cambridge 1989), 68–9.
85. Hopkinson, op. cit., 260; Calton Younger, *Ireland's Civil War* (London 1970; repr. 1979), 325.
86. Ibid., 45–6.
87. Boyce, *Nationalism in Ireland*, 332.
88. Hopkinson, op. cit., 274.
89. Ibid., 46.
90. A. T. Q. Stewart, *Edward Carson* (Dublin 1981), 120.

Chapter 10: Stability and Strife in the Nineteenth-Century Ireland (pp. 281–296)

1. Marianne Elliott, *Wolfe Tone: Prophet of Irish Independence* (New Haven/London, 1989), 246–50.
2. W. B. Hodgson (trans.), *Count Cavour on Ireland: Thoughts on Ireland, its Present and its Future* (London 1868), 2–3, 62, 72, 90–1, 105, 107.
3. Ibid., 110.
4. J. C. Beckett, Commentary on paper by Nicholas Mansergh, in David Watt, *The Constitution of Northern Ireland: Problems and Prospects* (London 1981), 28.
5. D. G. Boyce, 'Edward Carson and Irish Unionism' in Ciarán Brady (ed.), *Worsted in the Game: Losers in Irish History* (Dublin 1989), 150.
6. Terence Brown, *Ireland's Literature: Selected Essays* (Mullingar 1988), 52–3.
7. Thomas Croskery, *Irish Presbyterianism: Its History, Character, Influence and Present Position* (Dublin 1884), 62.
8. W. T. Latimer, *A History of the Irish Presbyterians*, 2nd ed. (Belfast 1902), 5–6.
9. Elizabeth Malcolm, 'The Catholic Church and the Irish Temperance Movement, 1838–1901', *I.H.S.*, xxiii, no. 89 (May 1982), 1–16.
10. For a fascinating study of the revolutionary breed see Tom Garvin, *Nationalist Revolutionaries in Ireland, 1858–1928* (Oxford 1987).
11. D. G. Boyce, *Nationalism in Ireland* (London 1982), 236, quoting Archbishop Croke; see also C. M. Candy, 'Popular Irish Literature in the Age of the Anglo-Irish Revival: Four Case Studies' (M.A. thesis, St Patrick's College, Maynooth, 1987), 52, 139, 176.
12. R. Finlay Holmes, *Our Irish Presbyterian Heritage* (Belfast 1985), 134.
13. W. E. Vaughan, *N.H.I.*, v, 745–6.

14. Anthony Trollope, *The Kellys and the O'Kellys* (1848), repr. (London 1906), 637ff.
15. Alan O'Day, 'The Irish Problem' in T. R. Gourvish and Alan O'Day (ed.), *Late Victorian Britain, 1867–1900* (London 1988), 235–41.
16. Keith Robbins, *Nineteenth-Century Britain: Integration and Diversity* (Oxford 1988), 181–5.

Bibliography

The most recent and comprehensive bibliographies of Irish history are T. W. Moody (ed.), *Irish Historiography, 1936–70* (Dublin 1971), and Joseph Lee (ed.), *Irish Historiography, 1970–79* (Cork 1981). The Irish Committee of Historical Sciences has published *Writings on Irish History* (annual lists of which were carried in *Irish Historical Studies*); the 1984 list includes addenda for the period 1973–83. G. R. Elton, *Annual Bibliography of British and Irish History* is valuable, as is L. M. Brown and I. R. Christie (ed.), *Bibliography of British History, 1789–1851* (Oxford 1977), and H. J. Hanham, *Bibliography of British History, 1851–1914* (Oxford 1977).

This bibliography is divided into the following sections: (1) General works; (2) Contemporary and near-contemporary publications; (3) Later works, covering 1798–1868; (4) Later works, covering 1869–1923; (5) Newspapers and periodicals; (6) Novels and creative literature; (7) Photographs. It is not an exhaustive list, but is intended as a guide to the literature, incorporating as wide a range as possible.

1. General Works

Akenson, D. H., *Small Differences: Irish Catholics and Irish Protestants, 1815–1922* (Kingston/Montreal 1988)

Beckett, J. C., *The Making of Modern Ireland, 1603–1923* (London 1966 and later editions)

Boyce, D. G., *Nationalism in Ireland* (London 1982)

Cullen, L. M., *The Emergence of Modern Ireland, 1600–1900* (London 1981)

Daly, Mary E., *Social and Economic History of Ireland since 1800* (Dublin 1981)

Foster, R. F., *Modern Ireland, 1600–1972* (London 1988)

Garvin, Tom, *The Evolution of Irish Nationalist Politics* (Dublin 1981)

Hoppen, K. T., *Ireland since 1800: Conflict and Conformity* (London 1989)

Kearney, Hugh, *The British Isles: A History of Four Nations* (Cambridge 1989)

Kee, Robert, *The Green Flag: A History of Irish Nationalism* (London 1972)

Kennedy, Liam, and Ollerenshaw, Philip (ed.), *An Economic History of Ulster, 1820–1940* (Manchester 1985)

Lee, Joseph, *The Modernisation of Irish Society, 1848–1918* (Dublin 1973)

Lyons, F. S. L., *Ireland since the Famine* (London 1971 and later editions)

McCartney, Donal, *The Dawning of Democracy: Ireland, 1800–1870* (Dublin 1987)

MacDonagh, Oliver, *Ireland: the Union and its Aftermath* (London 1977)
——*States of Mind: A Study of Anglo-Irish Conflict, 1780–1980* (London 1983)
Mansergh, Nicholas, *The Irish Question, 1840–1921*, repr. (London 1975)
New History of Ireland, Vol. IV: *Eighteenth Century Ireland, 1691–1800*, ed. T. W. Moody and W. E. Vaughan (Oxford 1986); Vol. V: *Ireland under the Union, I: 1801–70*, ed. W. E. Vaughan (Oxford 1989)
Norman, E. R., *A History of Modern Ireland* (London 1971)
O'Farrell, Patrick, *Ireland's English Question, 1534–1970* (London 1971)
——*England and Ireland since 1800* (London 1975)
Ó Tuathaigh, Gearóid, *Ireland before the Famine, 1798–1848* (Dublin 1972)
Strauss, Erich, *Irish Nationalism and British Democracy* (London 1951)

2. Contemporary and Near-Contemporary Publications

Barrington, Sir Jonah, *Rise and Fall of the Irish Nation*, repr. (Dublin 1853)
Butt, Isaac, *A Plea for the Celtic Race* (Dublin 1866)
——*Irish Federalism: Its Meaning, Its Objects and Its Hopes* (Dublin 1874)
Cloney, Thomas, *A Personal Narrative of those Transactions in the County Wexford in which the Author was Engaged during 1798* (Dublin 1832)
Croker, T. Crofton, *Researches in the South of Ireland* (1824), ed. Kevin Danaher (Shannon 1969)
Croskery, Thomas, *Irish Presbyterianism: Its History, Character, Influence and Present Position* (Dublin 1884)
Davis, Thomas, *Prose Writings*, repr. (London 1890)
Davitt, Michael, *The Fall of Feudalism in Ireland; or The Story of the Land League Revolution* (1904), ed. Seán Ó Lúing (Shannon 1970)
Dicey, A. V., *England's Case against Home Rule* (1886), ed. E. J. Feuchtwanger (Surrey 1973)
Duffy, Sir Charles Gavan, *My Life in Two Hemispheres* (1898), repr. (Shannon 1968)
Ferguson, Lady, *Sir Samuel Ferguron in the Ireland of His Day* (Edinburgh/London 1896)
Gaughan, J. A. (ed.), *Memoirs of Constable Jeremiah Mee* (Dublin 1975)
Gibson, William, *The Year of Grace* (Belfast 1860)
Gordon, James, *History of the Rebellion in Ireland* (Dublin 1803)
Grattan, Henry, *Speeches*, Vol. IV (London 1842)
Hall, Mr and Mrs S. C., *Hall's Ireland: Mr and Mrs Hall's Tour of 1840* (1841), ed. Michael Scott (London 1984)
Healy, T. M. *Letters and Leaders of My Day*, 2 vols (London 1928)
Hodgson, W. B. (trans.), *Count Cavour on Ireland: Thoughts on Ireland, its Present and its Future* (London 1868)
Jones, Tom, *Whitehall Diary*, Vol. III: *Ireland, 1918–25*, ed. Keith Middlemass (London 1971)
Lalor, J. F., *Selected Writings*, ed. Nathaniel Marlowe (Dublin 1918)
Latimer, W. T., *A History of the Irish Presbyterians*, 2nd ed. (Belfast 1902)

Lecky, W. E. H., *Leaders of Public Opinion in Ireland*, repr., 2 vols (London 1912)

Lewis, G. C., *On Local Disturbances in Ireland and on the Irish Church Question* (London 1836)

McElroy, S. C., *The Route Land Crusade: being an Authentic Account of the Efforts made to Advance Land Reform by the Route Tenants' Defence Association . . .* (Coleraine n.d.)

MacKnight, Thomas, *Ulster As It Is, or Twenty-Eight Years' Experience as an Irish Editor*, 2 vols (London 1896)

Musgrave, Sir Richard, *Memoirs of the Different Rebellions in Ireland*, 3rd ed. (Dublin/London 1802)

Nelson, Isaac, *The Year of Delusion* (Belfast 1859)

O'Connor, T. P., *Memoirs of an Old Parliamentarian*, 2 vols (London 1929)

O'Donnell, F. H., *History of the Irish Parliamentary Party*, 2 vols (London 1910)

Parnell, William, *Historical Apology for the Irish Catholics* (Dublin 1807)

Plowden, Francis, *Historical Letter to Charles O'Conor* (Dublin 1812)

——*Historical Reply to Charles O'Conor* (Dublin 1813)

Plunkett, Sir Horace, *Ireland in the New Century* (London 1904)

Porter, J. L., *The Life and Times of Henry Cooke* (London 1871)

Senior, Nassau, 'Ireland', *Edinburgh Review*, lxxix (1844), 189–266

Taaffe, Denis, *Vindication of the Irish Nation* (Dublin 1801)

Trench, William Steuart, *Realities of Irish Life* (1868), repr. (London 1966)

Wyse, Thomas, *Historical Sketch of the Late Catholic Association of Ireland*, 2 vols (London 1829)

Yeats, W. B., *Autobiographies* (London 1926)

3. Later Works (i): 1798–1868

Akenson, D. H., *The Irish Education Experiment: The National System of Education in the Nineteenth Century* (London 1970)

——*The Church of Ireland: Ecclesiastical Reform and Revolution, 1800–1885* (New Haven 1971)

Baker, Sybil E., 'Orange and Green: Belfast, 1832–1912' in H. J. Dyos and Michael Wolff (ed.), *The Victorian City: Images and Reality* (London 1973), ii, 789–814

Beames, Michael, 'Rural Conflict in Pre-Famine Ireland: Peasant Assassinations in Tipperary, 1837–47', *P.&P.*, no. 81 (1978), 75–91

——'The Ribbon Society: Lower-Class Nationalism in Pre-Famine Ireland', *P.&P.*, no. 97 (1982), 128–43

——*Peasants and Power: The Whiteboy Movements and their Control in Pre-Famine Ireland* (Brighton 1983)

Bell, P. M. H., *Disestablishment in Ireland and Wales* (London 1969)

Bolton, G. C., *The Passing of the Irish Act of Union* (London 1966)

Bowen, Desmond, *Souperism: Myth or Reality?* (Cork 1970)

——*The Protestant Crusade in Ireland, 1800–1870* (Dublin 1978)

Brooke, Peter, *Ulster Presbyterianism: The Historical Perspective, 1610–1970* (Dublin 1987)

Brose, O. J. *Church and Parliament: The Reshaping of the Church of Ireland, 1826–60* (London 1959)

Brynn, Edward, *The Church of Ireland in the Age of Catholic Emancipation* (New York/London 1982)

Buckley, Mary, 'Thomas Davis: A Study in Nationalist Philosophy' (Ph. D. thesis, U.C.C., 1980)

Burke, Helen, *The People and the Poor Law in Nineteenth-Century Ireland* (Dublin 1987)

Campbell, Mary, *Lady Morgan* (London 1988)

Chenevix Trench, Charles, *The Great Dan: A Biography of Daniel O'Connell* (London 1984)

Clarkson, L. A., 'Irish Population Revisited, 1687–1821' in J. M. Goldstrom and L. A. Clarkson (ed.), *Irish Population, Economy and Society: Essays in honour of the late K. H. Connell* (Oxford 1981), 13–35

Comerford, R. V., *The Fenians in Context: Irish Politics and Society, 1848–82* (Dublin 1985)

Connell, K. H., *The Population of Ireland, 1750–1845* (Oxford 1950)

——*Irish Peasant Society: Four Historical Essays* (Oxford 1968)

Connolly, S. J., 'Catholicism in Ulster, 1800–1850' in Peter Roebuck (ed.), *Plantation to Partition: Essays in Ulster History in honour of J. L. McCracken* (Belfast 1981), 157–71

——*Priests and People in Pre-Famine Ireland, 1780–1845* (Dublin 1982)

——*Religion and Society in Nineteenth Century Ireland* (Dundalk 1985)

Corish, P. J., 'Political Problems, 1860–78' in P. J. Corish (ed.), *A History of Irish Catholicism*, v, fasc. 3 (Dublin 1967)

Crotty, R. D., *Irish Agricultural Production: Its Volume and Structure* (Cork 1966)

Cullen, L. M., 'The 1798 Rebellion in its Eighteenth-Century Context' in P. J. Corish (ed.), *Radicals, Rebels and Establishments* (*Historical Studies XV*) (Belfast 1985), 91–113

Curtin, N. J., 'The Transformation of the Society of United Irishmen into a Mass-based Revolutionary Organisation, 1794–6', *I.H.S.*, xxiv, no. 96 (Nov. 1985), 463–92

D'Alton, Ian, 'A Contrast in Crises: Southern Irish Protestantism, 1820–43 and 1885–1910' in A. C. Hepburn (ed.), *Minorities in History* (*Historical Studies XII*) (London 1978), 70–83

——*Protestant Society and Politics in Cork, 1812–44* (Cork 1980)

Daly, Mary E., *The Famine in Ireland* (Dublin 1986)

D'Arcy, F. A., 'The Artisans of Dublin and Daniel O'Connell, 1830–47: An Unquiet Liason', *I.H.S.*, xvii, no. 66 (Sept. 1970), 221–43

Davis, Richard, *The Young Ireland Movement* (Dublin 1987)

Deane, Séamus, *A Short History of Irish Literature* (London 1986)

de Vere White, Terence, *The Road of Excess* (Biography of Isaac Butt) (Dublin 1946)

Dewar, M. W., Brown, John, and Long, S. E., *Orangeism: A New Historical Appreciation* (Belfast 1967)

Donnelly, J. S., jnr., 'Pastorini and Captain Rock: Millenarianism and Sectarianism in the Rockite Movement of 1821–4' in Samuel Clarke and

J. S. Donnelly, jnr (ed.), *Irish Peasants: Violence and Political Unrest, 1780–1914* (Manchester 1983), 102–39

——'The Social Composition of Agrarian Rebellions in Early Nineteenth-Century Ireland: The Case of the Carders and Caravats, 1813–16' in P. J. Corish (ed.), *Radicals, Rebels and Establishments (Historical Studies XV)* (Belfast 1985) 151–69

Edwards, Robin Dudley, and Williams, T. Desmond (ed.), *The Great Famine: Studies in Irish History, 1845–52* (Dublin 1956)

Elliott, Marianne, *Partners in Revolution: The United Irishmen and France* (New Haven/London 1982)

——*Wolfe Tone: Prophet of Irish Independence* (New Haven/London 1989)

Fitzpatrick, David, 'The Disappearance of the Irish Agricultural Labourer, 1841–1912', *I.E.S.H.*, vii (1980), 66–92

——*Irish Emigration, 1801–1921* (Dublin 1984)

Flanagan, Thomas, *The Irish Novelists, 1800–1850* (Westport, Conn. 1976)

Fogarty, Lilian, *James Fintan Lalor: Patriot and Political Essayist* (Dublin 1918)

Garvin, Tom, 'Defenders, Ribbonmen and Others: Underground Political Networks in Pre-Famine Ireland', *P.&P.*, no. 96 (1982) 133–55

Goldstrom, J. M., 'Irish Agriculture and the Great Famine' in J. M. Goldstrom and L. A. Clarkson (ed.), *Irish Population, Economy and Society: Essays in honour of the late K. H. Connell* (Oxford 1981), 155–71

Hempton, David, 'The Methodist Crusade in Ireland, 1795–1845', *I.H.S.*, xxii, no. 85 (Mar. 1980), 33–48

——*Methodism and Politics in British Society, 1750–1850* (London 1984)

——'Methodism in Irish Society, 1770–1830', *T.R.H.S.*, 5th ser., xxxvi (1986), 117–42

Hill, J. R., 'The Protestant Response to Repeal: The Case of the Dublin Working Classes' in F. S. L. Lyons and R. A. J. Hawkins (ed.), *Ireland under the Union: Varieties of Tension: Essays in honour of T. W. Moody* (Oxford 1980), 35–68

——'National Festivals, the State and "Protestant Ascendancy" in Ireland, 1790–1829', *I.H.S.*, xxiv, no. 93 (May 1984), 30–51

——'Popery and Protestantism, Civil and Religious Liberty: The Disputed Lessons of Irish History, 1690–1802', *P.&P.*, no. 118 (1988), 96–129

Holmes, R. Finlay, *Henry Cooke* (Belfast 1981)

——'Ulster Presbyterianism and Irish Nationalism' in Stuart Mews (ed.), *Religion and National Identity: Studies in Church History* (Oxford 1982), 535–55

——*Our Irish Presbyterian Heritage* (Belfast 1985)

Hoppen, K. T., 'Tories, Catholics and the General Election of 1859', *H.J.*, xiii (1970), 48–67

——'Landlords, Society, and Electoral Politics in Mid-Nineteenth-Century Ireland', *P.&P.*, no. 75 (1977), 62–93

——'Politics, the Law, and the Nature of the Irish Electorate, 1832–50', *E.H.R.*, xcii (1977), 746–76

——'National Politics and Local Realities in Mid-Nineteenth-Century

Ireland' in. Art Cosgrove and Donal McCartney (ed.), *Studies in Irish History presented to R. Dudley Edwards* (Dublin 1979), 190–227

——*Elections, Politics and Society in Ireland, 1832–85* (Oxford 1984)

Jupp, P. J. 'Irish Parliamentary Elections and the Influence of the Catholic Vote, 1801–20', *H.J.*, x (1967), 183–96

Keenan, D. J., *The Catholic Church in Nineteenth-Century Ireland* (Dublin 1983)

Kennedy, T. P. 'Church-Building' in P. J. Corish (ed.), *A History of Irish Catholicism*, v, fasc. 8 (Dublin 1970)

Kerr, Donal, *Peel, Priests and Politics: Sir Robert Peel's Administration and the Roman Catholic Church in Ireland, 1841–6* (Oxford 1982)

——'Under the Union Flag: The Catholic Church in Ireland' in *Ireland after the Union*, intro. Lord Blake (London 1989)

Lee, Joseph, 'On the Accuracy of the Pre-Famine Irish Census' in J. M. Goldstrom and L. A. Clarkson (ed.), *Irish Population, Economy and Society: Essays in honour of the late K. H. Connell* (Oxford 1981), 37–56

Leonard, D. W., 'John Mitchel, Charles Gavan Duffy, and the Legacy of Young Ireland' (Ph.D. thesis, University of Sheffield, 1975)

McCartney, Donal, 'Writings on Irish History in the Early Nineteenth Century' (M.A. thesis, U.C.D., 1955)

——'The Writing of History in Ireland, 1800–1830', *I.H.S.*, x, no. 40 (Sept. 1957), 347–62

McCourt, Margaret, 'Belfast Liberals: The 1865 and 1868 Elections' (M.A. thesis, Q.U.B., 1987)

MacDonagh, Oliver, *The Heriditary Bondsman: Daniel O'Connell, 1775–1829* (London 1988)

——*The Emancipist: Daniel O'Connell, 1830–47* (London 1989)

McDowell, R. B., *Public Opinion and Government Policy in Ireland, 1801–1846* (London 1952)

——*Ireland in the Age of Imperialism and Revolution, 1760–1800* (Oxford 1979)

Machin, G. I. T., *Politics and the Churches in Great Britain, 1832–68* (Oxford 1977)

MacIntyre, Angus, *The Liberator: Daniel O'Connell and the Irish Party, 1830–47* (London 1965)

McNiffe, Liam, 'The Politicisation of Leitrim, Sligo and Mayo in the General Election of 1852' (M.A. thesis, St Patrick's College, Maynooth, 1979)Mac Suibhne, Peadar (ed.), *Paul Cullen and his Contemporaries*, 5 vols (Naas 1961–77)

Maguire, W. A., *The Downshire Estates in Ireland, 1801–1845: The Management of Irish Landed Estates in the Early Nineteenth Century* (Oxford 1972)

Malcolm, Elizabeth, 'The Catholic Church and the Irish Temperance Movement, 1838–1901', *I.H.S.*, xxiii, no. 89 (May 1982), 1–16

——'*Ireland Sober, Ireland Free*': Drink and Temperance in Nineteenth-Century Ireland (Dublin 1986)

Miller, D. W., 'Irish Catholicism and the Great Famine', *J.S.H.*, ix (1974), 81–98

——'Presbyterianism and "Modernisation" in Ulster', *P.&P.*, no. 80 (1978), 66–90

Mokyr, Joel, *Why Ireland Starved: A Quantitative and Analytical History of the Irish Economy, 1800–1850* (London 1983)

Moody, T. W. (ed.), *The Fenian Movement* (Cork 1968)

Murphy, J. A., 'The Support of the Catholic Clergy in Ireland, 1750–1850' in J. L. McCracken (ed.), *Historical Studies V* (London 1965), 103–21

Murphy, Maura, 'Municipal Reform and the Repeal Movement in Cork, 1833–44', *Jn. Cork Hist. & Arch. Soc.*, lxxxi (1976), 1–18

Murray, A. C., 'Agrarian Violence and Nationalism in Nineteenth-Century Ireland: The Myth of Ribbonism', *I.E.S.H.*, xiii (1986), 56–73

Norman, E. R., *The Catholic Church and Ireland in the Age of Rebellion, 1859–73* (London 1965)

——'The Maynooth Question of 1845', *I.H.S.*, xv, no. 60 (Sept. 1967), 407–37

——*The Catholic Church and Irish Politics in the 1860s* (Dundalk 1969)

Nowlan, K. B., *The Politics of Repeal: A Study in the Relations between Great Britain and Ireland, 1841–50* (London 1965)

O'Brien, George, *The Economic History of Ireland from the Union to the Famine* (London 1921)

Ó Broin, León, *Fenian Fever: An Anglo-American Dilemma* (London 1971)

O'Connell, Daniel, *Correspondence*, ed. M. R. O'Connell, 8 vols (Dublin 1972–80)

O'Ferrall, Fergus, *Catholic Emancipation: Daniel O'Connell and the Birth of Irish Democracy, 1820–30* (Dublin 1985)

Ó Gráda, Cormac, *Ireland Before and After the Famine: Explorations in Economic History, 1800–1925* (Manchester 1988)

O'Neill, T. P., 'The Irish Land Question, 1830–50', *Studies*, xliv (1955), 325–36

Ó Tuathaigh, Gearóid, *Thomas Drummond and the Government of Ireland, 1835–41* (Dublin 1978)

Postgate, Raymond, *Robert Emmet* (London 1931)

Reynolds, R. J., *The Catholic Emancipation Crisis in Ireland, 1823–9* (New Haven 1954)

Roebuck, Peter, 'Landlord Indebtedness in Ulster in the Seventeenth and Eighteenth Centuries' in J. M. Goldstrom and L. A. Clarkson (ed.), *Irish Population, Economy and Society: Essays in honour of the late K. H. Connell* (Oxford 1981), 135–54

Ryan, Desmond, *The Fenian Chief: A Biography of James Stephens* (Dublin 1967)

Senior, Hereward, *Orangeism in Ireland and Britain, 1795–1836* (London 1966)

Sheehy, Jeanne, *The Rediscovery of Ireland's Past: The Celtic Revival, 1830–1930* (London 1980)

Steele, E. D., *Irish Land and British Politics: Tenant Right and Nationality, 1865–70* (Cambridge 1974)

——'Cardinal Cullen and Irish Nationality', *I.H.S.*, xix, no. 75 (Mar. 1975), 239–60

Vaughan, W. E., 'Landlord and Tenant Relations in Ireland between the Famine and the Land War, 1850–78' in L. M. Cullen and T. C. Smout (ed.), *Comparative Aspects of Scottish and Irish Economic and Social History, 1600–1900* (Edinburgh 1977), 216–26

——*Landlords and Tenants in Ireland, 1848–1904* (Dublin 1984)

Wall, Maureen, *The Penal Laws, 1691–1760* (Dundalk 1961)

Ward, Bernard, *The Eve of Catholic Emancipation*, 3 vols (London 1911–13)

Whelan, Kevin, 'The Religious Factor in the 1798 Rebellion in County Wexford' in Patrick O'Flanagan, Patrick Ferguson, and Kevin Whelan (ed.), *Rural Ireland, 1600–1900: Modernisation and Change* (Cork 1987), 62–85

Whyte, J. H., *The Independent Irish Party, 1850–59* (Oxford 1958)

——'The Influence of the Catholic Clergy on Elections in Nineteenth-Century Ireland', *E.H.R.*, lxxv (1960), 12–32

——*The Tenant League and Irish Politics in the 1850s* (Dundalk 1966)

——'Political Problems, 1850–60' in P. J. Corish (ed.), *A History of Irish Catholicism*, v, fasc. 2 (Dublin 1967)

4. Later Works (ii): 1869–1923

Baker, Sybil E., *Edwardian Belfast: A Social Profile* (Belfast 1982)

Beckett, I. F. W. (ed.), *The Army and the Curragh Incident, 1914* (London 1986)

Bennett, Richard, *The Black and Tans* (London 1964)

Bew, Paul, *Land and the National Question in Ireland, 1858–82* (Dublin 1978)

——*C. S. Parnell* (Dublin 1980)

——'The Land League Ideal: Achievements and Contradictions' in P. J. Drudy (ed.), *Ireland: Land, Politics and People (Irish Studies II)* (Cambridge 1982), 77–92

——*Conflict and Conciliation in Ireland, 1890–1910* (Oxford 1987)

——'Sinn Féin, Agrarian Radicalism and the War of Independence, 1919–21' in D. G. Boyce (ed.), *The Revolution in Ireland, 1879–23* (London/Dublin 1988), 217–34

Bowman, John, *De Valera and the Ulster Question, 1917–73* (Oxford 1982)

Boyce, D. G., *Englishmen and Irish Troubles: British Public Opinion and the Making of Irish Policy, 1918–22* (London 1972)

——(ed.), *The Revolution in Ireland, 1879–1923* (London/Dublin 1988)

——*The Irish Question and British Politics, 1868–1986* (London 1988)

——'They Have Got Yeats', *Text and Context*, no. 111 (1988), 39–54

——'Edward Carson and Irish Unionism' in Ciarán Brady (ed.), *Worsted in the Game: Losers in Irish History* (Dublin 1989), 145–57

Brown, Malcolm, *The Politics of Irish Literature* (London 1972)

Brown, Terence, *Ireland's Literature: Selected Essays* (Mullingar 1988)

Buckland, Patrick, *Irish Unionism 1: The Anglo-Irish and the New Ireland, 1885–1922* (Dublin 1972)

——*Irish Unionism 2: Ulster Unionism and the Origins of Northern Ireland, 1886–1922* (Dublin 1973)
——*Irish Unionism, 1885–1923: A Documentary History* (Belfast 1973)
——*The Factory of Grievances: Devolved Government in Northern Ireland, 1921–39* (Dublin 1979)
——*James Craig, Lord Craigavon* (Dublin 1980)
——*A History of Northern Ireland* (Dublin 1981)
——'Irish Unionism and the New Ireland' in D. G. Boyce (ed.), *The Revolution in Ireland, 1879–1923* (London/Dublin 1988), 71–90
Budge, Ian, and O'Leary, Cornelius, *Belfast: Approach to Crisis* (London 1973)
Bull, Philip, 'The United Irish League and the Reunion of the Irish Parliamentary Party, 1898–1900', *I.H.S.*, xxvi, no. 101 (May 1988), 51–78
Cairns, David, and Richards, Shaun, *Writing Ireland* (Manchester 1988)
Callan, Patrick, 'Voluntary Recruitment for the British Army in Ireland during the First World War' (Ph.D. thesis, U.C.D., 1984)
Candy, C. M., 'Popular Irish Literature in the Age of the Anglo-Irish Revival: Four Case Studies' (M.A. thesis, St Patrick's College, Maynooth, 1987)
Canning, Paul, *British Policy towards Ireland, 1921–41* (Oxford 1985)
Clark, Samuel, 'Social Composition of the Land League', *I.H.S.*, xvii, no. 68 (Sept. 1971), 447–69
——'Agrarian Class Conflict and Collective Action in Nineteenth-Century Ireland', *B.J.S.*, xxix (1978), 22–40
——*Social Origins of the Land War* (Princeton 1979)
Coldrey, B. M., *Faith and Fatherland: The Christian Brothers and the Development of Irish Nationalism, 1838–1921* (Dublin 1988)
Colum Pádraic, *Arthur Griffith* (Dublin 1951)
Coogan, T. P., *The I.R.A.* (London 1970)
Cooke, A. B., 'A Conservative Party Leader in Ulster: Sir Stafford Northcote's Diary of a Visit to the Province, October 1883', *P.R.I.A.*, lxxv, sect. C, no. 4 (1975), 61–84
——and Malcomson, A. P. W., *The Ashbourne Papers, 1869–1913* (Belfast 1974)
Coxhead, Elizabeth, *Lady Gregory* (London 1961)
Curtis, L. P., jnr, *Coercion and Conciliation in Ireland, 1880–92* (Princeton 1963)
——'Incumbered Wealth: Landed Indebtedness in Post-Famine Ireland', *American Historical Review*, lxxxv (1980), 332–67
D'Alton, Ian, 'Southern Irish Unionism: A Study of Cork Unionists, 1884–1914', *T.R.H.S.*, 5th ser., xxiii (1973), 71–88
——'Cork Unionism: Its Role in Parliamentary and Local Elections, 1885–1914', *Studia Hibernica*, xv (1975), 143–61
Daly, Dominic, *The Young Douglas Hyde* (Dublin 1974)
Daly, G. C., 'Church Renewal, 1869–77' in Michael Hurley (ed.), *Irish Anglicanism, 1869–1969* (Dublin 1970)
Daly, Mary E., *Dublin, the Deposed Capital: A Social and Economic*

History, 1860–1914 (Cork 1985)

Davis, Richard, *Arthur Griffith and Non-Violent Sinn Féin* (Dublin 1974)

——*The Young Ireland Movement* (Dublin 1987)

Donnelly, J. S., jnr, *The Land and the People of Nineteenth-Century Cork* (London 1976)

Dwyer, T. Ryle, *Eamon de Valera* (Dublin 1980)

Edwards, Owen Dudley, and Pyle, Fergus, *1916: The Easter Rising* (London 1968)

Edwards, Ruth Dudley, *Patrick Pearse: The Triumph of Failure* (London 1977)

Ellman, Richard, *James Joyce*, repr. (Oxford 1983)

Ervine, St John, *Craigavon: Ulsterman* (London 1949)

Fallis, Richard, *The Irish Renaissance: An Introduction to Anglo-Irish Literature* (Dublin 1978)

Fanning, Ronan, *Independent Ireland* (Dublin 1983)

Farrell, Brian, *The Founding of Dáil Éireann: Parliament and Nation-Building* (Dublin 1971)

Feingold, W. L., *The Revolt of the Tenantry: The Transformation of Local Government in Ireland, 1872–86* (Boston 1984)

Fergusson, Sir James, *The Curragh Incident* (London 1964)

Fitzpatrick, David, *Politics and Irish Life, 1913–21: Provincial Experience of War and Revolution* (Dublin 1977)

——'The Geography of Irish Nationalism, 1910–21', *P.&P.*, no. 78 (1978), 113–44

——*Irish Emigration, 1801–1921* (Dublin 1984)

——'Unrest in Rural Ireland', *I.E.S.H.*, xii (1985), 98–105

——*Ireland and the First World War* (Dublin 1986)

Forester, Margery, *Michael Collins: The Lost Leader* (London 1971)

Foster, R. F., *Charles Stewart Parnell: The Man and his Family* (Sussex 1976)

——'To the Northern Counties Station: Lord Randolph Churchill and the Prelude to the Orange Card' in F. S. L. Lyons and R. A. J. Hawkins (ed.), *Ireland under the Union: Varieties of Tension: Essays in honour of T. W. Moody* (Oxford 1980), 237–89

——'Anglo-Irish Literature, Gaelic Nationalism and Irish Politics in the 1890s' in J. M. W. Bean (ed.), *The Political Culture of Modern Britain: Studies in memory of Stephen Koss* (London 1987), 91–101

Gailey, Andrew, *Ireland and the Death of Kindness: The Experience of Constructive Unionism, 1890–1905* (Cork 1987)

——'Failure and the Making of the New Ireland' in D. G. Boyce (ed.), *The Revolution in Ireland, 1879–1923* (London/Dublin 1988), 47–70

Gallagher, Michael, 'The Pact Election of 1922', *I.H.S.*, xxi, no. 84 (Sept. 1979), 404–21

Garvin, Tom, *The Evolution of Irish Nationalist Politics* (Dublin 1981)

——'Priests and Patriots: Irish Separatism and Fear of the Modern, 1890–1914', *I.H.S.*, xxv, no. 97 (May 1986), 67–81

——'The Anatomy of a Nationalist Revolution: Ireland, 1858–1928' *Comparative Studies in Society and History*, xxviii (1986), 468–501

——*Nationalist Revolutionaries in Ireland, 1858–1928* (Oxford 1987)

Geary, L. M., *The Plan of Campaign, 1886–91* (Cork 1986)

Gibbon, Peter, *The Origins of Ulster Unionism: The Formation of Popular Protestant Politics and Ideology in Nineteenth-Century Ireland* (Manchester 1975)

Gilley, Sheridan, 'The Catholic Church and Revolution in Nineteenth-Century Ireland' in Yonah Alexander and Alan O'Day (ed.), *Terrorism in Ireland* (London 1984), 121–45

——'The Catholic Church and Revolution' in D. G. Boyce (ed.), *The Revolution in Ireland, 1879–1923* (London/Dublin 1988), 157–72

Goldring, Maurice, *Faith of Our Fathers: The Formation of Irish Nationalist Ideology, 1890–1920* (Dublin 1982)

Greaves, C. Desmond, *The Life and Times of James Connolly* (London 1961)

Gwynn, D. R., *The Life of John Redmond* (London 1932)

——*The History of Partition* (Dublin 1950)

Gwynn, Stephen, *John Redmond's Last Years* (London 1919)

Harrison, Henry, 'The Other Half Million' in Owen Dudley Edwards and Fergus Pyle (ed.), *1916: The Easter Rising* (London 1968), 101–15

Hepburn, A. C. (ed.), *The Conflict of Nationality in Modern Ireland* (London 1980)

Higgins, M. D., and Gibbons, J. P., 'Shopkeeper-Graziers and Land Agitation in Ireland, 1895–1900' in P. J. Drudy (ed.), *Ireland: Land, Politics and People (Irish Studies II)* (Cambridge 1982), 93–118

Holt, Edgar, *Protest in Arms: The Irish Troubles, 1916–23* (London 1960)

Hone, Joseph, *William Butler Yeats, 1865–1939* (London 1942)

Hopkinson, Michael, *Green Against Green: The Irish Civil War* (Dublin 1988)

Howie, Josephine, 'Militarising a Society: The Ulster Volunteer Force, 1912–14' in Alan O'Day and Yonah Alexander (ed.), *Ireland's Terrorist Dilemma* (Dordrecht 1986), 211–30

Hutchinson, John, *The Dynamics of Cultural Nationalism: The Gaelic Revival and the Creation of the Irish Nation State* (London 1987)

Jackson, Alvin, 'Irish Unionism and the Russellite Threat, 1894–1906', *I.H.S.*, xxv, no. 100 (Nov. 1987), 376–404

——*The Ulster Party: Irish Unionists in the House of Commons, 1884–1911* (Oxford 1989)

Jalland, Patricia, *The Liberals and Ireland: The Ulster Question in British Politics to 1914* (Brighton 1980)

Jones, D. S., 'The Cleavage between Graziers and Peasants in the Land Struggle, 1890–1910' in Samuel Clark and J. S. Donnelly, jnr (ed.), *Irish Peasants: Violence and Political Unrest, 1780–1914* (Manchester 1983), 374–417

Jones, Emrys, 'Late Victorian Belfast, 1850–1900' in J. C. Beckett and R. E. Glasscock (ed.), *Belfast: The Origin and Growth of an Industrial City* (London 1967), 109–19

Kendle, John, *Ireland and the Federal Solution: The Debate over the United Kingdom Constitution, 1870–1921* (Kingston/Montreal 1989)

Keogh, Dermot, *The Vatican, the Bishops, and Irish Politics, 1919–39* (Cambridge 1986)

Kirkpatrick, R. W., 'The Origins and Development of the Land War in Mid-Ulster, 1879–85' in F. S. L. Lyons and R. A. J. Hawkins (ed.), *Ireland under the Union: Varieties of Tension: Essays in honour of T. W. Moody* (Oxford 1980), 201–35

Laffan, Michael, 'The Unification of Sinn Féin in 1917', *I.H.S.*, xvii, no. 67 (Mar. 1971), 353–79

——*The Partition of Ireland, 1911–25* (Dundalk 1983)

Larkin, Emmet, *James Larkin: Irish Labour Leader, 1876–1947* (London 1965)

——*The Roman Catholic Church and the Creation of the Modern Irish State, 1878–86* (Dublin 1975)

——*The Roman Catholic Church and the Plan of Campaign, 1886–8* (Cork 1978)

——*The Roman Catholic Church in Ireland and the Fall of Parnell, 1888–91* (North Carolina 1979)

Lawlor, S. M., 'Ireland from Truce to Treaty: War or Peace? July to October 1921', *I.H.S.*, xxii, no. 85 (Mar. 1980), 49–64

Lee, Joseph, *Ireland, 1912–1985* (Cambridge 1989)

Longford, Earl of, and O'Neill, T. P., *Eamon de Valera* (London 1970)

Loughlin, James, 'The Irish Protestant Home Rule Association and Nationalist Politics, 1886–93', *I.H.S.*, xxiv, no. 95 (May 1985), 341–60

——*Gladstone, Home Rule and the Ulster Question, 1882–93* (Dublin 1986)

Lubenow, W. C., *Parliamentary Politics and the Home Rule Crisis: The British House of Commons in 1886* (Oxford 1988)

Lucey, D. J., 'Cork Public Opinion in the First World War' (M.A. thesis, U.C.C., 1972)

Lyons, J. B., *The Enigma of Tom Kettle: Irish Patriot, Essayist, Poet, British Soldier, 1880–1916* (Dublin 1983)

Lyons, F. S. L., *The Fall of Parnell* (London 1960)

——*John Dillon: A Biography* (London 1968)

——*Charles Stewart Parnell* (London 1977)

——*Culture and Anarchy in Ireland, 1890–1939* (Oxford 1979)

McDowell, R. B., *The Church of Ireland, 1869–1969* (London 1975)

Mac Giolla Choille, Breandán, *Intelligence Notes, 1913–16* (Dublin 1966)

Magee, John, 'The Monaghan Election of 1883 and the "Invasion of Ulster"', *Clogher Record*, viii, 2 (1974), 147–66

McMinn, J. R. B., 'Presbyterianism and Politics in Ulster, 1871–1906', *Studia Hibernica*, xxi (1981), 127–46

——'Liberalism in North Antrim, 1900–1914', *I.H.S.*, xxiii, no. 89 (May 1982), 17–29

——'The Myth of Route: Liberalism in County Antrim, 1869–1900', *Éire/Ireland*, xvii (1982), 137–49

Mandle, W. F., 'The I.R.B. and the Beginnings of the G.A.A.', *I.H.S.*, xx, no. 80 (Sept. 1977), 418–38

Martin, F. X., *The Irish Volunteers, 1913–15* (Dublin 1963)

——*The Howth Gun-Running, 1914* (Dublin 1964)

——(ed.), *Leaders and Men of the Easter Rising: Dublin, 1916* (London 1967)

——'1916: Myth, Fact and Mystery', *Studia Hibernica*, vii (1967), 7–126

——and Byrne, F. J., *The Scholar Revolutionary: Eoin MacNeill, 1867–1945, and the Making of the New Ireland* (Shannon 1973)

Matthew, H. G. C., *Gladstone, 1809–74* (Oxford 1988)

Miller, D. W., *Church, State and Nation in Ireland, 1898–1921* (Dublin 1973)

——*Queen's Rebels: Ulster Loyalism in Historical Perspective* (Dublin 1978)

Mitchell, Arthur, *Labour and Irish Politics, 1890–1930: The Irish Labour Movement in an Age of Revolution* (Dublin 1974)

Moody, T. W., 'The Irish University Question of the Nineteenth Century', *History*, xliii (1958), 90–109

——*Davitt and Irish Revolution, 1846–82* (Oxford 1981)

Murphy, J. A., 'Identity Change in the Republic of Ireland', *Études Irlandaises*, v (1976), 143–58

Nowlan, K. B. (ed.), *The Making of 1916: Studies in the History of the Rising* (Dublin 1969)

O'Brien, C. C., *Parnell and his Party, 1880–90* (Oxford 1964)

O'Brien, J. V., *William O'Brien and the Course of Irish Politics, 1881–1918* (Berkeley 1976)

O'Brien, R. B., *The Life of Charles Stewart Parnell, 1846–91*, repr. (London 1910)

Ó Broin, León, *Dublin Castle and the 1916 Rising* (London 1970)

——*Revolutionary Underground: The Story of the Irish Republican Brotherhood, 1858–1924* (Dublin 1976)

——*Michael Collins* (Dublin 1980)

O'Connor, Frank, *The Big Fellow: Michael Collins and the Irish Revolution* (London 1965)

O'Connor Lysaght, D. R., 'County Tipperary: Class Struggle and National Struggle, 1916–24' in William Nolan an T. G. McGrath (ed.), *Tipperary: History and Society* (Dublin 1985), 394–409

O'Day, Alan, *The English Face of Irish Nationalism: Parnellite Involvement in British Politics, 1880–86* (Dublin 1977)

——*Parnell and the First Home Rule Episode, 1884–7* (Dublin 1986)

——(ed.), *Reactions to Irish Nationalism* (London 1987)

——'The Irish Problem' in T. R. Gourvish and Alan O'Day (ed.), *Late Victorian Britain, 1867–1900* (London 1988), 229–49

O'Flanagan, Neil, 'Dublin City in an Age of War and Revolution, 1914–24' (M.A. thesis, U.C.D., 1985)

O'Halloran, Clare, *Partition and the Limits of Irish Nationalism* (Dublin 1987)

O'Halpin, Eunan, *The Decline of the Union: British Government in Ireland, 1892–1920* (Dublin 1987)

Pakenham, Frank (Lord Longford), *Peace by Ordeal: An Account from First-Hand Sources of the Negotiation and Signature of the Anglo-Irish*

Treaty, 1921 (London 1935; repr. 1972)

Patterson, Henry, *Class Conflict and Sectarianism: The Protestant Working Class and Belfast Labour Movement, 1868–1920* (Belfast 1980)

——'Industrial Labour and the Labour Movement, 1820–1914' in Liam Kennedy and Philip Ollerenshaw (ed.), *An Economic History of Ulster, 1820–1940* (Manchester 1985), 167–79

Pimley, Adrian, 'The Working-Class Movement and the Irish Revolution, 1896–1923' in D. G. Boyce (ed.), *The Revolution in Ireland, 1879–1923* (London/Dublin 1988), 193–215

Ramsden, John (ed.), *Real Old Tory Politics: The Political Diaries of Sir Robert Sanders, Lord Bayford, 1900–1935* (London 1984)

Rumpf, Erhard, and Hepburn, A. C., *Nationalism and Socialism in Twentieth-Century Ireland* (Liverpool 1977)

Ryan, A. P., *Mutiny at the Curragh* (London 1956)

Savage, D.C., 'The Origins of the Ulster Unionist Party, 1885–6', *I.H.S.*, xii, no. 47 (Mar. 1961), 185–208

Shannon, Richard, 'Gladstone and Home Rule: 1886' in *Ireland after the Union*, intro. Lord Blake (London 1989), 45–59

Solow, B. L., *The Land Question and the Irish Economy, 1870–1903* (Cambridge, Mass. 1971)

Stewart, A. T. Q., *The Ulster Crisis* (London 1967)

——*Edward Carson* (Dublin 1981)

Thompson, Francis, 'The Armagh Elections of 1885–6', *Seanchas Ardmhacha*, viii (1977), 360–85

——'Land and Politics in Ulster, 1868–86' (Ph.D. thesis, Q.U.B., 1982)

——'Attitudes to Reform: Political Parties in Ulster and the Irish Land Bill of 1881' *I.H.S.*, xxiv, no. 95 (May 1985), 327–40

Thomson, D. I., *The Imagination of an Insurrection: Dublin, Easter, 1916* (New York 1967)

Thornley, David, *Isaac Butt and Home Rule* (London 1964)

Tierney, Michael, *Eoin MacNeill: Scholar and Man of Action*, ed. F. X. Martin (Oxford 1980)

Towey, Thomas, 'The Reaction of the British Government to the 1922 Collins–de Valera Pact', *I.H.S.*, xxii, no. 85 (Mar. 1980), 65–76

Townshend, Charles, *The British Campaign in Ireland, 1919–21: The Development of Political and Military Policies* (Oxford 1975)

——*Political Violence in Ireland: Government and Resistance since 1848* (Oxford 1983)

Vaughan, W. E., and Fitzpatrick, A. J. (ed.), *Irish Historical Statistics: Population, 1821–1971* (Dublin 1978)

Walker, B. M., 'The Irish Electorate, 1868–1915', *I.H.S.*, xviii, no. 71 (Mar. 1973), 359–406

——*Parliamentary Election Results in Ireland, 1801–1922* (Dublin 1978)

——'Party Organisation in Ulster, 1865–92: Registration Agents and their Activities' in Peter Roebuck (ed.), *Plantation to Partition: Essays in Ulster History in honour of J. L. McCracken* (Belfast 1981), 191–209

——'The Land Question and Elections in Ulster, 1868–86' in Samuel Clark and J. S. Donnelly, jnr (ed.), *Irish Peasants: Violence and Political*

    Unrest, 1780–1914 (Dublin 1988) 230–65
——*Ulster Politics: The Formative Years, 1868–86* (Belfast 1989)
Watson, G. J., *Irish Identity and the Literary Revivial: Synge, Yeats, Joyce, O'Casey* (London 1979)
Welch, Robert, 'Constitutional, Language and Politics in Nineteenth-Century Irish Poetry' in Terence Brown and Nicholas Grene (ed.), *Tradition and Influence in Anglo-Irish Poetry* (London 1989), 7–30
West, Trevor, *Horace Plunkett: Co-operation and Politics: An Irish Biography* (Gerrards Cross 1986)
Williams, T. Desmond (ed.), *The Irish Struggle, 1916–26* (London 1966)
Williams, Martin, 'Ancient Mythology and Revolutionary Ideology in Ireland, 1878–1916', *H.J.*, xxvi, 2 (1983), 307–28
Winstanley, M. J., *Ireland and the Land Question, 1800–1922* (London 1984)
Woods, C. J., 'The General Election of 1892: The Catholic Clergy and the Defeat of the Parnellites' in F. S. L. Lyons and R. A. J. Hawkins (ed,), *Ireland under the Union: Varieties of Tension: Essays in honour of T. W. Moody* (Oxford 1980), 289–319
Wright, Frank, 'Protestant Ideology and Politics in Ulster', *European Journal of Sociology*, xiv (1973), 213–80
Yeats, W. B., *Collected Letters*, Vol. I: *1865–95*, ed. John Kelly and Eric Domville (Oxford 1986)
Younger, Calton, *Ireland's Civil War* (London 1970; repr. 1979)
——*Arthur Griffith* (Dublin 1981)

5. Newspapers and Periodicals

This section does not list all, or even most, of the vast number of newspapers and periodicals that were published in Ireland in the nineteenth century; such an enterprise would require a bibliography to itself. It offers a selection of some of the most interesting and important publications, so that the reader can, if he wishes, make a start and sample the very rich store of print that helps us re-create the world of Ireland in the last century.

Two useful guides are Royal Irish Academy, *Irish and Anglo-Irish Periodicals* (Dublin 1970), and V. E. Glandon, 'Index of Irish Newspapers, 1900–1922', *Éire/Ireland*, xi (1976), 84–121; xii (1977), 86–115.

Belfast Monthly Magazine (1808–14): Protestant Irish cultural periodical
Belfast Newsletter: Ulster Unionist
Belfast Telegraph: Ulster Unionist
Coleraine Chronicle: Ulster Liberal and Tenant Right
Connaught Telegraph: useful source for Land League
Dublin Daily Express: southern Unionist
Dublin University Magazine (1833–77): Protestant Irish cultural periodical
Freeman's Journal: Irish nationalist
Irish News: Ulster nationalist
Irish People: Fenian newspaper
Irish Times: southern Unionist
Nation: Young Ireland newspaper

Northern Star: radical newspaper of late eighteenth century
Northern Whig: Liberal Unionist after 1886
Pilot: O'Connellite newspaper
United Ireland: nationalist
United Irishman: early Sinn Féin

6. Novels and Creative Literature
Like Section 5, this offers a brief selection which will introduce the reader to a rich and varied collection.

Novels
Banim, John, *The Boyne Water* (London 1826)
Birmingham, George A., *The Bad Times* (London 1908)
Bowen, Elizabeth, *The Last September* (London 1929)
Carleton, William, *Traits and Stories of the Irish Peasantry*, 2 vols (Dublin 1830–33)
——*The Black Prophet* (Belfast 1847)
Edgeworth, Maria, *Castle Rackrent* (London 1800)
Griffin, Gerald, *The Collegians*, 3 vols (London 1829)
Joyce, James, *Portrait of the Artist as a Young Man* (New York 1916)
——*Ulysses* (Paris 1922)
Kickham, Charles, *Knocknagow* (Dublin 1873)
Lever, Charles, *The Martins of Cro' Martin* (London 1856)
——*Lord Kilgobbin* (London 1872)
Moore, George, *A Drama in Muslin* (London 1886)
Morgan, Lady (Sydney Owenson), *The Wild Irish Girl* (London 1806)
Sheehan, Canon Patrick, *The Graves of Kilmorna* (Dublin 1915)
Somerville, E.Œ., and Ross, Martin, *The Real Charlotte* (London 1894)
——*An Enthusiast* (London 1921)
——*The Big House of Inver* (London 1925)
Trollope, Anthony, *The MacDermots of Ballycloran* (London 1847)
——*The Kellys and the O'Kellys* (London 1848)
——*Castle Richmond* (London 1860)
——*The Landleagurs* (London 1883)

Drama
O'Casey, Seán, *Juno and the Paycock* (London 1925)
——*The Shadow of a Gunman* (London 1925)
——*The Plough and the Stars* (London 1926)
Synge, J. M., *The Playboy of the Western World* (London 1907)

Poetry
Davis, Thomas, *Essays and Poems* (Dublin 1945)
Ferguson, Sir Samuel, *Lays of the Western Gael, and other poems* (London 1865)
——*Hibernian Nights' Entertainments* (Dublin 1887)
Mangan, James, *Poems of James Clarence Mangan*, ed. D. J. O'Donoghue (Dublin/London 1903)
Moore, Thomas, *Poetical Works* (London 1854)
Yeats, W. B., *Selected Poetry*, ed. A. Norman Jeffares (London 1964)

Lennox Robinson (ed.), *A Golden Treasury of Irish Verse* (London 1927)

Montague, John (ed.), *The Faber Book of Irish Verse* (London 1974)

Kinsella, Thomas (ed.), *The New Oxford Book of Irish Verse* (London/New York 1986)

7. Photographs

Byrne, Art, and McMahon, Seán, *Faces of the West, 1875–1925* (Belfast 1976)

Walker, B. M., *Faces of the Past: A Photographic and Literary Record of Ulster Life, 1880–1915* (Belfast 1974)

Index